A Tale of Four Cities

New York

NINETEENTH CENTURY BASEBALL'S MOST EXCITING SEASON, 1889, IN CONTEMPORARY ACCOUNTS

Jean-Pierre Caillault

Foreword by David Nemec

Boston

Brooklyn

St. Louis

(1889) Boston, Brooklyn, New York, St. Louis.

The 1889 baseball season is special in the history of baseball. Both leagues—the veteran National League and the upstart American Association—featured thrilling pennant races that were not decided until the final day of the season. There was excitement off the field as well; the players' union (known then as "the Brotherhood") sowed the seeds of the boldest player revolt in baseball history.

This work presents accounts from

York Times, the *Brooklyn Daily Eagle*, the *Boston Herald*, and the

1889 pennant race and the passion that the press and public had for baseball. The National League race pitted the New York Giants, the reigning world champions, against the Boston Beaneaters, the team with 10 future Hall of Famers and three players that spearheaded the player revolt. The American Association race was just as exciting and even more controversial, as team presidents Chris Von de Ahe of the St. Louis Browns and Charles H. Byrne of the Brooklyn Bridegrooms hated each other

A Tale of Four Cities

A Tale of Four Cities

Nineteenth Century Baseball's Most
Exciting Season, 1889,
in Contemporary Accounts

JEAN-PIERRE CAILLAULT

foreword by David Nemec

McFarland & Company, Inc., Publishers
Jefferson, North Carolina, and London

LIBRARY OF CONGRESS CATALOGUING-IN-PUBLICATION DATA

Caillault, Jean-Pierre.
   A tale of four cities : nineteenth century baseball's most
exciting season, 1889, in contemporary accounts / Jean-
Pierre Caillault ; foreword by David Nemec.
      p.   cm.
   Includes index.

   ISBN 0-7864-1678-5 (softcover : 50# alkaline paper)

   1. National League of Professional Baseball Clubs—
History—19th century—Sources.   2. American Association
(Baseball league : 1882–1891)—History—19th century—
Sources.   I. Title.
GV875.A3C35   2003
796.357'0973'0934—dc21   2003013497

British Library cataloguing data are available

Cover image *(clockwise from top):* John Montgomery Ward, New
York Giants; "Parisian Bob" Caruthers, Brooklyn Bridegrooms;
Charlie Comiskey, St. Louis Browns and John Clarkson, Boston
Beaneaters *(Library of Congress, Prints and Photographs Division)*

Manufactured in the United States of America

McFarland & Company, Inc., Publishers
   Box 611, Jefferson, North Carolina 28640
      www.mcfarlandpub.com

In loving memory of my father,
and best friend, Pierre

Acknowledgments

There are many people who helped me during the process of putting this book together and to whom I owe a great debt. The staff of the National Baseball Hall of Fame Research Library in Cooperstown, NY, in particular Tim Wiles, Russell Wolinsky, Rachel Kepner, and Bill Burdick, were especially helpful and generous with their time in guiding me through their labyrinth of files and photos. Mark Rucker of Transcendental Graphics quickly found and sent the handful of photos I needed from Transcendental's collection. Mike Caplinger of the University of Georgia helped me to acquire the numerous images from the Library of Congress. The staff of the University of Georgia libraries, especially Virginia Feher in the Inter-Library Loans Department and Katie Brower of Photographic Services, helped me obtain much of the raw material that makes up the core of the book.

I would also like to express my gratitude to authors G. H. Fleming, James D. Hardy, Jr., and Daniel M. Pearson for unwittingly providing, through their own books, much of the inspiration for this book. My very good friend, Loris Magnani, has provided almost 30 years of stimulating baseball discussions, some of which led indirectly to this book. And, of course, I must thank 19th-century baseball expert David Nemec for very graciously agreeing to write the foreword.

And, finally, I'd like to thank my wife Kristen, not only for tolerating my absence during all of the time I spent reading copies of microfilm with a magnifying glass and typing hundreds of thousands of words written by 19th-century newspaper reporters, but for helping to reproduce a number of the images used in the book.

Table of Contents

Foreword

Writing about and researching the early history of baseball have been part of my professional life for more than thirty years now. Yet I still experience the same enthusiasm and sense of expectation each time I know I'm on the verge of learning something new about the game, as I did the very first time I stumbled on a row of ancient baseball guides from the 1890s in the Cleveland Public Library way back in the fourth grade. Whether it's a biography of John Montgomery Ward, a long-buried team photograph of the 1890 Cleveland Players' League club, or an account of a bizarre on-field incident that led to a subsequent change in the playing rules, a deep sense of satisfaction rises up within me whenever I make an important new discovery.

In *A Tale of Four Cities*, Jean-Pierre Caillault has magically inspired all of those feelings. With his careful selection of capsule game reports, interviews and "think" pieces from the sports pages of 1889, the author has constructed a unique and multi-layered re-creation of one of the most pivotal seasons in major league history. Not only was the 1889 campaign a period of intense excitement and one volatile game after another in both the then-existing major circuits, the National League and the American Association, but it was the last season before the long-simmering war between players and owners erupted into a full-scale conflagration as well as the first season that the current four-ball and three-strike limitations were enforced. What's more, the events of 1889 were instrumental both in spelling the end of the St. Louis Browns, baseball's longest-running dynasty up to the time, and in depriving Boston's John Clarkson of what otherwise would almost certainly have been universal recognition for assembling the greatest season ever by a major league pitcher.

Caillault's exhaustive research and complete knowledge of his subject are apparent to me in his authorial decisions. While seeming to remain detached from his subject matter, with each and every piece of material he chooses to weave into his overall pattern Caillault succeeds

1

admirably at the very difficult task he has set for himself. His strategy of allowing his readers to draw their own conclusions from his story ends in steering all who read his material to its dramatic conclusion into exactly the corners that he knows hold the richest rewards from the 1889 season as well as its darkest secrets.

To complement the text, Caillault has assembled an outstanding selection of photographs. In its combination of incisive text and extensive visual record, *A Tale of Four Cities* raises the bar a full notch for future books about the nineteenth-century game.

David Nemec
San Francisco
August 2003

Preface

The 1889 baseball season was unique in the history of baseball. Both leagues, the veteran National League and the upstart American Association, featured thrilling, tumultuous pennant races that were not decided until the final day of the season. And the players union, the Brotherhood, sowed the seeds of the boldest and most ambitious player revolt in baseball history.

The race in the National League, between the New York Giants, the reigning world's champions, and the Boston Beaneaters, featured 10 future Hall of Fame players, two of whom, William "Buck" Ewing of the Giants and Mike "King" Kelly of Boston, were generally acknowledged to be the game's best players but captained their teams in controversial and provocative manners. Three others, John Montgomery Ward and Tim Keefe of the Giants and Dan Brouthers of the Beaneaters, spearheaded the Brotherhood movement. And another, Boston pitcher John Clarkson, had what might have been the greatest single-season pitching performance in the annals of baseball. Along the way, the Giants were faced with the extraordinary situation of having lost access to their home park, the original Polo Grounds, and had to play "home" games in New Jersey and Staten Island before returning in mid-season to begin play at the New Polo Grounds in upper Manhattan. The 1890 edition of the *Spalding Guide* concisely summed up the National League season with this statement: "Never had there been so exciting a finish to a League championship race, and the base ball public was roused up to an enthusiastic pitch of excitement over the close contest between New York and Boston."

The American Association race was just as exciting as the National League's, but far more controversial. The two contestants' team presidents, Chris Von der Ahe of the St. Louis Browns and Charles H. Byrne of the Brooklyn Bridegrooms, hated each other passionately. And many of Von der Ahe's players hated him, too. The Browns' season was peppered with player suspensions handed out by Von der Ahe and in some

3

cases the team responded by intentionally losing, or so it seemed. Highly-respected Charlie Comiskey, the Browns' first baseman and captain, had to act as peacemaker between the players and Von der Ahe. The Bridegrooms ran into controversy over playing of Sunday games at Ridgewood Park, and the grandstand of their non–Sunday home grounds, Washington Park, burned down in mid-season. Toward the end of the campaign, games between the Browns and Bridegrooms were forfeited and the resulting dispute rocked the American Association to its very core. As the *Spalding Guide* remarked: "Up to the last day of the race it was doubtful as to which of the two clubs [St. Louis or Brooklyn] would win the pennant."

Throughout the season the umpires in both leagues were verbally assailed and occasionally in real danger of being physically assaulted, as record-setting crowds attended the games. The on-the-field climax to the 1889 season saw the Giants meet Brooklyn in a nine-game, pre-subway "subway series" that was the beginning of their famous rivalry that continues to this day. And off-the-field, John M. Ward was leading the Brotherhood rebellion against the magnates which led to the creation of a third major league, the Players' League, causing all three leagues to wage against each other a war that ultimately resulted in the demise of both the American Association and the Players' League.

In the spirit of G. H. Fleming's classic book, *The Unforgettable Season*, I have used contemporary newspaper accounts to capture the sustained, day-by-day excitement of the 1889 pennant races and the passion that the press and public had for baseball in that thrilling season. I have made no interpretations or syntheses of those accounts, just editorial selections, allowing the newspaper writers of the day to tell the tale in their own words. The accounts were taken from major newspapers representing each of the four teams' cities: the New York *Times*, the Brooklyn *Daily Eagle*, the Boston *Herald*, and the St. Louis *Post-Dispatch*. The illustrations come from the Library of Congress Baseball Card Collection, the National Baseball Hall of Fame Library, Transcendental Graphics, and microfilm copies of the New York *Clipper*.

I hope that *A Tale of Four Cities* will magically transport the reader back to the nineteenth century, bringing the 1889 season's players, managers, and owners to life through both the words and illustrations of the time.

—Jean-Pierre Caillault

The Season, 1889,
in Contemporary Accounts

Thursday, October 18, 1888

New York, October 17—"It's betting dollars to peanuts," said President Reach of the Philadelphia club to your correspondent this afternoon, "that Boston will get Brouthers and Richardson. I wanted both men badly, and offered $15,500 for them—$8000 for Richardson and $7500 for Brouthers—but Mr. Stearns told me it was no use, that they were as good as sold." The feeling in New York is of satisfaction, for they want to see Boston equipped as thoroughly as possible for the season of 1889.

—Boston *Herald*

Friday, October 19

The baseball event of 1888 will be Spalding's grand tour to Australia with the Chicago team and a picked team of league players, which leave San Francisco for Australia next month. It will be the most noteworthy tour ever undertaken by base ball players.

—Brooklyn *Daily Eagle*

The purchase of the releases by the Boston club of Dennis Brouthers, Harding Richardson, Charles Bennett and Charles W. Ganzel from the Detroit club completes what is by far the greatest deal ever perfected in the history of the national game. From the character of the men acquired as gentlemen and ball players, and from the price paid for their release, this transaction will be regarded as a stupendous piece of enterprise that may well appall the entire base ball world. Before it the securing of Kelly and Clarkson at the price of $10,000 each is a very insignificant

5

Left: Dan Brouthers, first baseman, Boston Beaneaters (Library of Congress, Prints and Photographs Division [LOT 13163-05, no. 107]). *Right:* Hardy Richardson, second baseman and left fielder, Boston Beaneaters (Library of Congress, Prints and Photographs Division [LOT 13163-05, no. 120]).

transaction. Base ball men here are all glad of the news and predict the championship of the league and of the world for Boston in 1889. They all say Boston deserves it as being the best base ball city in the country.
—Boston *Herald*

No player in this country is better known than Dennis Brouthers, the first baseman of the Detroit team, who stands 6 feet 2 inches in height and weighs about 200 pounds. He has led the league in batting during his connection with it, and as a first baseman he holds a high position. It will rejoice all Boston base ball lovers to learn that this powerful player is to come to this city. Harding Richardson is as good an all-around player as there is in the country. He is a terrific batter, and can fill any position in a nine, even to pitching and catching. He is 5 feet 8 inches in height and weighs 160 pounds. He will prove a powerful addition to the Boston team. Bennett is most favorably known. As a catcher he has few if any superiors in the country. Ganzel is also considered one of the best catchers in the league. He is a remarkably fine thrower and he can stand any amount of punishment at the hands of pitchers.

—Boston *Herald*

Sunday, October 21

Jim Mutrie said that he wanted to congratulate Boston on the acquisition, because nothing could suit New York better than to have Boston strong. "We have had too soft a thing with you," he said, and his eyes danced in his head as visions of ducats swam before them. When Tim Keefe was told the news he said: "I guess I can stand it; I won't have to choose the balls."

—Boston *Herald*

Wednesday, October 24

Michael J. Kelly came on from New York last evening arriving in this city at 9 o'clock and going at once to the place of business of a friend. A *Herald* representative came across the great ball player soon after his arrival, and had a long chat with him. He found Kelly willing to talk, and, as ever, ready to freely express his opinion on any matters pertaining to the national game and the Boston club in particular.

"Why," said Kelly, "talk about your base ball cities! Boston beats them all. There's no other city in the country like it. And then they treat a player here like a man. Those three men (the Boston directors) know how to use a man well. I tell you I'm stuck on the place, and as long as I play ball I will be found in Boston. When I get done with the Boston club I'm done playing ball. I'm ready to retire then from the business. Those three men have done a big thing getting those Detroit players. They come high, the same as all good things do. We'll have a dandy team here next year, and don't you forget it. I came on from Poughkeepsie with Dan Brouthers, and he's delighted at the idea of playing in Boston. Clarkson is dead stuck on Boston, too. He'll be here next year, and you'll see him pitch great ball with the slugging team he'll have behind him."

Kelly had a conference last evening with Directors Conant and Billings, during which he was offered and accepted the position of captain of the Boston nine for next season. He said that he would have a good nine to work with, and he will see to it that the men earn their salaries.

—Boston *Herald*

Wednesday, November 14

The American Association appears to be in an unenviable position just at this time, from the fact that none of the members thereof seem willing to trust the others. The management of the Brooklyn club has been repeatedly represented in print as remaining loyal to the association, and as having no intention of withdrawing therefrom. President Byrne, however, has been very guarded in his response to all inquiries as to what Brooklyn proposes to do next season. Yet his club is paying out large sums of money for new players. The question naturally arises, Why this outlay of money in strengthening a team that is already strong enough to cope with any in the association, if it is not preparatory to contests with the more powerful teams in the league; in short, is not the Brooklyn club preparing to take Washington's place in the national league?

President Von der Ahe of the St. Louis Browns is an obstacle to harmony in the association. He is fond of rushing into public print, from time to time, with his alleged grievances, and he narrates them regardless of the effect of his language or the soundness of the basis on which he builds his complaints. There is no love lost between Messrs. Byrne and Von der Ahe, and it is an open secret that several of the association magnates would like to get rid of the doughty St. Louis president, but the latter is entrenched behind a club which has not only made a great deal of money for him, but has won the championship of the association four years in succession.

—Boston *Herald*

Thursday, November 15

President Von der Ahe of the Browns is home again after a flying trip East connected with the American Association. A *Post-Dispatch* reporter accosted him this morning, after his arrival, and had a very pleasant chat with him.

"Do you regard the outlook for the Association as encouraging?"

"Decidedly so. Our prospects are in some respects better than ever, and we will again be on deck with as strong a circuit and as big attractions as ever. You can say that the stuff that has gone out—that Brooklyn and Cincinnati are watching each other, both eager to make a jump to the League—is all bosh. Both will remain loyal to the Association, not only because they regard it equal to the League, but they would not be foolish enough to sacrifice a good paying patronage with Sunday games for the uncertainty of satisfying a favored few, backed up by the buncombe of new faces, new games, and new attractions."

—St. Louis *Post-Dispatch*

Wednesday, November 21

New York, November 21—At the meeting of the rules committee yesterday at the Fifth Avenue Hotel an important change was made in base ball rules. The number of balls was reduced to 4, the strikes remaining 3. It will be 4 balls, 3 strikes next year.

—St. Louis *Post-Dispatch*

"The Brooklyn Club will not go in the League," says President Byrne. "We are perfectly contented as we are. Not only have we not been invited to enter the League, but we would not enter if we had been. We did not secure our great team with an idea of becoming a League club, but for the sole purpose of winning the championship of the Association of which we are now a member."

—St. Louis *Post-Dispatch*

Friday, November 23

After making threats for half a dozen years, the Baseball League passed what is known as the salary-graded list at the meeting at the Fifth Avenue Hotel yesterday, and from present appearances a war between managers and players is imminent.

President Young invited the reporters to the parlor where the meeting was held, and made known the cause for secrecy by giving them what he termed amendments to the constitution. Section 30 is the one that caused all the players in the corridor of the hotel to make exclamations not of a complimentary character. In the future it will read as follows:

The compensation for all League players for services as players shall be limited, regulated, and determined by the classification and grade to which such players may be assigned by the Secretary of the League, after the termination of the championship season, as follows:

Class A, compensation $2,500; Class B, compensation $2,250; Class C, compensation $2,000; Class D, compensation $1,750; Class E, maximum compensation $1,500. But this section shall not prohibit the payment of extra compensation for the services of the person to each club as field Captain or team manager.

In determining such assignment, batting, fielding, base-running, battery work, earnest team work, and exemplary conduct, both on and off the field, at all times, shall be considered as a basis for classification.

Of course, if carried into effect, this rule will abolish the fancy salaries paid to the ball players. Ten-thousand-dollar beauties will be a thing of the past, and instead of asking a princely income the average ball player will have to content himself with $2,500 for his labor. This will afford no small amount of surprise to such men as Ward, the shining light of the Brotherhood of Ball Players who is on his way to Australia. The rule next season will not affect men who have already made contracts for 1889, but Ward has not signed and he will feel it. It is more than likely that he will make strenuous objections and try and create a revolution among the players.

—New York *Times*

Saturday, November 24

The effect of this classification of players will work most advantageously principally in two ways. First, it will place the league clubs more on a financial equality. It will enable Indianapolis, Washington, Pittsburg and Cleveland to cope more successfully with Boston, New York and Chicago in securing new and strong players. The second advantage to be gained will be in the increased quality of ball playing. Every player will naturally strive to be placed in the first class. This will prove to be an incentive to put forth his best efforts, and be always in condition to play good ball.

—Boston *Herald*

The athletic and stalwart form of Tim Keefe, the well known pitcher of the New York Base Ball Club, but now more of an object of interest to the base ball world on account of his position as secretary and treasurer of the National League Brotherhood of Base Ball Players, displayed itself to the base ball editor of the *Herald* yesterday. Mr. Keefe appeared in excellent spirits as he exchanged salutations with the writer. "The action of the league this year is in direct violation of our contract clause, which states that a player, when resigned, shall not receive less than he received the previous season. It certainly is time to act. There will be plenty of fun ahead for the league. Do you think that Ewing is going to play for any $2500 next season, or that this rule is going to hasten his signing? Do you suppose that the New York club is going to be without his services on account of this rule? Not a bit of it, depend upon it. I shall not lose any sleep about the matter. I shan't rush to sign, and I don't thing that any of my comrades and friends will. We won't assemble until next spring, but when our houses of Parliament do assemble, let them tremble."

—Boston *Herald*

Sunday, November 25

A writer in the Louisville *Courier-Journal* says:

"The peculiar manner in which some of the crack pitchers deliver the ball is well worthy of note. Every twirler

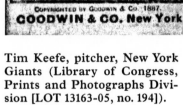

Tim Keefe, pitcher, New York Giants (Library of Congress, Prints and Photographs Division [LOT 13163-05, no. 194]).

possesses a style of pitching which belongs to himself only.

Caruthers first advances his right leg, fumbles the ball on his hip a second and then with a sour look throws to the batter. He pitches without effort and seemingly does not care whether the batter hits the ball or not. His delivery looks like it would be easy to bat, but the reverse is the case.

Welch, of the New Yorks, is always smiling. He plants his right foot forward and scrapes a pile of dirt, then expectorates, and a moment later wipes the perspiration from his brow, when suddenly he doubles himself up and throws with all his might. Batters say that he is the best pitcher in the league.

Clarkson, of Boston, faces second base first, then quickly whirls around and throws the ball over the plate, startling the batter. He is a swift thrower."

—Brooklyn *Daily Eagle*

Thursday, December 6

The principal matter before the Association at its meeting this morning was the graded salary plan, originated and adopted by the League at its meeting in November. The Association managers are nearly all in favor of the graded salaries because of their peculiar force upon certain players rather than the generally good effect they might have on base ball. Everybody knows that the resolution will not prevent clubs from paying big salaries to new men if they so desire, and, so far as the managers are concerned, the law need never have been passed. It will be a one-sided affair all through, and it is probably this fact which recommends it so strongly to the good graces of the base ball men. The Association took up this question this morning, and decided to appoint a committee of three to examine the scheme thoroughly and report upon it for action to the spring meeting of the Association.

—St. Louis *Post-Dispatch*

Manager W. H. Watkins of Kansas City, familiarly called "Wat," was asked today what he thought of the Association for next season:

"The Association will be all right. I do not think that St. Louis will win the pennant again. You see it is weak in some spots, and although it has the same club as last year, some other teams have been strengthened at their weak spots, and it will not be the same old story."

"What's your idea of the League?"

"Well, that's pretty hard to tell. If New York holds out with the same people it now has and plays the game it put up last year, it will get there again sure. Boston has the people to win with if they only get a manager to handle them properly, but I do not believe there is a manager in the country capable of doing it. There are some of the meanest elements in the business right in that club, and they will be sure to get up a fight on something. Suppose that Kelly is the captain of the team. Well, do you think a man like Brouthers is going to sit down and let a man like Kelly talk to him? If the New Yorks do not get swelled heads too, they will have their own way next season. I believe that Boston will be a great deal better than she was but I don't think she can win the championship with the crowd of growlers she's picked up recently."

—St. Louis *Post-Dispatch*

Wednesday, January 2, 1889

It must be conceded that in base ball the pitcher's position is an important one, and on that functionary depends much of the future success of the game. It is admitted that there is no position in the nine that requires a higher state of perfection than that of the pitcher. There are a great variety of pitchers. Some use head work, while others depend chiefly on their strength, and the great speed with which they can send the ball over the home plate. It is claimed that there is a great strain on the pitcher, but if a pitcher takes good care of himself outside of his regular work, he can easily endure the little strain put upon him during an afternoon's work on the ball field. It must also be remembered that at the most he does not pitch more than three times in one week on an average through the season, and about an hour's work at each game.

Many knowing ones claim that there is but one real successful class of pitchers—the head-worker. Of this class Timothy J. Keefe of the New York Club is undoubtedly the greatest wonder the base ball profession has ever produced. He has been one of the leading pitchers in the profession for the past eight or nine seasons. How well he has succeeded the history of the game will tell. Keefe's most effective ball is his slow drop. He uses the same movement in delivering a speedy ball that he does a slow one, which greatly deceives the batsman.

Michael Welch, more familiarly known as "Smiling Mickey," is another remarkable pitcher. He, like Keefe, has made a very fine record for himself. Since he has joined the New Yorks he has pitched great ball and is rarely out of form. It is amusing to see "Mickey" apply all his arts to induce the batsman to hit at a bad ball, and when he has succeeded his face lights up and he wears the smile for which he is famous. Welch has good speed, which he uses with the curves to great advantage.

Another and a very important person who took part in the world's championship series was Charles King of the St. Louis Browns, who is familiarly known in the profession as "Silver." President Von der Ahe purchased his release for a small figure from the National League. It was seen that King was the making of a great pitcher, his work in the box being as good as either Caruthers or Foutz. King is a young man with good habits, and by taking care of himself should last for some years.

Elton Chamberlain, who is more familiarly known as "Ed," is one of the rising young pitchers of the profession. For a young man in the business, Chamberlain has gained a great reputation, and his work has certainly been of the highest order.

—St. Louis *Post-Dispatch*

Sunday, January 6

Here is Clarkson's story of his opening work as a pitcher. Clarkson said: "I have always been a strong thrower (which is quite essential for first class pitching) since I can remember, and it was while attending school at my home in Cambridge, Mass., that I first began to throw a ball, for the position of pitcher was forced upon me, with no way out of it. So I began practice in dead earnest. I got a few points on curving a ball from George Wright. I mastered them fairly well and pitched my first game and won. By constant practice I got the balls so that I could control them at will, until at last I found myself in one of the strongest, if not the strongest, amateur clubs in Massachusetts, viz., the Beacons. I pitched for this club three years and got good practice as well as appearance. We played not more than twice a week, and I pitched every game the club played during that period."

—Brooklyn *Daily Eagle*

George Pinkney, of the Brooklyn team, in speaking of third base play, says: "In playing the base, or rather when I take my position on the field, I stand from ten to twelve feet from the base—down the line toward the shortstop and about three to five feet behind the line. Of course I vary my position according to the batsman. A good third baseman should

be an accurate thrower, both overhand and underhand, and a sure catch, on account of the peculiar twist on the high balls hit up around third base. Those balls must be grabbed and held firmly until they have settled in your hands or they are apt to twist out and shoot away from you in such a manner that you cannot recover them before they reach the ground. A good third baseman should be a wideawake and lively man, because he has little time to consider after a ball is hit to him, for they are of the hot and sharp kind."

—Brooklyn *Daily Eagle*

George Pinkney, third baseman, Brooklyn Bridegrooms (New York *Clipper*, April 17, 1886).

Tuesday, January 8

Buck Ewing admits the claim made some time ago that his success as a throwing catcher was due to the fact that he compelled the pitcher to pitch to him instead of the batter. Ewing said: "If I know a man has a reputation of being a base runner, and that he will go down on the first or second ball, he is my meat every time. All I do is to get the pitcher to hold him tight and to pitch to me instead of the batter. Then a good throw is bound to get him every time."

—St. Louis *Post-Dispatch*

Thursday, January 10

A very warm friend of the prospective captain of the Boston Base Ball Club said to the writer yesterday: "I notice that about everybody is pitching into Mike, and that there are very few to say a good word for him. Now it is a fact that Mike is the only available candidate that there is for captain. Who else is there? Morrill is not to be a member of the team, for it was on this condition that Kelly signed a contract. Mike has had no such chance as this to handle a team. If he can't make a success of this club, it will be because he is not fit to handle a base ball club. His pride has been aroused and he is determined to make a good showing. He has it in him to do well, and you will find out that he is the right man in the right place if he is not backcapped and is supported as he should be. All he wants, and all his friends ask for him, is a fair and square show. He ought to get it."

—Boston *Herald*

Friday, January 11

It is preposterous for the friends of Kelly to say that he has not had a fair show in this city. No player that ever wore a Boston uniform has been treated so fairly or so courteously, or had more encouragement by press and public to do his best at all times and under all circumstances. The fact is the "fair show" business in his city, as far as it pertains to Kelly, has been overdone.

—Boston *Herald*

Sunday, January 13

As regards Kelly being selected to captain the Boston team next season the matter has not by any means been settled in his favor, and the

Boston directors should go exceedingly slow before placing him in that position. Evidence is accumulating every day, of a most emphatic and convincing character, of the existence of firm, deep-seated, and almost universal opposition to his appointment as team captain for 1889. His former administration of that office was a failure; his habits are of a character not to command the respect of men under him; the erratic character of his own playing is not such as to inspire confidence in him as a leader, and if he has no control over his own conduct, he cannot be expected to control the conduct of his men. To select him as captain would be to violate the feelings of a vast majority of the patrons of the game in this city, who are now looking forward for a grand struggle for the championship by the team of 1889, under competent leadership.

—Boston *Herald*

While in New York President Von der Ahe signed Arlie Latham, his celebrated third baseman. Secretary Munson said the "freshest man on earth came to the Grand Central hotel, and offered to sign without being asked." Latham was in need of advance money and was given some last evening.

—St. Louis *Post-Dispatch*

Monday, January 14

"Oh, Johnny Morrill is a nice fellow, and all that, but he can't play ball with the Bostons this year. Just put it down in large italic letters that he will not play there, or else I do not. I'm not sore on Morrill, but we do not need him, and I guess we'll not run the team on a charitable basis, at least not for this season. Tra-la-la, old sport, and don't forget to say that Kel will be captain of the Bostons and that my friend Johnny Morrill will not play with that team, anyway."

The above are the words alleged to have been used by M.J. Kelly, candidate for the captaincy of the Boston team of 1889, in an interview with a reporter of the *Sporting Times* of New York, and published in its issue of yesterday.

—Boston *Herald*

Thursday, January 17

"I see there is an evident effort to create a prejudice against Shortstop Fuller in advance of his appearance here," said President Von der

Ahe this morning. "There is a good deal more in Fuller than people who know him as a ball-player want to concede. He is known as 'Shorty' Fuller, because he usually does his work neatly, with alacrity and dispatch; in fact, makes short work of the duties outlined in his territory. Comiskey wanted me to sign him two years ago. I think he will prove a good man for the Browns. We hope to win the championship the coming season with Fuller at shortstop."

—St. Louis *Post-Dispatch*

Friday, January 18

One of the Cincinnati pork policemen said the other day: "The 'bleachers' have a funny way of playing on Comiskey's name. They call him 'Common Whisky'."

—St. Louis *Post-Dispatch*

OLD JUDGE CIGARETTES Goodwin & Co., New York.

"Shorty" Fuller, shortstop, St. Louis Browns (Library of Congress, Prints and Photographs Division [LOT 13163-13, no. 20]).

Sunday, January 20

President Day of the Giants is still too ill to leave his home, and in consequence the much-talked-of series between the Giants and Brooklyns has not been arranged. "There will be no trouble about selecting dates," said Manager Mutrie yesterday. "If the Brooklyns want to play us we will meet them. As regards the outcome, I have no doubt as to the ability of the New-Yorks to whip the Brooklyns, or any club in the country."

—New York *Times*

The American Association have secured the services of Umpire Gaffney for their staff as umpire for 1889, and there is only one more umpire required, as Ferguson, Gaffney and Holland are now engaged and Goldsmith will probably be the fourth. On Friday Gaffney telegraphed Manager Barnie, chairman of the American Association Committee on Umpires, accepting the terms offered for next season and signifying his willingness to sign the usual contract. It is understood that his salary will be $1,800.

—Brooklyn *Daily Eagle*

Monday, January 21

The captain of the Brooklyn team of 1889 will not be chosen until the team are all together next April, when the men themselves can indicate their preference. The choice will be between the veteran Corkhill and Foutz, the two fully competent for the position.

—Brooklyn *Daily Eagle*

Dave Foutz said of the Brooklyn team: "The prospects for our nine the coming season look to me to be very flattering. I don't see where there is a nine in the country better equipped for the coming championship struggle than the Brooklyn Club. If we pull together, as we undoubtedly will, we will reach the goal first. I shall endeavor to hold down my new position, first base, as it should be done, and it won't take me very long to relieve the pitcher if the other side gets too familiar with his delivery. I have not given up pitching entirely and I guess I will be in the box pretty often before the season is over." Foutz favors the new rules. He says: "I think they will make batting heavier; at least they will make more runs in a game as there will be more bases on balls, and you know they are productive of runs to a more or

Dave Foutz, pitcher, Brooklyn Bridegrooms (Transcendental Graphics).

less extent. The successful pitcher will be the one that has the best control of the ball, with plenty of speed and good change of pace."

—Brooklyn *Daily Eagle*

The *Sporting Life* says: "It is reported that another bridegroom is to be added to the Brooklyn party," and that Dave Foutz is to be the happy man. It is said that David was caught napping at first base by a fair one of Baltimore.

—Brooklyn *Daily Eagle*

Wednesday, January 23

Bid McPhee, when asked who he thought would win the pennant in the Association next season, said: "The Brooklyns ought to win it, and I thought they would last year, but you see I missed my guess. Base ball is a mighty uncertain game, as one can never tell what is going to happen. It is even more uncertain than a presidential election, and that's saying a good deal. Take the Brooklyns as they are organized for next season, and you can't pick out a weak batter in the whole combination. They have a good fielding team and are particularly strong in pitchers."

—St. Louis *Post-Dispatch*

Saturday, January 26

Merchant Tim Keefe is to put on the base ball market a glove which he has named "The Ewing."

—Boston *Herald*

Monday, January 28

When Messrs. Byrne and Day met at the uptown residence of Mr. Day last week—Mr. Byrne calling on the league club's president to learn how his health was—they, of course, had a talk about the proposed meeting of their respective club teams on the field next April. In their desultory conversation on the subject Mr. Day expressed his opposition to the proposed games, as all the gain likely to result from the contest—outside of the gate receipts—would be in favor of Brooklyn, which club, Mr. Day said, would occupy the position "of having all to win and nothing to lose by the series. But," he added, "if you challenge my team I shall have to respond."

The two clubs will probably reply to the public demand for a meeting by the arrangement of a series of best two out of three games, each club to take the whole gate receipts of each game they win, the only fair arrangement possible. The players of the two teams are anxious for the games, and the newspaper talk—largely encouraged by the two clubs for advertising purposes—has roused up considerable local excitement on the subject, and when the two teams meet next April, as they undoubtedly will there will be the largest gatherings seen at Washington Park and the Polo Grounds ever seen at any Spring exhibitions.

—Brooklyn *Daily Eagle*

Wednesday, January 30

Dave Foutz's friends among the base ball fraternity in this city are of the opinion that under his leadership the Brooklyn Club would win the pennant. Dave himself is very modest regarding his ability to land the club at the head of the procession. Said he: "Our batteries are superior to any in the American Association. With the support that the batteries will receive from the strongest field in the Association, it seems impossible for us to lose. I think the St. Louis and Athletic Clubs will trouble us most."

When asked whether he would captain the team, Dave replied that he had as yet received no intimation of such an appointment. "I have heard from outsiders and read in the newspapers that it was the intention of the management to put me in charge, but from no other source. If I were selected I would do my utmost to merit the confidence reposed in me. Of course to be successful the captain of a nine must act with the manager, otherwise there will be discord. It will not do for the manager sitting on the bench to direct a batsman one way and then for the captain on the coaching lines to give a different order. With McGunnigle I am on the best of terms. We understand each other perfectly, and would work together in harmony."

—St. Louis *Post-Dispatch*

Thursday, January 31

Hub Collins, the second baseman of the Brooklyn Club, will retire from the ranks of the bachelors to-day, as he will be united in marriage to Miss Lillie Williams.

—Brooklyn *Daily Eagle*

In reviewing the Brooklyn Club, the "coming champions" of the American Association, a dispatch from New York to the Cincinnati *Enquirer* says: Beginning with the key to the position, Caruthers, Terry and Thos. J. Lovett will do the pitching. The latter is a new acquisition, whose record last season was of the phenomenal order. Bushong, Clark and Joseph P. Visner, another man of whom great things are expected, will "pick 'em off the bat." Foutz will fill the Orr vacancy at first, Hub Collins will meander around second, while Pinckney gathers beechnuts at third. Geo. Smith whose injured arm is as good as new, will resume business at short. Darby O'Brien, John Corkhill and Tom Burns will do picket duty in left, center and right fields respectively. McGunnigle will do the managing and thinking. President Byrne declared that the Association pennant would surely float over Washington Park next year, provided all the plans mapped out are followed.

—St. Louis *Post-Dispatch*

Sunday, February 3

The three dates between New York and Brooklyn have been selected and the clubs will battle for the championship of the two cities on April 9, 11, and 13. Manager Mutrie is sure of the success of his team, and is willing to wager money on the result. "Why," he said, "it's just like finding money to bet on the Giants. They are bound to win. Of course, Brooklyn plays a fair game, but when the series begins there will be only one club in the race." Manager Byrne of Brooklyn says but little on the subject. He thinks that, according to public form and performances, the New Yorks ought to be the favorites, but he has faith in his club.

—New York *Times*

Short Stop Ward has written to the manager of the Washington Club, it is said, and made known his intention of accepting the offer of the Senators. This rumor has caused no small amount of uneasiness in Boston, as it was thought that Ward would surely accept the terms of the Boston team. Bostonians have been counting on Ward for this year, but it looks as if the wiry little short stop would disappoint them. "We would like to have him in our club," said Mike Kelly, "and I am sure our Directors will pay as much for his release as Washington will, if not more. If Ward doesn't go to Boston he will make a sad mistake."

—New York *Times*

The *Philadelphia Times* in a paragraph about the veteran Corkhill says: "One of the Quaker City's most famous natives on the ball field is

John Corkhill. John is bald-
headed and the boys kindly
allude to him as Pop. He
played ball upon the old
horse market grounds
twenty years ago and when
he was appointed a policeman he patrolled a beat in
that vicinity. John hankered
after the diamond, how-
ever, and he soon dropped
his star and billy. He accepted a position with the
Philadelphia Club, but the
next season he migrated to
Cincinnati. In Porkopolis
Corkhill made a reputation
second to none as a center
fielder. Near the close of
last season Brooklyn pur-
chased Corkhill's release
from Cincinnati.

—Brooklyn
Daily Eagle

"Pop" Corkhill, center fielder, Brooklyn
Bridegrooms (New York *Clipper*, January
19, 1889).

Charlie King, the silver-haired cannon-ball twirler, who has pitched
himself into fame in the Brown Stocking camp, called on President Von
der Ahe yesterday and stated that at any time he was ready to sign for
the coming season. When asked what he thought the Browns' chances
were for the pennant King said: "Well, I guess we will not be very far in
the rear of the leader throughout the season, and will have something to
say as to who will carry off the coveted flag. I expect to work even harder
than I did last season toward getting the honors again, if possible."

—St. Louis *Post-Dispatch*

New York, February 2—The coming base ball season bids fair to
eclipse any preceding year in the history of the game. In a great mea-
sure this will be accounted for by the remarkable and successful tour
around the world of the Chicago and All-America teams.

The tour now being made under the management of Mr. Spalding
will have the same effect upon the base ball crank that Hasheesh has
upon a Turk. It will stimulate public interest in the game to a point never
before attained. In professional circles the whirl is greater both in volume

and extent than it has ever been before. The mills that grind professional grist have not been idle during the winter months. Boston, for instance, has a much stronger club at present than it could possibly have put into the field last season. Yet the Boston Club is more likely to fall to pieces through internal dissensions than any other club in the League.

In the matter of harmony combined with strength the New York Club undoubtedly holds the whip hand. Manager Mutrie is confident the club will lose no strength through the loss of Ward, but upon this point the public is still in doubt.

—St. Louis *Post-Dispatch*

Friday, February 8

It is well known that at the Ridgewood ball ground, where the Brooklyn Club plays its championship games on Sunday, there is a large local police force on hand to preserve order when necessary; but thus far there has been no need for their services, as the large assemblages of spectators which are gathered there to see the Brooklyn team play are of a character very different from the rather tough crowds who congregate at most of the cheap ball fields of Queens County.

—Brooklyn *Daily Eagle*

Saturday, February 9

Inspector McGinnis of the Bureau of Incumbrances spent the greater part of yesterday at the Polo Grounds watching the demolition of those portions of the high board fences that stood in the way of the proposed opening of One Hundred and Eleventh-street.

The work of demolition on the Sixth-avenue side of the grounds was done yesterday by a dozen sturdy men under the direction of Manager Mutrie of the New-York Baseball Club. Inspector McGinnis had the men and the disposition to continue the work begun by him on Thursday, but he gracefully gave way to Manager Mutrie, who said that, if the fence must come down, he preferred to take it down himself and save the lumber.

The action of the city authorities in clearing a way through the playground of the Giants was a grievous surprise to the baseball men, although it had been threatened for a long time. The refusal of the courts to grant an injunction against the Commissioner of Public Works left the coast clear, and the Commissioner promptly ordered the Bureau of

Incumbrances to remove every obstacle in the way of a 60-foot street that is to pass through the centre of the famous polo and baseball grounds.

There is much curiosity as to where the champions will play ball in this vicinity this Summer. Both President Day and Manager Mutrie declared yesterday that they did not know. Mr. Day remarked that even if a site should be selected at once it would not be possible to get it ready by the time the baseball season opened. Satisfactory grounds, it is said, can be secured at One Hundred and Fifty-fifth-street, overlooking the Hudson River.

—New York *Times*

Monday, February 11

Mr. R.L. Caruthers, the celebrated base ball pitcher, accompanied by his wife, arrived in the city yesterday, on his way to Hot Springs. Caruthers is looking well—about the same as he usually appears at this season of the year—and has not changed in any important feature since he was last seen in this city with his team, the Brooklyns. Of course Robert had only one way of thinking concerning the championship this year. In his opinion the Brooklyns would get it, barring accident. The team was never so strong and well equipped as it is at present, and if the Bridegrooms did not grasp the flag they would catch at it anyhow.

"As for St. Louis," said the old Brown-stocking pitcher, "I do not consider it safe to hazard an opinion. They are one of those teams you can tell nothing about. They are apt to jump in, take the bit between their teeth and go right ahead to the front and win hands down as they have done before; and then again, they are apt to fall down and get badly left. They are a good club, however, and I believe that St. Louis and the Athletics will prove to be the hardest clubs we will have to beat."

"What kind of pitching will you do this year?"

"I'm going to try to pitch better than I ever did. Last season I did not do as well as I should have done in pitching. I was not in the best of condition."

"What do you think of Foutz being made captain of the Brooklyns?"

"I think well of it. Foutz is a mighty good man and will do well in the place given him. I think the management could not have done better than to put him in to play first base regularly. In my opinion Foutz is one of the best first basemen in the country."

Caruthers said he was well pleased at the outlook for the season of 1889, and thought that it would be a bigger year for sport and money than base ball has ever seen since it was played under the present system.

He and Mrs. Caruthers left last night for Hot Springs, where he will stay and "boil out" until reporting time.

—St. Louis *Post-Dispatch*

Saturday, February 16

It may be definitely announced that there is not the slightest danger that the ball champions will carry on their season's games except on this island. The property in regard to which negotiations have begun is certainly quite as desirable as were the Polo Grounds. It is much more accessible, and it affords infinitely better opportunities for gathering and dispersing crowds of people.

It is situated across the Harlem River at One Hundred and Fifty-fifth-street, within about two blocks of the elevated station at that point. It is quite as easily reached by boats on the Harlem River, by trains on the New-York and Northern Road, and by trains on the New-York Central and Harlem Roads, the Central Company having promised to run a side track directly to the grounds. Boats by way of the Harlem River can, of course, come from downtown, affording quick and easy opportunity for the contingent of baseball enthusiasts in the business centres to reach the grounds with very little trouble.

—New York *Times*

The *Philadelphia Press*, in speaking of the probable league winners in 1889, says: "If individual strength in base ball was the criterion, Boston would get there beyond doubt. But individual strength counts for little. Team work is the most essential element in the success of a ball club, and team work is a stranger to that crew of veterans and youngsters who intend to make Boston their home this Summer. Dissensions have already arisen in the ranks of their club, and by the time the season opens Mike Kelly and his clique will have the Boston Club in a ferment of insurrection and insubordination, with the result we can all so easily predict."

—Brooklyn *Daily Eagle*

Arlie Latham's favorite expression is "Rasmatas." He says Chris has given him the "rasmatas" on the $200 he received last fall for playing the world's series. Chris now informs Arlie that the amount was advance money. Latham's rage is comical, and he says he will play in California this summer. All the same, he will turn up as chipper as ever when the Browns are ready for business.

—St. Louis *Post-Dispatch*

Mike "King" Kelly, Captain, catcher and right fielder, Boston Beaneaters (Library of Congress, Prints and Photographs Division [LOT 13163-08, no. 1]).

Monday, February 18

It is about settled that Kelly will captain the Boston team next season. Kelly will have a splendid set of men to handle, but he must learn to control his tongue if he wishes to be a colossal success. One thing is certain: If Kelly runs the team next season, the boys won't have to ride in antiquarian 'busses and dilapidated horse cars, which are occasionally pulled by an old mule.

—Boston *Herald*

Tuesday, February 19

The *St. Louis News*, in an article on wealthy ball players, has this to say about Caruthers: "Bob Caruthers, the $13,000 beauty of the Brooklyns, has far more wealth than any player in the country. Parisian Bob did not earn his big lump of United States dollars by the sweat of his brow, however. He came into possession of it through inheritance. Bob is a child of fortune. He belongs to one of the richest families in Chicago. About three years ago he was left about $30,000 by a grandfather, and his mother is now worth ten times that amount. Bob is one of three heirs, so that he is rich in prospects."

—Brooklyn *Daily Eagle*

Arlie Latham, surnamed "Monkey," is credited with having circulated the report that the Brooklyn Club management was desirous of securing his services. President Byrne declared the report untrue, and says that George Pinckney is about as good a third baseman as Brooklyn wants.

—St. Louis *Post-Dispatch*

An innovation in the score-card line will be made at Washington Park, Brooklyn, next season. It will be more in the line of a book, and consist of sixteen pages. Portraits of all the players of the home club will adorn the pages, with the records of each and the date of their joining the team. A schedule of the games will also be printed. It is promised that they will be very handsome and worthy of being retained as keepsakes.

—St. Louis *Post-Dispatch*

Thursday, February 21

Judging from recent developments the Giants are to be homeless. A resolution is before the Board of Aldermen, directing the grading of One Hundred and eleventh-street from Fifth to Lenox avenues, and if it is passed the Polo Grounds, dear to the memory of all lovers of out-door sports, will be a thing of the past. The resolution is in the hands of the committee on Public Works.

"If they decide to pave the street," said Manager Mutrie mournfully, when he was asked about the resolution by a *Times* reporter, "that will settle our diamond, as the street will take in a portion of Richardson's territory at second base. It's evident that the Aldermen are not in favor of physical culture. It's hard to part with the old grounds—the scene of hundreds of well-fought games—but such is fate, and I suppose that we will have to get a new diamond."

The management of the New-York Club is making an effort to hire or buy the Coogan estate at Eighth-avenue and One Hundred and Fifty-fifth-street. It would make a grand site for a ball ground. Something definite will be done in a few days. Ex-Assemblyman Joseph Gordon, a stockholder of the New-York Club, said that while Staten Island was a good place to play temporarily, he did not favor the scheme and would prefer to have the Giants' diamond in the upper portion of the city.

—New York *Times*

Saturday, February 23

Henry Chadwick says: "It is to be hoped that the custom of publishing club averages once a month during the season will be hereafter done away with, as it is undoubtedly a big incentive to play for record instead of the side. Aside from the effect of such publication in making players neglect team work in the field in order to play for their individual records, the fact remains that the statistics of players' averages—especially those of their batting—present the most unreliable data imaginable on which to base an estimate of a player's skill, either at the bat or in the field. By these averages the batsman who strives the most to make a show for his record is given the place of honor in the statistical table, while the batsman who really did the most to win the games against the record player, finds himself left out in the cold."

—St. Louis *Post-Dispatch*

Two years ago Mike Kelly was the hero of space writers. Last year Clarkson engrossed their attention, and now John Ward has the call. These three players have received more attention from base ball writers and base ball men than they deserve.

—St. Louis *Post-Dispatch*

Sunday, February 24

The unmistakable form of Director "Bill" Conant of the Boston Base Ball Club was seen on Columbus avenue yesterday within sight of the airy towers of the grand stand that cost such a fabulous amount, and that has been such a good "ad." for the Boston club. The writer thus addressed him:

"Mr. Conant, do you share the confident feeling of your partner, Mr. Billings, that the Boston club will be able to secure the great short-stop, John Montgomery Ward?"

"No," was the answer. "I do not. I do not believe for one instant that Mr. John B. Day is going to allow Ward to play in Boston. He thinks that we are strong enough already. He does not want to give us a team that would be practically invincible, as we would be if we signed Ward. I do not think there would be the least difficulty in our winning the pennant if we got Ward. Of course I would like to see Ward play in Boston for many reasons, but I am afraid that it will be no go."

—Boston *Herald*

Monday, February 25

Johnny Ward has been heard from, and according to his own statement nothing would suit him better than to be a member of the hub aggregation of 1889. "There are many reasons," says Ward, "why I am not likely to be a member of the Washington team next season." In the first place, if Ward goes to Washington Mr. Hewitt will have to pay him nearly double the salary of any man in the team. Ward received $4000 from New York last season to play shortstop, and if he is going to captain and manage a team nothing short of $5000 will satisfy him, although he may be secured for a little less. He wanted John B. Day to give him $5000 last season, which almost took the genial John B.'s breath away. If Ward does not play at Washington next season—and it is doubtful— the game will receive a black eye in the national capital; and this is to be deplored, as Washington is fast becoming one of the very best ball towns in this country.

—Boston *Herald*

Tuesday, February 26

Mr. J.F.G. Blackhurst, the New York lawyer who drew up the Brotherhood contract, says: "According to the terms of the Brotherhood contract, it is provided that a player can be reserved for the same figure that he received for the season just ended. The contract with reservation is a quasi-perpetual one, and it is well settled that the rights of either party cannot be determined impaired without its consent. Despite this fact, two league clubs are endeavoring to reduce the salaries of reserved players without their consent. Players who have signed the Brotherhood contract, and who have been reserved, need not be alarmed. The absence of Mr. Ward, President of the Brotherhood, is particularly unfortunate to those members who are in doubt about their rights."

—Boston *Herald*

Friday, March 1

New York, Feb. 28, 1889—Dark clouds are rolling up in the base ball sky, and, as the season draws near, the prospect for trouble becomes more threatening. The great horsecar strike of this city will be small compared with the strike that is promised by the base ball players, for they say that not a ball will be turned by a league player next season unless the present trouble is settled. The whole trouble comes from the new grading system, which cuts down many of the players' salaries, whereas the league contract specifies that a player shall not sign a contract for less than the amount of salary that he received during the season before.

—Boston *Herald*

Sunday, March 3

The American Association season this year promises great things in the way of interesting and close struggles, and a harder fight than ever for championship honors. There is a feeling of determination begot of demure reflection in the Association ranks against the planting of the "Five-Time Flyers" flag on St. Louis Territory, and the people of St. Louis will see one of the grandest championship battles on record in consequence.

Capt. Comiskey and his men are cordially hated by his Association competitors, because success makes then weary. They are crying out from the bottom of the consomme in desperation over their inability to get on top. The *Post-Dispatch* predicts that the base ball season of 1889 will be the most brilliant in the point of attractiveness and patronage seen in St. Louis since the famous days of 1883. The Browns may not win the pennant, but they'll be within earshot of the guns fired in celebration of the victory in October next.

—St. Louis *Post-Dispatch*

Base ball, particularly on Sunday, is a boon to the working man, clerk, business or professional man, who finds himself so occupied on week days that he is only too glad to embrace the fresh air, together with the opportunity, to enjoy the benefits derived from association with the national game and the solid enjoyment it affords. He finds enthusiastic expression in the return of the 25-cent rate of admission, and Sportsman's Park will once again resound with the huzzas of tens of thousands of patrons.

—St. Louis *Post-Dispatch*

Monday, March 4

An interesting question arises and that is "What have the New York Club's players been doing this winter?" Mr. Langdon M. Smith, base ball editor of the *World*, says of Ewing and Connor that "Ewing is rather fond of an easy time, and from all reports has become rather aldermanic. This has ever been the case with Buck. He becomes as fat as a prize ox during the Winter, and repents in sackcloth and sweaters in the Spring. He is a hard trainer, and on bright Spring mornings can be heard loudly bewailing the evil effects of Cincinnati beer as he trots around the cinder path. Roger Connor has been having high old times in Waterbury this Winter. He, too, has put on enough flesh to build an ordinary man outright, but Roger's colossal frame does not seem hampered in the least. He has made ineffectual efforts for several months to reduce his weight by playing dominoes every night with a choice set of cronies, but has finally given up the scheme in disgust and will go into a gymnasium next week."

—Brooklyn *Daily Eagle*

Tuesday, March 5

Washington, D.C., March 4, 1889—The delegates to the schedule meeting of the National League are coming in on every train, and by morning all will have arrived and the meeting will convene at the Arlington at noon. The topic that appears to be most in favor is the announced return of John Montgomery Ward. Some of the delegates believe he has been sent for by the brotherhood to settle the matter regarding the disgruntlers who refuse to sign under the new graded salary list. Others say he comes to settle definitely with Mr. Day as to his own location for this season, not wishing to remain in a state of uncertainty any longer.

—Boston *Herald*

Wednesday, March 6

The report of the committee selected to revise the Association constitution was presented by Mr. Byrne. A change provides that in case none of the substitute umpires are present at the game when the regular umpire is absent a list of three persons from the audience shall be furnished, and should either captain refuse to accept one of these the game shall be declared forfeited to the club willing to accept the services.

As regards the classification of salaries, the association took no action, and proposes to benefit by the experience of the league, and will take no action before the Fall at least.

—Brooklyn *Daily Eagle*

Monday, March 11

New York, March 10—On Friday I dropped in to see "Brother" Mike Kelly at his saloon. It is a gem of a place, and is getting more and more popular. It is the universal verdict that he has a gold mine here. Of course, having become the proprietor of a place of this kind, rumors thick and fast must spread about his ways, but it can be truthfully said that the great and only Mike never looked finer than he is looking now.

"How do you like the business, Mike?" I asked him. "I can't say that I am over enthusiastic over it," was his answer. "I do not like this rolling around doing nothing. Day before yesterday I walked eight miles. I expect to be in good condition by the time the season opens. I am coming over to Boston this week to take part in the Elks' benefit, where I will recite 'Casey at the Bat.' I haven't begun to learn it yet. I suppose that I will have to begin, but I assure you that I would rather be excused."

There are many here, more than in Boston, who think that Kelly will make a far better captain than Ward or Morrill. As a gentleman in Spalding's said: "When you get a captain of a nine, one of the very first things that you want is one who has plenty of snap and go. There are plenty of captains who would act in a half-afraid, half-asleep way if they had the strongest nine on the diamond. Now, Kelly is no one of that kind."

—Charles J. Foley, Boston *Herald*

Tuesday, March 19

Nine muscular men, stripped to the waist, occupied the gymnasium of the Brooklyn Athletic Association, on DeKalb avenue, this morning. They were Manager McGunnigle's boys, and a pleasing spectacle they presented to the exacting manager. A more robust, bronzed faced crew of ball tossers, trim from heel to crown, more completely equipped in physical proportions, never before reported for a campaign on the diamond in this city. Bright eyes, knotty, muscular frames, quick movements, with a firm tread, indicate that the Winter has been spent in constant practice. Every man is trained down to his gristle and bone weight.

Towering above them all is Dave Foutz, a giant in stature, with an overhead reach that will corral a sky scraper. In form he is spare and sinewy, weighing but 162 pounds; in marked contrast as regards weight with the heavy man of the club, Pitcher William Terry, who carries about with him 186 pounds of humanity. Altogether Brooklyn will be represented in the pennant contest by over two thousand pounds of as hard a team to conquer as ever played base ball.

—Brooklyn *Daily Eagle*

The Browns' manager-captain, Charles Comiskey, arrived in town this morning from Chicago looking like a four-time winner. He was in high spirits when a *Post-Dispatch* reporter met him down town.

"Will the Browns win the pennant this season?" the reporter asked.

"I'll tell you better in October," said Champion Charley. "But you can rest assured that with the team we will have this season we will have a little something to say as to the ultimate outcome of the race."

"What do you think of the Brooklyns, Athletics and Cincinnatis?"

"What do I think of them? Well, they are a lot of daisies, and they'll be in the race from beginning to end. Old Davie Foutz will handle the reins as captain in a manner that will surprise the country. He's a good one."

Comiskey is looking the picture of health, and will at once start in to get down to business for the coming season.

—St. Louis *Post-Dispatch*

Thursday, March 21

Brooklyn Base ball Club players rode astride bicycles in the park Tuesday afternoon. These athletic young men, dashing furiously along the drives on Schwallbach's web spoked machines, attracted the attention of fair promenaders, who seemed to admire very much the splendid appearance of Manager McGunnigle's pets, sitting erect upon their dizzy seats. It was better than a matinee at the theater.

The question of choosing a captain for the team was broached to some of the players yesterday and the sentiment seems to be in favor of Foutz. "He is the proper man for the place," said Tommy Burns. "I don't know of any other man who is looking for it. I think Foutz will be our captain."

—Brooklyn *Daily Eagle*

Sunday, March 24

The base ball players who have signed contracts with the Boston club for the season of 1889 have received instructions to report at the gymnasium of the Y.M.C.A. at 10 o'clock tomorrow morning, preparatory to taking a course of exercise preliminary to the more active service on the diamond. The Boston club will open the season with the following players:

Pitchers, Clarkson, Radbourn, Madden, Sowders; catchers, Bennett, Ganzel, Sommers; 1b., Brouthers; 2b., Quinn; 3b., Nash; s.s., Morrill, Wise or Ray; l.f., Richardson; c.f., Johnston; r.f., Kelly. It is, therefore, on these 16 men that Bostonians will base their hopes for the winning of the league pennant of the season of 1889.

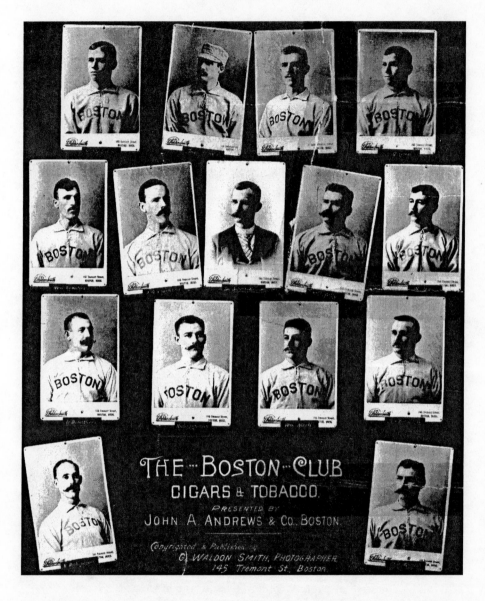

Boston Beaneaters, 1889. *Top row, left to right:* "Kid" Madden, Tom Brown, Charlie Ganzel, Joe Quinn; *second row, left to right:* Billy Sowders, John Clarkson, Manager James Hart, "King" Kelly, Irv Ray; *third row, left to right:* Dan Brouthers, Dick Johnston, Billy Nash, Hoss Radbourn; *bottom row, left:* Hardie Richardson, *right:* Charlie Bennett (National Baseball Hall of Fame Library, Cooperstown, NY).

On paper it looks like a formidable array of base ball talent, and such it undoubtedly is. In its battery department the club is as well equipped as a whole as any club in the league. On the bases the team is strong in both batting and fielding ability, and the same may be said of the outfield.

—Boston *Herald*

Monday, March 25

The noted ball tosser, John M. Ward, arrived early at New York Saturday morning on the steamer Saale. He seemed to be in excellent health, though he appeared a bit travel worn and had a foreign air about him that will probably soon wear away. He was neatly dressed, wearing a high hat, patent leather shoes and carried a natty cane. He said about his release: "I cannot tell anything about the matter until I receive more definite information about the course that is to be pursued. I learn that there is some talk about my playing in Boston. I have heard nothing whatsoever from the Boston management in relation to this matter, so that if they are trying to secure my services, they are negotiating with the Washington end of the string."

"What do you think of the Boston nine?"

"The addition of the Detroit players will undoubtedly greatly strengthen them, and if there are no factions in the team, and harmony prevails, the club will stand a pretty good show for the pennant. Between the cities of New York, Boston, and Washington, however, I prefer them in the order named. I refer to the city, bear in mind, and not the club. It is the city that I like."

"How about the classification scheme?"

"That is a matter that I will have to study carefully before I care to venture upon an opinion. You may rest assured that the brotherhood will take no step until there has been a thorough discussion of the matter. It is not true that my early arrival in advance of the rest of the party was caused by this classification idea. I came home on personal business and for no other reason. Regarding my destination, it will be entirely a matter of salary. If I am to be sold for $12,000, I think that I ought to have, say, half of the purchase money. Base ball is a business and I will go where I can do the best. I have no sentimental ideas about the city that will get me."

Many are of the opinion here that, after all, Ward will play in New York.

—Boston *Herald*

The Brooklyn team will open with Pitchers Caruthers, Terry, Foutz, Hughes and Lovett, all with their pitching arms in good order, Terry especially being in splendid form. Catchers Bushong and Visner will do the catching for April, and Clarke will no doubt report before Saturday. Their infield is the strongest they have yet placed in the field at the beginning of a season, including, as it does, Foutz, Collins, Pinkney and Smith, and as for the outfield, with O'Brien, Corkhill and Burns in position, it has no superior in the Association.

—Brooklyn *Daily Eagle*

Tuesday, March 26

Tim Keefe and Ward had a consultation yesterday as to the affairs of the brotherhood. No meeting will be convened until the annual meeting in May. The probability is that everything will be settled amicably between the league and the brotherhood. Their interests are, to a certain extent identical, as what injures the league hurts the brotherhood.

—Brooklyn *Daily Eagle*

The Polo Ground question is yet unsettled. It is the old Aldermanic point of the amount of "sugar" required to secure the privilege of using the ground one more season. The property owners want the street opened; the public want the club to hold the field until October. The committee and the Board of Aldermen, if they consulted only public interest in the matter, could settle it in an hour; but in these days of "boodle" deals it requires time to get out the highest bids for votes. As Marc Antony says, the Aldermen are "all honorable men." Yet each man has his price, apparently, with a few exceptions.

—Brooklyn *Daily Eagle*

Friday, March 29

Tim Keefe, in commenting on Ward's remaining in the New York team, said: "I hope John will stay in New York. I feel sure that the boys all wish him to remain. Whatever differences there may be between Ward and other players, there is not one of them but appreciates his magnificent work on the field. If he should go the club would be very greatly weakened."

—Brooklyn *Daily Eagle*

Saturday, March 30

This morning Foutz was unanimously elected captain of the team for the season, Corkhill, as the senior player, having charge of the outfield.

The new score sheet book was issued this afternoon and the sale was great, as it was such a decided improvement over the old score card. It contains page portraits of all the players, with sketches of each, as also the full schedule of the season's games and a picture of the great crowd present last Decoration Day at Washington Park. The book is a credit to Charley Ebbetts, who edited it.

—Brooklyn *Daily Eagle*

Buffalo's star attraction, who has divided the honors with Grover Cleveland, has arrived in town. He showed up at President Von der Ahe's office this morning and was readily recognized in the person of Elton Chamberlain, the Browns' handsome young pitcher. Chamberlain has certainly taken great care of himself the past winter, and he looks as though he could jump in and pitch the game of his life.

—St. Louis *Post-Dispatch*

Monday, April 1

Mr. Day has offered to give $10,000 to the city's charities for the privilege of using the Polo Grounds up to October 15. If this fails to give the club the grounds, they will play at Staten Island.

—Brooklyn *Daily Eagle*

Tuesday, April 2

The Brooklyn team have the hardest campaign to go through with of any since they have been in the association. In the first place their seven opponents in the arena are stronger than they ever were before, and all are bent upon downing the Brooklyn team above all others. The three leaders, the St. Louis, Athletic and Cincinnati clubs, will leave no stone unturned to whip the "Bridegrooms," no matter how they may stand with each other. What a crowd there will be at the Athletic grounds on April 17 to see the first championship match of the season between the Brooklyn and Athletic teams.

—Brooklyn *Daily Eagle*

President Von der Ahe stated this morning for the special benefit of the players of the Browns who have not yet signed, that only those who have signed will be allowed to wear the new uniforms provided for the team. Some of the men are holding off for outrageously high salaries, and they will be wallowing in the soup before President Von der Ahe will submit to their high-horse terms. Those who are holding off will be denied all the privileges of the park, and when they do sign they will do it at a very considerable reduction from the original terms offered by President Von der Ahe.

—St. Louis *Post-Dispatch*

Wednesday, April 3

Washington, D.C., April 3—Washington is all torn up over the press dispatches received here to-day stating that John Ward had declared he would not come to this city. He is quoted as saying: "I have as yet made no arrangements with Mr. Day. I don't know whether I will play here or not. That depends on Mr. Day himself. I certainly shall not go to Washington."

Since the annual meeting of the League last autumn the local management has been banking entirely on Ward and the blow occasioned by the failure to secure his services will be keenly felt.

—St. Louis *Post-Dispatch*

It costs something to put a first-class nine in the field nowadays. The Brooklyn Club rented Washington Park five years ago for $2,000 a year. Now the club pays $6,000 a year according to a new lease.

—St. Louis *Post-Dispatch*

Thursday, April 4

How will the Boston nine do this year is the question that has been agitating the base ball fraternity, and the interest taken in the answer increases as the time approaches for the men to take the field. As far as can be said of the immense sums of money that the Boston management has spent, and is willing still further to spend, to place the best ball nine in the world in this city, if the acquisition of the cream of the famous Detroit players is any criterion, Boston will have a nine that will play better ball than has been seen here for many a day. So strong is it that it is conceded that if Ward were to come to Boston the club would be almost invulnerable, and President Day acknowledges this fact by refusing to allow that player to come.

—Boston *Herald*

Friday, April 5

To-morrow the great series begins for the championship of the Metropolis between the American team of Brooklyn and the league team of New York. Every arrangement has been made to accommodate the vast crowd which will be present. The weather promises to be favorable, and as there is ample room for 20,000 spectators the scene is likely to be one to be remembered. Both teams are sanguine of success and the contest will be an exciting one beyond doubt. All three of the games will be played at Washington Park, the second on Thursday next and the last on Saturday. What an excitement there would be if each should win one and then end the series in a draw.

—Brooklyn *Daily Eagle*

John M. Ward is determined to retire from ball playing after the close of 1890, if not before. He is fixed upon entering the legal profession, which he has been training for for the past three years. His experience in managing the All America team has taken all the romance out of his head in regard to taking upon himself the control of a league team, and he is now likely to finish his career in the New York Club.

—Brooklyn *Daily Eagle*

New York and Brooklyn have thirty conflicting dates, and yet Byrne doesn't care. Last year he tried to avoid as many conflicts as possible, going to considerable awkward jumping, all of which might have been avoided had the schedule been made out like the present one, regardless of the League schedule, as the New York's opposition doesn't hurt Brooklyn much, and vice versa. It is only in Philadelphia where conflicts pinch both clubs badly.

—St. Louis *Post-Dispatch*

Saturday, April 6

The announcement on the *Herald* bulletin yesterday that Wise and Morrill had been released to Washington took the city by storm. The cranks gazed at the bulletin open-mouthed, and could scarcely credit

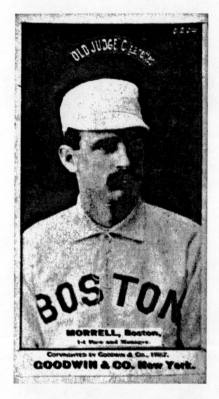

John Morrill, first baseman, Boston Beaneaters (Library of Congress, Prints and Photographs Division [LOT 13163-05, no. 11]).

their eyes. The fact that Morrill had signed, and especially his playing on Fast day, had caused them to believe that he was as valuable a man as ever. The blow is a severe one to thousands of lovers of the game in this city. They could have stood it had Morrill been retained in the team, even though not as captain, but his release was too much. One excited individual prophesied that the action of the directors would lead to a boycott of the team. "Mark my words," he said, "such action means disaster to the Boston club."

President Soden was genial and non-committal when a *Herald* man sought an interview yesterday. He said: "We have decided to release these two players to promote harmony in the nine. After the contest of Fast day it was very evident that Kelly and Morrill could not play in the same team in this city, so we allowed that man to go we felt could be the best spared."

If a little inside history could be revealed to the public, it would show that Morrill on Fast day did a very indiscreet act, and which was the very step which decided his fate in this city. On Fast day, before the games, Morrill saw President Soden and Director Conant, and mildly, yet firmly, informed them that he refused to captain the picked team that had been selected to pit against the Bostons on that day. Clarkson was thereupon selected as captain of the picked nine. By this act Morrill stood in his own light.

—Boston *Herald*

Sunday, April 7

Not content with winning first honors of the League and the world's championship, the New York Giants yesterday paved the way to adding new laurels to their list by defeating the Brooklyn Club in the opening game for the local championship. It was a grand game, and 10,000 persons witnessed it. The scores were far from being close, but this did not altogether have the effect of diminishing interest. The earnest manner in which the men played showed that they were straining every nerve to win, and their efforts were heartily applauded.

New Yorkers journeyed to Brooklyn in hundreds to witness the battle, and they yelled themselves hoarse cheering their favorites on to victory. Brooklynites, on the other hand, were as silent and mute as lambs. They expected to see their club take a game from the haughty Giants and had backed their opinion with cash. They could stand the loss of the money, but the jeers of the Gothamites irritated them and they left the grounds sad and forlorn and fully convinced that the Giants are, as Manager Mutrie put it, the same old Giants. While all of the New Yorkers played good ball great credit is due to Edward Crane, the big pitcher. He had just finished a tour of the world, but he did not appear a bit tired. He shot the ball across the plate with the speed of the wind so fast that the Brooklyn men almost wrenched the sockets of their arms hitting the atmosphere.

—New York *Times*

The big red ball of fire, which later resolved itself into the morning sun, had just made its appearance above Governor's Island yesterday morning, and had just received its daily welcome from the booming cannon there, when the steamer Laura M. Starin sped swiftly by Fort Williams, loaded with lovers of baseball and of baseball players on their way to welcome the returning players, who had arrived at Quarantine on the Adriatic a few hours before.

All of the ball players and the ladies who had accompanied them in their tour through many foreign countries were well and glad to get back to New-York. They seemed somewhat chagrined when they learned that neither President Harrison nor Mayor Grant nor the Board of Aldermen had come to bid them welcome, but otherwise they were quite pleased with the reception given them. It was a most demonstrative welcome, full of cheers and digs in the ribs and champagne.

Arrived at the foot of the West Twenty-second street, the players were landed, hustled into "coaches," and driven to the Fifth-Avenue Hotel, where everybody had breakfast. In the afternoon some of the party went over to see the game in Brooklyn, and in the evening they all went to Palmer's Theatre to see De Wolf Hopper. The theatre was elaborately decorated in honor of the returned players, flags of the different countries which had been visited by them being conspicuous in the adornments.

Mr. Hopper introduced so many baseball "gags" during the evening that the audience were not only treated to a very funny opera, but were given much practical information concerning our national game.

The baseball players since their departure from Chicago have played games in St. Paul, Minneapolis, Cedar Rapids, Des Moines, Omaha, Salt Lake City, and San Francisco, in America; at Honolulu, with King Kalakaua as a spectator, and in cities in Australia, New-Zealand, Ceylon, Egypt, Italy, France, England, and Ireland.

—New York *Times*

If President Day can get a lease of the grounds at Eighth-avenue and One Hundred and Fifty-fifth-street the Giants will play there as soon as a fence and a grand stand can be erected.

—New York *Times*

The Boston management has made two formal appointments—one of Michael J. Kelly as captain of the club, and the other of Mr. James A. Hart, as manager. Mr. Hart is 34 years of age, and a native of Girard, Pa. He is of medium height, slim, and his looks and manners indicate him to be of firm disposition and a man well calculated to fill the position to which he has been appointed. He has the reputation of being a successful financier and a strict disciplinarian.

—Boston *Herald*

The difference between the New York and Brooklyn clubs as they stand at present amounts to very little. In fact there are many people at both ends of the big bridge who are willing to wager good cold cash that the Association team will win the series.

—St. Louis *Post-Dispatch*

The Bostonians are beginning to think they have a great team and are already counting chickens that are yet in the shell. Outside people who are disposed to figure the thing up will possibly agree with them. They have a great aggregation of stars and no mistake about it, but the question that agitates the thoughtful Bostonian mind is whether the stars will agree to revolve in the same orbit or swing about in little groups without cohesion enough to make them effective.

Little faction fights are almost impossible of detection. It would be foolish to prophesy such a state of things in the Boston club, but of the entire eight clubs in the League the Bean-eaters appear to be the most likely victims of the virus of internal strife.

—St. Louis *Post-Dispatch*

Monday, April 8

DeWolf Hopper's recitation of "Casey at the Bat," at Palmer's Theater, on Saturday night, brought down the packed house in enthusiastic applause.
—Brooklyn *Daily Eagle*

Tuesday, April 9

Baseball has heretofore been regarded as an athletic game, in which muscle and a desire to dispute with the umpire have been potent factors. But that is all a mistake. Baseball is an intellectual pursuit, which is indulged in

De Wolf Hopper, comedian (New York *Clipper*, July 28, 1888).

only by gentlemen of the highest mental caliber, and by those whose minds have undergone a singularly stringent training in the matter of intellectuality. This fact was established last night at a dinner given in the great banquet hall at Delmonico's to the players whose tour through various foreign lands gave the American national game a world-wide fame.

The banquet hall was jammed with people and enthusiasm and champagne went hand-in-hand. Champagne sometimes got the better of enthusiasm, but the intellectuality of the gathering was its most conspicuous feature. Among the speakers calling the deepest and heartiest cheers from the lungs of the listeners were Mr. "Baby" Anson, Mr. "Johnny" Ward and Alfred C. Chapin, Mayor of Brooklyn.

Mayor Chapin was the first speaker. The fact that he hadn't seen a game of baseball for 25 years seemed to weigh upon Mr. Chapin's mind, and he said he only felt justified as appearing at this flow of reason by the fact that Brooklyn was familiarly regarded as the birthplace of baseball, and he lived in Brooklyn.

Mr. "Baby" Anson was considerably embarrassed when he rose to his feet, but was also thankful that he had been permitted to assist in teaching the world what it most needed to know, and Mr. "Johnny" Ward seemed glad of the opportunity given him to display his singularly correct knowledge of the English language.

Other speeches were made by gentlemen to whom the less intellectual habit of talking was most familiar, and the erudite persons present made generous allowance for their shortcomings. Mr. De Wolf Hopper and Mr. Digby Bell, gentlemen who combine an intellectual knowledge of baseball with a physical knowledge of how to be funny, came in late and made speeches.

The baseball season has begun.

—New York *Times*

Wednesday, April 10

New York, April 10—Helen Dauvray, after having, according to her agent, engaged nearly all her company and booked her tour for next season, has now, it is announced on the best authority, decided to not return to the stage at all, but to return instead to domestic life with her husband, John Montgomery Ward, the ball player. It is said that she and her husband had so serious a quarrel that they agreed to separate and that this was the reason that Mrs. Ward did not accompany the players on their recent tour of the world and for her determination to return to the stage. Man and wife have just been reconciled, and it is said that Ward's reason for wishing to sign with the New York Club is that his wife agreed to renounce her intention of acting again if he would do so and thus secure more time in the vicinity of New York during the ball season than he would have as a member of another club.

—St. Louis *Post-Dispatch*

Friday, April 12

New York's ball team is the proud possessor of three championships. Last season the Giants won first honors in the League, outplayed the St. Louis Browns in the world's series, and yesterday they carried off the deciding game for the local championship by defeating the Brooklyn team.

It was a contest that will long

Miss Helen Dauvray, actress and wife of John Montgomery Ward (New York *Clipper*, January 30, 1886).

be remembered by the admirers of the game of both cities. For nine innings both clubs struggled manfully without gaining any advantage, the scores at that period being even at 6 to 6. In the tenth, however, the New-Yorkers went to work with a will, and by good batting on the part of Ewing and Connor, each hitting the ball for three bases, scored two runs and won the game. In the last half of the tenth Brooklyn made a grand rally, and for a time matters looked gloomy for New-York, but a double play when three men were on bases ended the game in New-York's favor.

—New York *Times*

Something like seven thousand base ball enthusiasts went to Washington Park yesterday afternoon to witness the second game of the series for the local championship between the New York Giants and Brooklyn Bridegrooms. There have been games and games of ball, but yesterday's was a game of games. It was decidedly one of the most exciting contests ever played in this or any other vicinity.

—Brooklyn *Daily Eagle*

Saturday, April 13

Manager Hart, as it may not be known, has not the authority to select the team to play from day to day. This power has been delegated to the captain of the club. Mr. Hart, therefore, has no authority at all on the field, as is the case with all the other managers.

—Boston *Herald*

Sunday, April 14

After losing two games in succession to New York the Brooklyns somewhat retrieved themselves yesterday when they gave the Giants a dose of "whitewash." To Hughes's clever pitching can the victory be attributed. Keefe made his first appearance with the Giants and he was warmly welcomed. He pitched fairly well, but he was out of practice and failed to handle the sphere with his accustomed skill.

—New York *Times*

The Brooklyn team achieved the most noteworthy victory yesterday known in the history of the club, for they defeated the world's champion team with its strongest battery in position, not only winning the game, but adding to the triumph by retiring their powerful adversaries without a single run to their credit. The crowd in attendance was the largest ever gathered at a Spring exhibition game, over eight thousand people passing the gates.

—Brooklyn *Daily Eagle*

The heroes of the hour in New York, the observed of all observers for the past ten days, have been the returned base ball players. Victorious troops coming home from foreign countries could not have been more feted and petted than these heroes of the diamond. The leading men of the land, such as Chauncey Depew, for example, who has been spoken of seriously for the Presidency, the leading orator of the country, felt the importance of popularizing himself by speaking at their dinner; for he had never seen but one base ball game in his life and knew nothing whatever about the subject. Mark Twain did not know very much more about it than Depew, but considered it worthwhile to come all the way from Hartford and lend his humorous presence to the occasion. Everything at the dinner given in their honor contained a suggestion of the field, from the diamond shaped tables to the celluloid menus decorated with a miniature ball and bat. There were nine courses—called on the menu the "Innings"—nine toasts were proposed and responded to, and the ices were all frozen in shapes of pyramids and sphinxes, in memory of their Egyptian experiences, or of balls and bats, and the table decorations were all in the patriotic colors of red, white and blue. John Ward looks well and seems in the highest spirits. He apparently does not exert himself much to settle any of the controversies regarding his future, resting secure in the pleasant consciousness that he is valuable enough to be squabbled over, and that when competition has increased his opportunities he has simply to reach out his hand and choose the offer most agreeable to him. Apparently he has abandoned all idea of the law, for which he studied in Columbia College, and given himself entirely up to the profession of base ball, which at first he took up merely as a means of support until he could prepare himself for admission to the bar. Success in base ball is reached much more quickly, and he would toil at the legal profession many a long year before he could make as much money or hold as prominent a position in that difficult calling as in the business of ball twirling. His wife, Helen Dauvray, is hard at work getting ready for her appearance on the stage, which is to take place shortly, according to all the predictions of the theatrical people when she left the boards to take a leading part in the play of matrimony.

—*The Talk of New York*, Brooklyn *Daily Eagle*

Contrary to the usual custom of opening up the championship season in Louisville, in vogue for four years past, the Browns will start out this season at Cincinnati. Possibly the usual spring attack of excitement in that Ohio burg has superinduced the conclusion reached there, that the entrée of the champions will be in the nature of a picnic party for the red-hosed warriors. This seems to be the state of feeling over forthcoming meeting with the champions in Cincinnati, and so often has this feeling been given expression that the cranks of that town actually believe it.

While the porkers are overconfident there is nevertheless no gainsaying the fact that the Browns will have a hard fight in the coming conflict with the Cincinnati so-called coming champions. The high state of local interest in the coming games can be fairly estimated by the orders given in several mercantile houses to have the score bulletined by innings. It is a hard matter to down the red hot American enthusiasm on the deservedly popular national American pastime.

—St. Louis *Post-Dispatch*

Monday, April 15

President Von der Ahe accompanied the Browns to Indianapolis this morning. "We open the American Association championship season at Sportsman's Park on April 25. We propose to have a grand opening on that day, inaugurating what I am confident will be the greatest base ball season St. Louis will have ever seen. Sportsman's Park will be gaily decked with American flags with forty stars and the diamond will be resplendent with eleven stars from the town of Ohio pork."

"What do you think of the coming season?"

"I think the American Association Championship fight will be the hottest on record. Brooklyn is putting up a hard game to beat, and their team is unquestionably one of the greatest in the land. As for the Browns they'll be in the race from start to finish, and they'll make a hard fight to get there again."

—St. Louis *Post-Dispatch*

Thursday, April 18

On April 17, Opening Day in the American Association,
St. Louis won at Cincinnati 5–1 (King 1–0).
AA: St. Louis 1–0, Brooklyn 0–0.

There is a slight hitch between Timothy J. Keefe, the star pitcher of the New York Club and John B. Day, the President of that organization, caused by a difference of opinion. The difference amounts to just $1,000. Keefe thinks that his services for the coming year are worth $5,000, and President Day values them at $4,000. Keefe says that he will not play for less than the amount he asks, and President Day asserts that he will not increase the price he offers.

"Yes, it is true that I have asked for an increase," said Mr. Keefe yesterday. "I have played good ball for the New York Club, the organization has made money, and I do not think that my demands are unjust. As regards the classification system, I don't care a snap of my finger. If my terms are not agreed to I will attend to my sporting goods business and give up the diamond until matters are arranged to my satisfaction. The officers and managers of the New York Club are gentlemen; they have always treated me properly, and I do not feel inclined to sever my connection with the club. But for all that I want what I think I am worth and will not play for less."

"I had a talk with Keefe this morning," said President Day. "But he did not appear to be in a hurry to affix his signature to a contract. I offered Keefe $4,000 for the season, but he thinks he is worth $1,000 more. Keefe is a nice gentleman and a clever ball player, but I don't think his services or those of any other baseball player are worth more than my figure."

It is hoped by enthusiasts that the New-York President and the Giants' star pitcher will soon come to some agreement so that the genial "Tim" will be in harness when the championship season opens next week.

—New York *Times*

The largest crowd ever assembled in a Cincinnati ball park was present yesterday to witness the opening game of the American Association season between the Cincinnatis and the St. Louis Browns. People were standing fifteen and twenty deep around the park, and it is estimated that there were close to fifteen thousand people in attendance. King, who pitched for the Browns, was in magnificent form and pitched with wonderful speed, the red legs being unable to do anything with his delivery.

—St. Louis *Post-Dispatch*

Friday, April 19

On April 18, Brooklyn lost at Athletic 2–3 (Hughes 0–1).
St. Louis won at Cincinnati 12–4 (Chamberlain 1–0).
AA: St. Louis 2–0, Brooklyn 0–1.

After fighting in the courts and the Legislature for the past seven months the Giants have finally decided to give up their home on the Polo

Grounds, the scene of many a well-fought game, and move down to Staten Island to occupy the diamond vacated by Erastus Wiman's Metropolitan Club.

It was necessary to secure the St. George Grounds for the Spring and early Summer series. The Giants will pay a rental of $6,000 for St. George, and they have been promised that everything possible will be done for the convenience and transit of the patrons. If necessary boats will be run every five minutes to accommodate the large crowds.

"It is hard to be compelled to leave New York," said President Day yesterday. "But until we get new grounds no other course could be pursued. The club will begin the schedule of games on the island and perhaps stay there altogether if the place proves desirable. If it does not, why nothing remains for me to do but buy a plot of ground in the upper district adjacent to the elevated roads out of the jurisdiction of greedy real estate men."

The Boston club will meet the New Yorks in the opening game at St. George on Wednesday next.

—New York *Times*

Philadelphia, April 18—Smith, Brooklyn's shortstop, made a misplay to-day and lost the opening championship game to the Athletics. A bad throw to first gave Welch two bases, and he cleared the circuit when Stovey made a base hit.

—New York *Times*

The Browns gave the Cincinnati club another bad drubbing yesterday, defeating them by a score of 12 to 4. Only one hit was made by the Cincinnatis off Chamberlain's delivery in the first six innings. A feature of the game was the batting of Duffee, who made two home run drives, bringing in men from the bases both times. Duffee also made a remarkable catch in the seventh inning. The Browns ran bases ab libitum.

—St. Louis *Post-Dispatch*

Saturday, April 20

On April 19, Brooklyn won at Athletic 9–8 (Lovett 1–0).
St. Louis won at Cincinnati 4–3 (King 2–0).
AA: St. Louis 3–0, Brooklyn 1–1.

The Brooklyns defeated the Athletics at Philadelphia yesterday. A great throng had congregated on the outside of the gates long before the ticket offices were opened and from 2 o'clock to 3 o'clock a steady stream

American Association Opening Day, April 18, 1889, in Philadelphia, PA: Brooklyn Bridegrooms, *standing, left to right:* George Pinkney, Mickey Hughes, "Oyster" Burns, Darby O'Brien, Hub Collins; *sitting, left to right:* "Pop" Corkhill, Tom Lovett, Bob Clark, Manager Bill McGunnigle, Dave Foutz, Joe Visner, "Germany" Smith (National Baseball Hall of Fame Library, Cooperstown, NY).

of humanity was winding its way to the enclosure. On the inside every available seat was occupied by 3 o'clock and boxes were filled to their utmost capacity, forcing the late comers to climb on the roofs of the boxes, only to be pulled down by one of Lieutenant Lyon's big policemen. Ropes were strewn around the outfield and fully four thousand spectators were accommodated with standing room.

—Brooklyn *Daily Eagle*

This thing of the St. Louis Browns doing up the Cincinnatis is becoming very monotonous—to the Cincinnatis. It was a close contest, however, yesterday, the score standing 4 to 3. It was a game of kicks and wrangles, and Latham, Robinson and McCarthy all had trouble with Umpire Gaffney.

—St. Louis *Post-Dispatch*

Home-run Duffee is his name, and centerfield his station. Duffee will keep Tip O'Neill guessing this season on the leadership in the Association batting. He knows how to smash a ball and makes no apologies in smashing it.

—St. Louis *Post-Dispatch*

Sunday, April 21

On April 20, Brooklyn lost at Athletic 6–15 (Hughes 0–2).
St. Louis won at Cincinnati 2–0 (Chamberlain 2–0).
AA: St. Louis 4–0, Brooklyn 1–2.

Philadelphia, Pa., April 20—To-day's game, like that of yesterday, was characterized by heavy hitting, but this time it was the local players who did the slugging. Hughes was hit hard from the start, and in the sixth he was lifted out of the box. Captain Foutz then relieved Hughes and Terry went to first.

—Brooklyn *Daily Eagle*

Nothing could be more cruel and heartless than the conduct of the St. Louis Browns at Cincinnati the past week. They went to the Ohio metropolis and found its citizens rejoicing in the belief that they possessed a team that was certain to capture the American Association championship this season—ay, they believed them to be world-beaters. It was cruel and inhuman to disturb this belief, but the Browns did it. The good people of Cincinnati had warned their visitors that the red legs would get four straight games from them. And they did. They got them in the neck. A peculiarly excruciating feature of the action of the Browns was that they did this all while visitors to the Queen City and partaking of the hospitality and oleaginous butter of Cincinnati hostelries. They walloped the pride of the village of pork in their introductory meeting in the presence of over twelve thousand true and tried Ohio base ball cranks. Had it been any club but the Browns there would have been some limit to their thirst for pork blood, and they would have given the Reds at least one little game as a silver lining to their dark cloud of adversity and sorrow; but they in their insatiable greed, like Shylock, insisted on having every ounce of their pound of flesh. Alas that such monsters should claim this fair city as their home!

—St. Louis *Post-Dispatch*

There is no club in the Association which possesses so many good players as that from the City of Churches. Even strong players, however, do not always make strong clubs. The Brooklyns ought to show much better team-play this season than they did last, as the players were new to each other then. It will very likely be either them or the Athletics that the Browns will have to race home.

—St. Louis *Post-Dispatch*

Monday, April 22

On April 21, Brooklyn lost at Athletic 1–6 (Caruthers 0–1).
St. Louis won at Louisville 12–10 (King 3–0).
AA: St. Louis 5–0, Brooklyn 1–3.

The concluding game in the first Athletic-Brooklyn series was played at Gloucester, N.J., yesterday afternoon, and was won by the local team by better all-around play. Caruthers was hit hard and at the proper time, and his support was indifferent.

—Brooklyn *Daily Eagle*

Mr. Albert Mott, the "T.T.T." of the *Sporting Life*, and one of the most accomplished journalists of Baltimore, says: "Mike Kelly did himself no good in Baltimore. He was not a bit funny, and just a shade rowdyish. There is a vast difference between Kelly and Latham in this respect. Latham's antics are quick and graceful, Kelly's heavy and loaferish. Latham's sayings have a homely wit or an audacious interest, but never offend the proprieties, while Kelly's appear unnatural and stagey. Kelly appears to be straining to pose for effect; Latham's sayings and doings appear as the spontaneous effervescence of animal spirits. Kelly has deteriorated in the last year in play and manner, and people are asking themselves if the saloon business has anything to do with it."

"Backward, turn backward, oh time in thy jump; Make Kel a kid again, 'stead of a chump."

—Charles J. Foley, Boston *Herald*

The Browns are now alone in the lead in the American Association championship race, and they are apt to remain there. The Kansas City Club, which was tied with them for first place, lost at Cincinnati yesterday, while the Browns defeated Louisville. It was the largest crowd ever seen on the Louisville grounds which assembled there yesterday to witness the first appearance of the Association champions. So great was the gathering that play had to be suspended several times on account of the crowd encroaching on the field.

—St. Louis *Post-Dispatch*

Tuesday, April 23

On April 22, Brooklyn lost at Baltimore 4–6 (Lovett 1–1).
St. Louis won at Louisville 13–6 (Chamberlain 3–0).
AA: St. Louis 6–0, Brooklyn 1–4.

Every man in the team made errors except Foutz, and he erred in useless kicking on a point which only the umpire's judgment was concerned. This is bad enough in a player, but still worse in a captain. Owing to the percentage plan all the games have been pecuniarily profitable, the only consolation for the four defeats sustained in Philadelphia and Baltimore.

—Brooklyn *Daily Eagle*

Pitcher Caruthers says that "the new rules compel pitchers to send in balls over the plate, and that is what I propose to do, depending upon the excellent field behind me to catch the hit balls." In other words Caruthers will do a great deal of pitching for catches, and with the splendid outfield he has his point will be well taken provided he can make his batting opponents fungo balls. The pitcher who can do this effectively has heavy hitters at his mercy.

—Brooklyn *Daily Eagle*

The Browns kept up their winning streak at Louisville yesterday, when they defeated the home team by a score of 13 to 6. Chamberlain did very effective work in the box for the champions, all the hits made off him being scattered.

—St. Louis *Post-Dispatch*

AMERICAN ASSOCIATION STANDINGS

	W	L	PCT.	GB		W	L	PCT.	GB
St. Louis	6	0	1.000	—	Cincinnati	2	4	.333	4
Athletic	4	1	.800	1½	Brooklyn	1	4	.200	4½
Baltimore	4	1	.800	1½	Columbus	1	4	.200	4½
Kansas City	4	2	.667	2	Louisville	0	6	.000	6

Wednesday, April 24

On April 23, Brooklyn lost at Baltimore 4–5 (Terry 0–1).
St. Louis lost at Louisville 7–17 (Hudson 0–1).
AA: St. Louis 6–1, Brooklyn 1–5.

Albany, April 23—Gov. Hill vetoed the Polo Ground bill today, and the Giants will have to look for a new diamond to meet their opponents in contests for baseball supremacy.

"Unless the Board of Aldermen interfere in our behalf," said President Day yesterday, "the Giants will be compelled to desert New York and move down to Staten Island. For the present, however, I have arranged the two opening championship games to be played on the grounds of the Jersey City Club. On Friday, if I learn nothing favorable, preparations will be made to play at St. George. The latter is a beautiful place, but not as convenient to reach as our old grounds. Next year, however, you can rest assured the Giants will have a new diamond on Manhattan Island, second to none in the country and where we are not likely to be interfered with by grasping real estate men who have a pull in politics."

—New York *Times*

Baltimore, April 23—In a pitcher's game today the Brooklyns were defeated after a closely contested struggle. The attendance was 2,473, and the crowd wildly cheered as Hornung threw Foutz out at the plate in the ninth inning and preventing a "tie."

—New York *Times*

The managers of the New-York Club have come to the conclusion that they can dispense with the services of Short Stop Ward this year, and if any club wants to engage him an offer for his release will be entertained at once. Last season Ward received a big salary; his work was not of satisfactory character, and he was considered a drawback to the success of the club. His actions on and off the field did not suit his clubmates, and some of them openly avowed their intentions of never again playing in a team with him.

"Ward is a very jealous man," said one of the players to a *Times* reporter, "and he could not bear to see the club win with Ewing as Captain while he had made failures year after year. He clearly showed this last season, and nearly all the boys felt sore. Ward, while a good ball player, is afflicted with self-esteem, and thinks he knows more than anybody else about the game, while in reality Ewing knows more in one minute than the little short stop will ever know. I voice the sentiment of nearly all the players when I say that the Giants can play good ball and win the championship without the services of Ward."

"For some reason or another there appears to be a strong opposition to Ward," said President Day, "and for the best interests of the club I think it advisable to get another man in his place. Washington and Boston offered $12,000 for his release last Fall, but I did not care to let him go to Boston. Ward wouldn't go to Washington, but intimated that Boston would suit him. Now, if Boston wants him I will withdraw my objection and let him go there or anywhere."

Ward has been a member of the New-York Club since its organization in 1883. He has pitched, played centre field, second base, third base, and short stop, and was captain for four seasons.

—New York *Times*

"Yes, I'm feeling quite well, thank you," said the boss President, in response to the query of a *Post-Dispatch* reporter as to the condition of his health, both from a "game" point of view and physically.

"Did you lose any sleep in Cincinnati over the condition of affairs there?"

"No, the Browns put the Cincinnatis to sleep in a couple of rounds, and the city is in a state of innocuous desuetude over the calamity. The story has been well told in the newspapers, and it will prove an interesting page in the 'Tale of Two Cities.'"

—St. Louis *Post-Dispatch*

Thursday, April 25

On April 24, Opening Day in the National League,
New York lost to Boston 7–8 (Welch 0–1 and Clarkson 1–0).
Brooklyn lost at Baltimore 8–11 (Hughes 0–3).
NL: Boston 1–0, New York 0–1. AA: St. Louis 6–1, Brooklyn 1–6.

At 3:30 the bell rang, a signal for the New Yorks to appear. They marched down the field clad in their fine new habiliments of white knit jerseys, shirts and tights, black stockings, belts and caps, with "New York" in black letters across the front of the shirt. They presented a fine appearance, and naturally the champions awoke feelings of patriotic pride in the spectators, who applauded.

—Boston *Herald*

Centre fielder Gore of the Giants hit a ball for two bases at Oakland Park yesterday afternoon, a shout went up from the assemblage, and the championship season of the National Baseball League of 1889 had begun. There was a large crowd in the park, composed mainly of New Yorkers, who had followed their favorites to Jersey City in hopes of seeing them take a game from Boston's aggregation of culture and muscle.

—New York *Times*

New York Giants, 1889. *Back row, left to right:* George Gore, Elmer Foster, Mike Slattery, "Buck" Ewing, Willard "Bill" Brown, Bill George, Gil Hatfield, Jim O'Rourke, Mike Tiernan, Ed "Cannonball" Crane; *front row, left to right:* Danny Richardson, "Cannonball" Titcomb, Roger Connor, "Smiling" Mickey Welch, Manager Jim Mutrie, Art Whitney, Tim Keefe, Pat Murphy, John M. Ward (National Baseball Hall of Fame Library, Cooperstown, NY).

New York, April 24, 1889—With one run to tie, "Buck" Ewing was on third base in the ninth inning. There were two men out, and Dan Richardson at the bat. "Buck" cast an anxious eye toward the home plate. He is one of the "never sweats," and he fully expected that he would score that run. The number of sympathizers was not a few. With bated breath they saw three bad balls speed by Richardson. The Bostonians in the crowd felt blue. Then came one strike, two strikes, and the next ball went in the direction of Quinn, but Nash wouldn't let him take it. Quinn had seemed all thumbs in the game, and had let in one run, and Nash was determined to prevent further kindness. He made a clean pick-up, took deliberate aim, and the sphere in its winged course sped across the diamond and nestled in big Dan's eager, expectant and longing grasp just before Richardson crossed the base. The game was over, and many Bostonians present hurrahed themselves hoarse. It was a close shave.

—Boston *Herald*

The followers of the Giants sighed, buttoned up their coats, and started for the ferry displeased at the result of the first game of the season.

National League Opening Day, April 24, 1889, in Oakland Park, Jersey City, NJ: New York Giants vs. Boston Beaneaters, John Ward (batting) vs. John Clarkson (National Baseball Hall of Fame Library, Cooperstown, NY).

Good ball players are hard losers, and the Giants were the most unhappy men in the metropolis last night. Short Stop Ward, while not under contract, agreed to play with his team. When the announcement was made and Ward appeared on the field he was greeted with a round of applause.
—New York *Times*

Evidently Brooklyn opens the season in fearfully hard luck. All who saw the game admit that the element of luck was largely with the home club and against the visitors. They seem to be playing against fate.
—Brooklyn *Daily Eagle*

Manager Gus Schmelz and his Cincinnati Nadjies arrived here this morning from Dayton. Good-natured Gus has a reform he wishes to introduce into ball playing. It is to eliminate all coaching.

"There is very little difference nowadays between the actual playing strength of the various clubs and it is the coaching and bulldozing of the umpire which makes one team appear so much superior to another. Take,

for instance, the St. Louis team. Comiskey has got the umpires so bull-
dozed that his club gets the better of nearly every decision. So it is with
Anson of the Chicagos and Ewing of the New Yorks. Clubs see that it is
bulldozing that wins and they are employing men who they know will
play what is termed 'dirty ball.' Abolish coaching and bullying and you
will have a nice, genteel game and close and exciting games."

—St. Louis *Post-Dispatch*

Friday, April 26

On April 25, New York beat Boston 11–10
(Titcomb 1–0 and Madden 0–1). Brooklyn tied Columbus 9–9.
St. Louis beat Cincinnati 10–5 (King 4–0).
NL: New York 1–1, Boston 1–1. AA: St. Louis 7–1, Brooklyn 1–6.

Eleven to ten was the result of the New-York-Boston game yesterday, and as the Giants secured the greater number of runs joy reigned
in the metropolitan baseball circles last night. The Giants held the lead
from start to finish. With the exception of the last inning the on-lookers
never felt fearful of the result. At that stage, however, with two men out,
Hardie Richardson hit over the left-field fence for a home run, but preferred to remain at third base so as to make Catcher Brown get close to
the batter. The latter, however, did not bite at the bait. He paid no attention to Richardson, but retired the batsman after the occupant of third
base had walked home.

—New York *Times*

New York, April 25—The contest was played on Oakland Park, Jersey City, on the heights, which are always cold and the wind did blow
considerably. Umpire McQuaid again gave grave offence to the Bostons.
This seems to be, however, what must be expected in close games away
from home. Ten men—and under the double umpire system 11 men—
must beat. Friday's game will be played at Staten Island. As a stage runs
from second base to the outfield, the players in that territory will wear
rubber-soled shoes.

—Boston *Herald*

"Which is the home team, the dark blues or the light grays?" was a
question asked by a stranger at yesterday's contest at Washington Park;
and it was not a surprising question under the circumstances, for never
before did our local team receive the cold shoulder from the home crowd
as they did yesterday. A piece of stupid work by the captain gave the

visitors an advantage by giving them the last chance at the bat, and but for the rain this latter blunder would have given Columbus the game.

—Brooklyn *Daily Eagle*

After music by the band, a speech from Mayor Noonan and cheers from 8,000 people the Browns opened up on the Cincinnatis yesterday afternoon and fairly annihilated them. It was a gala occasion. The grand stand was crowded with ladies in handsome toilettes and the structure was richly decorated with bunting and flags. A new pennant floated from the flag-pole in the northern corner of the grounds. King pitched well for the Browns, and Boyle gave him good support.

—St. Louis *Post-Dispatch*

Saturday, April 27

On April 26, St. Louis beat Cincinnati 8–2 (Chamberlain 4–0).
AA: St. Louis 8–1, Brooklyn 1–6.

New York, April 26—It will be a great battle this year between the two league clubs now in this city, and the champions seem to have decidedly the better chances. They are stronger in the infield, outfield, in the box, in base running, sacrifice hitting and team work. This leaves only batting a mooted question. As a well known base ball expert, in speaking of the matter, has put it: "The Boston club is just strong enough to lose many games this year by one run. If certain players were worth $10,000, John Ward was worth every cent of that amount, if not more."

—Boston *Herald*

New York, April 27—At the Park Avenue Hotel yesterday there was a consultation among the members of the Base Ball Players' Brotherhood. Ward, Brouthers, Nash, Ganzel, Radbourn and several others were present. It leaked out that in future demands will be made upon the magnates during the championship season when, if necessary, a strike could be made effective. All the players in the League will be brought into the order and before next October the base ball money makers will know what concessions the players will demand. It is pretty certain the players will make a fight against the classification rule.

—St. Louis *Post-Dispatch*

Yesterday's game at Sportsman's Park was another easy victory for the Browns. Chamberlain pitched a wonderful game and had the visitors completely at his mercy. In one inning he retired the side on strikes, two of the men sawing wind after three balls had been called on the little pitcher.

—St. Louis *Post-Dispatch*

Such language as "Say, yer rotten, yer stinkin'," as Tebeau yelled frequently at Latham yesterday is rather coarse to be used in the presence of ladies and should not be tolerated on the ball field. That sort of hoodlum billingsgate is not calculated to elevate the game.

—St. Louis *Post-Dispatch*

Sunday, April 28

On April 27, St. Louis lost to Cincinnati 10–12 (King 4–1).
AA: St. Louis 8–2, Brooklyn 1–6.

The prediction that it would be a cold day when the Cincinnati Club downed the Browns was verified yesterday afternoon at Sportsman's Park. A strong wind, which at times almost approached a gale, was blowing from the northwest, and it was decidedly frigid in the open, exposed park, and the Cincinnatis won. The wind made ball playing decidedly difficult and interfered materially with the pitchers, who were unable to keep the ball over the plate.

—St. Louis *Post-Dispatch*

New York, April 27—Whatever may be said of the new four-ball rule there is no doubt that it increases the batting. No matter whether the pitchers are wild or not they are forced to drive the ball as nearly over the plate as possible, and it is a poor pitcher, indeed, who is unable to put a fast, straight ball over the rubber. The scores are noticeably heavy already, and those who have been longing for heavier batting and quickly moving games will find all they have been looking for before the end of the season.

—St. Louis *Post-Dispatch*

New York, April 27—Much surprise was occasioned late last week when it was announced that Foutz was no longer captain of the team and that O'Brien had been appointed to the position. The opinion seemed to be general that Foutz was admirably suited to the office, some even going so far as to predict that he would be a second Comiskey. He, however, has given up the captaincy voluntarily and he was relieved of it at his own request. Manager McGunnigle says: "Foutz asked to be excused on the ground that he could take care of first base better if he

were not captain. We therefore decided on O'Brien, as his work as captain last fall was satisfactory. We had great trouble in getting him to consent to take Foutz's place, but he finally did so."
—St. Louis
Post-Dispatch

Monday, April 29

On April 28,
St. Louis beat
Cincinnati 5–2
(Chamberlain 5–0).
AA: St. Louis 9–2,
Brooklyn 1–6.

Darby O'Brien, captain and left fielder, Brooklyn Bridegrooms (New York *Clipper*, June 23, 1888).

For a long while I have contended that ball players, as well as club owners, would be better off and have less wrangling if players would sign contracts to hold good for two, three or five years. As far as the length of time is concerned, it amounts to nothing, for at the present time a player can be held forever by a club under the present reserve rule. But by signing men for a certain period it would stop players from demanding exorbitant salaries every spring, as has been the case for the past few years with the New York club. The New Yorks won the world's championship, and this has caused the craniums of some of the players to swell.
—Charles J. Foley, Boston *Herald*

Mr. Mott, the able Baltimore correspondent of the *Sporting Life*, says of O'Brien as captain that "just what Darby will do remains to be seen, but Mr. Byrne has a jewel of a field director in Tom Burns, and, perhaps, in the end he may be tried. Tom has a violent temper, and sometimes makes himself disagreeable to the players, but he gets the work out of them when not hampered in his views. Beside, Tom is now older and more experienced and might not offend so much. Anyway, Brooklyn has the material for a team director, and in time will get there. The club is a strong one, and susceptible of the prettiest kind of field work and the heaviest of batting, and if anyone sizes them up for the season by what they have accomplished so far in the race he will be apt to get badly left in his reckoning."

—Brooklyn *Daily Eagle*

The Cincinnatis went down before the Browns for the seventh time yesterday and there was an audience of over 10,000 people to witness their humiliation. Chamberlain and Cyclone Duryea were the opposing twirlers and the little St. Louis pitcher proved himself the better man. Both pitched splendid games, however, and strangely enough, it was a home run drive by the St. Louis twirler which won the game.

—St. Louis *Post-Dispatch*

Tuesday, April 30

On April 29, New York beat Washington 4–2 (Crane 1–0).
Boston won at Philadelphia 8–3 (Clarkson 2–0).
Brooklyn beat Baltimore 7–5 (Terry 1–1).
NL: New York 2–1, Boston 2–1. AA: St. Louis 9–2, Brooklyn 2–6.

Even a centennial celebration cannot drown the enthusiasm of the baseball admirer. Over 3,000 journeyed to Staten Island yesterday to see New-York's ball players take possession of the diamond at St. George and win their opening game on their new grounds from the Washington Club. From the start to finish it was a battle of pitchers in which Crane excelled. The Senators once held the lead, but near the termination of the game the Giants made one of those spurts for which they are famous and carried off a victory.

In the last inning Whitney

Art Whitney, third baseman, New York Giants (Library of Congress, Prints and Photographs Division [LOT 13163-13, no. 9]).

OLD JUDGE CIGARETTES Goodwin & Co., New York.

and Crane sent two balls over the fence, each for a home run. Whitney's went over on a bound, and its progress was stopped by some debris, but the one hit by Crane was last seen making a bee line for the Narrows.

The ground is not in good condition to play on at present, but a force of men will be put to work and everything possible will be done to make needed improvements. In the outfield the old stage used in the spectaculars was occupied by the players, who were forced to wear rubber-soled shoes in order to prevent slipping while running after batted balls. Until the stage is removed the Giants will get big batting records. Balls bound by fielders with increased speed after they strike the woodwork, and hits that would ordinarily prove good for two bases will yield home runs.

—New York *Times*

Philadelphia, Pa., April 29, 1889—First blood in Philadelphia. The season opened gloriously here today, as far as the weather and the Bostons were concerned. They did some great playing, putting up such a stiff game as to astonish the spectators.

—Boston *Herald*

AMERICAN ASSOCIATION STANDINGS

	W	L	PCT.	GB		W	L	PCT.	GB
Athletic	8	1	.889	—	Cincinnati	4	7	.300	5
St. Louis	9	2	.818	—	Brooklyn	2	6	.250	5½
Baltimore	6	2	.750	1½	Louisville	2	8	.200	6½
Kansas City	6	4	.600	2½	Columbus	1	8	.111	7

NATIONAL LEAGUE STANDINGS

	W	L	PCT.	GB		W	L	PCT.	GB
New York	2	1	.667	—	Chicago	2	2	.500	½
Boston	2	1	.667	—	Philadelphia	1	1	.500	½
Cleveland	3	2	.600	—	Indianapolis	2	3	.400	1
Pittsburg	2	2	.500	½	Washington	0	2	.000	1½

Wednesday, May 1

On April 30, New York beat Washington 9–7 (Welch 1–1). Boston lost at Philadelphia 6–7 (Madden 0–2). Brooklyn lost to and beat Baltimore 3–5 and 7–2 (Lovett 1–2; Hughes 1–3). St. Louis beat Louisville twice 3–2 and 10–4 (Devlin 1–0; Chamberlain 6–0). NL: New York 3–1, Boston 2–2. AA: St. Louis 11–2, Brooklyn 3–7.

Fortune favored the Giants yesterday. The Senators played ball good enough to win nine games out of ten, but the New-Yorkers had the luck on their side, and in consequence the visitors had to bow to the inevitable and gracefully accept defeat. The leadership alternated several times, and it was not until the eighth inning, when the local players made one of their rallies, that the onlookers felt sanguine of success.

—New York *Times*

The infield work of Burns, Collins and Pinkney was excellent, two pretty catches by Burns being noteworthy. He is evidently the best man for captain of the team when he controls his temper.

—Brooklyn *Daily Eagle*

Keefe and the New-York Club have not yet come to any agreement. The probabilities are, however, that he will sign a contract to-day. Keefe was one of the spectators at Staten Island yesterday, and had a pleasant interview with Manager Mutrie.

—New York *Times*

Ten innings were required yesterday morning to decide the game between the Browns and the Louisvilles, and it proved to be the prettiest contest of the season. From the time the game opened until the last ball was pitched the result of the contest was as uncertain as the sun, which was playing hide-and-seek with the clouds all morning.

—St. Louis *Post-Dispatch*

Thursday, May 2

On May 1, New York beat Washington 16–3 (Crane 2–0).
Boston lost at Philadelphia 8–10 (Sowders 0–1).
Brooklyn beat Baltimore 6–2 (Caruthers 1–1).
St. Louis beat Louisville 9–1 (Devlin 2–0).
NL: New York 4–1, Boston 2–3. AA: St. Louis 12–2, Brooklyn 4–7.

For New-York Crane was at his best and he was given first-class support. The big pitcher sent the ball over the plate with the speed of the wind, and completely puzzled the Senators. Big Brown stood behind the bat and handled the fast delivery without flinching.

—New York *Times*

Philadelphia, Pa., May 1, 1889—Few expected that a game would be played, for it began to rain at about 3 o'clock, and it kept up almost the entire afternoon, slackening only toward the end of the game. The players went reluctantly on the grounds, which were thoroughly wet down before play began, so that the ball was very slippery and hard to use. As is usual, the wet ball was harder for the Bostons to handle than for their opponents. The combination of weather, wet ball, errors by Boston and terrific hitting gave Philadelphia a perfect picnic.

It looks as if Clarkson was our only winning pitcher, and it need not be at all surprising if he were to go into the box on Thursday. He has to work awfully hard to win games, even with the aggregation of batters behind him, but he is very willing, and he never grumbles when called upon.

—Boston *Herald*

The Brooklyn batsmen in this game hit fewer fungo balls than they have done in any game this season, they giving but three chances for catches in the entire game; and for the first time that they have supported Caruthers' pitching they lay well out in the field for the chances for catches he gave them. His pitching makes a lively batting and a beautiful fielding game, and if he is well backed up by skill and judgment in the outfield, especially when he faces a slugging batting nine, there is sure to be pretty work in the way of fielding as a rule.

—Brooklyn *Daily Eagle*

OLD JUDGE CIGARETTES Goodwin & Co., New York.

Bob Caruthers, pitcher, Brooklyn Bridegrooms (Library of Congress, Prints and Photographs Division [LOT 13163-13, no. 11]).

Friday, May 3

On May 2, New York beat Washington 16–3 (Welch 2–1).
Boston won at Philadelphia 5–4 (Clarkson 3–0).

Brooklyn beat Athletic 4–2 (Terry 2–1).
St. Louis beat Louisville 5–1 (King 5–1).
NL: New York 5–1, Boston 3–3. AA: St. Louis 13–2, Brooklyn 5–7.

Washington's League team proved its inability to cope favorably with the Giants yesterday. The latter hit the ball at will and scored runs until they tired. They made singles, doubles, and triples, to the intense delight of the spectators, and Connor and Gore created no small amount of enthusiasm by knocking the ball over the fence for home runs.

Welch has lost none of his effectiveness. In yesterday's contest he seemed to pitch in his old form, and his work was favorably commented upon in all parts of the grand stand.

—New York *Times*

Philadelphia, Pa., May 2, 1889—Another one-run game, the fourth thus played in six games by Boston, two of which have been won and two lost. It was a great game to win, and John Clarkson deserves about as much credit for winning it as anyone. Boston has now won three games out of six played, and Clarkson has been the pitcher in each of these.

—Boston *Herald*

It is true that the team did not handle the ash with such good effect as they did in their last Baltimore game, too many chances for catches being given the field yesterday, for one thing; and they failed in another point of play in batting, and that was in their not being ready to meet good balls when they came in. Judicious waiting for a base on balls is a good point for a batsman to play, but to play it properly he must keep himself ready for the first ball over the plate. This is no easy task in the face of a hot fire from an ill directed battery which obliges the batsman to look out for the ball too close to his person; but batsmen, under the existing rules, find this one of their regular duties. There was too much slugging at swiftly pitched balls and too little effort made to tap them safely over the heads of the infielders. This is not easy of accomplishment, but the effort to succeed leads to better results than follow the fungo hitting of the endeavor to slug for home runs.

—Brooklyn *Daily Eagle*

The Browns will play in Kansas City to-day without the services of Robinson, their second baseman. He went on a strike last night and refused to accompany the team to the City by the Kaw. Almost the entire club were on a strike with him last night, but now Robbie is holding out all by himself. The trouble all arose over Mr. Niehaus, who keeps the carriage gate at the park, refusing to admit a small boy and pair of Mr. Robinson's trousers to the base ball park free of import duty. Yesterday afternoon Robinson concluded that he would don a padded pair of playing trousers so before the game he sent a small boy over to his room right across from the park to get him a pair. When the boy returned with the trousers in his arm Mr. Niehaus refused to admit him, remarking that he could not get in even if he had them on his legs, as he had strict orders to let no one pass the gate without a ticket.

To say that the second baseman of the Browns was angry and indignant when he learned of the action of Mr. Niehaus is a mild, genteel way of putting it. He was frothing at the mouth. Niehaus received a call from the ball player and for a while listened to language that made his gray hairs stand on end. Robinson made no attempt to restrain his own or protect the old man's feelings. When he had finished the gate-keeper had a pretty fair idea of the second baseman's state of mind. Niehaus went to Mr. Von der Ahe with tears in his eyes, so the latter says, and complained of Robinson's action. The "Boss President" hunted up the ball tosser and proceeded to lecture him about the manner in which he had abused the gate-keeper. Robbie did not take kindly to Mr. Von der Ahe's remarks, and the result was a tongue-lashing match, which cost the ball player $25. Now this did not please Robinson any better than Mr. Niehaus' action. He did not think his speech was so bad that he should be charged $25 for delivering it, and he so informed Mr. Von der Ahe. He told him the fine was unjust, and if not removed he would not accompany the team to Kansas City. Mr. Von der Ahe refused to remove it. Then the fun commenced in real earnest.

The Browns' President had secured passage to Kansas City for the club over the Chicago, Burlington & Quincy road. At the depot Robinson took a firm stand that either the fine imposed must be remitted or he would play no more ball for the club and would not accompany them to Kansas City. Nearly all the members of the team agreed with him that the fine should not have been imposed, and they declared they would stick to him and remain here until the Browns' President gave in to his second baseman. Now it is a well-known fact that Mr. Von der Ahe has a fondness for running his team in his own way, and if there is anything he does not like it is to be dictated to by his players. He positively refused to remit the fine and Robinson was just as firm in his refusal to make the trip unless the fine was remitted. The result was that both sides held out and the Chicago, Burlington & Quincy train pulled out with President Von der Ahe, his son Eddie, Comiskey, the captain, and Duffee, the center-fielder, as the only representatives of the Champion Browns aboard. All the other players remained standing on the platform. As the clubs in the American Association are all under contract to play their games on schedule things looked pretty bad. Comiskey and Duffee could not hope to make any sort of a stand against the Cowboys, even if Mr. Von der Ahe and his son should jump in and help them out. How they should play was probably fully discussed by the quartette on the way up. After a great deal of argument and persuasion, Mr. Munson, the Secretary of the club, succeeded in getting all the balance of the men except Robinson to make the trip on the Missouri Pacific train, which left at 9:15 P.M., some time after the C., B. & Q. He had to purchase new tickets for them, however, so that the trip cost the organization double fares for all the men, except Comiskey and Duffee. O'Neill and Latham, it is alleged, missed the train by accident, having got off to look for Comiskey, who had stepped off and got aboard again just as the cars were pulling out. Robinson claims, however, that they were with him in the trouble and that all the players except the two who were in the car with the Browns' President would have been here yet if he had not persuaded them to go. He says that they will all stick to him until the trouble between Mr. Von der Ahe and himself has been settled.

Robinson when seen in reference to the trouble remarked: "I would rather not say anything about it, but as I suppose you will publish something anyhow, I will tell you how it occurred. Comiskey told me to get a pair of O'Neill's base ball trousers as my own are too small for me. About a half hour before the game I sent a boy over for the trousers and so that Niehaus would know he was not attempting to get in to see the game, I gave him a note explaining matters. Still the old man refused to let him in. Such a small, contemptible thing as that would anger anybody, I think, particularly when I was obeying my captain's orders in getting the pants. I did abuse the old man some and swore at him, and I suppose I should not have done so, but I was very angry. During the game Mr. Von der Ahe, who had received Niehaus' complaint, walked down the field to where I sat on the players' bench and commenced abusing me there before the people in the grand stand. I did not think that was right and I told him it was no place to talk about the matter. He said that I was no gentleman, and I retorted that I was as much of a gentleman as he was. Then he left, and afterward told me that I had been fined $25. If he had asked me to apologize to Niehaus I should have done so, although I think the old man gave me cause to get angry, but I think the fine was very unjust. I had nothing to do with the other players striking. They thought the fine an outrage and decided among themselves not to go to Kansas City unless it was remitted. They would not have left last night either, I don't think, if I had not gone away from the depot, where they could not talk to me and learn what I intended doing. I know Mr. Von der Ahe has it in his power to expel me, but I will never play with his team again unless he remits the fine. Of course, they can get along without me, and so can

I live without playing ball, although I cannot make anything like the same money at anything else."

—St. Louis *Post-Dispatch*

The Baltimore papers favor orange and black as the colors for their club. It would serve to give the nine a distinctive character all over the country, and would especially fit with the team name of "Orioles," besides reviving the glories of the old "Lord Baltimores," who wore the local colors and, for a time at least, did honor to them. President Stern of the Cincinnatis has decided to return to the old red stocking uniforms, regarding the black suits as "Jonahs." "Never again as long as I am at the head of the Cincinnati Club," he remarked yesterday, "will it depart from the red and white uniform."

—St. Louis *Post-Dispatch*

"Yank" Robinson, second baseman, St. Louis Browns (Library of Congress, Prints and Photographs Division [LOT 13163-13, no. 26]).

Saturday, May 4

On May 3, New York lost at Philadelphia 4–9 (Crane 2–1).
Boston won at Washington 9–6 (Madden 1–2).
Brooklyn beat Athletic 12–6 (Lovett 2–2).
St. Louis lost at Kansas City 3–16 (Chamberlain 6–1).
NL: New York 5–2, Boston 4–3. AA: St. Louis 13–3, Brooklyn 6–7.

Philadelphia, May 3—One bad inning ruined the Giants' chance of success to-day. It was the first. Crane, Ward, and Brown made several misplays before they got warmed up to their work, which the Philadelphia men took advantage of by scoring 7 runs. The visitors tried hard to overtake the Quakers, but without success, and were forced to succumb.

—New York *Times*

Washington, D.C., May 3, 1889—When the game began there were about 1000 people present. The wind blew strongly toward left field, and the weather was decidedly inclement. The players wore their cardigans, while the spectators buttoned their coats up to their chins, and shivered at that. The scorers wore gloves, and had an uncomfortable time of it.

—Boston *Herald*

Despite the fact that Manager McGunnigle is in favor of placing the opposing team first at the bat in every game he allows his men to overrule him on this point and to still keep in the old rut of having "the first crack at the new ball." What possible advantage there is in this rule is as much at command of the side last at the bat in the first inning as it is for those who go in first; but under the rule of using two new balls neither party have any advantage. Granting, however, that the rule does work the way the rutty ball captains claim it does, it does not compare with the far more important advantage of being last at the bat, thereby having the benefit of an opportunity for a winning rally.

—Brooklyn *Daily Eagle*

Robinson again refused to go to Kansas City last night to join the Browns unless the fine imposed upon him by Mr. Von der Ahe was remitted. This was not done and he remained here. The trouble has created considerable alarm among the admirers of the Browns, who fear it will cost St. Louis the championship. A number of friends advised the little second baseman to go to Kansas City and talk the matter over with Von der Ahe, but this he refused to do, saying he knew it would be of no use, and that if he gave in to the Browns' President he would always be treated badly. The trouble between President Von der Ahe and Robinson was unquestionably the underlying cause of the Browns' ignominious defeat at Kansas City yesterday afternoon. With one or two exceptions, the players' sympathies were with Robinson, and to "get even" with Mr. Von der Ahe, make him repent his action and remit the second baseman's fine, the team allowed the Cowboys to defeat them. Chamberlain pitched the first two innings of the game, and ten runs were made off him. The whole St. Louis team fielded miserably, Latham and O'Neill making several inexcusable errors, which proved conclusively with whom they were sympathizing. If the trouble is not settled it is more than likely that the Browns will lose every game in Kansas City. This will give them a setback that they may never be able to overcome. With proper playing they could almost clinch the pennant right now, as all the other clubs in the association have been sustaining frequent defeats. While Mr. Von der Ahe is blamed for talking to Robinson in front of the grand stand yesterday, the admirers of the team will score the little second baseman for the defeat the club sustained at Kansas City. If their poor play keeps up it will undoubtedly cause Robinson to lose what public sympathy he now has. Something should be done to settle the trouble. This is difficult, however, for if Mr. Von der Ahe gives in the players would do as they pleased hereafter, and Robinson is unwilling to recede from his stand. Comiskey, as captain of the team, the players would naturally expect to side with the President, but they will probably all be down with Duffee for not entering their combine, and are apt to make things disagreeable for the young center fielder, who is just establishing a reputation for himself. Very likely, as Comiskey stated in Kansas City in an interview, the bad play was due in part to the fact that there was no one on the train with the men, and they probably remained up all night playing cards and drinking so that they were in no condition to play ball. There must have been a pre-arranged play also to lose the game, and this work may be kept up until the trouble is settled. If so it will cost the nine the pennant unless the settlement is made very soon.

—St. Louis *Post-Dispatch*

Sunday, May 5

On May 4, New York lost at Philadelphia 2–11 (Titcomb 1–1).
Boston won at Washington 3–2 (Clarkson 4–0).
Brooklyn beat Athletic 9–5 (Hughes 2–3).
St. Louis lost at Kansas City 9–16 (King 5–2).
NL: New York 5–3, Boston 5–3. AA: St. Louis 13–4, Brooklyn 7–7.

Washington, D.C., May 4, 1889—Another one-run victory gained after a great struggle of pitchers, after a desperate battle. Clarkson again pitched, and had no easy task, for there was little hitting to help him. He showed as consummate skill as was ever seen on the ball field. Clarkson worked the batsmen to perfection, and his magnificent efforts evoked the commendation of all of the spectators. He is pitching in unprecedently fine form, and he will undoubtedly make a great record this season.

—Boston *Herald*

Kansas City, Mo., May 4—President Von der Ahe telegraphed Robinson this morning to report here for to-morrow's game. Robinson telegraphed back that he would come when the fine was remitted. Von der Ahe then announced that, beginning with to-morrow and continuing for four days, Robinson would be fined $25 a day, unless the second baseman "came to time" in the meantime. If, by the end of the four days Robinson did not come he would be expelled. When asked for an explanation of the two successive "Waterloos" Von der Ahe said that the Browns had simply been outplayed, a thing that was liable to happen to the best clubs in the world at times; that no club had ever been so good but what the poorest club could beat it occasionally. He scorned the idea that the Browns had deliberately "thrown" the games. "If I thought for a moment that they had done such a thing I would fire the whole club," he said. The only player who seemed, according to "der boss," to have not played as well as he could was O'Neill, and his case would be investigated, and he would probably be disciplined.

—St. Louis *Post-Dispatch*

New York, May 4—The Brooklyns have struck their gait and have begun to show that they are able to play winning ball. The fielders have regained confidence, and are playing in the best form. The pitchers have limbered up and the whole team is handling the stick with excellent effect. The consequence is that victories are taking the place of defeats,

Chris Von der Ahe, president, St. Louis Browns (Library of Congress, Prints and Photographs Division [LOT 13163-05, no. 418]).

and the boys will start on the first Western trip to-night with every prospect of a successful tour. Whether this improvement is due to Capt. O'Brien's regime or not is unknown, but certain it is that the nine has played better ball all round since he took charge. Life and energy seem to have been infused into their work and their playing is marked by a dash and determination that bear good fruit.

—St. Louis *Post-Dispatch*

Monday, May 6

On May 5, Brooklyn game versus Athletic declared a tie by umpire.
St. Louis lost at Kansas City 12–18 (King 5–3).
AA: St. Louis 13–5, Brooklyn 7–7.

The fine Spring weather yesterday and the promise of a very exciting contest led to the largest gathering of spectators ever seen at the Ridgewood Base Ball Park, no less than 12,614 people passing the gates on the occasion. A more orderly Sunday gathering was never seen on a ball field. In fact at no period since the grounds have been occupied by the Brooklyn Club has a better assemblage of spectators been present at the park; and yet the crowd put a stop to play in the sixth inning of the contest by rushing in on the outfield until it was impossible to proceed with the game. There was no disturbance and no excitement beyond the fact that the spectators encroached upon the field, one portion starting the move and the other following like a flock of sheep.

The ground officers went down to induce the crowd to stand back as they had done the previous five innings, and Mr. Byrne and O'Brien tried their best to get them back, while Stovey and Welch—as dozens of men were ready to testify—told the crowd they could move in if they liked, and they did so, and soon the Athletic players, who had gathered back of second base in a bunch, were surrounded, and it then became impossible to place the crowd back in their former position. Umpire Holland, seeing that the ground officials and Mr. Byrne had done their best to clear the field, and also that there was no possibility of having the contest resumed, called the game back to the last even five innings played, which left the game a draw, 1 to 1.

—Brooklyn *Daily Eagle*

There is something decidedly "queer" about the play of the Browns at Kansas City. When the team left here Thursday night they were in the best of trim, and both King and Chamberlain had been pitching magnificently. They never were in better shape. They met the Kansas City Club the next day and were beaten by a score of 16 to 3. Chamberlain started in to pitch for the Browns and 10 runs were scored off him in two innings. Saturday, King entered the box, and in the fifth, sixth and seventh innings 10 runs, 5 of them earned, were made off him. Yesterday these teams met for a third time and despite the apparent efforts of the Browns to lose they took a long lead and would certainly have won had not Devlin, who started out to pitch, been injured. Not a hit was made off him in the two innings he was in the box and five men had been struck out by him. Then King was brought in. The score was 11 to 7 in their favor at the end of the eighth. But King, who had been pitching rather poorly, let down completely in the ninth and eleven earned runs were made off him in that one inning, the Cowboys eventually winning by a score of 18 to 12. They would probably be batting yet had not Comiskey gone into the box and retired them.

No one who has ever seen the Browns play will believe for a moment that the Kansas City Club can bat either Chamberlain or King as they have done in this series provided those pitchers are playing ball. They have done what no other club has ever done or can do. Not only have the pitchers been batted hard, but the other players have made most outrageous errors in fielding. But one construction can be placed in the matter, and that is that the Browns are not trying to play ball. They are endeavoring to get "even" with Mr. Von der Ahe for fining Robinson and to force their employer to come to the second baseman's terms. However just any grievance they may have, it does not warrant them in throwing games. If Mr. Von der Ahe's methods are distasteful to them they can quit him, but they should not go through the semblance of playing and intentionally lose.

There is no question about the matter. The club is trying to lose as a club. It is hard to name individuals, but neither King nor Chamberlain can be held blameless. President Von der Ahe and the team will be back to-morrow, and the most rigid investigation should follow. It is better to play ball with an entire new nine than to have "crooked work" done by good players. The *Post-Dispatch* makes no charge of crookedness, but if it is plain that the Kansas City games are "on the dead," the Brown Stocking players should be made to show that such is the case. As for Robinson, he is still here. He drove through Forest Park and along the Boulevard yesterday behind a double team, with three friends, and stated that he would never play ball with the Browns until his fine of $25 was remitted.

—St. Louis *Post-Dispatch*

The Bostons are now on the road to victory, and before the month is out they should be snugly ensconced in first position. Clarkson seems to be the mainstay of the team, so far as the pitching department is concerned, and the boys feel confident of victory every time he is in the box. Radbourn needs warm weather; then he begins to thaw out and the rheumatism doesn't trouble him. Brouthers is hitting the ball on the nose, and drawing the claret right along. Big Dan has an engagement to put a couple over the centre field fence at the Boston grounds this season. Kelly has got settled down to business, and is playing like a Trojan (Kel was born in Troy). We have a great team, and the club that beats us out will be out of breath at the finish.

—Charles J. Foley, Boston *Herald*

Tuesday, May 7

On May 6, New York won at Philadelphia 13–9 (Welch 3–1).
Boston won at Washington 23–3 (Radbourn 1–0).

St. Louis won at Kansas City 11–9 (Chamberlain 7–1).
NL: New York 6–3, Boston 6–3. AA: St. Louis 14–5, Brooklyn 7–7.

Philadelphia, May 6—At last the Giants won a game here. They
started in with a vim to-day and scored 5 runs in the first inning. Satisfied
that the Giants had a commanding lead, Capt. Ewing retired in the fourth
inning and Brown went behind the bat.

—New York *Times*

Washington, D.C., May 6, 1889—"Rad" was in to pitch and the boys
to slug. "Rad" did pitch and the boys did slug. Such hitting, such pound-
ing, such running all over the lot by the Washington fielders.

It was not only one of the greatest batting exhibitions ever seen in
Washington, but one of the heaviest ever seen in the country, for the hitting was very clean and sharp. The men would have pounded anybody.
Brouthers' batting was simply awful. He is said to be the first one who
ever sent the ball over the centre field fence. That fence, it may be borne
in mind, is as far from the home plate as the Boston centre field fence.
The hit would have undoubtedly gone over our fence at Boston, and was
worth making the whole trip to see. The pitchers were afraid of Dan after
that, but when they put it there, how he did hit it.

—Boston *Herald*

The Browns managed to win a game at Kansas City yesterday
despite a seeming determination on their part to lose. Eleven to 9 was
the final score and the Browns had a number of their runs literally forced
upon them.

—St. Louis *Post-Dispatch*

President Chris Von der Ahe and the "quitters" arrived home early
this morning, fresh from the Waterloo at Kansas City. The Browns do
not enjoy the way the people here have been talking of their play in
Kansas City, and Mr. Von der Ahe and all his players claim they did their
best in the games and lost purely through hard luck.

Chamberlain remarked: "The claim that we were not trying to play
is all nonsense. The players did not think Robinson should be fined and
felt sore about it, but that did not prevent them from playing the best
ball they could. We are not foolish enough to do such a thing as that, as
we all know what the penalty would be."

Tip O'Neill, the long left fielder of the champions, who distinguished
himself in Kansas City as an error-maker, said: "I think that charge made
that the Browns threw the games at Kansas City is a most serious one
and is certainly unjust. It is no trifling matter to charge a club with

crookedness. We played miserable ball up there, it is true, but it could not be helped. We simply played in hard luck. It was such a streak as any team is apt to have, only we had ours at a most unfortunate time."

Latham, the Browns' third baseman, who also distinguished himself by miserable play at Kansas City, said: "It was all hard luck that beat us, and those miserable grounds. The charge that the team did not try to play is all bosh. We did our best. It is strange that King and Chamberlain should have been batted so hard, but the Kansas City club certainly hit them on their merits."

—St. Louis *Post-Dispatch*

AMERICAN ASSOCIATION STANDINGS

	W	L	PCT.	GB		W	L	PCT.	GB
St. Louis	14	5	.737	—	Brooklyn	7	7	.500	4½
Kansas City	11	6	.647	2	Cincinnati	7	10	.412	6
Athletic	8	5	.615	3	Columbus	4	10	.286	7½
Baltimore	9	6	.600	3	Louisville	3	14	.176	10

NATIONAL LEAGUE STANDINGS

	W	L	PCT.	GB		W	L	PCT.	GB
New York	6	3	.667	—	Cleveland	6	6	.500	1½
Boston	6	3	.667	—	Indianapolis	5	6	.455	2
Pittsburg	7	4	.636	—	Chicago	4	6	.400	2½
Philadelphia	5	3	.625	½	Washington	0	8	.000	5½

Wednesday, May 8

On May 7, New York lost at Philadelphia 4–6 (Crane 2–2).
Brooklyn won at Louisville 13–3 (Lovett 3–2).
St. Louis beat Columbus 21–0 (King 6–3).
NL: Boston 6–3, New York 6–4. AA: St. Louis 15–5, Brooklyn 8–7.

Philadelphia, May 7—With three defeats charged against them, the big New-York Giants left this city to-night for Boston in anything but a happy frame of mind. Crane was effective, but the local players' hits were more timely than those of the visitors.

—New York *Times*

What a pull up in the race the Brooklyns have made since their April trip to Philadelphia and Baltimore. One defeat out of nine games played has fully made up for their unlucky start in April.

—Brooklyn *Daily Eagle*

President Byrne, in speaking of the exaggeration indulged in by the Philadelphians about the crowds at their grounds, says of the large attendance the Brooklyns had in one game there: "There was a big crowd there, and the lowest number I have heard estimated is 12,000, and I am informed the Athletic management gave out 15,000 as the figure. As a matter of fact there were about 10,000 people on the ground. This much I am certain of, and that is that the Brooklyn Club was paid for 9,935 admissions. It is these false reports about the sizes of crowds," continued Mr. Byrne, "that sets the ball players crazy and makes them jump up in salaries. Now, over in Brooklyn we never lie about our crowds. There are the turnstiles, and the exact number of persons passing through then are given to the press and the public. That is what the turnstiles are for."

Charles H. Byrne, president, Brooklyn Bridegrooms (Transcendental Graphics).

—Brooklyn *Daily Eagle*

The trouble between Mr. Von der Ahe and Robinson has finally been settled, and the Browns have again settled down to playing ball. Mr. Von der Ahe states that Comiskey came to him yesterday and asked for permission to settle the matter with Robinson. Mr. Von der Ahe says he gave him permission to do so, stipulating that the fine should be paid by Robinson. As a result of Comiskey's intercession Robinson played in his old position at second base yesterday and the club put up a remarkably fine game of ball. The second baseman, however, alleges that Comiskey came to him and told him to play, stating that the fine would not go. However the settlement was made, it was a good thing for the club. If the trouble had never occurred they would have had a long lead for the championship, but by dropping three games at Kansas City they will now have a hard fight for it.

—St. Louis *Post-Dispatch*

Thursday, May 9

On May 8, New York lost at Boston 0–7
(Crane 2–3 and Clarkson 5–0). Brooklyn won at Louisville 21–2
(Caruthers 2–1). St. Louis beat Columbus 9–4 (Chamberlain 8–1).
NL: Boston 7–3, New York 6–5. AA: St. Louis 16–5, Brooklyn 9–7.

Boston, May 8—A delay caused by an accident on the railroad prevented the New-Yorks from getting here on time to-day. As soon as they arrived at the station they were driven to the grounds, where 10,000 persons saw the pride of New-York succumb to the superior playing of Boston's cultured ball tossers. Defeat was bad enough, but the Bostonians made it doubly painful by adding the stigma of a "whitewash."

—New York *Times*

Bostons, 7; New Yorks, 0. That was the score by which the Boston league team won the opening championship game in this city of the season of 1889. The season was inaugurated in a most brilliant manner, as far as weather and attendance of spectators were concerned. The sight from the pavilion was a grand one. That immense structure was tested to its fullest seating and standing capacity, while to the right and left, on what are known in base ball parlance as the "bleaching boards," a dense sea of faces was seen, till it seemed impossible to crowd another one in.

The game itself proved a walkover for the Bostons. Clarkson pitched a remarkably effective game, especially with men on bases. Brouthers and Kelly carried off the honors at the bat, the latter making the first home run of the season in this city, the ball going over the right field fence.

Crane had a left leg that bothered him seriously, and in the eighth inning he retired, Ewing going in to pitch and Brown to catch. The crowd laughed good-naturedly when the New York captain entered the box, and evidently expected he would prove a soft snap for the Boston batsmen. He proved to be the contrary. In the inning and a half that he pitched but one hit was made off his delivery, and he struck out Clarkson, Kelly and Richardson.

The feature of the game that most marred its pleasure was the unprofessional and disgusting conduct of Capt. Ewing. No fault can be found with any captain or player who resorts to legitimate work to win a game for his side, but the actions of Ewing yesterday call for a most vigorous protest. His actions were a disgrace to the profession and an insult to the spectators. He frequently delayed the game on a pretense of giving instructions to Crane, and he kept up a continual wordy warfare with the umpire and the spectators. He protested at the slightest provocation, and gave an ugly exhibition of temper when a decision was given in favor of Boston. He finally became so unbearable and so persistent and annoying to Umpire Fessenden that the latter imposed on him a fine of $20, and if he had added another cipher to the sum, the outraged spectators would have voted it a just punishment.

—Boston *Herald*

Friday, May 10

On May 9, New York won at Boston 10–9
(Ewing 1–0 and Madden 1–3). St. Louis lost to Columbus 4–6
(King 6–4). NL: Boston 7–4, New York 7–5.
AA: St. Louis 16–6, Brooklyn 9–7.

Boston, May 9—With Welch sick, Crane injured, and George and Titcomb out of condition the Giants were without a pitcher to-day. Capt. Ewing, however, was equal to the emergency. He resolved to do some curving himself, and put big "Bill" Brown behind the bat.

When the Boston players saw New-York's Captain in the box they regarded the undertaking as a huge joke, and got themselves in readiness to lose the ball. But they didn't. Ewing remained there for nine innings, and although the Boston men hit the ball at times very hard, the Captain of the Giants would not surrender his position, and to the intense discomfort of the 5,900 spectators in the South End ground piloted his club to victory.

The boys received news of the engagement of Keefe before the game to-day, and joy reigned in the heart of every Giant.

—New York *Times*

The day was most unusually warm for the time of year, and it was a strange sight to see hundreds of people sitting on the bleaching boards, some of them coatless and many with handkerchiefs around their necks or with umbrellas over their heads. It was a sight that one would expect to see in the middle of July rather than at this time of the year.

—Boston *Herald*

Saturday, May 11

On May 10, New York won at Boston 7–5
(Keefe 1–0 and Radbourn 1–1). Brooklyn won at Louisville 10–6
(Hughes 3–3). St. Louis beat Columbus 16–5 (Chamberlain 9–1).
NL: New York 8–5, Boston 7–5. AA: St. Louis 17–6, Brooklyn 10–7.

Boston, May 10—Keefe pitched his first League game to-day and the Giants won in handsome style. The appearance of the genial expert curver seemed to inspire the boys with confidence, and they played with rare vim and determination. Good batting won the game. In the fourth inning the Giants were four runs to the bad, but they braced up and by clever work sent five men around, took the lead and held it throughout

George Gore, center fielder, New York Giants (Library of Congress, Prints and Photographs Division [LOT 13163-05, no. 192]).

the game. The features of the game were Gore's clever fielding, and the batting of Gore, Richardson, and Ewing. Altogether the Giants played good ball, and although the spectators were disappointed at the result, they were forced to applaud the magnificent work of the visitors.

The fourth inning changed the complexion of the game, and caused sorrow to reign in the breast of every Bostonian present. Ward started by going to first on a fumble by Ray, and Richardson sent the sphere over Johnston's head for three bases. O'Rourke ran to first on balls, Whitney went out at first and Keefe hit the ball safely. Then big George Gore came to the rescue. To use the vernacular of the profession, he hit the ball in the nose, and before it was returned to the diamond O'Rourke and Keefe had touched the home plate, the score was tied, and New-York's successful batsman was at third base, with good prospects of finishing the circuit. "Now line her out, Mike," said Capt. Ewing to Tiernan. The latter did as requested, Gore scored, and the Giants had the game won.

—New York *Times*

A correspondent desires to know what point the Athletics were likely to gain by the action of Stovey and Welch in urging the crowd to come in on the field. The answer is, to prevent the Brooklyn team from having time to rally by cutting the game short by delay, the Athletics knowing that the Brooklyn team had to take the 6:30 train for Louisville, even if they had to lose the game by it. Rule 26, section 2, states that "if after the game has begun, one side refuses or fails to continue playing—unless such game is suspended or terminated by the umpire—a forfeited game shall be declared by the umpire in favor of the club not in fault." It will be seen how advantageous it was for the Athletics to delay the game and thereby lessen the number of innings for the Brooklyns to pull up their

WELSH, C. F. Athletics
COPYRIGHTED BY GOODWIN & CO. 1888.
OLD JUDGE
CIGARETTES.
GOODWIN & CO., New York.

Curt Welch, center fielder, Philadelphia Athletics (Library of Congress, Prints and Photographs Division [LOT 13163-05, no. 384]).

score in, and this was the object of Welch and Stovey in trying to induce the crowd to come in. They began their tactics in the fourth inning, after the game had been tied, the crowd then rushing in back of Welch.

—Brooklyn *Daily Eagle*

Sunday, May 12

On May 11, New York lost at Boston 3–4 (Hatfield 0–1 and Clarkson 6–0). Brooklyn's tie game of May 5th ruled a forfeit loss (Terry 2–2). St. Louis beat Baltimore 20–4 (King 7–4). NL: Boston 8–5, New York 8–6. AA: St. Louis 18–6, Brooklyn 10–8.

Boston, May 11—The Bostons looked for an easy victory against Hatfield's pitching, but they made a big mistake. Only four hits were made in the nine innings, and the Bostonians had about given up the game when Murphy and Connor made two errors that allowed them to win. Clarkson was hit hard, but, with the exception of one inning, the hitting was scattered and of but little value in run scoring. On the whole luck played an important part in the game to-day, and to that only can the home team attribute the victory.

—New York *Times*

Dan Brouthers was about the only Bostonian who seemed able to gauge the delivery of young Hatfield, and as soon as the ball was put over the plate he hit hard and safely. When the break came, as it did come in the eighth inning, and the Bostons not only tied the score but forged ahead, the pent-up feelings of the crowd found vent in torrents of cheers, and almost every one rose to his feet in a frenzy of ecstasy. The victory was most desirable, as it sent Boston into the first position and New York to third place.

—Boston *Herald*

Cincinnati, May 11—The Brooklyns were knocked out this morning by the directors of the association. A special meeting of the Board was held at the Grand Hotel to take action on the Brooklyn and Athletic wrangle that took place at Ridgewood Park last Sunday. The law was plain and the evidence far from conflicting. Treasurer W.H. Whitaker, of the Athletic Club; President C.H. Byrne, of the Brooklyns, and Umpire Holland all gave their versions. After it was all in the directors adopted the following:

Resolved. That it is the opinion of the Board of Directors that Umpire Holland erred in deciding the game a draw; and the Board of Directors hereby reverses the decision and gives the game to the Athletic Base Ball Club by a score of nine runs to none, as provided in Rule 61 of the joint playing rules, which is herewith appended:

Rule 61. Every club shall furnish sufficient police force upon its grounds to preserve order, and in the event of a crowd entering the field during the progress of a game and interfering with the play in any manner the visiting club may refuse to play further until the field be cleared. If the ground be not cleared within fifteen minutes thereafter the visiting club may claim and shall be entitled to the game by score of nine runs to none, no matter what number of innings have been played.

—Brooklyn *Daily Eagle*

Baltimore played its first game in St. Louis with the Browns yesterday afternoon and wore convict suits of alleged Lord Baltimore colors, black bagging breeches and striped black and old gold stockings, shirts and caps.

—St. Louis *Post-Dispatch*

New York, May 11—Said a recognized authority to-day: The American Association is not as well off in the matter of official umpires as was supposed at the beginning of the season. Of the four who at present hold the positions but two are reliable—Ferguson and Gaffney. Unless the Association succeeds in strengthening these weak points there is bound to be trouble before the season is well over.

—St. Louis *Post-Dispatch*

Monday, May 13

On May 12, Brooklyn won at Cincinnati 10–7 (Terry 3–2).
AA: St. Louis 18–6, Brooklyn 11–8.

"No player on the field has to work as hard as the umpire," remarked Gaffney, the king of umpires, this morning in conversation with a *Post-*

John Gaffney, umpire, American Association (Library of Congress, Prints and Photographs Division [LOT 13163-05, no. 307]).

Dispatch reporter. "I don't bar the pitcher, catcher or any of them. Umpiring was never so difficult as this season, and yet when we should have had our salaries increased they were cut instead. What the Association did with the other umpires I do not know, but I do know very well that they cut me $500 on the season. A pitcher works for nine innings and has a lay off of at least a day or two between games, whereas an umpire works for eighteen innings and does it seven days in the week. He cannot sit on the bench during half the game, but is kept on his feet the entire two hours, and is kept running about from back of the pitcher to back of the plate and to bases the greater part of the time. Umpiring is especially hard this season, because more runs are being made than ever before, and this of course keeps more men on bases and makes more base decisions necessary. It is base decisions which cause us to do lots of running, and in which there is most difficulty in satisfying the players and people. Then one is kept constantly hollering and you have no idea how wearing it is. A man must yell so as to be heard all over the grounds every time he speaks or people are dissatisfied and will say: 'What's the matter with Gaff? He is losing his voice.' Why, when I get up in the morning my lungs are sore from the hollering, and yet I was never so strong as I am now."

"Does the guying of the crowd rattle you any?"

"No, I never pay any attention to them. They always tire before I do. Then I have been very fortunate, somehow, in not being jeered much. The sport loving public of America are very fair, and they are always with a man if they see he is capable and endeavoring to do his best. They realize that all umpires are bound to make some mistakes."

"What club in your opinion will win the pennant this season?"

"That is a question I am asked at least twenty times a day, but never answer. I don't think an umpire should express an opinion on such a question."

—St. Louis *Post-Dispatch*

Tuesday, May 14

On May 13, New York lost to Cleveland 7–8 (Hatfield 0–2).
Boston beat Pittsburg 7–5 (Clarkson 7–0).
NL: Boston 9–5, New York 8–7.

Cleveland's new League team made its first appearance in this vicinity yesterday before a large crowd at St. George, and characterized the event by taking a ball from the Giants. They won, or, rather, the New-Yorks lost, because of poor field work.

—New York *Times*

Mr. Clarkson pitched out his seventh consecutive victory yesterday, and the Pittsburg club figured as mourners in a very interesting game, marked by clean hitting and fine fielding.

—Boston *Herald*

Byrne's far-famed Brooklyn $50,000 gilt-edged aggregation will be the recipients of a rousing welcome upon their opening at Sportsman's Park on Thursday. The Brooklyns consider themselves as sure pennant winners, and they spurn the mere mention of the Browns beating them out. Bob Caruthers and Dave Foutz are outspoken in their claims for Brooklyn, and they ridicule the idea of any other team landing the pennant this season.

—St. Louis *Post-Dispatch*

AMERICAN ASSOCIATION STANDINGS

	W	L	PCT.	GB		W	L	PCT.	GB
St. Louis	18	6	.750	—	Athletic	11	10	.524	5½
Baltimore	12	8	.600	4	Cincinnati	10	12	.455	7
Brooklyn	11	8	.579	4½	Columbus	6	14	.300	10
Kansas City	13	10	.565	4½	Louisville	5	18	.217	12½

NATIONAL LEAGUE STANDINGS

	W	L	PCT.	GB		W	L	PCT.	GB
Philadelphia	9	5	.643	—	Chicago	8	8	.500	2
Boston	9	5	.643	—	Pittsburg	8	9	.471	2½

	W	L	PCT.	GB		W	L	PCT.	GB
Cleveland	10	8	.556	1	Indianapolis	7	10	.412	3½
New York	8	7	.533	1½	Washington	3	10	.231	5½

Wednesday, May 15

On May 14, New York lost to Cleveland 0–5 (Titcomb 1–2).
Boston beat Pittsburg 13–9 (Radbourn 2–1).
Brooklyn won at Cincinnati 4–0 (Lovett 4–2).
St. Louis beat Baltimore 7–2 (Chamberlain 10–1).
NL: Boston 10–5, New York 8–8.
AA: St. Louis 19–6, Brooklyn 12–8.

Not one of the New-York players succeeded in reaching the home base yesterday, and the world's champions suffered defeat of the worst character—a "Chicago"—at the hands of the infant of the League, the Cleveland Club. In seasons gone by tradition says that pitchers trembled in their boots at the thought of facing the far-famed Giants. They have been known, in the language of the profession, to "knock pitchers out of the box," lose the ball, keep outfielders busy chasing triples and home-runs, and, in fact, perform various other marvelous feats indicative of the brawn and muscle. But a change has taken place, and the Giants of to-day are comparatively harmless. They cannot be charged with losing the ball—in fact, they fail to find it—and opposing pitchers no longer fear the big "sluggers" of Gotham.

Yesterday the Clevelands gave the champions a neat coat of "white-wash." The cause can easily be explained. It is not hard luck or the glorious uncertainty of the game, but weak batting. In two games the high-salaried players of the New-York team have only made six base hits—a poor showing for an amateur nine—and until they make some improvement in the batting department they cannot hope to win. This work causes them to lose game after game until now they are fifth in the League race. Their field work, too, has not been up to the standard. If a player makes an error or half a dozen no fault should be found with his work, as the best of players make errors. But misplays, bad plays, and errors of judgment should not be tolerated on a first-class team, and several have been made in the last two games.

—New York *Times*

"What's the matter with the Brooklyns? Oh, they're all right. Well, I should smile." These remarks just about express the feeling which prevailed in local base ball circles last night as the score of the second

Cincinnati-Brooklyn game was posted on the bulletin board at the *Eagle* office. How sick the croakers do feel, and especially the New York scribes who reside in Brooklyn, yet are down upon the local team. And they have not even the consolation of seeing their pets, the Giants, victorious. The Brooklyn team feels so sorry for them. On their return from Staten Island yesterday, when they were greeted with the records in the evening extras of "Cleveland vs. New York, 5 to 0; Brooklyn vs. Cincinnati, 4 to 0," and all their bets lost, the party felt sick.

—Brooklyn *Daily Eagle*

One of the most gratifying evidences of the Browns' success as a team is the constant watchfulness of Capt. Comiskey in the playing of his men. He is constantly encouraging them with good cheering words which have a bracing effect upon them.

—St. Louis *Post-Dispatch*

Thursday, May 16

On May 15, New York beat Cleveland 16–2 (Hatfield 1–2).
Boston beat Pittsburg 8–7 (Radbourn 3–1).
Brooklyn won at Cincinnati 10–6 (Caruthers 3–1).
St. Louis beat Baltimore 9–7 (King 8–4).
NL: Boston 11–5, New York 9–8.
AA: St. Louis 20–6, Brooklyn 13–8.

Beatin, a young man who learned the art of curving a ball in the coal mining districts of Pennsylvania, pitched against the Giants yesterday at St. George. In the language of Mr. "Buck" Ewing he was just "pie" for the boys. He tried his stock of curves, in and out shoots, drops and raises, slow and fast balls, but the Giants hit them all.

Capt. Ewing led in the work with two doubles and a like number of singles, and Gore made a pretty home run. To add to their good batting the Giants played in the field as of yore and delighted the spectators with their clever work.

—New York *Times*

Decidedly, the honors of the day belonged to Charles Radbourn, who pitched a superb game, and was a stumbling block to the heaviest hitters on the other side. His support was simply disheartening, but he never rattled, and his slow drops, rising balls and curves, delivered with beautiful accuracy, were well worth witnessing. Dan Brouthers didn't monopolize all the space in the base column, but managed to get in a single and a great triple to right centre.

—Boston *Herald*

One element of strength exhibited by the Brooklyn team this season is their ability to do good uphill fighting in their games. They are never whipped until the ninth inning ends all chances for a rally to recover lost ground. They have not only shown this in individual games, but especially in the work in the pennant race since their unlucky April start in the contest. Their pull up from seventh place to second position in the race within fifteen days presented ample evidence of their ability in this respect, and yesterday they won the game by splendid uphill fighting at Cincinnati.

—Brooklyn *Daily Eagle*

The Browns took one from the Baltimores yesterday, but had to work hard for it. Gaffney did not give satisfaction, and Latham and Comiskey told him so in very plain terms. Latham was fined $5 and made to sit on the bench like a naughty school boy. Comiskey sassed back and was put down beside Latham on the bench.

—St. Louis *Post-Dispatch*

Long Dave Foutz, the old pitcher of the Browns, who is now playing first base for the Brooklyns, looks as natural as of old. "I never care to make predictions," he said, "but I will say that I think our chances for the championship are as good as those of any other club. It looks to me at present as if the race would be between us and the Browns."

"I think our chances of winning the pennant are fully as good if not better than those of any other club," said Bob Caruthers. "We certainly have a very strong team." Caruthers wears the same Parisian smile that he contracted while in Paris several years ago.

—St. Louis *Post-Dispatch*

Friday, May 17

On May 16, New York beat Cleveland 6–3 (Ewing 2–0).
Boston beat Pittsburg 14–4 (Clarkson 8–0).
Brooklyn lost at St. Louis 7–9 (Hughes 3–4 and Chamberlain 11–1).
NL: Boston 12–5, New York 10–8. AA: St. Louis 21–6, Brooklyn 13–9.

Capt. Ewing didn't have on a mask or chest protector yesterday. He faced the assemblage, curved the ball out of the reach of the Cleveland

OLD JUDGE CIGARETTES Goodwin & Co., New York.

Jim O'Rourke, left fielder, New York Giants (Library of Congress, Prints and Photographs Division [LOT 13163-13, no. 5]).

bats, and New-York won another game from the infants of the League. Ewing thinks that he is something of a pitcher, and unless good judges are mistaken he will make batters think so before the season is over if he is called upon to go in the box often. Everybody applauded the popular Captain of the Giants, and it was agreed that he is the greatest of all general ball players.

In the seventh inning O'Rourke made the best play of the game. Twitchell hit a hard line ball to left field, which looked good for several runs but for Lawyer O'Rourke's agility. He ran like a deer, caught the ball with one hand, and retired the side.

—New York *Times*

Boston rubbed it in again yesterday afternoon, gaining the fourth consecutive victory of the week over Pittsburg, and an easy one it was. The invincible, Clarkson and Bennett, formed the Boston battery, and the former participated in his eighth consecutive victory. Clarkson fielded his position with that snap and vigor that is characteristic of him, and other members of the club might well take pattern by him. He always plays ball, no matter what the score may be.

It was a great day for foul balls, and without doubt more were batted than ever in any game on the grounds, to the great annoyance of the people in the grand stand, for the balls kept coming in there at a great rate.

Kelly made one of the greatest slides to the plate yesterday ever seen on a ball field. Maul had the ball waiting for him, but Kelly made a side slide, tearing the cloth off his uniform around the knees. It was wonderful work.

—Boston *Herald*

Perhaps the most fashionable audience which ever attended a base ball match in St. Louis was present at the opening game yesterday between the Brooklyns and Browns. There were about six thousand people in the park, and a number of society's fairest belles watched the contest with interest from the grandstand. Ferguson umpired his usual miserable game, giving the Browns the worst of it as is his custom. He was particularly hard on Chamberlain on balls and strikes, but there was little kicking by the players, as they knew all complaints would be met by fines.

—St. Louis *Post-Dispatch*

President Byrne was very unhappy yesterday. He expected to see his Brooklyn Bridge Brightlights walk away from the Browns in a canter. Bob Caruthers, the great and only Parisian Bob, will pitch against the Browns on Sunday. Bob will have the biggest crowd of people to entertain he has seen in years.

—St. Louis *Post-Dispatch*

Saturday, May 18

On May 17, New York beat Pittsburg 11–7 (Hatfield 2–2).
Boston beat Cleveland 14–4 (Radbourn 4–1).
Brooklyn lost at St. Louis 2–11 (Lovett 4–3 and King 9–4).
NL: Boston 13–5, New York 11–8.
AA: St. Louis 22–6, Brooklyn 13–10.

The champions kept up their winning streak and disposed of the visitors in handsome style. New York's star pitcher, the genial Timothy Keefe, started to play, but retired at the end of the first inning on account of a lame arm. Hatfield took his place and pitched another good game.

—New York *Times*

The Bostons made 13 runs in the first two innings today against the Clevelands, and interest in the game went at once below par. After that the home team did not exert itself, though they made hits in every inning but one.

—New York *Times*

The Browns played with all their old-time vim yesterday and won from the Brooklyns hands down. They batted Lovett all over the field, hitting him just as they pleased. In the fifth inning Clark, who was catching for the visitors, called to Manager McGunnigle to take Lovett out of

the box, but McGunnigle refused to do so, as there was no hope of winning the game and he did not want to tire another pitcher. King pitched
a magnificent game.

　　　　　　　　　　　　　　　　　　　　—St. Louis *Post-Dispatch*

　　The celebrated City of Churches' delegation, whose achievements
are of the diamond order, will bid farewell to-morrow to the cold, cruel
mortals of the Mound City, who have so relentlessly shattered their
hopes, and Sportsman's Park will be tested to its utmost capacity to
accommodate the people who want to witness the departure of Byrne's
Brooklyn beauties. The farewell ceremonies will be thoroughly interesting and the St. Louis pet, Parisian Bob Caruthers, will in all probability
fire up the pitcher's box with all his old-time zeal and ambition. Silver
King, with his cannon-ball speed, will defend the St. Louis fortifications
and the battle will be waged with the fierceness of a civil war. Play will
be called at 3:30 P.M.

　　　　　　　　　　　　　　　　　　　　—St. Louis *Post-Dispatch*

Sunday, May 19

On May 18, New York lost to Pittsburg 2–3 (Welch 3–2).
Boston beat Cleveland 10–8 (Clarkson 9–0).
Brooklyn won at St. Louis 5–3 (Terry 4–2 and Chamberlain 11–2).
NL: Boston 14–5, New York 11–9.
AA: St. Louis 22–7, Brooklyn 14–10.

　　As usual, Dan Brouthers proved to be the most efficient coadjutor
of Clarkson, and had he not been in the game, it is, indeed, doubtful
whether victory would have perched on the Boston banner. Every one
of his hits counted in the run getting, and he was the only one on his
side who did any successful hitting. He fielded, too, in great shape, and
made several fine pick-ups.

　　　　　　　　　　　　　　　　　　　　—Boston *Herald*

　　All the Browns said last evening, "It was a mighty hard game to
lose." It was certainly a mighty hard game to win. Brooklyn did not win
it until eleven innings were played. The 3,000 spectators who braved the
chilly air and threatening clouds, which promised to put a veto on yesterday's game, were well repaid for their trip to Sportsman's Park. They
saw the grandest game played there this year. Comiskey, Foutz, Duffee,
Latham, Terry and several others covered themselves with glory. Three
elements contributed to the Browns' defeat. The first and greatest,

perhaps, was the error of judgment of Umpire Ferguson. In the opening inning he declared Comiskey's hit over the right fence foul when it had flown fair by several feet. This virtually robbed the Browns of two runs. An error of judgment in base running by McCarthy injured the Browns' prospects of a run at an important stage. The third and last element, which contributed to the Browns' defeat, was Terry's magnificent pitching. He proved effective at the most critical stages and thus helped carry his side to victory.

—St. Louis *Post-Dispatch*

St. Louis, Mo., May 18—When the announcement was made on the *Eagle* bulletin board that the Brooklyns had won the game the large crowd which read it broke out in enthusiastic cheers. Hats were thrown in the air, and men and boys screamed with delight. The cheers could be heard several blocks away.

—Brooklyn *Daily Eagle*

The last game between the Browns and Brooklyns will take place to-day at Sportsman's Park and it promises to be a most bitterly fought contest. The Brooklyns are a great team and with their pitchers in shape will give the Browns and all other teams a hard fight for the pennant. The great Bobby Caruthers, the star pitcher of the old Browns, will pitch for Brooklyn to-day, with Doc Bushong catching. If the day is pleasant the biggest crowd that has attended a game at Sportsman's Park since 1883 will turn out. The attraction is a grand one, and lovers of the game will enjoy a rare treat. Silver King and Jack Milligan will be the Browns' battery. Play will be called at 3:30 P.M. Bob Ferguson will umpire.

—St. Louis *Post-Dispatch*

Monday, May 20

On May 19, Brooklyn won at St. Louis 2–1
(Caruthers 4–1 and King 9–5). AA: St. Louis 22–8, Brooklyn 15–10.

No one saw Clarkson pitch ball last season as he is doing this year. The reason is most evident. He has some catchers to support him this season, and last year the club was in a most poor way behind the bat. Then he has some hitters to help inspire him. Look to Clarkson and Radbourn to make the greatest records of any of the league pitchers, as far as games won and lost are concerned. These are the only records that a pitcher need care anything about. What does he care about earned runs and all that sort of rubbish? When his club is well ahead he is not going to pitch his arm off for the sake of a record.

—Boston *Herald*

The largest crowd that has been on a baseball ground here since the memorable Browns-Athletic Sunday game of 1883 assembled at Sportsman's Park yesterday to witness the closing game of the opening series between the Browns and Brooklyns. Long before 3 o'clock all the seats in the park had been taken and when play was called the roof of the grand stand, the players' dressing-room and all other buildings in the park were black with people, and men were standing four or five deep inside the field. It was a great game, the visitors winning by the close margin of 2 to 1. Ferguson had many close decisions to give and generally gave them against the Browns. The crowd guyed and hissed him unmercifully. It was a great victory for Bobby Caruthers, the Browns' old pitcher, who did the twirling for the visitors. Both he and King pitched brilliantly, but with Ferguson's able assistance the Brooklyns won.

—St. Louis *Post-Dispatch*

The Brooklyn Base Ball Association met with quite a misfortune yesterday at home in the destruction of the club's fine grand stand by fire at a time when it needs every facility to accommodate the immense crowd which will gather at Washington Park on Decoration day to see the team play on home grounds with the only rivals they have in the association. But this piece of hard luck at home was offset by a stroke of good fortune abroad in the club team achieving the most noteworthy victory of their Western campaign, and that was in defeating the St. Louis Club's strongest team by the close score of 2 to 1, thus ending the home series at St. Louis with a record of two victories to two defeats, a victory in itself, for the Browns were in to do their level best to make it four straight.

The game of yesterday was one to be remembered and it was fortunate for Brooklyn that the right umpire was in position, who had the courage to withstand the bulldozing tactics of the St. Louis captain and his players and who could not be cowed by the insults, abuse and howls of the poolroom gang who were on the bleaching boards. There is no umpire who excels Ferguson in the courage of his convictions and no bulldozing will cause him to shrink from his duty in impartially deciding disputed points. It was a great triumph for Caruthers. He knew his men and outwitted them by his fine strategic pitching. Everything was propitious for an exceptional contest and it is estimated there were fully 15,000 people on the grounds.

—Brooklyn *Daily Eagle*

Bob Ferguson may be a very good umpire, but he failed to display any evidence of the fact in his work in this city. No doubt he has meant well, but as the lawyer would say, there has been a fatal variance between his intention and decisions. Somehow he has always been assigned to umpire here when the Brooklyn Club plays the Browns, and his work has been uniformly bad. His umpiring here last season created the greatest dissatisfaction, and in the Brooklyn series which closed yesterday his work has been simply execrable. In the first game the Browns got the worst of nearly all close decisions, and most decidedly the worst of the calling of balls and strikes. The home team really had slightly the best of the umpiring in the second game, but they did not need it, as they won hands down. In Saturday's and yesterday's games Ferguson's umpiring was most outrageous. Everything was a strike for a Brown Stocking batsman, while nothing was a strike for a Brooklynite. A fair hit of Comiskey's in the eighth inning, which Ferguson declared foul, unquestionably lost the Browns Saturday's game as it was a home run drive against the players' dressing-room in right field, and would have brought in another run besides his own. Ferguson's eyesight is said to be defective, and he is certainly woefully incompetent to umpire a game of ball. It speaks well for the St. Louis audience that they made no attempt to interfere in any way with the game. In almost any other city they would certainly have made an attempt to mob him.

—St. Louis *Post-Dispatch*

President Von der Ahe was seen by a *Post-Dispatch* reporter this morning regarding Ferguson's erratic umpiring in the Brooklyn series, and particularly his decidedly Brooklyn favoritism in the games of Saturday and Sunday. "I did not see much of yesterday's game, as I was attending to the business at the office," said Mr. Von der Ahe, "but I heard enough of kicking and derogatory comments from people whom I saw as they were leaving the grounds, to convince me that his umpiring was decidedly Brooklyn. Ferguson gave the Browns the worst of it on Saturday and literally beat us out of the game in declaring Comiskey's home run hit foul. The ball hit the players' dressing-room directly under the west window so hard that it marked the board. Still, viewed through his Brooklyn eye-glasses, Mr. Ferguson could not see that it struck as fairly as any home-run hit ever landed in the right field territory. The trouble with Ferguson is that his old age has affected his eyesight and he can scarcely see at any stage of the game. His poor sight is especially bad when he officiates in games between the Browns and Brooklyns. He is not competent in my opinion to umpire and he ought to be laid on the shelf. His decisions are so glaringly bad at times that they are disgusting to the clubs playing and to the patrons of the game."

"Do you think Ferguson is otherwise fair?"

"Yes, he is no doubt honest, and means to do what is right, but his judgment and eyesight are so poor that he is thoroughly incompetent to officiate as umpire. I have never accused him or any other umpire of being dishonest, and think Ferguson a first class fellow outside of his erratic judgment and poor abilities as an umpire. He certainly deprived the Browns of two games by his rank decisions."

—St. Louis *Post-Dispatch*

Bob Ferguson himself was seen at the Planters' House this morning: "I made no mistakes," he remarked, "in that series, and Comiskey's kicking was totally uncalled for. I like Charley first-rate and he is a good fellow, but he is constantly kicking and abusing umpires, whether justly or not, everybody knows that. I only regret that in my good nature I stood all the abuse I did from him yesterday. It is shameful the way he talked. Whenever I make a mistake in a game it hurts me much worse than it does any of the players. I feel it most keenly. In umpiring, I try to satisfy myself. When I have done that I don't care what other people think. My conscience is thoroughly at ease so far as my work in this series is concerned, and if the American Association is not satisfied with me they can easily get rid of me. So long as I satisfy my own conscience I don't care a—for the American Association or any man or any body of men. That ball hit by Comiskey Saturday struck foul and the English on it caused it to bound inside the line and hit the house. It did not strike the house on a fly, but landed between the inner fence and house and bounded to the house. Anybody who says differently either did not see it or maliciously misrepresents matters, and has not a particle of honesty and fairness in his composition. I have three more games, I believe it is, to umpire between the Browns and Brooklyns, and the best thing to be done is to let somebody

Bob Ferguson, umpire, American Association (New York *Clipper*, July 14, 1888).

else umpire them, so that I can't give the Browns the worst of it. The Browns manage to beat the Brooklyns on the latter's grounds with me umpiring and there seems to be no complaint. Now if I favored Brooklyn why would I not do so on their home grounds?"

—St. Louis Post-Dispatch

President Von der Ahe's innovative plan of admitting ladies free when accompanied by escorts, one escort having the privilege of two ladies, is an excellent one, and is meeting with a great deal of favor. It will again be in operation on Thursday next, when the Athletics make their farewell appearance.

—St. Louis Post-Dispatch

New York, May 19, 1889—The Base Ball Brotherhood held its annual spring meeting at the Fifth Avenue Hotel today. The players discussed the classification rule question, but no definite action was agreed upon. The players are opposed to the rule, but there is not much chance ordering a strike, when the objectionable features can be removed in a less boisterous, but more sensible, manner.

—Boston Herald

Tuesday, May 21

On May 20, Brooklyn lost at Kansas City 12–18 (Hughes 3–5). St. Louis beat Athletic 4–1 (Chamberlain 12–2). AA: St. Louis 23–8, Brooklyn 15–11.

Work was commenced at Washington Park yesterday in reconstructing the burnt fence on Fifth street, and to-day all the debris of the destroyed grand stand will be removed from the grounds and thrown in the vacant lots on Fifth street for the benefit of the neighboring poor, who will thereby be given plenty of fire wood for weeks to come. The work of reconstruction was begun by the

Charles Ebbetts, secretary, Brooklyn Bridegrooms (New York *Clipper*, April 16, 1892).

energetic secretary of the club, Charles Ebbetts, a few hours after the fire had been put out. After being authorized by President Byrne and Directors Abel and Doyle, Mr. Ebbetts went to work, notified the insurance agents, the Building Superintendent and the municipal authorities, and before sundown yesterday the insurance had been settled, the official permits secured, contracts made for rebuilding and extra laborers engaged. Mr. Ebbetts has shown himself to be a valuable man to the club in this critical emergency.

—Brooklyn *Daily Eagle*

AMERICAN ASSOCIATION STANDINGS

	W	L	PCT.	GB		W	L	PCT.	GB
St. Louis	23	8	.742	—	Athletic	12	13	.480	8
Kansas City	17	11	.607	4½	Baltimore	12	14	.462	8½
Brooklyn	15	11	.577	5½	Columbus	9	17	.346	11½
Cincinnati	14	15	.483	8	Louisville	7	20	.259	14

NATIONAL LEAGUE STANDINGS

	W	L	PCT.	GB		W	L	PCT.	GB
Boston	14	5	.737	—	Cleveland	11	12	.478	5
Philadelphia	13	6	.684	1	Pittsburg	9	13	.409	6½
New York	11	9	.550	3½	Indianapolis	8	13	.381	7
Chicago	11	10	.524	4	Washington	4	13	.235	9

Wednesday, May 22

On May 21, New York beat Pittsburg 5–4 (Welch 4–2).
Brooklyn won at Kansas City 14–13 (Terry 5–2).
St. Louis lost to Athletic 2–3 (King 9–6).
NL: Boston 14–5, New York 12–9.
AA: St. Louis 23–9, Brooklyn 16–11.

Playing baseball in the mud is something of a novelty, but the Giants proved that they are good at the game by disposing of the Pittsburg players at St. George yesterday in fine style. The clay diamond was transformed into a mud puddle, and it was with the greatest difficulty that the men fielded the ball.

Welch this season has showed a marked improvement in his command of the ball. He has thus far given but few men bases on balls, which is a good indication, considering the change in the rules limiting the number of unfair balls to four. The genial little pitcher appears to have recovered his old form and bids fair to make matters unpleasant for big batters this year.

—New York *Times*

Thursday, May 23

On May 22, New York beat Chicago 11–4 (Keefe 2–0).
Boston lost to Indianapolis 4–5 (Clarkson 9–1).
Brooklyn won at Kansas City 13–7 (Caruthers 5–1).
St. Louis beat Athletic 9–5 (Devlin 3–0).
NL: Boston 14–6, New York 13–9.
AA: St. Louis 24–9, Brooklyn 17–11.

Big, robust Capt. Anson and his around-the-world combination made their appearance at St. George yesterday bent on taking a ball from the Giants. They felt confident of success until they saw genial Timothy Keefe, the king of curvers, walk into the box. His presence sent a chill through the big Captain, for he knew from experience that the New-Yorkers, with Keefe in the box and Ewing behind the bat were foemen worthy of his steel. And he was right. Keefe pitched in his old form, allowing the visitors to make only two base hits, and New-York won with ease.

Gore in particular distinguished himself. He led in the batting with Tiernan and Ewing and played centre field as it has never been played before at St. George. A double play which he made in the first inning brought the spectators to their feet and for several minutes the enclosure was transformed into a modern Bedlam. The bases were all occupied when Anson hit a low line ball to right centre. Gore started for the ball, caught it on a hard run a foot from the ground, and sent it like a rocket into

"Cap" Anson, captain and first baseman, Chicago White Stockings (Library of Congress, Prints and Photographs Division [LOT 13163-05, no. 30]).

Ewing's outstretched hands in time to put out Ryan, who had run in from third base.

—New York *Times*

Manager Frank Bancroft of the Indianapolis club had his wife in the grand stand yesterday. She sat in the front row, just where she could smile her prettiest at her favorites, and, encouraged by her presence, the visitors put up the finest game of ball that has been seen here this season.

—Boston *Herald*

Boston, May 22—This was Clarkson's first defeat this season.

—New York *Times*

Caruthers was put in the box and he did masterly work there. Indeed it is very evident that he has got back to his old effective style of pitching again. The superior play of the visitors and the one-sided character of the game afforded no loophole for the Associated Press reporter to attribute the defeat to the umpire, as is usually done out West.

—Brooklyn *Daily Eagle*

Friday, May 24

On May 23, New York lost to Chicago 17–18 (Hatfield 2–3).
Brooklyn won at Kansas City 17–3 (Lovett 5–3).
St. Louis lost to Athletic 8–9 (King 9–7).
NL: Boston 14–6, New York 13–10.
AA: St. Louis 24–10, Brooklyn 18–11.

New-York's aggregation of Giants bowed to the superiority of Anson's around-the-world combination at St. George yesterday afternoon. It was one of the poorest games played this season, although ten innings were required to decide the contest. This simple fact, however, did not lessen the glory of a victory in the eyes of the big Captain from Chicago, and last night he was, perhaps, the happiest man in the metropolis. As he left the field his honest, sunburned face fairly beamed with smiles, and he laughed one of those hearty laughs for which he is peculiar.

While the game did not suit the average on-looker, it was a source of delight to the "old-timers." Thirty-five runs, 34 base hits, and 23 errors recalled memories of bygone days when the Eckfords, Mutuals, and Atlantics struggled for diamond field honors, and the Elysian Fields, the Union and Capitoline Grounds were in their prime.

—New York *Times*

The Brooklyn Club ended their first Western tour yesterday with a slashing victory over the Kansas City team, making the best record in the West since their organization. Out of fourteen games played they won eleven, taking three straight from Louisville and Cincinnati, breaking even with the champions and winning three out of four with Kansas City.

—Brooklyn *Daily Eagle*

There has been something decidedly queer about the play of Tip O'Neill, the Browns' left fielder, for some time back. From champion batsman of the American Association for the last two seasons he has dropped to one of the very worst. Instead of slashing away at the ball in his old time style he strikes as though he wanted to get out. He often permits himself to be called out on strikes, usually sulking after he gets two strikes and hitting at the next ball pitched no matter how wide it is or doing something equally foolish. When he makes a hit he seems to secure it against his wishes. His batting is particularly weak when something is depending on him. O'Neill's fielding has been even worse. Unless a ball is knocked right into his hands he does not get it. He will wait for it on the bound and will generally occupy so much time in fielding it in that the batsman makes two bases on the hit. The officials of the Browns claim they have no difficulty with O'Neill, but he certainly seems to be sulking about something or else playing for his release. Possibly some other club has made him an offer. Playing as he is, the big left fielder is worse than a wooden man on the nine, for the wooden man would not be expected to bat and thus furnish an out.

—St. Louis *Post-Dispatch*

"Tip" O'Neill, left fielder, St. Louis Browns (Library of Congress, Prints and Photographs Division [LOT 13163-05, no. 416]).

Saturday, May 25

On May 24, New York beat Chicago 9–7 (Welch 5–2).
Boston beat Indianapolis 5–3 (Radbourn 5–1).
NL: Boston 15–6, New York 14–10.

Boston won by a hair yesterday, and, indeed, it is remarkable how hard this strong aggregation of hitters has to battle for victory.

—Boston *Herald*

President Von der Ahe was very indignant this morning over the references to the Browns' pitchers in a morning paper, and stated that he could not understand why King and Chamberlain should be regarded as being overworked when they were pitching only in their regular turns.

"Both King and Chamberlain prefer to pitch whenever the club needs them," said President Von der Ahe, "and they are not in the least overworked."

—St. Louis *Post-Dispatch*

Sunday, May 26

On May 25, New York lost to Chicago 8–9 (Keefe 2–1).
Boston beat Indianapolis 8–4 (Clarkson 10–1).
Brooklyn won at Columbus 6–3 (Terry 6–2).
St. Louis beat Kansas City 10–7 (Chamberlain 13–2).
NL: Boston 16–6, New York 14–11.
AA: St. Louis 25–10, Brooklyn 19–11.

By just one run Capt. Anson won another game from the New-York Giants yesterday. There was a large crowd at St. George, and judging from the applause bestowed upon the players they enjoyed everything but the results.

—New York *Times*

In the Brooklyns' half of the second inning was where the kicking commenced. Visner was given his base on balls, stole second and started for third. He got there, but Captain Orr thought different and immediately entered a vigorous protest. Umpire Goldsmith told him to desist, but he continued to protest. Goldsmith then fined him. More talk ensued and Goldsmith ordered him to leave the field. To this Columbus objected and the game was given to the Brooklyns by 9 to 0. This, of course, put Columbus in a bad position and left them with a fine of some $1,500 to pay. Through the courtesy of the Brooklyn manager, however, the teams again went upon the field, Mr. Byrne not wishing to do anything to injure the Columbus management.

—Brooklyn *Daily Eagle*

The game at Sportsman's Park yesterday was a slugging match, in which the Browns excelled. Chamberlain was batted very hard by the visitors during the first two innings, but after that became effective. O'Neill, who has been fielding and batting poorly of late, caught three flies and made three hits. Like coffee, he appears to be useless until roasted.

—St. Louis *Post-Dispatch*

New York, May 25—While the New Yorks have not advanced materially during the past week, there is a certain amount of satisfaction in the fact that they have averted, for the time being, a disastrous exhibition of ground and lofty tobogganing. There are many things that have a handicapping tendency on the St. George diamond. The infielders long to play on diamonds where they can meet a hot ground hit with some degree of confidence, and the outfielders are dreaming of planting their kangaroos once more on the green turf of a civilized field.

—St. Louis *Post-Dispatch*

The Brotherhood of Base Ball Players held their annual meeting at the Fifth Avenue Hotel on Sunday last, and although nothing authoritative can be learned of their action, enough has been heard to warrant the belief that the Brotherhood will soon assert itself. It is likely that the League will be asked to form an Arbitration Committee for the purpose of discussing various grievances with the Brotherhood. While the Brotherhood objects to the classification and graded salary schemes, the chief fight will be made on the purchase and sale of players. On this question the Brotherhood will make a decided stand. It is not likely, however, that it will be found necessary to resort to extreme measures in the matter. While a strike is within the bounds of possibility there is every reason to believe that the whole question will be settled by an amicable discussion. Several of the League officials affect to laugh at such a thing as a ball players' strike.

—St. Louis *Post-Dispatch*

Monday, May 27

On May 26, Brooklyn lost at Columbus 4–5 (Hughes 3–6).
St. Louis beat Kansas City 12–3 (King 10–7).
AA: St. Louis 26–10, Brooklyn 19–12.

The triumvirs strengthened the club not a bit too soon, and the $20,000 they paid for the Detroit players was not one cent too much. Bless you, that team is not yet playing the ball of which it is capable. This is especially true of the batting.

—Boston *Herald*

The decisive action of Umpire Goldsmith in Saturday's game at Columbus, in ordering Orr off the field for his excessive kicking, resulted in one of the prettiest exhibitions of playing without a single kick in yesterday's game. If all umpires would act in the same manner in such cases the game would become what it should be and the rowdy players—they are becoming fewer every season—be suppressed.

—Brooklyn *Daily Eagle*

A Kansas City delegation numbering about fifteen, all young and enthusiastic and decorated with plug hats, canes and buttonhole bouquets, sat in the front row down stairs of the grand stand at Sportsman's Park yesterday afternoon. They had come here to see the Cowboys wipe up the earth with the Browns. Their enthusiasm was great, and when their pets scored the first run of the game in the second inning their Wild West yells made the welkin ring. Then the Browns scored a run in the next inning, and the Kawites became sad. Their emotions were absolutely distressing when the Browns scored six more in the following inning, and the addition of still two more runs in the fifth to the champions' score caused the young men from the West to drop their tired heads on their breasts. When the Browns piled up three more runs in the ninth, the Kansas City brigade sorrowfully tore off their floral decorations and adorned themselves with crepe. They had come out in carriages but returned in hearses, a woe-stricken, but enlightened delegation. The Kansas City players had been boasting that they could kill swift pitching. King gave it to them, but they failed to commit any homicide. They were completely at his mercy.

—St. Louis *Post-Dispatch*

Tuesday, May 28

On May 27, Brooklyn won at Columbus 10–4 (Lovett 6–3).
St. Louis lost to Kansas City 5–8 (Devlin 3–1).
AA: St. Louis 26–11, Brooklyn 20–12.

The Brooklyn team are traveling rapidly toward the goal and if they keep up their present good playing at home as they have abroad it is safe to predict that they will be in the lead by the first week in June. Elaborate preparations are being made to receive them on their return on Thursday, when they play two games with the team from St. Louis. The new stand is about finished, and the seating capacity will be about 3,000.

—Brooklyn *Daily Eagle*

The Browns played a miserable game yesterday and it was the most listless game they have played here for years. During the greater part of the game there were no coaches on the lines, and even when McCarthy, who with Comiskey was on base, called to Latham to get up and coach, the latter refused to do so, but remained seated on the bench chatting to O'Neill. Even Comiskey appeared to take no interest in the game and did no coaching whatever.

—St. Louis *Post-Dispatch*

AMERICAN ASSOCIATION STANDINGS

	W	L	PCT.	GB		W	L	PCT.	GB
St. Louis	26	11	.703	—	Athletic	15	14	.517	7
Brooklyn	20	12	.625	3½	Baltimore	14	16	.467	8½
Cincinnati	20	15	.571	5	Columbus	10	22	.313	13½
Kansas City	18	16	.529	6½	Louisville	8	25	.242	16

NATIONAL LEAGUE STANDINGS

	W	L	PCT.	GB		W	L	PCT.	GB
Boston	16	6	.727	—	Chicago	13	13	.500	5
Philadelphia	14	9	.609	2½	Pittsburg	11	15	.423	7
New York	14	11	.560	3½	Indianapolis	9	15	.375	8
Cleveland	14	13	.519	4½	Washington	6	15	.286	9½

Wednesday, May 29

On May 28, New York beat Indianapolis 7–0 (Welch 6–2).
Boston beat Chicago 10–3 (Clarkson 11–1).
Brooklyn lost at Columbus 4–7 (Hughes 3–7).
NL: Boston 17–6, New York 15–11.
AA: St. Louis 26–11, Brooklyn 20–13.

Little Welch as usual was all smiles, and he had the batsmen of the visiting team completely at his mercy. They couldn't gauge his curves at any stage of the game, and had to content themselves with two singles and a "whitewash."

—New York *Times*

Those who missed the opening contest of the season on the South end grounds yesterday afternoon between the Bostons and Chicagos missed the finest pitching exhibition that has been seen in any contest of the big clubs this season. Mr. John G. Clarkson was the fortunate young man who accomplished the feat, and to say that he surprised and delighted the many friends of the home club would be putting the matter lightly. In the second inning Clarkson struck out the side. In the third inning he struck out the first two batsmen, making five men that he struck out in succession. In the fourth he struck out Anson and Pfeffer, making seven strike-outs out of eight men to bat. In the fifth he struck out Tener and Bastian, making ten men who struck out in five innings. Clarkson was decidedly on his pitch, and seemed to have his opponents completely at his mercy. He was applauded again and again throughout the contest for his brilliant work.

—Boston *Herald*

The Brooklyn Club have wisely placed tickets for sale at the various sporting goods houses for to-morrow's games, so as to avoid a crush at the ticket offices, for there will be the largest crowd present ever seen on the grounds. A hearty reception awaits the home team, one they well merit, and the champions will also be welcomed.

The men were working on the grand stand all night last night by electric light. The heavy rain on Monday was a drawback. The ground can accommodate 18,000 people. No horses or wagons will be allowed on the field to-morrow.

—Brooklyn *Daily Eagle*

Thursday, May 30

On May 29, New York beat Indianapolis 8–6 (Keefe 3–1).
Boston beat Chicago 3–2 (Radbourn 6–1).
NL: Boston 18–6, New York 16–11.

For six innings the Indianapolis men held a lead over the Giants yesterday, but in the lucky seventh the latter forged to the front and held the lead during the remainder of the contest. Roger Connor, the biggest of the Giants, led in the batting. Besides getting his base on balls once he hit safely four times.

—New York *Times*

Short-stop Ward did not play yesterday. His wife sailed for Europe on the Germanic and he went to see her off.

—New York *Times*

When Hardy Richardson, with a sweep of his brawny arms, sent the ball flying into left centre field in the ninth inning yesterday afternoon, and sent in two runs, winning the game for the Bostons, over 4000 people went fairly wild with joy, and for some minutes the applause and demonstrations continued. Richardson was the hero of the hour. He had pulled the game out of the fire at the eleventh hour, when it seemed lost, and when most of those present had made up their minds to this fact. It was Richardson's day, too. His hit it was that started the first run for his club. In the field he was everywhere, and a large number of difficult chances fell to his lot. He took balls in right and centre fields, and his work on slow grounders was quick, sharp and sure. Then he stole two bases.

—Boston *Herald*

Friday, May 31

On May 30, New York lost to and beat Indianapolis 5–6 and 7–3 (Hatfield 2–4; Welch 7–2). Boston beat Chicago twice 10–8 and 4–2 (Radbourn 7–1; Clarkson 12–1). Brooklyn lost to and beat St. Louis 4–8 and 9–7 (Terry 6–3; Caruthers 6–1 and King 11–7; Chamberlain 13–3). NL: Boston 20–6, New York 17–12. AA: St. Louis 27–12, Brooklyn 21–14.

Roger Connor, first baseman, New York Giants (Library of Congress, Prints and Photographs Division [LOT 13163-05, no. 161]).

Decoration Day and the Fourth of July have always vied with each other for the distinction of being the best baseball day of the year. Up to yesterday the honors were about evenly divided, but now Memorial Day is in the lead. With one exception all the League and Association clubs played two games yesterday, and the contests were attended by larger crowds than ever before.

Down at St. George the New-Yorks did not draw as well as they would have done on their old diamond. The caliber of the club the Giants had to face, the opposition to the location of the grounds, and the counter-attraction in Brooklyn all had the effect of lessening the attendance, and only about eight thousand persons saw the New-Yorks win and lose a game. The management of the club is convinced that St. George will never attract big crowds, and efforts will be made to arrange matters so that the Giants will play once more on their Polo Ground diamond.

—New York *Times*

In spite of the immense attendance at the games of the morning and afternoon. the weather undoubtedly kept many away. The horse cars had all they could do, however, to accommodate the demands upon them from thousands of patrons, and from early morning to late in the afternoon they were literally packed with humanity. The attendance at the morning game was 7755, and at the contest of the afternoon 12,401, a total of 20,156 for the day. This would indicate gate receipts of $10,078, and, as the visiting club gets 25 per cent of this, Mr. Spalding will have as salve for his wounded feelings in losing both contests the snug little sum of a little over $2500.

It was with superior prowess at the bat that both games were won. Both Radbourn and Clarkson pitched superbly, and received the finest kind of support. But one fielding error marked the play of the coming champions in both games. The feature of the work of the Bostons was the great batting of Richardson. In both games he made three hits in succession. His six hits of the day included two singles, three doubles and a triple.

—Boston *Herald*

It would require a whole page of the *Eagle* even to catalogue the games of ball which were played on Memorial day in this part of the country, and as for this city, never, in the history of base ball, were so many thousands of people engaged either as spectators or players in the game as there were yesterday. At Washington Park, in spite of the inauspicious weather which prevailed during the early morning, nearly nine thousand people were present to greet the Brooklyn team and the St. Louis champions on the occasion of their first game together at the park this season, while at the afternoon game a scene was presented never before witnessed in Brooklyn, and that was the gathering of over twenty thousand spectators at the park and that, too, despite the fall of rain at the very time when the greatest rush was expected, the shower which occurred at 3:30 P.M. preventing some three or four thousand people from being added to the vast assemblage within the enclosure. It was a representative Brooklyn assemblage, too, such a one as only Brooklyn can gather at a match, one which was intelligent and consequently orderly, while at the same time impartial.

—Brooklyn *Daily Eagle*

Chamberlain evidently has a very sore arm. It was an unfortunate time for the team to become crippled, just as it is starting out on a long trip and opening a series with Brooklyn, its most dangerous rival for the pennant. The mishap falls with particular force on the Browns, because the only two pitchers they possessed whom they could put in the box with any degree of confidence were King and Chamberlain. Without a pitcher the strongest of teams is apt to lose to the very weakest. King cannot do all the work, and yet there is no good man to substitute in Chamberlain's place. Certain it is that the Browns will need some one to relieve King, and if neither Hudson nor Devlin pan out it is difficult to see where they are to get a man, as good pitchers are extremely rare, and it is next to impossible to obtain them unless a valuable find is accidentally secured out of a minor association. Unless the Browns are strengthened in the box they are apt to return home away behind in the race.

—St. Louis *Post-Dispatch*

Saturday, June 1

No games were played on May 31.

The *Mail and Express* recently stated that "Sunday in the neighborhood of Ridgewood Park has become a day of riot and revelry." There never was a greater falsehood uttered by that paper. During the past two seasons the immense base ball gatherings at Ridgewood Park have been as orderly as any seen either at the Polo Grounds or Washington Park. The patrons of Ridgewood know well enough that any disorder there by the crowd would cause the Brooklyn Club to stop their games there, and in self protection and to insure the continuance of their Sunday recreation in watching these contests they form themselves into a sort of committee of the whole on police and keep excellent order. Not even under the exciting conditions of the Athletic row last month at the park was there either rioting or disorder, the vast assemblage being a model one in the good humor they preserved under the circumstances. Had the same occurrence taken place at the Polo Grounds there might have been "riot and disorder."

The Brooklyn Club have never played a Sunday game at Washington Park and have never attempted to or wished to do so. That park is kept for those of their patrons who have the means and the leisure to visit the grounds on week days. The Sunday games are played in an out of the way district, where no one is disturbed and where the thousands who cannot get off on week days go to enjoy a harmless sport with far less opportunity for "riot and disorder" than are afforded on Sundays at Coney Island, Rockaway, Long Branch and the other watering place resorts.

—Brooklyn *Daily Eagle*

Sunday, June 2

On June 1, New York lost at Washington 5–9 (Whitney 0–1).
Boston beat Philadelphia 7–2 (Clarkson 13–1).
NL: Boston 21–6, New York 17–13.

Washington, June 1—Probably the most remarkable baseball game played here for many months was that between the Washington and New-York Clubs to-day, although it was neither a brilliant fielding nor a heavy batting contest, but was made unusual by the continuous kicking of the visitors upon the slightest provocation, to the delight of the spectators, though it grew monotonous.

The trouble and contention commenced in the second inning, when Ewing, who was declared out on strikes, used abusive language to Umpire Curry, and as his epithets became unbearable Mr. Curry ordered Ewing from the game. He then kept his peace but in other ways taunted the umpire. With Ewing retired Keefe from the game. In their place were substituted Crane and Brown. In the third inning Crane pleaded lameness and wanted to retire, and then O'Rourke, captaining the Giants, ordered Welch to pitch. A physician in attendance examined Crane, who was unmercifully "guyed" by the spectators, and the result of the consultation was that he was able to play. After half an hour's delay the umpire ordered the resumption of the game, and the positions of the players were shifted so that Whitney finished in the box and Crane played first.

—New York *Times*

It was a pleasure to most of the magnificent crowd of 7780 people who saw the game at the South end grounds yesterday afternoon to have the Bostons win. A great deal rested upon the shoulders of Clarkson, who had excellent command of the ball and great speed. Brouthers and Clarkson did the best batting, the latter making two singles, while Brouthers sent in four of the seven runs.

—Boston *Herald*

Monday, June 3

On June 2, Brooklyn lost to St. Louis 1–2
(Caruthers 6–2 and King 12–7).
AA: St. Louis 28–12, Brooklyn 21–15.

There were 11,721 people present at Ridgewood Park yesterday, making a total attendance of over 41,000 people at the three games played at Brooklyn, which is the largest attendance ever at three games of ball. Only one hit was secured off King, and he made three hits off Caruthers out of three times at the bat, Latham's hit sending him home once and another hit of his sending in Duffee. Thus King's batting yielded the Browns both their runs. His pitching and batting won the game.

—St. Louis *Post-Dispatch*

The Brooklyn Club should by all means set aside a portion of the grand stand—that back of third base would be best—for ladies and non smokers, leaving the cigar and cigarette slaves to sit behind the catcher. At present the ladies cannot escape the cigar nuisance, as the smokers are all over the grand stand.

—Brooklyn *Daily Eagle*

Tuesday, June 4

On June 3, Boston beat Philadelphia 10–6 (Radbourn 8–1). Brooklyn lost to Kansas City 6–9 (Terry 6–4). St. Louis won at Columbus 11–7 (Devlin 4–1). NL: Boston 22–6, New York 17–13. AA: St. Louis 29–12, Brooklyn 21–16.

The two successive defeats of Sunday and yesterday sustained by the Brooklyn team, accompanied by the two victories scored by their Eastern rivals in Philadelphia on Saturday and Sunday, sent Brooklyn back to third place, and the indications are that they will find it troublesome to get back to second

Will "Adonis" Terry, pitcher, Brooklyn Bridegrooms (New York *Clipper*, May 26, 1888).

position until the Louisvilles come to town and the St. Louis champions face the Athletics.

The new rules are damaging to all pitchers who lack command of the ball, and this happens to be Terry's one weak point. He has pluck and nerve in the box; is cool under trying circumstances; has great speed and effective curves at command and plenty of endurance. But with the small margin of but four balls against him his want of command of the ball comes in very costly at times, as it did in this game.

—Brooklyn *Daily Eagle*

In view of the phenomenal patronage bestowed on the Brooklyn Club at home this season the club will rate among the most profitable professional organizations in the base ball world this year. The cost of the fire under such circumstances is but a mere drop in the bucket. No wonder the league looks on with longing eyes on the Brooklyn Club as a coming member.

—Brooklyn *Daily Eagle*

Manager Frank Bancroft of Indianapolis is quoted as saying: "The League rules which compel a club to remain over in a League city and play off postponed games, instead of picnicking off to the country to give an exhibition game, no doubt saved our lives, and I thank God for the rule. We were to have played in Johnstown on Friday, having accepted a guarantee of $150 for the game there, but the League Club objected, and we cancelled the date. In the hotel, the Hurlbert House, where we intended stopping, only nine of the seventy guests were saved. You can see what we escaped."

—New York *Times*

AMERICAN ASSOCIATION STANDINGS

	W	L	PCT.	GB		W	L	PCT.	GB
St. Louis	29	12	.707	—	Cincinnati	21	19	.525	7½
Brooklyn	21	16	.568	6	Baltimore	17	18	.486	9
Athletic	19	15	.559	6½	Columbus	15	23	.395	12½
Kansas City	20	17	.541	7	Louisville	8	30	.211	19½

NATIONAL LEAGUE STANDINGS

	W	L	PCT.	GB		W	L	PCT.	GB
Boston	22	6	.786	—	Chicago	14	17	.452	9½
Philadelphia	19	12	.613	4½	Pittsburg	13	18	.419	10½
New York	17	13	.567	6	Indianapolis	10	21	.323	13½
Cleveland	17	14	.548	6½	Washington	7	18	.280	13½

Wednesday, June 5

On June 4, New York lost at Washington 3–5 (Keefe 3–2).
Boston beat Philadelphia 4–2 (Clarkson 14–1).
Brooklyn beat Kansas City 5–3 (Lovett 7–3).
NL: Boston 23–6, New York 17–14.
AA: St. Louis 29–12, Brooklyn 22–16.

Washington, June 4—The Washington-New-York game here to-day
was essentially a pitchers' battle between the two Keefes, and the Washington man fairly rivaled his famous opponent.

—New York *Times*

The Bostons won another game from the Philadelphias yesterday,
but had to work for it, and work hard. Dick Johnston made the hit that
broke the spell. There were two men on bases when he accomplished his
pretty hit. Clarkson accomplished the great and wonderful piece of pitching of striking out Fogarty, Thompson and Mulvey on nine balls pitched.

—Boston *Herald*

Thursday, June 6

On June 5, New York won at Washington 4–3 (Welch 8–2).
Boston lost to Philadelphia 4–5 (Madden 1–4).
Brooklyn beat Kansas City 4–2 (Caruthers 7–2).
St. Louis won at Columbus 4–3 (King 13–7).
NL: Boston 23–7, New York 18–14.
AA: St. Louis 30–12, Brooklyn 23–16.

Washington, June 5—Umpire Curry received a very painful injury
in the fourth inning by being hit with a sharp foul-tip ball and, although
he made an effort to finish the game, was compelled to leave the field in
the following inning. Wise of the Washingtons and George of the New-
Yorks proved acceptable to both clubs and they officiated during the
remainder of the game and no fault was found with their decisions.

—New York *Times*

The Bostons died hard yesterday, and it was not until after a pro-
tracted struggle of 11 innings that the Philadelphias succeeded in pulling
down their flag. It was the most exciting contest of the season, and the
3068 spectators present were continually kept on the anxious seat.

—Boston *Herald*

The home team's batting was weak, not because they did not make base hits, but for the reason that they went in for slugging at swiftly pitched balls too often instead of trying to tap them safely to short outfield. Take Caruthers' play in this respect, for instance. He struck at the ball as if he meant to knock it out of the lot, and this he did time and again, even when men were on the bases. What was the result? He struck out twice and when he did hit the ball he hit fungo and was easily retired.

Robert, from being one of the most effective batsmen of the team, is now the weakest, simply from his foolish effort to slug the ball instead of trying to place it safely, even at the cost of a sacrifice hit. His case is quoted for the reason that he is an intelligent player, and the patrons look for better work at his hands than is expected from others who have not the headwork at command which he has.

—Brooklyn *Daily Eagle*

Friday, June 7

On June 6, New York lost at Boston 7–10
(Keefe 3–3 and Clarkson 15–1).
Brooklyn lost to Kansas City 4–6 (Lovett 7–4).
St. Louis won at Columbus 9–3 (Hudson 1–1).
NL: Boston 24–7, New York 18–15.
AA: St. Louis 31–12, Brooklyn 23–17.

Boston, June 6—The Bostons took a strong lead in the first of to-day's game, and then by miserable playing aided by three hits allowed New-York to crawl dangerously near them in the seventh. Clarkson seemed to have no control of the ball and gave eight men their bases.

Umpire Barnum's work displeased the visitors. He declared Brouthers safe at first in the opening inning when everybody else thought that he was out. The mistake gave Boston 4 runs, and in consequence won the game. The attendance was 4,583.

—New York *Times*

St. Louis now has a lead which it will be difficult to overcome. In fact it now looks as if they would be five time winners, with the Athletics and Brooklyns fighting for second place. The season is early, however, and one or the other of these present leaders may weaken and Brooklyn go to the front.

—Brooklyn *Daily Eagle*

Saturday, June 8

On June 7, New York lost at Boston 4–9
(Welch 8–3 and Radbourn 9–1).
NL: Boston 25–7, New York 18–16.

Radbourn was lame and did not exert himself. He seemingly tossed
the balls over the plate. As a result, Johnston and Brown had chances to
show great speed in the outfield. It was the first time this season that Johnston has been able to show at his best, and he made some great catches
after long runs at racing speed.

Mr. Ewing is a great ball player, but he has thoroughly disgusted the
lovers of the game in this and other cities by the way that he struts around,
by his constant stream of abusive chatter, and by his otherwise outlandish
actions, all indulged in to attract attention.

—Boston *Herald*

Sunday, June 9

On June 8, Brooklyn beat Louisville 14–5 (Caruthers 8–2).
St. Louis lost by forfeit and won at Baltimore 0–9 and 5–1
(King 14–7). AA: St. Louis 32–13, Brooklyn 24–17.

The interest in base ball will be kept up to the boiling point while
the Bostons are away by a miniature representation of the game in Music
Hall. This scheme has proved immensely popular in New York; and there
is no doubt of its success in this city, where the base ball fever rages
more violently than in any other section of the country. The first bulletins comprehended by this new arrangement will be shown tomorrow,
when the Bostons play in New York.

—Boston *Herald*

Nash had not made an error between May 6 and June 7, a feat
almost unparalleled in base ball history. During that time he put out in
19 games 35 men, and had 37 assists.

—Boston *Herald*

Brooklyn's team both outfielded and outbatted the Louisvilles at
Washington Park yesterday and encountered little difficulty in winning
from the Colonels. It was a one-sided game. Caruthers pitched a good
game and was admirably supported. Corkhill, with two home runs, led
in the batting.

—New York *Times*

Billy Nash, third baseman, Boston Beaneaters (Library of Congress, Prints and Photographs Division [LOT 13163-05, no. 13]).

New York, June 8—The hope that the New York team will duplicate its last season's work is growing beautifully less. Commissioner Gilroy's decision to not rebuild the Polo Ground fence will have a most enervating effect on the men, and the depressing effects of Staten Island fog and mist will complete the iniquity. Goodbye to the flag. Bad luck seems to pursue the New York team abroad, as well as at home. Crane gave his knee another wrench in Washington and is laid up. Keefe has not yet rounded into his championship form, and at present Mike Welch seems to be the only fit twirler in the team. As a whole, however, the pitchers are doing as good work as the rest of the players. One day they bat like fiends and lose the game through errors. On the next they brace up and field perfectly, but are unable to bat, and, strange to say, their weakness in the latter respect always comes when their own twirler pitches winning ball. How long will this thing continue?

Credit should be given to the Boston Club for the manner in which they are playing ball. If they can keep it up their grip on the pennant will be exceedingly hard to shake off. It cannot be denied, however, that they have everything in the way of encouragement. Enthusiastic crowds, popular favor and perfect physical condition are factors necessary to the well being of any club, and all these the Bean Eaters possess in marked degree.

—St. Louis *Post-Dispatch*

Boston, Mass., June 8—The New York League nine is all torn up with internal dissension, and therein lies the chief reason for their poor playing of late. They are not the same lot of ball tossers they were last season. There is wanting that harmony among men that is so essential to success. The reason is hard to find, but it is more than probable that the reason is the petty jealousies existing between the men. In the first place some of the men think Johnnie Ward is made too much of by the papers. He is a good player but he isn't the best in the world. Ewing and Crane were left behind in Washington Wednesday night. That is to say, they missed the train and Ewing was on the score card to catch next day in Boston. Ewing didn't appear—the captain of the nine and Mutrie gave it out that Buck was at his hotel laid up with a sore finger. Buck was actually in Washington, and the account of his doings there, in print, look very bad for the morals of League captains.

—St. Louis *Post-Dispatch*

Baltimore, Md., June 8—There were thousands of spectators to welcome the arrival of the St. Louis club, but the latter failed to appear until after 5 o'clock, caused by the train being delayed and Umpire Gaffney declared the game forfeited to Baltimore, but Barnie waived the forfeit and the game was played. The visitors played with their usual vim and brilliancy and had their opponents beaten from the jump. Only seven innings were played, darkness stopping the game.

Umpire Gaffney announced to-night that the regularly scheduled game of to-day was forfeited to the Baltimore club owing to the non-appearance of St. Louis. The game played was a postponed game.

—St. Louis *Post-Dispatch*

Monday, June 10

On June 9, Brooklyn beat Louisville 12–2 (Lovett 8–4).
St. Louis forfeit from previous day annulled.
AA: St. Louis 32–12, Brooklyn 25–17.

It was a great day for base ball in this city when the four Detroiters were secured. They are all quiet men, who talk little and work a great deal. It is hard to estimate how much good their example has done the other members of the team. How different, His Majesty Michael J. Kelly has been, for instance, since these men came into the team. He attends to his business, and has eschewed those monkey shines that the people could not tolerate. As a result, he is respected, and he is now on the top wave of popular favor. People have begun to realize that this man is a winner. It takes a man with the aggressive nature of an Anson, an Ewing, a Comiskey and a Kelly to "get there." Few ever expected that he would play the ball that he has played this season. He has been batting hard, fielding as Bostonians never expected to see him field in the outfield, and has been running bases and making slides such as are not within the power of any player in the game

—Boston *Herald*

WELSH, P., New Yorks

COPYRIGHT BY GOODWIN & CO., 1888.

OLD JUDGE
CIGARETTE FACTORY.
GOODWIN & CO., New York.

"Smiling" Mickey Welch, pitcher, New York Giants (Library of Congress, Prints and Photographs Division [LOT 13163-05, no. 223]).

Welch is doing the best work of the New York pitchers, and must be ranked as one of the greatest of twirlers. This makes the thirteenth consecutive year for Welch as a pitcher, his first professional engagement being with the Volunteer club of Poughkeepsie, N.Y., in 1877. Dan Brouthers used to work a knot hole at that time to see Mickey curve the ball, and little did Dan think then that he would be a batsman whom Mickey would fear later on. Brouthers' home is at Wappinger Falls, a suburb of Poughkeepsie.

—Charles J. Foley, Boston *Herald*

One of last season's umpires says: "I have had considerable experience both as an umpire and ball player, but of all the base ball associations that I have ever struck the American stands first for kickers. There is as much difference umpiring in the league and association as there is between riding in a two horse wagon and a palace car. I can umpire a whole season in the league and give entire satisfaction, but I cannot go through one inning in the association without being called 'pet' names, both by the audience and the players. The players go in a game and try to win ball by bluffing the umpire. That is their chief object, and they never lose an opportunity to work it. They seem educated up to it, and the home club is always upheld by the crowd, whether it is correct or not. That makes the road of the umpire doubly hard to travel, and I can say that the life of an association umpire is not a pleasant one."

—Brooklyn *Daily Eagle*

Mr. Byrne says that O'Brien is a very unwilling occupant of the position he occupies and that he would vacate it to-morrow if he could. This being the case, O'Brien cannot justly be said to be responsible for the errors of judgment he may commit in the position. The fact has never been questioned as to O'Brien's skill as an outfielder, nor have his palpably earnest efforts to win in every match. There is one fact very apparent, and that is that he cannot stand impartial criticism any more than can others of the team. They can swallow any amount of newspaper taffy with infinite gusto, but, criticized, they at once forget every favor ever done them by the offending scribe. But of such are the majority of the fraternity; gratitude for favors done them is an unknown quality with them.

—Brooklyn *Daily Eagle*

The game forfeited by Umpire Gaffney to the Baltimores Saturday because the train on which the Browns arrived was late, will be played off. Manager Barnie of the Baltimores has magnanimously refused to take advantage of a technicality to secure a game and says he will not accept it. The clubs are to play off their postponed game next Wednesday, the contest of Saturday going down as the regularly scheduled game for that day. Gaffney under the rules had no right to forfeit the game, as the delay of the Browns was unavoidable. An umpire can only declare a game forfeited at the request of the team not at fault, and as Baltimore does not make the request, Gaffney has no power in this case to award them the game.

Evidently, Mr. Barnie does not wish to advance the chances of the Brooklyns or Athletics in the race, for if his sympathies were not with the Browns he would probably have made a demand for the game anyhow. Of course it will be more money in his pocket to play it Wednesday, as the Browns always draw well in Baltimore.

—St. Louis *Post-Dispatch*

New York, June 9, 1889—A quiet looking, lithe, neatly dressed young man, a little below the average height, stepped off the steamer Pilgrim this morning. A *Herald* writer had been waiting for him, his errand being to have a talk on the brotherhood question. The reader may have guessed from this that the gentleman in question was John M. Ward of the New York club to whom the subject is most important, and one to which he has given a great deal of thought and study. The probable action of the Brotherhood of National League Players relative to the classification system is the vital question in base ball today. The members of the body have been very close-mouthed on the subject, but the writer was able today to obtain information that will throw much light on the matter.

Mr. Ward spoke with great earnestness. He said: "The whole matter of this classification has been generally misunderstood. We are represented as a lot of disgruntled, dissatisfied players, and are held up as a disturbing element, while the managers of the club and the officers of the league are pictured as a body of liberal, generous gentlemen, having only the welfare of the game and of the players at heart. This is the way they want the public and the players to look at them. Now, what is the actual condition of things? What is our grievance? Simply this: Last year it was agreed, at a meeting of a committee of the league and of the brotherhood, that no player should be reserved for any ensuing season at a salary less than he had received the previous season. It was also agreed that the amount of this salary should be written in the contract. This was all that we wanted, but was it done? The league utterly ignored this agreement.

"The end of the season came and the players departed for their respective homes. Some of the players left for Australia. While we were gone the classification scheme came into existence. We were not consulted, and, therefore, were in entire ignorance of all that had occurred. We found, to our surprise, that our agreement had been violated and that many players had signed contracts. It has been asked why we did not do anything in the matter. What could we do? The contracts signed were perfectly legal, and the players could not go back on them, but we intend to insist that reparation shall be done those players affected. Why should the players support the league if such clubs as Indianapolis and Washington can't stand the pace? Why should first-class players be compelled to play for lower salaries than they can get elsewhere simply because Indianapolis can't afford it? I recognize the fact that clubs in every association are rich and poor, but I say let the rich ones pay the deficiencies of the weak ones. The National League of Base Ball Clubs is a partnership in everything save receipts. Why not receipts?

John M. Ward, shortstop, New York Giants (Library of Congress, Prints and Photographs Division [LOT 13163-05, no. 221]).

"Something like that has got to be done, because the player does not intend to be treated as has been the case. He has feelings and rights, and both have got to be respected. I am sure the public will sympathize with us once it has the facts. How has the league ever met us? If certain clubs cannot meet their obligations, and remedies must be adopted that affect the player, should he not be consulted? The league did not deal fairly with the player on the classification scheme. Why did we ask that a player not be reserved at a less salary than he had been receiving? First, so that a club could not hire a man at a good salary and then cut him down next season as has been done this year in many cases; second, so that a club could not handle a man like a piece of merchandise, and transfer him anywhere against his will. We shall insist that this rule shall be restored. Now that the effect of this pernicious classification rule doesn't hit the mark, clubs like Indianapolis can't make any money anyway, and the rich clubs will make more money. If, as the promoters of this iniquitous and unjust rule intimate, there would be an early death to base ball but for the classification rule, why don't they apply the proper remedy and make rich clubs pay the piper and not the poor player?"

—Boston *Herald*

Tuesday, June 11

On June 10, New York beat Boston 5–1
(Keefe 4–3 and Clarkson 15–2).
Brooklyn beat Louisville 7–5 (Caruthers 9–2).
St. Louis won at Baltimore 9–1 (Chamberlain 14–3).
NL: Boston 25–8, New York 19–16.
AA: St. Louis 33–12, Brooklyn 26–17.

After administering three defeats to the Giants on the Boston grounds the representatives of the city of culture attempted to repeat the dose on the diamond of the champions, but they failed. In fact, the Giants had the easiest kind of victory, and came within an ace of shutting out the aspirants for championship honors.

The New-Yorkers played with their old time vim and determination; Keefe pitched good ball; the boys took all chances on the bases, and in a word they showed form that if continued will land them in first place. The Bostons, however, never quit, but continued making efforts to overhaul their more speedy opponents, and were not beaten until the last man was retired in the ninth inning. Under Capt. Kelly's command the Bostons seem to have plenty of heart and play with an air of confidence. This is a strong point, and no doubt is one of the secrets of the success of the team. If a little of the same material could be infused into some clubs in this vicinity, our nines would make a much better showing.

—New York *Times*

New York, June 10, 1889—The Staten Island grounds are, indeed, a curiosity. The ground clear to the boards back of second base is perfectly bare and very rough indeed, making good fielding very difficult. About 20 feet back of second base the stage laid last year for the spectacular representation of "Nero" by the Kiralfys begins. This stage has quite a pitch, and the fielders wear rubber-soled shoes. Behind the stage is the fence, and surrounding the fence is the lofty scaffolding used in the play. The fence is not a very high one, and often balls bound over, allowing a home run. On the left field side, back of third, in foul territory, is a declivity, and here no little time is lost by the fielders running down after foul balls.

—Boston *Herald*

The third game of the series between Brooklyn and Louisville, played yesterday at Washington Park, was witnessed by the smallest attendance of spectators of the month, and on the bleaching boards back of first base the crowd was the roughest seen there this season, a gang of toughs being present who, by their language to the umpire, did enough to have half a dozen of them promptly ejected from the grounds. If such roughs are allowed to indulge their habitual propensities with impunity, as they were yesterday, it will not take long to thin the attendance of the better class of patrons of the grand stand.

—Brooklyn *Daily Eagle*

Baltimore, Md., June 11—The Browns are playing magnificent ball and are being royally received everywhere. Capt. Comiskey has not only infused life into his men, but is batting, fielding and running bases in marvelous style.

—St. Louis *Post-Dispatch*

AMERICAN ASSOCIATION STANDINGS

	W	L	PCT.	GB		W	L	PCT.	GB
St. Louis	33	12	.733	—	Kansas City	21	22	.488	11
Athletic	26	15	.634	5	Baltimore	19	21	.475	11½
Brooklyn	26	17	.605	6	Columbus	16	25	.390	15
Cincinnati	22	22	.500	10½	Louisville	8	37	.178	25

NATIONAL LEAGUE STANDINGS

	W	L	PCT.	GB		W	L	PCT.	GB
Boston	25	8	.758	—	Chicago	17	20	.459	10
Cleveland	24	14	.632	3½	Pittsburg	13	22	.371	13
Philadelphia	23	14	.622	4	Indianapolis	10	24	.294	15½
New York	19	16	.543	7	Washington	9	22	.290	15

Wednesday, June 12

On June 11, New York beat Boston 2–1
(Welch 9–3 and Radbourn 9–2).
Brooklyn beat Louisville 4–2 (Lovett 9–4).
St. Louis lost at Baltimore 5–7 (King 14–8).
NL: Boston 25–9, New York 20–16.
AA: St. Louis 33–13, Brooklyn 27–17.

Boston has the distinction of being the only club in the League that has not suffered the stigma of a "whitewash" this season and the New-Yorks made a mighty effort to break that record yesterday. For six innings they succeeded wonderfully well, but in the seventh big Dan Brouthers made a hit over the centre-field fence for four bases and prevented the Giants from accomplishing their task.

All eyes were centered on "Mike" Welch, New-York's pitcher. Since the season began the smile that was wont to adorn his face in years gone by was missing, and it was replaced with a troubled expression. Yesterday, however, a broad smile was seen on the pitcher's face as he stepped into the box, and this change caused joy to reign among the small army of cranks at St. George.

And they were not victims of misplaced confidence. Welch pitched one of those games that have gained for him fame and dollars, and the Bostonians nearly wrenched the sockets of their arms in their efforts to hit the ball. Brouthers had a record that he was forced to part with yesterday. For thirty-three games he had not fallen a victim to three strikes, but Welch's work was too much for him, and he had to give way.

—New York *Times*

The batting and base running were seriously interfered with by the heavy condition of the grounds. They resembled a big quagmire, and were in simply horrible condition. It had rained heavily in the morning, and this converted the grounds into a miniature lake. It was very bad near the home plate, and almost every batsman who started to run stepped in the mire. The fielders, therefore, had plenty of time to fumble the ball, again and again, and still get their man out.

—Boston *Herald*

Umpire Gaffney has sent in his resignation as an umpire of the American Association, it being his intention to enter the hansom cab business at Worcester, Mass., his home. Gaffney's retirement will be a loss to the Association, as good umpires are extremely scarce and he was certainly the best in the country. The Association cut his salary $500 or

John Gaffney, umpire, American Association (New York *Clipper*, February 13, 1892).

$600 this year and he has been dissatisfied ever since.
—St. Louis *Post-Dispatch*

Thursday, June 13

On June 12, St. Louis lost at Baltimore 3–8 (Hudson 1–2). AA: St. Louis 33–14, Brooklyn 27–17.

The writer called upon Director Conant yesterday to ascertain what was his opinion on Ward's article on the classification scheme. He said: "I have read Mr. Ward's latest effusion on classification and regard it as the ablest thing that he ever wrote, but I cannot agree at all with him in many of his conclusions, and I do not think that Ward would have given utterance to many of his statements if he had taken the time to think the matter over on all sides. His is but the utterance of a ball player who is thinking of but today, who does not realize that his condition today is due to the classification scheme such as we have just adopted. What do men like Ward, Brouthers and others of their kind want to bother their heads about this classification scheme for? They are getting big salaries, and most of the men are perfectly contented with their treatment; at least that is my experience with our men. Why, base ball would be impossible without such a classification scheme as we have adopted. What clubs in the country could afford to pay such fancy prices as some of the league clubs are paying? Why, under any other condition of things, base ball on the present scale of salaries and expenses would be impossible. Of 16 big clubs last season only three made any money.

"Mr. Ward says that, taking all the clubs together, there is a great deal of money made in base ball. No, this is not a fact. Most of the clubs found it very hard to make both ends meet last year, and the same will be true this year. The clubs save something this season through the classification rule. Mr. Ward is getting more money than ever. The salaries of players were never so great as they now are, and it is plain that limit must be reached. Unless something was done to bring the clubs weaker financially on the same plane with the strong ones, the game would have to go to the wall. Mr. Ward says that if the company is too fast for such clubs as Washington and Indianapolis, these clubs ought to get out. Not so fast, young man. I would like to hear from Mr. Ward how he can replace any of the league cities that he now considers weak. You cannot grade the means of a city to support a club any more than you can grade the playing strength of the clubs."

—Boston *Herald*

Friday, June 14

On June 13, New York beat Philadelphia 3–2 (Keefe 5–3).
Boston beat Washington 7–1 (Clarkson 16–2).
Brooklyn beat Cincinnati 2–1 (Terry 7–4).
St. Louis tied at Athletic 2–2.
NL: Boston 26–9, New York 21–16.
AA: St. Louis 33–14, Brooklyn 28–17.

Genial Timothy J. Keefe, the star pitcher of the Giants, was in an unusually happy frame of mind yesterday, and he amused himself by curving the ball in such a manner that the Philadelphia players couldn't find its whereabouts. One after another they fell victims to the skill of the New-York twirler, and when the nine innings were finished thirteen men had been retired on strikes and the Giants won the game by a very narrow margin.

In the last half of the ninth inning, when nearly everybody had given up the game, Tiernan distinguished himself by making a base hit. Ewing faced Buffinton and contented himself with making a sacrifice, which advanced Tiernan to second. Ward then followed and proved that he was the right man in the proper place by knocking the ball for two bases, sending in Tiernan and making the score even at 2 to 2.

The cheers that greeted this achievement had scarcely subsided, when the daring little short stop, seeing a good opportunity, stole to third base, to the delight of the spectators and the discomfiture of the visiting players. An air of confidence seemed to pervade the atmosphere when the biggest of the Giants, Roger Connor, grabbed his bat and walked to the plate. In the vernacular of the profession he hit the ball "square in the nose," sent in Ward, won the game, caused a feeling of joy to reign in the hearts of the spectators, and gave the enthusiasts a chance to yell in a manner new to Staten Island.

—New York *Times*

The tail of the league tried to wag the head yesterday afternoon at the South end grounds, and the attempt was a signal failure. The strong, tried, horny-fisted veterans of so many seasons literally played with the youngsters from Washington. It was by superior work of the stick that the home club won the game. The visitors could not bat Clarkson even a little bit. The big man, Brouthers, was on hand, and batted in three out of the seven runs scored by his side.

—Boston *Herald*

Saturday, June 15

On June 14, New York beat Philadelphia 14–4 (Welch 10–3).
Boston beat Washington 9–3 (Radbourn 10–2).
Brooklyn beat Cincinnati 7–4 (Caruthers 10–2).
St. Louis lost at Athletic 5–8 (Chamberlain 14–4).
NL: Boston 27–9, New York 22–16.
AA: St. Louis 33–15, Brooklyn 29–17.

The Bostons were able to give the Washingtons cards and spades yesterday, and then beat them with consummate ease. Compared with the brawny representatives of the modern Athens, the base ballists of the capital city were as naught, and availed as little as the strength of a pigmy against a giant.

—Boston *Herald*

Capt. Mike Kelly of the Bostons, who is the greatest "guy" on the ball field, was fined $10 by Umpire Curry yesterday because when the latter declared Daily of the Washingtons safe at first base Kelly, in right field, balanced himself on his hands, waved his feet in the air and behaved like a mule.

—St. Louis *Post-Dispatch*

Clever field work saved Brooklyn yesterday. The Cincinnati men had on their batting clothes and made matters rather lively for Caruthers, but the home players handled the ball in great shape and by doing so managed to keep down the run column of the Porkopolitans.

—New York *Times*

Sunday, June 16

On June 15, Boston beat Washington 3–2 (Clarkson 17–2).
NL: Boston 28–9, New York 22–16.

It was a stiff game that the visitors put up, and the Bostons had to work like beavers to win. Clarkson had a great game to pitch, and it is safe to say that there is no pitcher in the country who could have given such a magnificent exhibition as he did. It was artistic and scientific in the extreme, and it was a treat to be present and watch such playing. It was the quintessence of all there is fine in base ball.

—Boston *Herald*

New York, June 15—While the team was on its Eastern trip the same old rumors of internal dissension arose from the same old sources and very likely for the same old moth-eaten purposes. They were telegraphed on to the metropolitan press by the column, but strange to say the minds that originated the rumors abroad failed to publish them. As a matter of fact there is not a club in the league more entirely harmonious in root and branch than the New Yorks. If some of these scandal-mongers could step into the club-house either before or after a game they would soon realize that their tongues were wagging in vain.

—St. Louis *Post-Dispatch*

Brooklyn, June 15—The Louisvilles dropped four games while here, but it must not be supposed that the Brooklyns had much of a "snap" with the valorous gentlemen from the land of rye and ultra marine vegetation. On the contrary, the visitors played a much better game than had been expected, losing the last two contests by very close calls.

—St. Louis *Post-Dispatch*

New York, June 15—If President Day of the New York Club is correctly reported and will act upon what he says, he is by long odds the most liberal and progressive gentleman now connected with the business of baseball. To an interviewer at Washington recently he denounced the classification scheme as unbusiness like and unjust, and declared his willingness to pool the receipts of the game so that each club receive an equal share. Coming from the president of a club which has been and will again be one of the best paying, the proposition to pool receipts is advanced ground and stamps its leader as a man of far-seeing business intelligence. And yet why should not President Day and every other League official entertain these same views? Upon examination they will be found to express the very conditions which in the nature of things and in strict justice ought to be.

As for the classification scheme, I recently wrote a statement of the facts in connection with the formation of the present League contract for the purpose of showing wherein classification as applied had violated one of the most important agreements with the players. President Day, as one of the League committee that met the players, recognizes the truth of that statement and the consequent influence of a promise unfulfilled. What the players object to is the reservation of men at a reduction of salary. The promise not to do this was the principal agreement. President Day, as a man of principle, feels this, and to his credit be it said he alone of all the managers has sought no advantage by the use of classification. He knows that classification applied to men who feel it to be unnecessary and unjust, will only make poor ball players and eventually detract from the interest of the game. Moreover, he doubtless feels that, as a man of judgment, he is in a better position to conduct his own affairs, and determine how much he can afford to pay his own employees than anyone else, and he resents the attempt of others to dictate to him in these matters.

Finally, President Day realized that this classification is a mere subterfuge and a scheme by which it is sought to carry along a couple of weak cities at the expense of their players. It was said that classification was intended for the benefit of two alleged losing clubs. What business, then, have Boston, Chicago and Philadelphia to employ it? Plainly, the practice does not correspond with the profession, and players readily recognize the rule as a mere cloak.

The second portion of President Day's statement, namely, that he is willing to pool the receipts, is more remarkable than the first; not, however, because less in accordance with what ought to be, but because it involves an apparent sacrifice of personal interests for the general good. The New York Club holds one of the most valuable franchises in the League, and under ordinary circumstances is a veritable gold mine to its owners. The pooling of receipts (by which, I take it, he means 50 per cent to the visiting club) would mean that New York should give to visiting clubs 50 cents instead of 25 cents on every dollar of gate money, and receive the same when itself is away from home. But while the exchange might be nearly even with Boston, Chicago and Philadelphia, with the smaller cities it would be largely against New York. This is by no means so unfair as it may appear at first sight. What is it that makes the New York franchise so valuable? It is simply because it holds a monopoly of its territory, and that monopoly is created by the co-operation of all the other clubs. If it were not for the support of the Washington, Indianapolis, Cleveland, Pittsburg and other clubs, and their refusal to play against any rival club in New York, the New York Club alone could not keep out competitors. Why, then, are not Washington, Indianapolis and the others entitled to some substantial share of the benefits arising from a condition which they themselves create? It may be urged in reply that New York makes full return to Indianapolis by in turn supporting the latter in the monopoly of its territory. Such a claim, however, is untenable. Indianapolis' support to New York enables the latter to make many thousands of dollars while New York's support to Indianapolis helps the latter to lose several thousands. The returns to each are thus widely disproportionate and New York does not pay its debt, because it does not pay for value received. Again, it may be said that such a pooling of receipts offers no reward to the enterprise which develops or collects a strong team or provides attractions. This, too, is incorrect. Fifty per cent to visiting clubs does not mean that all receipts will be equal. It is true that, as between any two clubs, as, for instance, Boston and Washington, in their games together, each will receive the same amount of admission money, but as Washington must play seventy games on its own ground while Boston plays only ten there, it will easily be seen that Boston still has a big advantage from its own home games. It is true it would take a little from the revenue of the Chicago and other bonanza clubs, and hand it over to the weaker cities, but certainly none of the latter would thereby be ruined, and since it would act as a sliding scale it is hard to see just how any of the larger clubs would be seriously crippled.

John B. Day, president, New York Giants (1889 *Spalding Guide*).

There is, too, another side to the case. The League must have a certain number of clubs. Though not possible to have eight cities of equal drawing powers, the clubs must be evenly matched, and the players in the smaller cities are thus expected to put up just as good ball as those in the larger. This being the case, it is manifestly unfair to compel the former to play for less money than their more fortunate fellow players who happen to be located in the larger cities. And yet, with Boston making $100,000 and Indianapolis losing $5,000, the players of the latter city cannot expect as high salaries as the former club can afford to pay. Neither can the Boston players be expected to willingly see their salaries cut down to a scale which the Indianapolis Club must pay. What then is the reasonable way out of the dilemma? Equalize the financial strength of the clubs. Take away from the big clubs the power to buy up the strongest players and the playing strength will soon equalize itself. Give each club its almost equal share and the strongest incentive to ruinous competition for players is taken away. Give every club the means to pay the regular rate of salaries and the oppression of the reserve rule will be a thing of the past. Equalize as much as possible and nine-tenths of the evils which now beset the game will disappear. The genuineness of the contests would be in no wise affected, but, if thought necessary to assure the public, a system of graded prizes could be adopted such as has been already urged by the most thoughtful writers upon the game.

—John M. Ward, by telegraph to the St. Louis *Post-Dispatch*

Monday, June 17

On June 16, Brooklyn lost to Cincinnati 3–4 (Lovett 9–5).
St. Louis won at Athletic 9–5 (King 15–8).
AA: St. Louis 34–15, Brooklyn 29–18.

Tuesday, June 18

On June 17, Boston lost to and beat Washington 2–6 and 11–6
(Radbourn 10–3; Clarkson 18–2).
St. Louis lost at Athletic 2–11 (Devlin 4–2).
NL: Boston 29–10, New York 22–16.
AA: St. Louis 34–16, Brooklyn 29–18.

The greatest play of the first game was made in the third inning, when the Washingtons had three men on bases. Myers drove a wicked looking ball far down into right centre that looked as if it were good for three bases, but our little "dickey-bird" made one of the finest runs that he has made this season, and by a last superb effort clutched at the ball and got it, while the crowd fairly howled for joy.

—Boston *Herald*

Before starting for Cleveland last night Short Stop Ward, President of the Ball Players' Brotherhood, said that a conference in the West will be held shortly between committees representing the Brotherhood and the League. Ward of New-York, Hanlon of Pittsburg, and Brouthers of Boston will look after the interest of the players, and Day of New-York, Rogers of Philadelphia, and Spalding of Chicago the managers'.

The object of the conference is to take definite action in regard to the classification system. Since its adoption it has been a dead letter, nearly every club violating the rule, and the players are desirous of having it repealed. The majority of the managers, too, are in favor of abolishing the rule, and the probabilities are that in a short while the classification system will be a thing of the past. This is one of the many devices used by managers whose generosity is limited, to cut down salaries. It was only a pretext, and from the outset only one or two took advantage of it, the others paying their players just as they pleased.

—New York *Times*

AMERICAN ASSOCIATION STANDINGS

	W	L	PCT.	GB		W	L	PCT.	GB
St. Louis	34	16	.680	—	Cincinnati	24	24	.500	9
Athletic	29	16	.644	2½	Kansas City	21	25	.457	11
Brooklyn	29	18	.617	3½	Columbus	18	26	.409	13
Baltimore	25	21	.543	7	Louisville	8	42	.160	26

NATIONAL LEAGUE STANDINGS

	W	L	PCT.	GB		W	L	PCT.	GB
Boston	29	10	.744	—	Chicago	19	24	.442	12
Cleveland	28	16	.636	3½	Pittsburg	17	24	.415	13
Philadelphia	24	17	.585	6	Indianapolis	12	28	.300	17½
New York	22	16	.579	6½	Washington	11	27	.289	17½

Wednesday, June 19

On June 18, Brooklyn lost to St. Louis 4–5
(Terry 7–5 and King 16–8).
AA: St. Louis 35–16, Brooklyn 29–19.

Only a fly ball hit in the air,
Direct to the hands of the left field player;
Eagerly watched by thousands of eyes,
For on that catch depended the prize.
Hands were ready to give applause,
For Darby had ofttimes given them cause;
But for once—as luck would have it—he failed;
And the home team's flag in the dust was trailed.

This is the rhymester's story of yesterday's contest, in lines brief but to the point. There is no questioning the fact that the Brooklyn team is not the favorite of Dame Fortune. At Ridgewood and at Washington Park this week the least stroke of good luck would have given the Brooklyn team a position in the pennant race which would have been like taking the tide at the flood "which leads on to fame and fortune." But it was not to be; and instead they have been pushed further down in the list and given an uphill fight in the struggle for the pennant which will require their best efforts to enable them to recover the valuable ground lost within the past few days.

—Brooklyn *Daily Eagle*

Thursday, June 20

On June 19, New York lost at Cleveland 1–10 (Keefe 5–4).
Boston won at Pittsburg 6–1 (Clarkson 19–2).
Brooklyn beat Baltimore 9–0 (Caruthers 11–2).
NL: Boston 30–10, New York 22–17.
AA: St. Louis 35–16, Brooklyn 30–19.

The grounds in this city contain a "skin" diamond, and, as the visitors have been accustomed to one of turf, it was thought they would fall behind the home team in fielding display. Such was not the case by any means. No prettier infield work was ever done than that of Nash, Quinn, Richardson and Clarkson today. The balls went at them like a bullet from a rifle, only to be handled without the slightest break.

—Boston *Herald*

Friday, June 21

On June 20, New York won at Cleveland 1–0 (Welch 11–3).
Boston won at Pittsburg 2–1 (Madden 2–4).
Brooklyn beat Baltimore 14–3 (Lovett 10–5).
NL: Boston 31–10, New York 23–17.
AA: St. Louis 35–16, Brooklyn 31–19.

Cleveland, June 20—The New-Yorks won a hard fought contest today and fairly earned the victory. The only run was made by Ward in the eighth inning. After getting first on a hit, he started to steal second, and while Stricker rushed to cover the base Connor hit the ball over the ground he had just left.. Had Stricker remained, a double play would probably have settled both Ward and Connor, but as it happened Ward kept on to third. He afterward scored on a fine slide, amid hearty applause, on Richardson's hit toward first.

—New York *Times*

While hard to distinguish between so many brilliant catches as were made, perhaps the most electrifying was the one made by Johnston in the seventh inning. There was no one on bases when Smith hit the ball on its centre, and it sailed to left centre in a most wicked way. It appeared impossible for any one to get up to it, but Johnston made the effort. Brown gave him plenty of room, and close to the fence Dick's outstretched hands encircled the ball and held it. The crowd applauded. Such a catch as that would have wrung applause from a stone wall. The Boston correspondents bestowed their blandest smiles on their crestfallen brethren of the Smoky city, and paralyzed them by remarking that Dick made those catches every other game.

—Boston *Herald*

Yesterday was Ladies' day at Washington Park and the crowd of spectators was increased from 1,924 on Wednesday to 2,057 yesterday, the latter count excluding the invited guests of the club on the occasion. This shows pretty conclusively that the fair sex draw the masculine to the grand stand and that the Ladies' day investment was a good one. The day, too, will be more enjoyable than ever before, as the new rule went into effect yesterday, and that rule placed the selfish smokers in their own compartment of the grand stand, where they may smoke themselves into dried hams if they choose without annoying the ladies, as they did before. One other improvement should be made and then that part of the stand set aside for ladies and their escorts and non smokers will be complete, and that is to prohibit the waiters from passing between the seats.

—Brooklyn *Daily Eagle*

Dick Johnston, center fielder, Boston Beaneaters (Library of Congress, Prints and Photographs Division [LOT 13163-05, no. 7]).

Saturday, June 22

On June 21, New York won at Cleveland 17–6 (Keefe 6–4).
St. Louis won at Louisville 7–3 (Chamberlain 15–4).
NL: Boston 31–10, New York 24–17.
AA: St. Louis 36–16, Brooklyn 31–19.

The managers of the New-York Club have been looking for new
grounds ever since the old diamond at the Polo Grounds was taken away,
and the chances are that by the time the club reaches home from the present Western trip a new enclosure will be in course of erection. Poor attendance at St. George made this step necessary.

When the club played the opening games at Staten Island cold
weather was given as an excuse for the poor attendance. With warm
weather, however, the crowds increased but little, and the managers set
about to find a new ground in this city. They did not succeed until yesterday. Papers were drawn up, and the lease will be signed to-day. President Day was opposed to telling the whereabouts of the new home for
the Giants until all the papers are signed, but it is more than probably
that the grounds at One Hundred and Fifty-fifth-street and Eighth-
avenue, the property of James Coogan, will be the spot.

Work will be begun at once. The old grand stand and the "bleaching boards" at the Polo Grounds will be removed, and a force of workmen will be engaged to grade the property and erect the fence while the
stands are being placed in position. The new grounds can be reached by
the west elevated road, and will be a vast improvement over Staten Island.
The objection to the latter was the time occupied in getting home after
a game. With a ground in the upper portion of the city this will be
remedied, and the baseball crank, if his club loses, will have his wounded
feelings soothed with a warm dinner.

—New York *Times*

Sunday, June 23

On June 22, New York lost at Cleveland 6–8 (Welch 11–4).
Boston won twice at Pittsburg 1–0 and 4–3 (Clarkson 20–2;
Sowders 1–1). Brooklyn lost to Baltimore 5–9 (Terry 7–6).
St. Louis won twice at Louisville 7–6 and 3–2
(King 17–8; Hudson 2–2). NL: Boston 33–10, New York 24–18.
AA: St. Louis 38–16, Brooklyn 31–20.

Cleveland, Ohio, June 22—In the third inning, with three men on
bases and two out, Ewing dropped the ball over the left fence, 478 feet

from the plate and chased the three men home. The ball sped so swiftly that it was not seen, and nobody knew it was over the fence until Twitchell signaled to McQuaid. It was the longest hit ever made on the local grounds, and when the spectators realized it the applause was generous. The ball must have gone 250 yards.

—New York *Times*

John Clarkson seems to improve with every game he pitches. It is safe to say that in all his career he never did such superb twirling as he did in the fifth, sixth and seventh innings today. He not only struck out twelve men in the game, but he fielded out two men at the home plate, and finally made the hit in the tenth inning that brought in the winning run. In the fifth inning he struck out the side, Kuehne interspersing a safe hit. In the sixth, with two men out, one of whom he struck out, he struck out the third man, and in the seventh inning, with the bases full and no one out, he threw Sunday and Dunlap out at the plate, and caused Hanlon to be third out, with no runs in, on a fly to Brown.

The second game was a repetition of the first in its fighting character. Sowders did fully as well as Galvin. This may or may not have been due to an amusing fact that Capt. Dunlap did not "tumble" to until the game was nearly over. After Clarkson had dressed at the close of the first game, he took a seat on the players' bench within range of Sowders' eye. It was noticed that Sowders became unusually effective. Dunlap wondered what it all meant. He soon detected Sowders glancing slyly at Clarkson, who was sitting on the bench as innocent and demure as any one on the ground. Dunlap kept his eye on Clarkson and soon detected him giving Sowders the sign for a certain ball to the batsman. In an instant Dunlap called a halt, and Clarkson was "fired" off the bench.

—Boston *Herald*

Brooklyn, June 22—The opening of the new elevated road to the grounds had a decided effect on the attendance, many New Yorkers taking advantage of the rapid transit to see the game.

—St. Louis *Post-Dispatch*

President Von der Ahe has secured the crack pitcher of the York (Pa.) club, John Stivetts. The deal was concluded during the past week and Stivetts will come to St. Louis with the Browns. He is a little taller than King but is fully as speedy in his pitching as the Browns' silver-haired twirler. Stivetts went down to Gloucester, N.J., last Sunday, to show the Browns what he could do. Milligan caught him in practice, and the Browns big back-stop says Stivetts has plenty of speed, with good command of the ball. He will be quite an acquisition to the Browns' pitching department.

—St. Louis *Post-Dispatch*

New York, June 22—The subject of the Brotherhood's demands is being discussed very freely in base ball circles at present. Although a strike is within the bounds of possibility, it is very unlikely that the Brotherhood will be obliged to resort to such extreme measures. Both sides will probably concede many points rather than endure the mutual financial suffering that a strike will occasion. It is well-known that President Day, who is on the conference committee, favors the more important demands of the Brotherhood, and that Mr. John T. Rogers is not disposed to be blindly antagonistic. The chief snag which the Brotherhood will encounter is in the person of Mr. A. G. Spalding. In addition to being obstinate he is known to be opposed to almost every point demanded by them.

—St. Louis *Post-Dispatch*

Charles Comiskey, captain and first baseman, St. Louis Browns (Library of Congress, Prints and Photographs Division [LOT 13163-05, no. 392]).

Ren Mulford, in the *Cincinnati Times-Star*, says of Comiskey and his methods in captaining a team:

"Perhaps there is no captain in the business who possesses the head that rests on Comiskey's shoulders. There is a mystery about his management. He talks to his men to deceive the opposing team. His verbal orders amount to shucks! Did you ever see his position in the field? He invariably stands with his body well thrown forward and his hands behind him. He uses his mouth to hoodwink his opponents! To his men he telegraphs his orders with his fingers! With a base runner on first he will say:

"'Take your time there, now. Don't you run!'

"And that man gains a little more rope; is off a moment later in response to a twitching of Commy's digital, and as hair, dust and grass are mixed up in a slide at second and the traveler rises safe from the cloud Commy will remark:

"'Why, I told you not to run!'

"But he grins to himself and when his boy returns to the bench it is to meet with a complimentary word from the captain. Whenever a St. Louis player makes a double or three bagger the next man always has quite a time to find his bat. The delay enables the runner to regain his wind. There are tricks in all trades, and Captain Comiskey seems to have mastered all that there are in a base ball deck."

—Brooklyn *Daily Eagle*

Monday, June 24

On June 23, Brooklyn beat Columbus 8–2 (Caruthers 12–2).
St. Louis lost at Louisville 3–7 (Chamberlain 15–5).
AA: St. Louis 38–17, Brooklyn 32–20.

The all star Brooklyns will be the Glorious Fourth attraction at Sportsman's Park. The pyrotechnic display of skyrocket flies, batteries of variegated stars, bomb base hits, daisy cutters, grasshoppers, and a generally explosive demonstration due to the conflict when Greek meets Greek, etc. will form a kaleidoscope of base ball entertainment seldom witnessed by local patrons of the game. If the day is pleasant there ought to be 20,000 to 25,000 people at the two games.

—St. Louis *Post-Dispatch*

Tuesday, June 25

On June 24, New York lost at Chicago 0–6 (Crane 2–4).
Boston lost at Indianapolis 5–6 (Clarkson 20–3).
Brooklyn won by forfeit and lost to Columbus 7–13 (Lovett 10–6).
NL: Boston 33–11, New York 24–19.
AA: St. Louis 38–17, Brooklyn 33–21.

As was announced in *The Times* a few days ago, workmen started yesterday to get in condition the new grounds of the Giants at eighth-avenue and One Hundred and Fifty-fifth-street. They will be called the New Polo Grounds. Architect Deery feels confident that the grounds will be ready by July 8, when the club returns home. He said the grand stand when completed will seat about five thousand people. The entrance will be only about one hundred yards from the elevated station.

—New York *Times*

Umpire Goldsmith being too ill to officiate at the Brooklyn-Columbus game yesterday Substitute Paasch was called upon by President Byrne to fill the position. The Columbus men objected and said that they would not play with the umpire named. Thereupon Mr. Paasch gave the game to Brooklyn by the forfeit score of 9 to 0. After some wrangling, in order not to disappoint the spectators it was agreed to play off a postponed game and Columbus won easily.

The Columbus manager showed poor judgment in not agreeing to the substitute named by Brooklyn. Section 59 of the rules of the American Association is as follows: "Each club, shall, on or before the 10th day of April of each year, send to the President of the Association the names of three reputable persons, residents of the city where the club is located or in its immediate neighborhood; and when the regular umpire fails for any cause to be in attendance upon the field at the time specified for calling the game, the home club shall designate one of the said substitute umpires, who shall officiate during that game; and in the event that none of said persons are present, the Captains of the two clubs shall select an umpire, in the manner provided for by said section."

In Brooklyn the substitutes are Messrs. Pike, Daily, and Paasch, and only the latter was present at yesterday's game.

—New York *Times*

The worst exhibition of bad management of a team, of incompetent captaining and of rowdy ball playing seen at Washington Park this season was that shown at the hands of Manager Buckenberger, Captain Orr and a majority of the Columbus team yesterday. It only needs the repetition of such scenes as that of yesterday to reduce the attendance at the grounds to "a beggarly account of empty boxes," for it was enough to disgust every reputable patron of the game. If it were only the offenders against decent ball playing who suffered in the matter no one would regret it, but it is the Brooklyn Club that sustains the financial loss—a club which has been trying its best, with unprecedented outlays of money, to give its patrons gentlemanly exhibitions of the beauties of the game at the hands of the strongest gathering of base ball stars money could secure.

—Brooklyn *Daily Eagle*

That was a very strange and foolish act of Columbus to refuse to play a game at Brooklyn with Paasch as an umpire, and then after the game had been forfeited to play Brooklyn a postponed game with the same umpire. It looked very much as if Columbus wanted to present the Brooklyns with a game.

—St. Louis *Post-Dispatch*

AMERICAN ASSOCIATION STANDINGS

	W	L	PCT.	GB		W	L	PCT.	GB
St. Louis	38	17	.691	—	Cincinnati	28	24	.538	8½
Athletic	33	19	.635	3½	Kansas City	21	29	.420	14½
Brooklyn	33	21	.611	4½	Columbus	20	32	.385	16½
Baltimore	29	23	.558	7½	Louisville	9	46	.164	29

NATIONAL LEAGUE STANDINGS

	W	L	PCT.	GB		W	L	PCT.	GB
Boston	33	11	.750	—	Chicago	22	26	.458	13
Cleveland	31	18	.633	4½	Pittsburg	18	28	.391	16
Philadelphia	26	20	.565	8	Indianapolis	17	28	.378	16½
New York	24	19	.558	8½	Washington	11	32	.256	21½

Wednesday, June 26

On June 25, New York won at Chicago 12–8 (Crane 3–4).
Boston lost at Indianapolis 4–6 (Radbourn 10–4).
Brooklyn lost to Columbus 2–4 (Caruthers 12–3).
St. Louis beat Cincinnati 7–3 (Hudson 3–2).
NL: Boston 33–12, New York 25–19.
AA: St. Louis 39–17, Brooklyn 33–22.

A greater contrast between the discreditable exhibition of Monday at the hands of the visiting team from Columbus and the quiet conduct of their players yesterday has not been presented at Washington Park this season. On Monday they were engaged in bullying and bulldozing the small man who occupied the umpire's position, because they knew they could do it with comparative immunity from punishment. Yesterday they were controlled by an umpire who has made up his mind to stand no more insults from bulldozing kickers, and the gang who attacked little Paasch were as quiet as lambs before big Goldsmith.

Yesterday their hearts were in the game. It was beat Brooklyn or die, and they did not die. In but one inning was Caruthers' pitching punished, and that was in the fourth, when two hard hit balls went out to the carriages at center field—both in the same place—and two home runs were scored.

It will be plainly seen that this year the Columbus team is Brooklyn's *bete noir*, as Kansas City was last year. There is always one team out of the eight which an otherwise winning team cannot beat and this year Brooklyn finds it in Columbus. In fact they go in against that team half beaten at the start apparently, while playing pluckily enough against the far stronger teams of St. Louis, the Athletics and the Cincinnatis. On the other hand the Columbus team play against Brooklyn as they do against no other club.

—Brooklyn *Daily Eagle*

Indianapolis, Ind., June 25, 1889—Indianapolis base balldom is very jubilant tonight, for its pet team has won another victory over the Bostons. If there is anything on this terrestrial sphere that delights the average Hoosier, it is to win a game of ball over the representatives of the "Hub," and when this occurs the people in attendance are fairly wild with glee. Everybody joins in the hilarity. It has been a long time since the bleaching boards here have had a real good chance to "holler," but for two days they have had a sufficiency of opportunity, and have improved it.

—Boston *Herald*

Chicago, June 26—Monday Mr. Ward called on Mr. Spalding and asked him to name a day when the committee should meet. Mr. Ward went over the full list of grievances and a discussion of two hours took place. Mr. Spalding as chairman said he would confer with the other members of the committee and if they thought the matter urgent would call a special meeting, but at the present time he did not see why the whole matter could not be laid over till the League meeting in the fall. It is said Mr. Ward was opposed to any delay and demanded an immediate conference. The brotherhood, it is stated, has perfected plans to play ball under a new organization if this tie-up occurs.

—St. Louis *Post-Dispatch*

Thursday, June 27

On June 26, New York won at Chicago 12–7 (Welch 12–4).
Boston lost at Indianapolis 6–10 (Clarkson 20–4).
Brooklyn beat Columbus 10–3 (Terry 8–6).
St. Louis lost to Cincinnati 1–6 (Stivetts 0–1).
NL: Boston 33–13, New York 26–19.
AA: St. Louis 39–18, Brooklyn 34–22.

Indianapolis, Ind., June 26, 1889—Even Clarkson could not stem the tide. He got the worst lambasting he has been subjected to this season. Clarkson worked like a beaver. He tried every kind of pitching in the vocabulary, but hit him the Indians would.

—Boston *Herald*

Brooklyn had an easy victory over Columbus yesterday. Widner's pitching was hit rather hard, and the Bridegrooms took advantage of the numerous errors committed by the visitors. After the game Manager Byrne refused to pay the Columbus manager his share of the gate receipts, claiming that he violated the rules on Monday when he refused to play with Umpire Paasch. He will forward the money to the Secretary of the Association, prefer charges against the Columbus Club, and ask that the fine for leaving the field—$1,500—be imposed.

—New York *Times*

Manager Buchenburger of Columbus, by the action of Byrne, is left short of funds with which to meet his hotel and other bills, and says he is powerless to do anything until he gets back home. Columbus is a young club struggling for existence in a small town, while the Brooklyns are making more money than any team in the Association, if not in the country. They lost nothing by the action of Columbus, as after refusing to play the regular game, the Ohio boys played a postponed game that afternoon with the Brooklyns. The regular game was forfeited to Brooklyn and they were beaten in the postponed game that was played. Therefore they gained a game by the foolishness of Columbus, and the people who came to witness a contest were not disappointed. Although such sulkiness as Columbus displayed should be punished, it seems rather hard that the man they benefited with a victory should insist on adding $1,500 to his already well-stocked treasury by taking it from their depleted bank account.

—St. Louis *Post-Dispatch*

Stivetts, the new pitcher of the Browns, was pitted against the Cincinnatis yesterday, and, considering his support, did remarkably well. He has plenty of speed, and promises to prove a valuable man.

—St. Louis *Post-Dispatch*

The celebrated Brooklyns will be here Wednesday next. Old Dave Foutz, Doc Bushong and Bobbie Caruthers will meet with the reception they usually do—of a very kindly nature. Charlie King, with his cannonball arm, is still on top of the pitching records in the Association. King has done grand work this season and he wants to help win the pennant so as to have a "go" at Boston this fall.

—St. Louis *Post-Dispatch*

Friday, June 28

On June 27, New York won at Chicago 13–10 (Crane 4–4).
Boston won at Indianapolis 10–6 (Madden 3–4).

St. Louis lost to Cincinnati 6–8 (Stivetts 0–2).
NL: Boston 34–13, New York 27–19.
AA: St. Louis 39–19, Brooklyn 34–22.

No player in the New York club has been doing steadier hitting than the old Boston favorite, James H. O'Rourke, the "Marquis of Leggett."

—Boston *Herald*

Just at the conclusion of the second Cincinnati game a man jumped out of the grand stand and made a bee line for Pitcher Stivetts. With no other apology for his abruptness than his brazen "mug," he approached Stivetts and fired a volley of abuse at him for losing the game. Not satisfied with deliberately insulting Stivetts, the individual in question said: "If I'd a knowed you was goin' to pitch, I'der never come out."

Stivetts, who is a modest young man of a retiring disposition, told the "swell" that if he, Stivetts, had known that his presence in the box was distasteful to the individual in question and the few pals who were with him, that he would have requested that President Von der Ahe to let him retire in favor of some other man.

Although Stivetts did not pitch as well as he might under ordinary circumstances, his work did not warrant the abuse showered upon him. A few of those who are most insulting in their demeanor toward some of the Browns have been "spotted" and will be incontinently put out of the park, at the first provocation.

—St. Louis *Post-Dispatch*

Saturday, June 29

On June 28, New York won at Indianapolis 5–2 (Welch 13–4). Boston lost at Chicago 3–11 (Clarkson 20–5). NL: Boston 34–14, New York 28–19.

Chicago, Ill., June 28, 1889— The debut of the Boston team in this city this season was not very much to its credit; in fact, it was very much to its discredit. Not only did it receive

Jack Stivetts, pitcher, St. Louis Browns. (This picture is from later in his career, when he played for Boston.) (Transcendental Graphics)

the worst punishment it has thus far sustained, but it played the worst game it has been guilty of. The people sat and wondered if this was the same team that has the lead in the league race, and fondly hopes to win the championship.

—Boston *Herald*

Sunday, June 30

On June 29, New York won at Indianapolis 4–1 (Crane 5–4).
Boston lost at Chicago 2–8 (Sowders 1–2).
Brooklyn won at Athletic 3–2 (Caruthers 13–3).
St. Louis beat Louisville 10–1 (King 18–8).
NL: Boston 34–15, New York 29–19.
AA: St. Louis 40–19, Brooklyn 35–22.

Indianapolis, June 29—The contest this afternoon was an interesting one, and noteworthy from the fact that Mr. Connor, the robust young man who covers first base for the Giants, showed how hard he could hit. He set a ball out of the grounds like a rifle shot in the sixth inning, making the longest hit ever seen in this city.

—New York *Times*

New York, June 29—The spirit which sandpapered the feet of the New York team as they clambered up the greased pennant pole last season seems to be once more on the verge of materialization. Even in the absence of Keefe they have put up a game that has caused the cranks to squeak and gibber in New York streets. With the exception of the first game at Chicago the team has played ball that will, if continued, assuredly retain the pennant.

—St. Louis *Post-Dispatch*

Chicago, Ill., June 29, 1889—This has, indeed, been a disastrous week for Boston. To win a game out of six is not a very good record for a team that is out for the pennant. The team seems to be experiencing its turn at hard luck. When Radbourn rejoined the team this morning it was found he could hardly walk. It is feared he has broken a blood vessel in his leg, in which case his retirement from the box is uncertain as to time. This morning Kelly woke and found he had a severe pain in the upper left leg and he couldn't play. He was permitted to lay off. He was not seen at the grounds by the Boston newspaper men, and when one of the Boston players was asked where Kelly was, he muttered something about the races at the Chicago trotting track.

—Boston *Herald*

King's old-time speed, beautifully tempered by an exceptional command of the ball, came into play at the proper time and place, yesterday, in the game between the Browns and Kentucky Colonels, and the latter were handily vanquished in consequence. King's perfect control of the drop ball he occasionally uses gave him power over the opposing batsmen, which he put to excellent advantage. He struck out eight men, and of these he caught six nibbling on his fascinating drops.

—St. Louis *Post-Dispatch*

The far-famed Brooklyns will be here on Wednesday and will play the Browns three championship games, two of which will form the Fourth of July attraction at Sportsman's Park. There can be no better way to spend the glorious Fourth than by seeing the Browns and Brooklyns battling for supremacy, and as a great deal depends upon the outcome of this series the local interest in the games is very great. Bob Caruthers will pitch, it is expected, Wednesday, and Bob Terry and Lovett or Hughes on the Fourth. Silver King and Elton Chamberlain will look after the Browns' interests on these occasions.

—St. Louis *Post-Dispatch*

Monday, July 1

On June 30, Brooklyn won at Athletic 8–3 (Terry 9–6).
St. Louis beat Louisville 12–7 (Stivetts 1–2).
AA: St. Louis 41–19, Brooklyn 36–22.

The Brooklyns are playing great ball, and Comiskey's "pudding" is diminishing. It looks as if "Com" would eat "crow" before he will enjoy that pudding which he boasted his club had last May.

—Brooklyn *Daily Eagle*

Tuesday, July 2

On July 1, New York lost at Indianapolis 5–6 (Keefe 6–5).
Boston won at Chicago 7–3 (Clarkson 21–5).
St. Louis beat Louisville 8–2 (Chamberlain 16–5).
NL: Boston 35–15, New York 29–20.
AA: St. Louis 42–19, Brooklyn 36–22.

Chicago, Ill., July 1, 1889—John Clarkson was right on his pitching ball today, and, as his example was emulated by the men behind him, the

Bostons won with hands down. The Boston pitcher has not acted so much like his real self since the game at Pittsburgh, when he struck out 16 men, as he did this afternoon. Today 10 men fell victim to his marvelous work. Then Clarkson led his side at the bat. He put a ball over the fence in one inning, and in another he made a hit that sent in another run. In short, it was a great day for Clarkson.

—Boston *Herald*

President Byrne's team from the City of Churches will arrive to-morrow morning, and in the afternoon will start the ball rolling with the Browns. The games will have a large bearing on the championship race. The Brooklyns are playing in splendid form, and they will yet make a merry fight for the pennant. Dave Foutz, Bob Caruthers and Doc Bushong, of the Browns, are still with them, and they have gathered about them great players in Corkhill, Visner, Burns, Collins, O'Brien, Pinckney, Smith and Bob Terry.

—St. Louis *Post-Dispatch*

The Brooklyns have no use for Silver King. He is like a thorn in their side. Silver rather knocks their high hopes into smithereens. Arlie Latham yesterday broke his stoical silence on the art of batting by making three hits. Let him continue his good work on his old pal, Bob Caruthers.

—St. Louis *Post-Dispatch*

AMERICAN ASSOCIATION STANDINGS

	W	L	PCT.	GB		W	L	PCT.	GB
St. Louis	42	19	.689	—	Cincinnati	31	27	.534	9½
Brooklyn	36	22	.621	4½	Kansas City	26	31	.456	14
Athletic	33	22	.600	6	Columbus	23	35	.397	17½
Baltimore	32	25	.561	8	Louisville	10	52	.161	32½

NATIONAL LEAGUE STANDINGS

	W	L	PCT.	GB		W	L	PCT.	GB
Boston	35	15	.700	—	Chicago	24	30	.444	13
Cleveland	35	20	.636	2½	Pittsburg	23	29	.442	13
New York	29	20	.592	5½	Indianapolis	20	31	.392	15½
Philadelphia	27	26	.509	9½	Washington	13	35	.271	21

Wednesday, July 3

On July 2, New York won at Indianapolis 8–6 (Welch 14–4).
Boston lost at Chicago 4–5 (Madden 3–5).
NL: Boston 35–16, New York 30–20.

Indianapolis, July 2—The Giants kept within hailing distance until the seventh inning, when they made one of those spurts for which they are famous, took the lead, and held it until the finish. In the seventh Gore began with a double and Tiernan sent him home with a pretty single to right field. Then tall and muscular Connor hit the ball with all his might and the tiny buckskin was lost to sight outside of the enclosure.

—New York *Times*

Boston would have had another game to its credit tonight but for two singularly unfortunate errors, and such errors! Probably the most broken up ball player in the country at this moment is Joe Quinn. To his bad work in the sixth and ninth innings must the responsibility of today's defeat be credited.

Will the league baby be fractious when the Bostons come to fondle it tomorrow? All will admit that the infant has been altogether too frisky and ought to be spanked.

—Boston *Herald*

Gaffney, the king of umpires, arrived here this morning to officiate in the St. Louis-Brooklyn series. When here before, Gaffney complained of the hard work of umpiring under the present rules and spoke bitterly of the action of the Association in cutting his salary $500 from what he received last season. While in the East afterward he resigned his place as umpire and stated that he intended starting in the hansom cab business at Worcester, Mass., his home. He was requested to remain, and did so on condition that his salary should be returned to the old figure. This was done and Gaffney is to receive $2,500 for the season, instead of $2,000.

—St. Louis *Post-Dispatch*

Joe Quinn, second baseman and short-stop, Boston Beaneaters (Transcendental Graphics).

Brooklyn's representative base ball team arrived here this

morning and registered at the Lindell Hotel. They appear confident of taking at least two of the three games to be played here by them to-day and to-morrow, and if they do it will place them dangerously close to the Browns. Bob Caruthers, the old Browns pitcher, speaking of the team, remarked: "We have been playing a very strong game, and as the Browns appear to be somewhat weak just at present in the pitcher's box, I think we ought to get two of these three games. Of course, base ball is a very uncertain thing, and they may turn out otherwise, but it looks that way to me. No doubt the members of the Browns think just the other way. Now we have second place in the race, and I think have a very good chance to win the pennant. It is a close race between the three leading clubs, and if we can make as successful a trip as we did last time I think we will fly the bunting."

—St. Louis *Post-Dispatch*

Thursday, July 4

On July 3, Brooklyn won at St. Louis 7–4
(Caruthers 14–3 and King 18–9).
AA: St. Louis 42–20, Brooklyn 37–22.

It was worth the price of admission to the game yesterday to see Gaffney umpire. It was an awful sight. Those who have read about "Gaff" as the "King of Umpires" wouldn't have known him. He was not the king at all. He was not much bigger than the deuce. Four separate decisions on the bases were so glaringly bad that even the Brooklynites looked surprised. All of them were against the Browns. Fuller put out a man at second, Latham another at his bag, and Boyle a third man at the home plate, but in each instance the "King" shook his head. In one inning, two of these errors occurred, so that the Browns were really forced to put out five men. The decision putting out O'Neill at first when Foutz was a yard away from the bag was the fourth of Gaffney's ridiculous exhibitions. All through the game, too, he was very hard on King as to balls and strikes and very light on Bob Caruthers. Gaffney can umpire. Everybody knows that. He is square, too. Everybody knows that also. But a man who saw him yesterday and yesterday only would have laughed at either of these statements.

—St. Louis *Post-Dispatch*

As usual with defeat at St. Louis, some excuse has to be given for the defeat, and Gaffney's umpiring was made to answer for it. But Brooklyn's playing was the only cause.

—Brooklyn *Daily Eagle*

Friday, July 5

On July 4, New York lost and won
at Pittsburg 2–4 and 6–4 (Crane 5–5; Keefe 7–5).
Boston won and lost at Cleveland 6–0 and 7–11
(Clarkson 22–5; Radbourn 10–5).
Brooklyn lost and won at St. Louis 3–4 and 12–10
(Terry 9–7; Lovett 11–6 and Chamberlain 17–5; King 18–10).
NL: Boston 36–17, New York 31–21.
AA: St. Louis 43–21, Brooklyn 38–23.

Pittsburg, Penn., July 4—Exactly 5,279 people witnessed the first contest, the largest crowd that has ever attended a morning game in Pittsburg. In the afternoon about 8,000 people filled the grounds and crowded the outfield to such an extent that ground rules allowing a man three bases on a hit into the crowd had to be adopted.

—New York *Times*

Cleveland, O., July 4, 1889—According to the custom prevailing in the national league, two games were played in this city, and the best that either contestant could do was to break even with the other. When, in the arrangement of the playing schedule of the present season, the Bostons were assigned to play two games on the great national holiday with the Clevelands, the new member of the league family, there was a disposition on the part of the Boston gentlemen to object, but the objection was a slight one, and the triumvirs took what they thought was a severe dose of unpalatable medicine. Little did they or anyone else dream at that day that the Clevelands and the Bostons would be the two leaders in the race, and neck and neck in position; yet such is the fact, and it has proved a financial bonanza, especially to the plucky Cleveland management. The day was a gala one for the base ball admirers of pretty nearly all of northern Ohio. The people who were attracted to the great contests between these leaders came pouring into the city from every direction. Such an outpouring of spectators to a base ball game was never before known in Cleveland in its experience as a base ball city. There were 9015 people present at the morning game that passed through the turnstiles, and 8796 at the afternoon contest. So large were the crowds that they trespassed on the field, and a ground rule was adopted that a ball knocked or thrown into the crowd should only yield two bases.

—Boston *Herald*

Perhaps the largest crowd which has ever assembled at a base ball park in St. Louis at a morning game was present at the first game yesterday between the Browns and Brooklyns. The double umpire system was tried, Gaffney calling balls and strikes and Jack Kerins attending to the base decisions. Gaffney was very severe on Chamberlain in the matter of balls and strikes, and Kerins made several erroneous decisions, but they were about equally divided.

—St. Louis *Post-Dispatch*

The morning contest was one of the prettiest contests seen at the St. Louis grounds this season. McCarthy clinched the victory for St. Louis in the eighth inning by making a neat double play. Collins had made a hit and Boyle had muffed a short fly off Foutz's bat, when Burns stepped to the plate. The big right fielder drove the ball on a line for the right field seats. McCarthy ran back to the fence, and reaching up just managed to take the ball. He sent it like a shot to second and caught Collins off base. The play was recognized by continuous demonstration for five minutes.

Tommy McCarthy, right fielder, St. Louis Browns (New York *Clipper*, August 29, 1891).

—Brooklyn *Daily Eagle*

The League has given its answer to the request of the Brotherhood of Base Ball Players. A.G. Spalding has written John M. Ward that he has communicated with Messrs. Rogers and Day, the other members of the League Committee and that it is their unanimous opinion that it would be inadvisable to hold any meeting of the two committees at present. The committee of which he is chairman could do nothing, Mr. Spalding writes, except report the matter to the regular League meeting at the end of the season, unless a special meeting of the League should be called, and that is done only in cases of great emergency, and he does not think this particular matter is a case of that kind. If the League players have any grievances they can and will be righted at the regular annual League meeting, and the two committees can confer at the close of the championship season.

—St. Louis *Post-Dispatch*

Manager Buchenberger, who arrived at the Lindell this morning with the Columbus Club, states that the trouble between his organization and the Brooklyn team has been adjusted. The full story of the affair, as related by the Columbus manager, has never been published. "When we went to Brooklyn," he explained, "we, of course, expected that Goldsmith, the regular umpire, would be there. Instead of him we found Paasch, one of the substitute umpires. As I had heard my own players and other clubs complain of his strong partiality to the Brooklyns I objected to him and asked for one of the other substitute umpires, either Pike or Daily. They would not let us have them, and I finally agreed to accept Paasch. Just as McGunnigle and I were sending out our men to play Paasch forfeited the game. McGunnigle then asked us to play off a tie game we had with them, saying that they would be foolish to play us the regular game as that had already been given them by the umpire by a score of 9 to 0. Paasch ordered us to play off the tie and said if we did not he would forfeit it also. Of course he was working under Byrne's instructions. If we refused to play he would have forfeited the game although he has no power to forfeit such games and his action would not hold. But his threat will give you an idea of the man's nerve. We consented to play, I insisting that it should be the regular scheduled game, despite Paasch's action. We beat the Brooklyns badly, and I protested against Paasch's forfeiture of the game. Then Byrne claimed a $1,500 penalty for our refusing to play the first game. He held out our share of the gate receipts, but afterward he paid us the money and waived his claim to the fine on our withdrawing our protest against the award of the game to Brooklyn.

—St. Louis *Post-Dispatch*

Saturday, July 6

On July 5, New York lost at Pittsburg 2–5 (Welch 14–5).
Boston lost at Cleveland 0–2 (Clarkson 22–6).
NL: Boston 36–18, New York 31–22.

Pittsburg, Penn., July 5—The Pittsburgs outbatted and in many instances outplayed the Giants. "Smiling Mickey" Welch was "pie" for the locals.

—New York *Times*

Cleveland, O., July 5, 1889—John Clarkson is a disgusted base ball pitcher. After pitching one of the grandest games of his life, he met defeat at the last moment, because of the most inexcusable blunders of two men of long experience on the ball field, Richardson and Kelly. The chagrin of the Boston pitcher cuts deeper because his team, through no fault of his, received its first shutout of the season.

—Boston *Herald*

Sunday, July 7

On July 6, New York won at Pittsburg 7–1 (Keefe 8–5).
Boston lost at Cleveland 6–9 (Madden 3–6).
Brooklyn won at Kansas City 12–11 (Caruthers 15–3).
St. Louis beat Columbus 8–1 (Chamberlain 18–5).
NL: Boston 36–19, New York 32–22.
AA: St. Louis 44–21, Brooklyn 39–23.

Cleveland, O., July 6, 1889—Kelly erred in not going up close behind the bat after two balls had been called and no strikes. It would have had the tendency to have steadied Madden. He didn't do it, even after three balls had been called. The result was that Madden gave three men their bases on balls, and every one of them scored. It is not necessary for a catcher to go close to the plate after two and three balls have been called when pitchers like Clarkson and Radbourn, who have such excellent command, are in the box; but with Madden it is necessary. It steadies a young pitcher wonderfully to have his catcher shorten the distance, and holding up his hands to indicate a spot to pitch to.

—Boston *Herald*

The Bostons return home in the lead, to be sure, but their lead has been cut down in a most decided manner. The New Yorks, despite a crippled team, have more than held their own, and are a most dangerous foe in a most threatening position. The return to the Polo grounds and the encouragement of larger home crowds will undoubtedly be of benefit to them.

—Boston *Herald*

The Browns fortified their leading position in the Association race by their creditable defeat of Columbus yesterday at Sportsman's Park. One of the greatest catches ever seen on the field was made by Tip O'Neill. He had a big contract on hand to shut off two runs in the fifth inning, when Johnson lined out a beauty to leftcenter. Tip, with an eye like an eagle, and a gait like a Spokane, made a brilliant spurt in the direction in which the ball was coursing, and with one bound sprang into the air and choked its existence, shutting off two runs, and making one of the grandest captures ever seen in St. Louis.

—St. Louis *Post-Dispatch*

Monday, July 8

On July 7, Brooklyn lost at Kansas City 8–16 (Lovett 11–7).
St. Louis beat Columbus 8–3 (Stivetts 2–2).
AA: St. Louis 45–21, Brooklyn 39–24.

Stivetts is not only a good pitcher, but he is a batter of more than average ability. He made three cracking hits yesterday, two of which went safe. He improves as he grows accustomed to Association speed.

—St. Louis *Post-Dispatch*

It needs but a slight examination of the work of some of the players in the Boston nine to show that they are most decidedly overpaid. Now, a captain of a first-class nine, and a first-class captain, must be a pusher, as well as a leader. It does not make him a first-class executive officer because he can bat and run bases successfully, but he must be able to push his men as well as lead them. If he throws his whole life and soul into his play, his men will do the same, and no one will maintain that the present captain does this.

—Boston *Herald*

Tuesday, July 9

On July 8, New York beat Pittsburg 7–5 (Crane 6–5).
Boston beat Cleveland 6–1 (Clarkson 23–6).
Brooklyn won at Kansas City 8–4 (Caruthers 16–3).
St. Louis beat Columbus 14–0 (King 19–10).
NL: Boston 37–19, New York 33–22.
AA: St. Louis 46–21, Brooklyn 40–24.

Manager Mutrie's classic features were a study for an artist yesterday. He stood at the entrance of the New Polo Grounds at One Hundred and Fifty-fifth-street and Eighth-avenue, and as the thousands of the patrons of the national game filed into the enclosure he smiled as only a successful baseball manager can. Poor playing, bad weather, wretched grounds, and small attendance down at St. George have had a depressing effect upon the enterprising pilot of the Giants and he has been anything but himself. The jingling of the dollars, halves, and quarters as they fell into the treasury box of the New Yorks yesterday had the effect of restoring the genial "Jim" to his former self, and he stood in the broiling sun nodding and smiling at the old patrons, while he wiped the perspiration from his corrugated brow with a silk handkerchief. The new grounds promise to be a grand success. In the words of Mr. Mutrie, "The Giants have struck the right spot."

To add to the delight occasioned by the big crowd the Giants opened their new grounds with a victory, and this is looked upon by baseball "cranks," who are perhaps the most superstitious individuals in the world, as a good omen. The Pittsburgs have always drawn fair crowds in this city, but they were never looked upon as cards. Over 10,000 persons paid admission yesterday, which is by far the largest crowd that ever witnessed a contest in this city in which the Smoky City players opposed the Giants. The gates had to be closed before the game began.

When the gates were closed those denied admission went across the street to a beer garden and watched the game

MUTRIE, Manager, N. Y.
COPYRIGHTED BY GOODWIN & CO. 1888
OLD JUDGE
CIGARETTES.
GOODWIN & CO., New York.

Jim Mutrie, manager, New York Giants (Library of Congress, Prints and Photographs Division [LOT 13163-05, no. 201]).

from the windows. Others occupied positions on a hilly tract of land on the west side of the grounds, christened Dead-Head Hill, and they were bunched together as closely as checks in a dude's trousers. It was estimated that fully 5,000 persons saw the game free of charge. The grand stand was not completed and the rays of the sun bore down on the heads of the occupants of the seats and gave them an idea of what the small boy suffers all summer on the "bleaching boards." The surreptitious onlookers, however, enjoyed themselves to their hearts' content. Those in the beer garden sipped the amber colored fluid, and the occupants of "Dead-Head Hill" were under the shade of trees and foliage, and evidently enjoyed the efforts of their brethren who had paid admission and were trying to keep cool. Several times when good plays were made, and after the shouts of those in the grounds had died away the echoes of

New Polo Grounds, New York (*Frank Leslie's Illustrated Newspaper*, July 27, 1889).

applause from "Dead-Head Hill" could be heard distinctly, which proved that the onlookers from the lofty eminence could distinguish the fine points of the game.

All eyes, of course, were riveted on Mr. "Buck" Ewing, the catcher plenipotentiary of the New Yorks. His appearance on the field was the signal for a big cheer, and hundreds tried to grasp the hand of the clever but modest ball player. In the first inning several of the Stock exchange admirers of the New York Captain presented him with a gold watch with an inscription. He bowed in acknowledgment of the gift, blushed like a schoolgirl, and went out at first base.

—New York *Times*

The Brotherhood of League Players will be satisfied with President Spalding's letter, and will allow their grievances to go over until next winter.

—Boston *Herald*

AMERICAN ASSOCIATION STANDINGS

	W	L	PCT.	GB		W	L	PCT.	GB
St. Louis	46	21	.687	—	Cincinnati	35	30	.538	10
Brooklyn	40	24	.625	4½	Kansas City	29	36	.446	16
Athletic	37	25	.597	6½	Columbus	25	40	.385	20
Baltimore	35	29	.547	9½	Louisville	13	55	.191	33½

NATIONAL LEAGUE STANDINGS

	W	L	PCT.	GB		W	L	PCT.	GB
Boston	37	19	.661	—	Chicago	29	31	.483	10
Cleveland	39	22	.639	½	Pittsburg	26	35	.426	13½
New York	33	22	.600	3½	Indianapolis	22	34	.393	15
Philadelphia	30	29	.508	8½	Washington	14	40	.259	22

Wednesday, July 10

On July 9, New York beat Pittsburg 9–0 (Keefe 9–5).
Boston beat Cleveland 15–5 (Madden 4–6).
NL: Boston 38–19, New York 34–22.

It was a New-York day on the New Polo Grounds yesterday. From start to finish only one club was in the race, and the Pittsburgs never had a fifty-to-one chance. Only 1,800 persons paid to see the game, but double that number witnessed the contest from neighboring beer gardens and Dead Head Hill. Baseball here is at fever heat, but until the roof is erected on the grand stand the attendance will not be very large. Of course, the army of "cranks" will turn out en masse, but the sensible patrons of the game see no reason why they should risk being overcome by the heat or having their faces and necks tanned like oarsmen.

—New York *Times*

The first triple play in which the Bostons have figured took place in the seventh inning, when, with men on first and second and none out, the ball was hit to Tebeau by Kelly, the fielder not being obliged to move a step to touch his base, while in a twinkling the ball traveled around to second and first, and the play was made before the astonished spectators could make out what it was all about.

—Boston *Herald*

Mr. Byrne recently informed Mr. Von der Ahe and other American Association members of his determined opposition to an increase in Gaffney's salary, and now Mr. Byrne's organ grinds out seductively sweet music pealing forth praises for Byrne for his exertions in Gaffney's behalf. Byrne's double-dealing is again brought to the surface. His smooth, oily ways are captivating and his glib tongue wields a power to manipulate at will. Byrne is anxious to win the American Association pennant and a little thing like the altering of a few desultory facts to accomplish his end does not in the least bother him. In fact, his little scheme in the Gaffney deal seems to have afforded him untold pleasure. There is one

man in the business who is the bane of his existence. That man is Chris
Von der Ahe, who is a constant menace to Byrne's schemes.

—St. Louis *Post-Dispatch*

Thursday, July 11

On July 10, New York beat Pittsburg 14–1 (Crane 7–5).
Boston lost to Cleveland 5–8 (Clarkson 23–7).
Brooklyn won at Louisville 3–0 (Caruthers 17–3).
St. Louis lost to Athletic 2–4 (Chamberlain 18–6).
NL: Boston 38–20, New York 35–22.
AA: St. Louis 46–22, Brooklyn 41–24.

From the outset the Giants showed they were in a batting mood.
Connor carried off the honors of the day. After making two singles he
sent the ball over the centre field fence for a home run in the last inning,
and claims the distinction of being the first man to accomplish that feat.
De Wolf Hopper purchased the ball from a small boy who picked it up,
and will have it gilded.

—New York *Times*

The Brooklyn team succeeded in Chicagoing their Louisville opponents yesterday, but it was by superior fielding alone, as they were outbatted by the home team. Wet grounds had much to do with the fielding
errors. Rain began as play was called, and a smart shower fell for half an
hour. The bases were covered with tarpaulins, however, and in a quarter of an hour Umpire Goldsmith again began the game.

—Brooklyn *Daily Eagle*

Umpire Holland was simply rotten on his balls and strikes decisions
against Chamberlain and the Browns yesterday. It is about time the
champions are given a square deal in the umpirical end of the game.

—St. Louis *Post-Dispatch*

Prettier races for pennants were never seen than those going on at
present in the American Association and National League. The Browns,
Brooklyns and Athletics are neck and neck in the Association and half
the season is still before them. Even closer is the race in the League. Not
in the history of the associations have the three leading clubs kept so close
to each other, and there will be no walkover in either of them this year.

—St. Louis *Post-Dispatch*

Friday, July 12

On July 11, New York beat Cleveland 9–1 (Welch 15–5).
St. Louis beat Athletic 13–12 (Stivetts 3–2).
NL: Boston 38–20, New York 36–22.
AA: St. Louis 47–22, Brooklyn 41–24.

New-York's aggregation of Giants is playing great ball. Since they began to play on the new grounds they have not lost a game and in the four games the Giants made 39 runs, while their opponents tallied just 7.

Manager Loftus of the Clevelands looked on in wonderment yesterday as he saw the Giants score run after run, and at the termination of the game he had a high opinion of the ability of the champions.

"Just as sure as four unfair balls give a man his base," he said, "the Giants will get first honors again this year. They play better ball and use better judgment than any other club in the League. Of course, Boston is a strong team, but the club has only one pitcher—Clarkson—to rely on, and he cannot do all the work. It is only a question of time for the Giants to be in the lead."

—New York *Times*

The weather of yesterday gave the Bostons a most decided chance to gain a needed rest, if their work since their return has afforded any criterion. Our boys have appeared fagged out, and have not played with dash or spirit. To be sure, their leader has not, to all appearances, tried to infuse any enthusiasm into his men. Time was when there was no need to complain of listlessness in Kelly, but something is the matter, and many would like to know what it is

—Boston *Herald*

Saturday, July 13

On July 12, New York beat Cleveland 4–3 (Keefe 10–5).
Boston beat Pittsburg 13–1 (Clarkson 24–7).
Brooklyn lost and won at Louisville 3–4 and 8–1
(Terry 9–8; Lovett 12–7). St. Louis beat Athletic 4–2
(Chamberlain 19–6). NL: Boston 39–20, New York 37–22.
AA: St. Louis 48–22, Brooklyn 42–25.

The dish that the Bostons served to those present was very palatable, for it was about the best exhibition of heavy hitting seen here this year. The men went to the bat as if they meant business. Not a hit was made off Clarkson in the five innings in which he pitched, and but two men saw first base.

—Boston *Herald*

In the second game the Louisvilles tried a new pitcher, and the youngster lost them the game. The new man was Springer, and the Brooklyn batsmen made his discontent winterish in the most summary manner, as they scored seven runs in the first two innings. The pitcher was white as a sheet when he went on the grounds, and he was so nervous that he was pitied by every one who saw him.

—Brooklyn *Daily Eagle*

Sunday, July 14

On July 13, New York beat Cleveland 11–6 (Welch 16–5).
Boston beat Pittsburg 6–4 (Madden 5–6).
Brooklyn won at Cincinnati 15–5 (Caruthers 18–3).
St. Louis beat Baltimore 25–5 (Stivetts 4–2).
NL: Boston 40–20, New York 38–22.
AA: St. Louis 49–22, Brooklyn 43–25.

Six straight victories is the record achieved by the Giants on their new grounds last week. The clever work of the team seems to have increased the interest in the game, and when the bell sounded for the contest to begin the gates were closed and thousands were on the outside clamoring for admission. A canvas awning was placed over the grand stand, and the spectators viewed the game with comfort.

—New York *Times*

In the third inning of yesterday's contest between the Bostons and the Pittsburgs, there were three men on bases on the side of the visitors, and not a hand out, and such a hard and sure hitter as Miller at the bat. He caught the ball squarely, and sent it flying out to far centre field. Johnston caught it, and, by one of his marvelous recoveries, made a throw which sent the ball, with unerring precision, straight into the expectant hands of Catcher Kelly, and, though Smith made a fine slide, he was out. It was among the finest pieces of work of its kind that has been seen on the grounds this season, and the delight of the crowd was exactly in inverse proportion to what it expected, judging by the cheers, the shouts and applause that greeted the play, and that were kept up for some time and renewed when the little centre fielder walked in from his position at the close of the inning.

—Boston *Herald*

Monday, July 15

On July 14, St. Louis beat Baltimore 9–0 (Chamberlain 20–6).
AA: St. Louis 50–22, Brooklyn 43–25.

Cincinnati, July 14—The most destructive storm Cincinnati has
known for years visited this city this afternoon, coming up with a sud-
denness that was dazing. A torrent of rain leaped from the sky and swept
the city like a mighty wave. The sewers could not carry off the water fast
enough, and the streets were shallow but angry rivers. The rainstorm
lasted for two hours. About the middle of the storm a glare of light over-
spread the whole sky, lasting but a moment. This was followed by a rash
of thunder that seemed to shake the whole city. It had scarcely died away
when a mighty wave of wind swept by, lasting only an instant, but doing
immense damage.

At the ball park 5,000 were watching an exciting game between the
Cincinnatis and Brooklyns when this wind wave came. Its first move was
to pick up 150 yards of the high board fence and dash it down upon a
score of vehicles, completely wrecking half a dozen of them. Several
frightened horses dashed into the grounds and rushed madly about. The
women and children in the grand stand set up a cry of terror, which was
accentuated a moment later by a section of the roof going, while at the
same time the big canvas curtains in front were ripped into shreds with
a noise like a thousand rifles. A rush for the exits was made. By a prodi-
gious effort loss of life and limb was averted.

—New York *Times*

Baltimore was shut out by the Browns at Sportsman's Park yesterday by a score of 9 to 0. Chamberlain not only pitched a remarkable fine
game but he made a home run drive off Kilroy.

—St. Louis *Post-Dispatch*

The Brooklyns are the Browns' most dangerous rivals. The Champions now have a good lead on the Athletics, but the team from the City
of Churches is uncomfortably close and keep playing a winning game.

—St. Louis *Post-Dispatch*

Tuesday, July 16

On July 15, New York beat Chicago 7–4 (Keefe 11–5).
Brooklyn won at Cincinnati 6–4 (Foutz 1–0).
St. Louis lost to Baltimore 3–7 (Stivetts 4–3).

RICHARDSON, 2nd B,. New Yorks
Copyrighted by GOODWIN & CO. 1887
OLD JUDGE
CIGARETTES.
GOODWIN & CO., New York.

Danny Richardson, second baseman, New York Giants (Library
of Congress, Prints and Photographs Division [LOT 13163-
05, no. 207])

NL: Boston 40–20, New York 39–22.
AA: St. Louis 50–23,
Brooklyn 44–25.

Capt. Anson and his band of tourists were received on the New Polo Grounds yesterday by Capt. Ewing and his team of pennant winners. In the ninth inning all eyes rested on big Connor as he faced the Chicago pitcher. The New-York first base man has a national reputation as a "slugger," and Healy kept the ball out of his reach, preferring to give him his base. Then little Richardson surprised the Chicago men and sent a thrill of joy to the heart of nearly every onlooker. In the vernacular of the profession he hit the ball in the "nose," and its journey to the North River was stopped by the fence in left field. The sphere, however, rolled under the free seats, and before the Chicago fielder found it the bases were all empty, and New-York was in the lead 7 to 4.

—New York *Times*

Yesterday's contest was a very exciting one, as it was one of those uphill fights which snatch victory out of the jaws of defeat. In the ninth inning the home team—first at the bat—had runners on second and third bases with but one man out, the score standing at 6 to 4 in Brooklyn's favor. Holliday then hit a ball to the out field which looked perfectly safe and Mullane ran home, while McPhee had passed third on his way home, when Corkhill just managed to get his hands under the ball as it was close to the ground. It was a grand effort and it not only put Holliday out but Corkhill threw the ball into second, making double play and putting the side out. The stands were paralyzed when Umpire Ferguson called "You're out!" For five minutes the groans and hisses were frightful. The game ended then and there, Brooklyn having no need to play the ninth inning. As the players came off the field they had to get around Ferguson, who walked off as cool as possible, full of pluck and nerve and ready to defend himself if attacked. Of course, the hoodlums present abused and insulted him without limit. Mad with rage, several big fellows forced themselves upon him, and invited attention by asserting, in terms that were sufficiently emphasized, that he was an infernal thief. As he left the field two frenzied cranks threw glasses from the bleachers, which fell at his feet. He did not open his mouth to the multitude, and they exhausted their surplus rage by expletives more forcible than elegant.

—Brooklyn *Daily Eagle*

There is something very strange about the manner in which Bob Ferguson umpires a series in which the Brooklyn team are engaged. He denies being prejudiced in favor of the club which represents the city from which he hails, yet the opposing teams frequently complain of his decisions being decidedly in favor of the bridegrooms.

Now come tidings from Cincinnati that Ferguson was assaulted there for presenting a game to the Brooklyns. His decisions so incensed the crowd that several beer glasses were hurled at him at the conclusion of the game, though he escaped unhurt.

—St. Louis *Post-Dispatch*

AMERICAN ASSOCIATION STANDINGS

	W	L	PCT.	GB		W	L	PCT.	GB
St. Louis	50	23	.685	—	Baltimore	37	32	.536	11
Brooklyn	44	25	.638	4	Kansas City	31	39	.443	17½
Athletic	38	28	.576	8½	Columbus	27	45	.375	22½
Cincinnati	38	32	.543	10½	Louisville	15	58	.205	35

NATIONAL LEAGUE STANDINGS

	W	L	PCT.	GB		W	L	PCT.	GB
Boston	40	20	.667	—	Chicago	30	35	.462	12½
New York	39	22	.639	1½	Pittsburg	26	37	.413	15½
Cleveland	40	27	.597	3½	Indianapolis	23	39	.371	18
Philadelphia	35	29	.547	7	Washington	18	42	.300	22

Wednesday, July 17

On July 16, New York lost to Chicago 10–13 (Crane 7–6).
Boston lost to Indianapolis 4–6 (Clarkson 24–8).
Brooklyn lost at Cincinnati 3–4 (Lovett 12–8).
St. Louis beat Kansas City 4–2 (Chamberlain 21–6).
NL: Boston 40–21, New York 39–23.
AA: St. Louis 51–23, Brooklyn 44–26.

At last the New-Yorks have been beaten on their new grounds. For seven straight games the Giants were successful, but it remained for Capt. Anson and his team of tourists to accomplish the feat. "The New-Yorks are record makers," the big Captain remarked after the game, "but Mr. Ewing and his men seemed to have overlooked the fact that the White Stockings are record breakers."

—New York *Times*

Dan Brouthers' double in the first went farther down on the right field fence than any ball that has been sent in that direction this season. It struck the slats beyond the register and bounded back. It was Dan's 100th hit of the season, and it brought in two runs. Brouthers has shown that he has by far the best eye for the ball in the country. He has struck out but twice this season.

—Boston *Herald*

Thursday, July 18

On July 17, New York beat Chicago 8–3 (Welch 17–5).
Boston beat Indianapolis twice 10–5 and 7–5
(Radbourn 11–5; Daley 1–0).
NL: Boston 42–21, New York 40–23.

The baseball craze has probably struck the fair sex. Hundreds of ladies witnessed the contest yesterday, and the majority of them showed their familiarity with the game by using score cards.

—New York *Times*

There was a great deal more snap in the Bostons' work than there had been in past games, and even Mr. Kelly condescended to come out of his chrysalis condition and do some coaching, his voice being heard very often during the course of the afternoon. One can easily see that there is championship material in the Boston nine, if properly directed, and if it is not properly directed, it is the fault largely of the captain.

—Boston *Herald*

President Von der Ahe of the Browns received a telegram yesterday from the Louisville management asking if he would exchange Hudson for Ramsey. He immediately answered by telegraph that he would and the dicker will be made. It is difficult to see how the Browns are to be benefited any by the trade. Ramsey has the reputation of being one of the hardest drinkers and most difficult players to handle in the profession. He was a great pitcher in his day, but his day has long since passed.

—St. Louis *Post-Dispatch*

Friday, July 19

On July 18, New York beat Indianapolis 4–2 (Keefe 12–5).
Boston beat Chicago 8–1 (Clarkson 25–8).
Brooklyn beat Athletic 11–7 (Caruthers 19–3).
St. Louis lost at Cincinnati 1–5 (Chamberlain 21–7).
NL: Boston 43–21, New York 41–23.
AA: St. Louis 51–24, Brooklyn 45–26.

Capt. Mike Kelly showed his old captain that he still knew a thing or two about base ball yesterday afternoon. Something must have dropped, for the Boston captain was full of "ginger," and worked with a dash and a vim that were something new to home patrons. He batted hard and ran bases with the greatest success, having three steals of second to his credit, and one of third, and he scored three runs out of the eight for his side.

—Boston *Herald*

A report from St. Louis says that Third Baseman Latham and Pitcher King of the Browns have been charged with playing games in the interest of pool rooms. The story is founded on letters said to have been received from Omaha and Kansas City with regard to peculiar bets offered against the Browns on days when King was in the box and when Latham was doing some of the bad playing which he has exhibited on a number of recent occasions. It is said that Von der Ahe has charged both men with throwing games and has employed detectives to secure evidence.

—New York *Times*

If the Browns should be still in the lead in the championship race when they return home they will have made a remarkably successful trip. They now have a lead over Brooklyn of two games in the matter of games lost. It is true they have won six more games, but their rivals may make this up at any time, but the Brooklyns cannot reduce the number of games they have lost, and therefore the only safe lead a club can have is in the matter of games lost.

In the League the race is even closer. Boston still leads, but the New Yorks have been playing a strong game and gradually overhauling the

Bean-eaters. There is no question about the race being eventually between the Bostons and New Yorks, as this paper has all along stated it would.

—St. Louis *Post-Dispatch*

Saturday, July 20

On July 19, New York lost to Indianapolis 8–9 (Crane 7–7).
Boston lost to Chicago 6–13 (Radbourn 11–6).
NL: Boston 43–22, New York 41–24.

In order to win the Giants must put in their strongest team each day. If a player complains of a pain or an ache he should not be allowed to lie off whenever he feels so disposed. That sort of work will weaken any club. Capt. Ewing, Gore, Connor, Richardson, and perhaps one or two others are playing in the best possible manner. But more than that is necessary. If the Giants want to win every man in the team must put his shoulder to the wheel.

—New York *Times*

Sunday, July 21

On July 20, New York beat Indianapolis 8–5 (Welch 18–5).
Boston lost to Chicago 0–2 (Clarkson 25–9).
Brooklyn lost to Athletic 2–3 (Terry 9–9).
St. Louis won at Cincinnati 5–1 (King 20–10).
NL: Boston 43–23, New York 42–24.
AA: St. Louis 52–24, Brooklyn 45–27.

New-York defeated Indianapolis yesterday, and as the Bostons were beaten by Chicago the Giants are only one game behind the cultured players of the Hub.

—New York *Times*

Boston, Mass., July 20—The Chicago colts downed the Bostons again to-day. The game, which was one of the finest of the season, was full of brilliant plays, the greater part of them being made by the "Colts."

—St. Louis *Post-Dispatch*

New York, July 20—There is not a member of the New York team at present who does not firmly believe that they will win the flag of 1889.

OLD JUDGE CIGARETTES Goodwin & Co., New York.

Charles "Silver" King, pitcher, St. Louis Browns (Library of Congress, Prints and Photographs Division [LOT 13163-13, no. 21]).

This feeling gives them vim and snap and a personal interest in the team's success. When the players were dressing subsequent to the loss of Friday's game the silence was funereal and there was not a man there who did not feel like indulging in a volley of good plain English.

—St. Louis
Post-Dispatch

When the players were ready at 4 P.M. Umpire Gaffney was not on hand and the difficulty had to be faced of selecting an umpire in his place. After a discussion it was decided to place Cross, of the Athletics, and Bushong, of the Brooklyns, to act under the double umpire rule of the association. The absence of the three substitute umpires necessitated the adoption of this poor rule, which never can work satisfactorily except under very exceptional circumstances.

—Brooklyn *Daily Eagle*

Cincinnati, O., July 20—King was relieved by Chamberlain in the latter part of the game. The silver-haired twirler, about whose play so much has recently been made, pitched most effectively. His work was quite different from what it has been at St. Louis, where he had to be taken out of the box more than once.

—St. Louis *Post-Dispatch*

Monday, July 22

On July 21, Brooklyn beat Athletic 8–6 (Caruthers 20–3).
St. Louis lost at Cincinnati 1–10 (Chamberlain 21–8).
AA: St. Louis 52–25, Brooklyn 46–27.

There were 8,000 baseball enthusiasts in Ridgewood Park yesterday afternoon. The chief feature of the game was the batting and fielding of Collins. He had the very large number of fifteen chances at second with only a single error.

—New York *Times*

A telegram was sent out from Cincinnati yesterday stating that at the conclusion of the game President Stern had wired President Von der Ahe of St. Louis offering him $10,000 for the release of Comiskey. It was said that the Browns' captain was wanted to play first base and manage the club and that he had expressed his willingness to join the Reds and there was a belief prevalent that he would be secured.

A broad grin spread over Mr. Von der Ahe's face when the deal was mentioned to him.

"I guess Stern must have sent that telegram by mail, for it has not reached me yet," he remarked.

"Would you sell Comiskey for $10,000?"

"No, I would not. Stern would be safe in making me the offer. Brooklyn offered $12,000 for him, but Comiskey is not for sale, nor does he want to go anywhere else. He would rather play ball with the Browns than with any other club in the country. If you make that statement in the paper that Comiskey is not for sale half the clubs in the country will make offers for him just for the advertising they will receive out of it, they knowing full well there is no chance of my accepting their offer. Comiskey has always been a good, faithful, conscientious player, and I have no desire to part with him."

—St. Louis *Post-Dispatch*

Tuesday, July 23

On July 22, New York lost at Philadelphia 9–10 (Keefe 12–6).
Boston lost to Washington 2–3 (Daley 1–1).
St. Louis won at Columbus 5–1 (Stivetts 5–3).
NL: Boston 43–24, New York 42–25.
AA: St. Louis 53–25, Brooklyn 46–27.

The Bostons simply monkey with the championship. Such an exhibition as that of yesterday is the veriest travesty upon the sport. Few amateur pitchers would have been guilty of such work as forcing in two runs in the same inning by giving bases on balls. Three defeats in the last four home games is a very, very bad record. Matters are getting worse and worse.

—Boston *Herald*

AMERICAN ASSOCIATION STANDINGS

	W	L	PCT.	GB			W	L	PCT.	GB
St. Louis	53	25	.679	—	Cincinnati		42	33	.560	9½
Brooklyn	46	27	.630	4½	Kansas City		31	42	.425	19½
Athletic	39	30	.565	9½	Columbus		28	49	.364	24½
Baltimore	41	32	.562	9½	Louisville		17	59	.224	35

NATIONAL LEAGUE STANDINGS

	W	L	PCT.	GB			W	L	PCT.	GB
Boston	43	24	.642	—	Chicago		33	38	.465	12
New York	42	25	.627	1	Pittsburg		27	42	.391	17
Cleveland	42	29	.592	3	Indianapolis		26	43	.377	18
Philadelphia	40	30	.571	4½	Washington		21	43	.328	20½

Wednesday, July 24

On July 23, New York lost at Philadelphia 5–7 (Welch 18–6).
Boston beat Washington 10–4 (Clarkson 26–9).
Brooklyn beat Kansas City 4–3 (Caruthers 21–3).
St. Louis won at Columbus 9–3 (King 21–10).
NL: Boston 44–24, New York 42–26.
AA: St. Louis 54–25, Brooklyn 47–27.

Philadelphia, July 23—The Phillies won by good honest ball playing the second of their series with the Giants to-day, and the baseball cranks of the Quaker City are beside themselves with joy. The champions are greatly depressed over their two beatings, and the future looks as black to them as their famous Nadjy suits.

—New York *Times*

Bobby Caruthers won a very close and exciting game for the Brooklyns yesterday. The Kansas City team have always played a stiff game when opposed to the Bridegrooms. In the ninth inning O'Brien made a safe hit and Collins was given a base on balls. Two men were out and everything depended on Caruthers. He acquitted himself nobly by driving the ball down to the right field, bringing both the men on bases home and winning the game amid a tumult of cheers.

—New York *Times*

Thursday, July 25

BUCK EWING, Capt., New Yor s
Copyrighted by GOODWIN & CO. 1887
OLD JUDGE
CIGARETTES.
GOODWIN & CO., New York.

William "Buck" Ewing, captain and catcher, New York Giants (Library of Congress, Prints and Photographs Division [LOT 13163-05, no. 181]).

On July 24, New York lost at Philadelphia 6–15 (Keefe 12–7). Boston beat Washington 12–3 (Madden 6–6). Brooklyn beat Kansas City 7–6 (Terry 10–9). St. Louis lost at Columbus 0–5 (Stivetts 5–4). NL: Boston 45–24, New York 42–27. AA: St. Louis 54–26, Brooklyn 48–27.

A prominent baseball man yesterday said: "Ewing is the best catcher that ever handled a ball. In fact, I consider him the best all-round ball-player in the profession. As a catcher, batter, base runner, worker generally, and captain—everything combined—he has no equal." Ewing's home run over the left-field fence yesterday is said to be the longest hit ever made at Recreation Park. And still they couldn't win.

—New York *Times*

Friday, July 26

On July 25, New York beat Washington 7–5 (Welch 19–6). Boston won at Philadelphia 6–5 (Clarkson 27–9). Brooklyn beat Kansas City 7–5 (Caruthers 22–3). St. Louis won at Columbus 10–8 (King 22–10). NL: Boston 46–24, New York 43–27. AA: St. Louis 55–26, Brooklyn 49–27.

Philadelphia, Pa., July 25, 1889—Clarkson pitched superbly, and worked like a Trojan, as he had to. During the last part of the game he had to pitch with the sun in his eyes, and it was a wonder he could command the ball as he did. He never lost his head, however, and he confessed after the game that he has rarely worked to win as he did in this contest.

—Boston *Herald*

The most numerous and fashionable attendance of ladies ever seen at a ball match in Brooklyn graced the grand stand with their presence yesterday at Washington Park and but for the encouraging influence of their bright eyes the home team would have been defeated. But another victory was added to the list of successes which have hitherto marked these exceptional days of each month. The genial president of the club was in his element in seeing that his fair guests were duly attended to, and he was full of smiles as bevy after bevy of Brooklyn's fair ones passed him at the Grand stand entrance on their way to their seats.

—Brooklyn *Daily Eagle*

Saturday, July 27

On July 26, New York lost to Washington 1–9 (Keefe 12–8).
Boston won at Philadelphia 3–0 (Madden 7–6).
Brooklyn beat Cincinnati 20–6 (Foutz 2–0).
NL: Boston 47–24, New York 43–28.
AA: St. Louis 55–26, Brooklyn 50–27.

A week ago Manager Mutrie of the Giants prophesied that his club would be in the lead to-day. While Mr. Mutrie is a good manager he is a failure as a prophet. Instead of being in the lead the Giants are now four games in the rear of their Boston rivals, and unless they play better ball the young men from the City of Culture will have a lead that even the big New-York aggregation will be unable to overcome.

—New York *Times*

Dan Brouthers felt a little disconsolate. Some one walked off with his hat, by mistake, while he was at tea, and, though a superior Dunlap was left in the place of his derby, it was about two sizes too big.

—Boston *Herald*

Will some club stop the Brooklyns? They won eight out of the twelve games played by them on their recent Western trip, and have lost only one of the seven played on their home grounds since their return home. Brooklyn is certainly playing a remarkably strong game, and with the Browns doing as poorly as they have been, the Bridegrooms look like pennant winners just now.

—St. Louis *Post-Dispatch*

Sunday, July 28

O'DAY, P. Washington

COPYRIGHTED BY GOODWIN & CO. 1887.

GOODWIN & CO. New York.

Hank O'Day, pitcher, New York Giants (Library of Congress, Prints and Photographs Division [LOT 13163-05, no. 321]).

On July 27, Boston lost at Philadelphia 4–5 (Clarkson 27–10). Brooklyn beat Cincinnati 6–2 (Caruthers 23–3). St. Louis lost and won at Baltimore 2–4 and 3–1 (Chamberlain 21–9; King 23–10). NL: Boston 47–25, New York 43–28. AA: St. Louis 56–27, Brooklyn 51–27.

So as not to be handicapped by the scarcity of men the management of the New-York Club yesterday engaged O'Day, pitcher of the Washingtons. O'Day has been dissatisfied with his position in Washington and wanted to join a first-class club. He took pains to have that information carried to Manager Mutrie, who, after a consultation with President Day and Capt. Ewing, deemed it advisable to try and secure him.

—New York *Times*

New York, July 27—In his hours of leisure the suave manager of the New York team has pictured to himself the laurels that would rest upon his brow when, for the second time, the League pennant should fly from the Polo Grounds' flagstaff. Next to John L. Sullivan and President Harrison, James Mutrie would be the greatest of Americans. It is not astonishing, therefore, that "Truthful Jeems" should feel a trifle depressed over the recent losses of his club. He has not abandoned hope, however. In the innermost recesses of his heart he still believes the boys will brace up and play a game that will cause the most violent crank to use his lungs to their fullest capacity.

Boston has been very successful in Philadelphia, and the friends of the Bean Eaters are in high glee. Even now they see the pennant flying from the South End grounds, fanned by the customary and never-to-be-eluded east wind. If the Hubbites should win the flag their cup will be filled to overflowing with joy.

—St. Louis *Post-Dispatch*

Brouthers got five bases on balls in the three games. They are all afraid of the big fellow. The question has so often been asked about the weight of the three big first basemen. First comes Connor of New York, the heaviest of the lot, about 215; Anson, about 210; Brouthers, 190.

—Boston *Herald*

By strenuous efforts the field was placed in tolerable condition, considering the heavy rain of the morning, plenty of sawdust on the muddy part of the diamond making it in playable order.

The visitors went to the bat in the ninth with four runs to get to tie the game. With Caruthers in the box this was an almost impossible task and they failed to rally, going out in one, two, three order.

—Brooklyn *Daily Eagle*

Monday, July 29

On July 28, Brooklyn lost to Cincinnati 1–2 (Terry 10–10).
AA: St. Louis 56–27, Brooklyn 51–28.

In the sixth inning a pitched ball struck Pinkney on the head and stunned him for a few minutes, the ball rebounding back from his head to the pitcher as he bent to avoid the ball. The players, as he fell, rushed up to him to bathe his head with ice water, the worst thing possible under such circumstances.

—Brooklyn *Daily Eagle*

Speaking of Comiskey the Baltimore *American* says: When asked whether or not they feared Brooklyn's taking honors away from them, the tall and portly captain remarked, "They will never see daylight." Brooklyn, he thought, was being assisted by the umpires, who seem to think that Manager Byrne is the only member of the American Association. As an evidence that they believe this, all the Eastern clubs have been notified that St. Louis will tolerate no substitute umpires in the East, and they insist that the regular man officiate. In Brooklyn the desire is to get the regular man out of town, in order to let the substitutes get in their work, but it will not be so with the St. Louis Club, which he says will win the pennant hands down.

—St. Louis *Post-Dispatch*

Tuesday, July 30

On July 29, New York won at Washington 5–2 (Keefe 13–8).
Boston beat Philadelphia 7–6 (Clarkson 28–10).

SMITH, S. S. Pittsburg
COPYRIGHTED BY GOODWIN & CO., 1887.
GOODWIN & CO. New York.

Charles "Pop" Smith, shortstop, Boston Beaneaters (Library of Congress, Prints and Photographs Division [LOT 13163-05, no. 291]).

St. Louis won and tied at Baltimore 4–3 and 0–0 (King 24–10).
NL: Boston 48–25, New York 44–28.
AA: St. Louis 57–27, Brooklyn 51–28.

A telegram was received at the *Herald* office last evening from Manager Horace Phillips of the Pittsburgs announcing that he had accepted the offer of the Boston club for the services of Charles M. Smith of the Pittsburg club. The Boston management has for some time been aware of the weakness of the club in the position of shortstop. Smith is about 23 years of age and has seen long service as a player. He is acknowledged to be one of the finest infielders in the country. There will be no need of Messrs. Nash and Richardson looking out for any territory beside their own hereafter, and thus the work of the nine will be greatly improved, and they will be enabled to do much better team work.

—Boston *Herald*

The Browns played two games at Baltimore yesterday . In the third inning of the second game Umpire Goldsmith gave Kilroy, who had scored, out for cutting off third base. The crowd claimed he did not see the play and rushed in on the field to mob him. The police had to be called.

—St. Louis *Post-Dispatch*

AMERICAN ASSOCIATION STANDINGS

	W	L	PCT.	GB		W	L	PCT.	GB
St. Louis	57	27	.679	—	Athletic	41	33	.554	11
Brooklyn	51	28	.646	3½	Kansas City	31	47	.397	23
Baltimore	45	34	.570	9½	Columbus	30	53	.361	26½
Cincinnati	46	35	.568	9½	Louisville	19	63	.232	37

NATIONAL LEAGUE STANDINGS

	W	L	PCT.	GB		W	L	PCT.	GB
Boston	48	25	.658	—	Chicago	39	39	.500	11½
New York	44	28	.611	3½	Pittsburg	31	44	.413	18
Cleveland	43	33	.566	6½	Indianapolis	27	48	.360	22
Philadelphia	43	33	.566	6½	Washington	22	47	.319	24

Wednesday, July 31

On July 30, New York lost at Washington 1–5 (O'Day 0–1).
Boston beat Philadelphia 13–0 (Radbourn 12–6).
NL: Boston 49–25, New York 44–29.

Washington, July 30—Umpire Baker fined Ewing $25 and ordered him from the game in the eighth inning for using disrespectful language while remonstrating over a decision in that inning. Manager Mutrie and the members of the New-York Club say that the rulings of Umpire Baker were unfair and were the cause of the defeat. He is a Washington man, and it is asserted that his sympathies are with the local nine.

—New York *Times*

Kelly made the star play of the game in the sixth inning. Myers made a long hit to right field, and Kelly started so slowly for it at first that, in order to capture it, he had to race his prettiest when it was nearing the ground. He made a jump for it, and got it with outstretched hands, but his impetus was so great, and he was so close to the fence, that he literally jumped against the right field fence in order to avoid going into it with his body and thus, perhaps, lose the ball. The play was one of that kind never before seen on this or any other grounds and tickled the spectators immensely, and the Boston captain came in for a great demonstration when he came in from the field and took his place at the bat in the following inning.

—Boston *Herald*

There was not much of a crowd present yesterday, but those who were there were given rain checks. A specimen of the mean ways of a certain class of politicians was shown yesterday very conspicuously. Among those who had a season's pass in his possession was Assemblyman ___, and yet, in passing out, this fellow was dishonest enough to take a rain check, just as if he had paid his quarter for admission. President Byrne went after him, however, and made him return it.

—Brooklyn *Daily Eagle*

Thursday, August 1

On July 31, St. Louis lost at Athletic 3–7 (King 24–11).
AA: St. Louis 57–28, Brooklyn 51–28.

Friday, August 2

On August 1, Boston lost at Washington 2–3 (Clarkson 28–11).
Brooklyn beat Louisville twice 8–6 and 14–1
(Foutz 3–0; Lovett 13–8).
NL: Boston 49–26, New York 44–29.
AA: St. Louis 57–28, Brooklyn 53–28.

Washington, D.C., Aug. 1, 1889—The Bostons did not put much life in their work, especially at the bat. Some excuse may be found in this: That they were riding in cars from 11 o'clock Wednesday night till 2:45 o'clock this afternoon, had nothing to eat since 7:30 o'clock this morning, and went directly from the dinner table to the ball field. Therefore, they were not in as fresh condition as their opponents.

Smith played his first game at short for Boston. He accepted his two chances in a clean manner, one being a throw to the plate that cut off a run; but he did not show up strong at the bat.

—Boston *Herald*

Baseball was played under difficulties at Washington Park yesterday, but the exigency of the case warranted strenuous efforts to get the games off, and so the unpropitious weather had to be submitted to, and, in consequence, the players entered the field subject to a degree of unpleasantness in the form of mud and water under foot and rain overhead seldom seen in a contest. No one not of the class of enthusiastic admirers of the game known as base ball "cranks" expected to see the attendance exceed a few hundred, but the official count showed that over three thousand people were present, and half of that number had to sit on stands exposed to the rain, which fell almost intermittently after the first of the two games had been played. The fact is that what your crank will not submit to in order to see a game is something yet to be tested. The hot rays of a July sun do not deter him, nor any fall of rain. Even a chill November atmosphere has no preventive power to cause him to keep away.

It was the wettest kind of a game ever played on the field, the pitchers using towels to dry the ball as well as sawdust.

—Brooklyn *Daily Eagle*

Saturday, August 3

On August 2, New York beat Philadelphia 7–0 (Welch 20–6).
Boston won at Washington 10–6 (Madden 8–6).
Brooklyn lost to St. Louis 2–6
(Caruthers 23–4 and Chamberlain 22–9).
NL: Boston 50–26, New York 45–29.
AA: St. Louis 58–28, Brooklyn 53–29.

Harry Wright's boys, the young men who gave the Giants a set-back last week, appeared on the New Polo Grounds yesterday with the avowed intention of duplicating their feat. But they didn't. Revenge could be discerned on the faces of all the New-York players, and they went to work in a businesslike manner.

The ground looked like a pocket edition of the Johnstown flood. In the outfield the water in some places was two feet deep, and it was amusing to watch the players wade through in their efforts to capture batted balls. The Giants took to the water like spaniels and played a great fielding game.

After two men were out in the opening inning Ewing hit the ball over the centre field fence, making a home run that entitles him to the one-hundred-dollar prize for that feat.

—New York *Times*

Washington, D.C., Aug. 2, 1889— Madden was quite ill from an attack of summer complaint, and was really too weak to go into the box, but he was down on the score card, and rather than disappoint Manager Hart he went in. Brown and Brouthers are also suffering from the same trouble as Madden, but that didn't prevent them from committing several larcenies of bases, or Brouthers from doing some tremendous hard hitting.

—Boston *Herald*

"Kid" Madden, pitcher, Boston Beaneaters (Library of Congress, Prints and Photographs Division [LOT 13163-05, no. 10]).

The largest gathering of spectators ever seen on the Washington Park ball grounds at any Friday game was that of yesterday, on the occasion of the first appearance of the champions since last June. They came on the field early and found the infield in tolerably good condition, despite the rain of the previous night. But the outfield was like a skating pond, it was so slippery, and this condition of things proved to be far more costly to the Brooklyns than to St. Louis. A slip by Pinkney gave one run and falls by Collins and Burns virtually let in three more runs. It was not an error in either case, but it proved costly.

—Brooklyn *Daily Eagle*

There were nearly five thousand more people at Washington Park yesterday than at the New Polo Grounds, and, noting this fact, the New York and Philadelphia managers concluded they had better prepare a double attraction to offset the Brooklyn–St. Louis star match of to-day; so they doubled up with two games for one admission, so as to get a fair show in gate receipts, as the majority were sure to be at Washington Park.

—Brooklyn *Daily Eagle*

"Is it true, Mr. Byrne, as stated in one of the morning papers, that you offered and St. Louis refused $12,000 for Comiskey?" the *Eagle* reporter asked of the president of the Brooklyn Base Ball Club this morning.

"Not quite true. The price we finally offered was $15,000 for Comiskey and Mr. Von der Ahe refused that."

"Is that not the biggest price ever offered for a ball player?"

"Yes, far the biggest."

"What makes Comiskey so mighty valuable?"

"Oh, everybody knows why Comiskey is valuable. It is his ability to handle men and make them play ball. If a man has got base ball in him at all Comiskey gets it out of him. He handles his men as a good officer handles a body of soldiers. He is a wonderfully good judge of the capabilities of players and he has them playing up to the top notch every time. His phenomenal record last year shows how good the judgment of the St. Louis captain is. Duffee, the center fielder, is a boy who didn't cost the club a cent. See what a player Comiskey has made of him. McCarthy is another man whom Comiskey has made in the same way, and his spirit is the motive power of the team. He's worth $15,000 to us. You see he's not only a captain, he's also the finest kind of a manager on and off the field."

"That was pure ill luck that loss of the game to St. Louis yesterday," said Manager McGunnigle to the reporter. "They won the game in the first inning by making four runs. They should not have had any runs, but Collins slipped when putting the last man out for a blank in that inning. After that four men scored. Pinkney would have had Latham out but that he slipped in the same inning. Those two slips saved the game for St. Louis."

"We have a better ball team and we are going to win the pennant. We have been pulling up on them for the past six weeks. We have been doing very nicely lately and are going to keep it up."

—Brooklyn *Daily Eagle*

Sunday, August 4

On August 3, New York beat Philadelphia 18–8 (Keefe 14–8).
Boston lost at Washington 3–8 (Clarkson 28–12).
Brooklyn beat St. Louis 13–6 (Terry 11–10 and Stivetts 5–5).
NL: Boston 50–27, New York 46–29.
AA: St. Louis 58–29, Brooklyn 54–29.

The results of the ball games were favorable to the New-Yorks yesterday. They defeated the Philadelphia players, while Boston suffered a set-back at the hands of Washington, and the Giants are once more within hailing distance of the leaders. So near in fact that if they are successful against the Bostons this week the Gothamites may step into first place.

—New York *Times*

The veteran of the Brooklyn Club, genial, quiet Will Terry, aided by George Pinkney's fine exhibition of team work at the bat, gave Brooklyn a well earned victory yesterday over the champions, and if the remainder of the team will follow up George's style of hitting in this game and do the same fine work at the bat they will win the pennant sure.

Three men were on bases when Pinkney came to the bat in the first inning. Would he hit a fungo ball? was the question. This time, however, team work at the bat was of the order, and not efforts to "knock the stuffing out of the ball" by slugging, and Pinkney, by a beautiful tap of the ball to short center, earned his base and sent in two runs.

—Brooklyn *Daily Eagle*

New York, August 3—While the result of Friday's game with the Browns precluded the chance of Brooklyn's leaving here in the lead today, the players and base ball people of Brooklyn do not for a moment waver in their faith in the club's landing in first place yet. Not since the season began has the fight between them been so close and absorbing as it is now, and, judging by the playing strength of the two clubs as demonstrated during the past two weeks, it is not unreasonable to expect the Brooklyns to forge ahead in the immediate future. What the Brooklyn players lack in that quality called "ginger" by Arlie Latham, they make up in heavy batting ability and steady all-round work.

Charley Comiskey and Ted Sullivan, the latter the guest of the St. Louis club during its stay in the East, were talking over old times at the Grand Central Hotel yesterday. "Do you remember the day," asked Charlie, "when you told me you would make a professional player out of me?"

"Well do I remember it," answered Ted. "It was along in 1875 at St. Mary's College, near Kansas City. You had just entered college and I was about to finish. We were out in the college yard one day tossing the ball about and I spotted you at once as a likely player, although you couldn't have been more than 14 years old at the time. I put you in to catch that day and afterwards told you that I would get you on a professional team when you finished schooling, and did so, too, four years later. It was with the team of Dubuque, Io., and your salary was $50 a month. Things have changed in the intervening ten years, eh, Charlie?"

—St. Louis *Post-Dispatch*

Monday, August 5

On August 4, Brooklyn beat St. Louis 7–2
(Caruthers 24–4 and King 24–12).
NL: Boston 50–27, New York 46–29.
AA: St. Louis 58–30, Brooklyn 55–29.

The largest assemblage of spectators ever seen at a base ball match on Long Island outside of Washington Park and the second largest gathering to that of last Decoration day crowded the extensive grounds at Ridgewood yesterday to repletion; and a more respectable or orderly crowd was never seen at a match. In the first place, the weather was all that could have been desired, and as the occasion was one of exceptional interest there was an extraordinary rush of people to the scene of the contest. Society men from Hamilton, Brooklyn, Oxford, Carlton, Lincoln and Montauk clubs were there by the dozens; in fact, there was scarcely a residence of our best districts which had not one or more of its occupants there, many, of course, visiting the place sub rosa, but they were there all the same. The attraction was too great to resist, and the vast assemblage witnessed one of the most exciting and attractive exhibitions of the beauties of our national game yet seen at Ridgewood Park. Each of the contesting teams had won one game of the series and this

Joe Visner, catcher, Brooklyn Bridegrooms (New York *Clipper*, September 14, 1889).

game was to settle the question as to which would win the best two out of the three, and the result was to be a test of the relative strength of the two teams, the only rivals for the association pennant of 1889.

Captain Comiskey had his strongest team in the field, with King and Boyle in the battery positions, while Brooklyn presented what has this season been the team's most successful battery players, Caruthers and Visner, and as every thing was in order for a close contest, players in good form, field in first class condition, with order prevailing in a crowd of over 17,000 people, no game this season was ever begun under more auspicious circumstances for a fine exhibition of ball playing.

Caruthers was at his best yesterday. The St. Louis batsmen were at his mercy. Comiskey was the only one who could hit his pitching. Just think of it. Three single hits in a nine inning game by a team like St. Louis.

The scene at Ridgewood Park when the game began ought to have been photographed and a picture of it sent to the Sunday Observance Society as a memento of the attractive force of the national game in drawing a vast assemblage of law and order people, without a drunken man to mar the scene or the slightest disturbance of any kind. Even kicking was at a discount, the double umpire system working to perfection.
—Brooklyn *Daily Eagle*

The Brooklyns secured another victory over the Browns yesterday at Ridgewood Park, and they are now but a few points behind the champions. The contest for the pennant between these two clubs is now becoming intensely interesting to the lovers of the national game. This fact was attested by the immense crowd which witnessed yesterday's game. Every inch of space, excepting that necessary for the game was occupied.
—St. Louis *Post-Dispatch*

Cincinnati, O., Aug. 4, 1889—Shortly before reaching Cincinnati it leaked out that the train containing the Bostons came near meeting with an accident during the night. The train hands were very reticent when questioned, but from what could be learned it appears that at about 2 o'clock this morning the train was proceeding at a fair rate of speed, when on rounding a curve the headlight of an approaching locomotive suddenly burst in view. The engineer of the Bostons' train reversed his engine, the brakes were quickly applied and the train brought to a standstill. The engineer of the approaching train also reversed his engine, but in applying the brakes some of the gear broke, and a collision appeared inevitable. Happily a disaster was averted, but when the two trains came to a stop the locomotive of one was within eight feet of the other.

—Boston *Herald*

Tuesday, August 6

On August 5, New York won at Chicago 8–7 (O'Day 1–1).
Boston won at Indianapolis 4–2 (Daley 2–1).
Brooklyn won at Athletic 13–0 (Terry 12–10).
NL: Boston 51–27, New York 47–29.
AA: St. Louis 58–30, Brooklyn 56–29.

Chicago, Aug.5—After a highly interesting game the Giants won from the local club to-day, and another Chicago scalp dangles from the belt of Capt. Ewing.

—New York *Times*

The Brooklyn team played their fourteenth game with the Athletics yesterday and won their ninth victory. This time the defeat was a Waterloo one, as the score at the finish stood at 13 to 0. Terry was in the box for Brooklyn, and William was in winning form again, as he was against the St. Louis team last Saturday.

—Brooklyn *Daily Eagle*

An item started in the East has been traveling the rounds to the effect that if the St. Louis Club had such a schemer as "Charlie" Byrne to look after their interests they would not lose the pennant in a hundred years. This is a terrific in shoot into Byrne. What's the matter with the propagation of his schemes for Brooklyn for the past five years? Have they ever won Brooklyn the pennant? The item is a pretty severe commentary on Byrne's ball players. And, by the way, if Byrne is so great a schemer, why does he want to give $15,000 for Comiskey?

—St. Louis *Post-Dispatch*

AMERICAN ASSOCIATION STANDINGS

	W	L	PCT.	GB		W	L	PCT.	GB
St. Louis	58	30	.659	—	Cincinnati	47	40	.540	10½
Brooklyn	56	29	.659	½	Kansas City	34	51	.400	22½
Baltimore	49	36	.576	7½	Columbus	34	55	.382	24½
Athletic	45	35	.563	9	Louisville	20	67	.230	37½

NATIONAL LEAGUE STANDINGS

	W	L	PCT.	GB		W	L	PCT.	GB
Boston	51	27	.654	—	Chicago	42	41	.506	11½
New York	47	29	.618	3	Indianapolis	33	50	.398	20½
Philadelphia	44	36	.550	8	Pittsburg	32	50	.390	21
Cleveland	45	37	.549	8	Washington	25	49	.338	24

Wednesday, August 7

On August 6, New York won at Chicago 10–8 (Keefe 15–8).
Boston lost at Indianapolis 3–8 (Madden 8–7).
Brooklyn lost at Columbus 3–4 (Caruthers 24–5).
NL: Boston 51–28, New York 48–29.
AA: St. Louis 58–30, Brooklyn 56–30.

Chicago, Aug. 6—For eight innings the New-Yorks had everything their own way this afternoon, and it looked like an easy game for them. They had a lead of 7 runs when the White Stockings went to bat in the ninth inning. At that juncture Keefe seemed to lose his effectiveness and his curves were batted at will. After Chicago had scored 7 times and made the game even he recovered his form and saved the game.

The Giants never lost their nerve. On the contrary, the change of affairs seemed to make them desperate, and they began the tenth inning in fine style, scoring 2 runs, and winning the game.

—New York *Times*

Indianapolis, Ind., Aug. 6, 1889—Of the three runs made by Boston, two of them were made by knocking the ball outside of the grounds; in other words, they were "combers."

—Boston *Herald*

In every season's championship campaign—alike in the league as in the association—each of the contesting clubs invariably finds one of the opposing teams more difficult to cope with than the rest. There is, however, an important difference in this respect between the St. Louis and

Brooklyn teams: and that is that while the former generally find their snag among one or other of the leading teams Brooklyn's trouble is with the tail enders as a rule.

It is the same, too, in the league. While New York can cope successfully with every other league club except Philadelphia, Boston wins with ease against the Phillies; and while the former has no difficulty in defeating the Indianapolis team, the Bostons can do nothing with them.

This season there seems to be a special effort made by the Columbus team, from its manager and captain down, to do its best to defeat Brooklyn, while the most careless and indifferent playing the Columbus team does is against St. Louis, as the record of twelve defeats out of fourteen games amply proves. To down Brooklyn is the great ambition of Buckenberger, Orr & Co. If they had tried half as hard to win against St. Louis as they have done against Brooklyn our home team would now have been in the van.

—Brooklyn *Daily Eagle*

It was amusing to watch the men at work on the new grand stand at the Polo Grounds while the game was in progress. They only handled their tools between innings. At the rate the men worked yesterday it will be Christmas before the grand stand is completed. The new field is not deep enough. Such hits as do not go to the extreme of the center field at Washington Park will go easily over the center field fence at the Polo Grounds. The left field is still a pool of water and slippery with mud outside the pond. The arrangements for the accommodation of the public by the elevated road people are simply wretched.

—Brooklyn *Daily Eagle*

The Bridegrooms have made a new departure in the mascot line. A big black tabby cat now poses as a luck-bringer for the pets of Gowanus. Judging by the recent good work of the Bridegrooms the mascotic influences of "Tabby" could not well be improved upon. The Brooklyns ought to be well in front with their work encouraged in this feline manner.

—St. Louis *Post-Dispatch*

Thursday, August 8

On August 7, New York won at Chicago 4–2 (Crane 8–7).
Boston lost at Indianapolis 7–13 (Radbourn 12–7).
Brooklyn won at Columbus 10–8 (Terry 13–10).
St. Louis won at Kansas City 4–1 (Chamberlain 23–9).

NL: Boston 51–29, New York 49–29.
AA: St. Louis 59–30, Brooklyn 57–30.

Chicago, Aug. 7—To-night the New-Yorks left this city for Indianapolis after having accomplished half a week's good work. They won three straight games from the local club, and as Boston succumbed twice to the skill of the Hoosiers, the champions are within hailing distance of first place.

In the vernacular of the profession, Crane was on edge and he shot the ball across the plate with such speed that it resembled a pea. Ewing, as usual, played great ball, and he was the cynosure of all eyes.

—New York *Times*

Indianapolis, Ind., Aug. 7, 1889—The Bostons met another reverse today, and at a moment when they thought they had the game well in hand. The Hoosiers went in at the sixth inning, and how they did line out that ball! Whack! Whack! Whack! Not till eight hits and seven runs had been made did the slaughter cease.

—Boston *Herald*

At the bat the hitting of Tom Burns shone resplendent, his record being four telling hits. Smith at short and Pinkney at third base did admirably, and Corkhill's catch of McTamany's long hit in the sixth inning brought down the applause of the stand.

—Brooklyn *Daily Eagle*

Friday, August 9

On August 8, New York lost at Indianapolis 4–14 (Welch 20–7). Brooklyn won at Columbus 12–11 (Caruthers 25–5). St. Louis won at Kansas City 12–2 (King 25–12). NL: Boston 51–29, New York 49–30. AA: St. Louis 60–30, Brooklyn 58–30.

Tom "Oyster" Burns, right fielder, Brooklyn Bridegrooms (New York *Clipper*, February 2, 1889).

Manager Hart of the Bostons, before leaving Indianapolis, received the following telegram from one of the directors of the club: "What is the matter with the team? You are disgracing the Boston public and Music Hall is filled with hisses daily. You had better put Madden, Johnston, and Smith in cotton. What is the matter with Radbourn? Ain't he going to pitch any more? This kind of work is losing the club thousands of dollars. Do you want to force any of us to go West?" After reading the contents of the dispatch Manager Hart was all broken up. He sat down and wrote a six-page letter to President Soden and enclosed the telegram. "I am a business man," wrote Hart, "and as such want to be treated." "I never heard of such a thing as this in my life," he said afterward. "A club leading in the race getting a send-off like this from one of the owners of the club. Why, it's only worthy of a crazy man." "Pop" Smith felt the rebuke keenly. "I have made a few errors and happen to be unfortunate enough in joining the team away from home when they are losing," said he, "but my bad playing has not lost games." The more the men think about it the more they feel disgusted from Hart down.

James Hart, manager, Boston Beaneaters (New York *Clipper*, March 9, 1889).

—New York *Times*

A compactly built man, short in stature and of not a little girth, stood in front of the Boston and Albany depot on Kneeland street at 6:05 o'clock last evening, and for several minutes he poured forth a flood of indignation and looked as if he meant every syllable of scathing denunciation which bubbled up out of his wrathy mind. He was Mr. J.B. Billings of the Boston Base Ball Club triumvirate, and he was talking to a *Herald* reporter.

Not until the reporter showed Mr. Billings what had been published about the affair was he aware of such publicity of trouble in the camp, and then he said, sharply: "Well, what do you wish to know?"

"Only if you really did send Manager Hart such a dispatch."

"I sent a dispatch to Manager Hart, but it was of a confidential nature, and I am astonished to read of his showing it to anybody."

"And was the dispatch that you sent like this one printed?"

"Well, yes; that was practically what I wired to Hart, but I didn't tell him to show it to the boys. I tell you, I was mad at the way the boys were playing ball. Everybody in Boston was taunting me sarcastically about the team, and I couldn't stand it any longer. But Mr. Hart had not the slightest right to show that dispatch to anyone. It was a confidential communication to the manager of the club from me, and I can find not the least excuse for his violation of that confidence. And I'll send him another one tonight, too," and Director Billings' looks spoke volumes. "I own one third of the stick of the club, and I tell you Mr. Hart had better look out," was Director Billings' closing remark.

—Boston *Herald*

Chicago, Ill., Aug.8, 1889—Has Manager Hart's administration of the affairs of the team, and the playing of the team itself, been of that character which justified the employment of the language used in the dispatches referred to? The *Herald* correspondent was with the team on its first western trip, and is with it on the present one. He has had an opportunity to carefully observe Manager Hart's methods in the performances of his duties, to see the men in all their games, and to associate with them more or less at the hotels and on railroad trains. Frequent conversations have been held with the manager and players relative to Boston's chances for winning the pennant, and what they really feel as to their desires to see the pennant go to the Hub, and without an exception a deep and evidently sincere desire has been found that the team should bring the prize to Boston. While, undoubtedly, some of the views entertained by Manager Hart as to the best way to control a ball team may be open to honest criticism, yet the fact remains that he has brought his best judgment, acquired by years of experience, to his work. He has been thoroughly honest and conscientious in his endeavors to serve the directors of the Boston club and the Boston public as well. Under his administration the team has held first place continuously since May 17. He has caused the club to proceed without the slightest appearance of inharmony. He is popular with his men, looked out for their comfort on the road, and kept a sharp eye on the men when playing, and he naturally feels very sensitive over the intimation in the dispatches that confidence in him had about gone, and that one of the directors might be "forced" to join the team.

Your correspondent had an interview with Manager Hart and found him in anything but a calm mood. He has written to both President Soden and Mr. Billings. He has nothing but the highest feelings of respect for the former; he considers the latter has insulted him personally in an outrageous and unwarranted manner, and he has not heard the last of the matter.

—Boston *Herald*

It is quite the fad in New York to see handsome equipages drawn by fiery steeds done up in very English style going through the boulevards and Central Park, taking the little family pets—pugs and skye-terriers—out for an airing. A similar sight will probably be witnessed here to-morrow morning. Mr. Chas. Byrne, being a swell Gothamite, will engage a fine turnout and send his Brooklyn mascot black cat around town for an outing. The cat will, no doubt, enjoy the sights of the city.

—St. Louis *Post-Dispatch*

Bob Caruthers says Brooklyn will win the pennant, dead sure. Dave Foutz says they can't lose it. Corkhill says they've got a cinch on it. Burns spurns the thought of its going anywhere than to Brooklyn. Doc Bushing says it's like pulling teeth to beat the Browns, but Brooklyn will do it sure-pop. Collins don't make much of a hub-bub about it, but he's very confident of winning. Darby O'Brien laughs at the suggestion of its loss to Brooklyn. Pinkney says St. Louis is not in it. The black cat mascot doesn't say much, but according to latest advices it will come to the "scratch" in due time with an opinion.

—St. Louis *Post-Dispatch*

Saturday, August 10

On August 9, New York won at Indianapolis 8–1 (Crane 9–7).
Boston lost at Chicago 0–9 (Clarkson 28–13).
St. Louis lost at Kansas City 7–11 (Ramsey 0–1).
NL: Boston 51–30, New York 50–30.
AA: St. Louis 60–31, Brooklyn 58–30.

Indianapolis, Aug. 9—The victory achieved by the Giants is a precious one, as Chicago whipped Boston, and the New-Yorkers are only a few points behind the leaders.

—New York *Times*

Manager Hart's face brightened today, as he showed the newspaper men of the party the following dispatch:

Boston, Aug. 9, 1889.

To James A. Hart, Manager Boston Base Ball Club, Chicago: Do not let Billings's telegram worry you at all. We have the fullest confidence in you and the team. Go ahead and win six games out of the next eight.

Soden and Conant.

Mr. Hart and his men regard this dispatch as a repudiation on the part of Messrs. Soden and Conant of the telegrams sent by their associate in the ownership of the club, and they appreciate it accordingly.

—Boston *Herald*

From to-day the American Association race will be fought down the three quarter stretch with a bitterness unparalleled in the history of base ball.

—St. Louis *Post-Dispatch*

Sunday, August 11

On August 10, New York won at Indianapolis 9–6 (O'Day 2–1).
Boston won at Chicago 9–7 (Madden 9–7).
Brooklyn lost at St. Louis 2–4
(Caruthers 25–6 and Chamberlain 24–9).
NL: Boston 52–30, New York 51–30.
AA: St. Louis 61–31, Brooklyn 58–31.

Indianapolis, August 10—"I can't win today," said Pitcher Keefe about five minutes before the beginning of the contest between the Hoosiers and New Yorks this afternoon. He was still feeling indisposed from the effects, it is supposed, of malaria, and O'Day was called in to take his place.

—Boston *Herald*

Chicago, August 10—At last there is a silver lining to the cloud. After passing through the valley of the shadow of defeat, and all hope of retaining first place in the gigantic league having almost vanished, the Bostons are permitted to hold a little longer lease of the coveted position, and again has Jim Mutrie proven a false prophet. When he was in this city the first of the week he said that by tonight the New Yorks would be in first place.

Well, they came mighty near it, and, as it is, only a lap exists between that team and the Bostons. His prophecy would have been fulfilled but for the terrific hitting of Brouthers, Richardson, and Johnston in the 10th inning of today's game, which enabled the Bostons to come out victorious over the Chicagos.

—Boston *Herald*

Indianapolis, Ind., Aug. 10, 1889—Manager Mutrie of the New Yorks was in capital humor tonight, as he talked over the recent substantial progress made by the club, and intimated his belief that great things were in store for it in the near future.

"Do you think you will overhaul Boston?"

"I think we will. We are bound to, if hard work will accomplish it. We are only a few points behind them now."

"What are your chances for the pennant?"

"Excellent, and if our boys win this year it will be the grandest victory ever scored by a ball club."

"Why?"

"Well, at the beginning of the season we ran up against a continuous streak of ill-luck. Politicians, property holders, the loss of our grounds, illness of our players, inclement weather were dead against us and these are some of the reasons why I say to you that it will be a grand victory for New York if it wins the pennant."

—Boston *Herald*

A fine game between the two clubs tied in the Association race was naturally expected, but the contest between the Browns and Brooklyns at Sportsman's Park yesterday far exceeded anticipations in point of excellence. A better or more interesting exhibition of ball playing has seldom ever been witnessed in this city. Brilliant plays were frequent, and several were of the marvelous order. Duffee's catch of Corkhill's fly was simply wonderful. It occurred in the ninth inning, and had he missed it the ball would have in all probability bounded in to the seats and the game been lost to the Browns. Nobody expected him to get it, and when he got his hands on the sphere and clung to it, it was several seconds before the crowd could realize that he had actually caught it. Then the shout which went up could have been heard a mile away. Even the players looked out at the center fielder in blank astonishment. When the next man was retired and the Browns came in for their tenth inning, Duffee received an ovation that lasted more than a minute. His name was shouted by the enthusiasts as if nothing short of a speech would satisfy them. His catch, however, was not the only distinction Duffee earned. In the fourth inning Duffee lit on to the first ball pitched and sent it sailing towards left center. It bounced into the seats and he scored, setting the crowd wild. In fact it was Duffee's day. He covered himself all over with glory. McCarthy, too played in splendid style. One of his catches in right field was of an astonishing kind, and brought forth enthusiastic shouts of delight. At the bat, too, he distinguished himself. He had Caruthers almost crazy with his fouling tactics, and when in the tenth inning he made a number of attempts to bunt the ball, and, finally, after Caruthers kicked to the umpire, hit a long fly away over Corkhill's head for three bases, "Bobby" almost cried from vexation.

Every body went away vowing it was the greatest game they had ever seen in their lives. The game was for blood from start to finish and a better contest throughout has certainly not been seen here this year. It is doubtful indeed whether one was ever played on the grounds.

—St. Louis *Post-Dispatch*

Charlie Duffee, center fielder, St. Louis Browns (Library of Congress, Prints and Photographs Division [LOT 13163-13, no. 19]).

At the close of yesterday's game Latham was suspended until 10 o'clock Monday. President Von der Ahe, who sat on the players' bench throughout the game and kept his field glasses on the third baseman, was very much dissatisfied with his play, and at the close of the game went to the dressing rooms and informed "Arlie" that his work in the game had been very suspicious and for that reason he would lay him off until 10 o'clock Monday morning, at which time he would meet him in his office for a talk, and if his explanation of his play was not satisfactory his suspension would be made indefinite. Latham did not have a word to say, and received no sympathy from the players. The truth is, they were as sore at his play as was the president of the club, and Comiskey informed Mr. Von der Ahe that if Latham was not laid off that he would not put on his uniform to-day. Latham was hissed by the spectators for his work, which was of such a character to excite the gravest suspicions. He made a sorry exhibition of himself while at the bat and certainly acted in a queer way in the field.

Capt. Comiskey was red hot at Latham yesterday and gave the "freshest man on earth" a well-deserved roasting. Bob Ferguson, the umpire, told Latham to play ball yesterday, before he struck out the third time. Latham reached out for several balls that would have taken a barber pole to corral.

—St. Louis *Post-Dispatch*

Chicago, Ill., Aug. 10, 1889—The movement to have Cincinnati take the place of Indianapolis in the league next year is being pushed quietly but earnestly. A representative of a Cincinnati paper that is advocating that city joining the league called upon President Spalding of the Chicago club today to ascertain how favorably disposed he was toward Cincinnati. Mr. Spalding said that Cincinnati was a very desirable city to have in the league, and he should favor its admission, provided it would give up Sunday ball playing and the selling of beer on the grounds. These conditions the Cincinnati people are said to be ready to comply with.

—Boston *Herald*

Out of 375 votes received by the New York *Sporting Times* for the best general player, Ewing has 171, Kelly 48, Anson 33, Ward 29, Connor 25, Glasscock 17, Ganzel 14, Williamson and Buffinton 10, A. Irwin 8, Faatz 5, Denny 3 and Dunlap 2. In the association, Foutz 138, Comiskey 72, Stovey 46, Caruthers 35, Burns 21, O'Neill 16, Orr 12, Collins 6, Marr 5, Earle and Mullane 3, Long 2, Mack 1.

—Boston *Herald*

Monday, August 12

On August 11, Brooklyn lost at St. Louis 4–14
(Terry 13–11 and King 26–12).
AA: St. Louis 62–31, Brooklyn 58–32.

The Brooklyn team were outplayed at all points at St. Louis yesterday, alike at the bat, in the field, in base running and in the box. Terry was put in to pitch against the champions, and for the sixth time, and he lost his fourth game against them on the occasion, his pitching and that of Foutz combined being hit for fourteen runs and eighteen base hits. Ten fielding errors against one by the St. Louis team show how the visitors were outplayed in the field and to these were added six costly battery errors. That is the story in brief of yesterday's signal defeat of the Brooklyn team at St. Louis. To-day Caruthers goes in the box, and as he is the only pitcher who has been successful against St. Louis the Brooklyns may pull one game off out of the three.

The attendance was the largest of the season, the turnstile count showing the crowd to exceed eight thousand. Of course, the St. Louis papers had it 15,000. They always double up on the crowd there. The account sent to New York from St. Louis says: "The greatest crowd that has assembled in Sportsman's Park since 1883 was there to-day to witness the second game of the Brooklyn series. Every seat was occupied and a black ring fifty feet deep fringed the entire field. A conservative estimate of the attendance is 15,000."

—Brooklyn *Daily Eagle*

Pinkney, Collins and Corkhill have not missed a championship game this season, and the first named has participated in every game played by Brooklyn since the Spring of 1886. Pinkney's record is certainly a remarkable one, showing as it does not only faithful attention to duty, singular immunity from accident, but an excellent mode of life to keep in constant condition with.

—Brooklyn *Daily Eagle*

President Von der Ahe this morning notified Latham that his suspension, which had only been temporary, was now in effect for an indefinite period, without pay. Latham will soon be around begging like a whipped boy. He never has any money, and suspension without pay means that he will starve unless some of the people who have been advising him will support him while he is on his "vacation." This is not likely, because he can now do nothing in return. The chances are that his withdrawal will strengthen the team, because if Sweeney can keep up his batting streak of yesterday he is worth two Lathams.

—St. Louis *Post-Dispatch*

Arlie Latham, third baseman, St. Louis Browns (Library of Congress, Prints and Photographs Division [LOT 13163-05, no. 407]).

Tuesday, August 13

On August 12, New York won at Cleveland 4–3 (Keefe 16–8).
Boston won at Pittsburg 5–3 (Clarkson 29–13).
Brooklyn lost at St. Louis 0–11
(Caruthers 25–7 and Chamberlain 25–9).
NL: Boston 53–30, New York 52–30.
AA: St. Louis 63–31, Brooklyn 58–33.

Pittsburg, Pa., Aug. 12, 1889—Clarkson pitched his best game on
the trip. He showed more speed and better judgment than of late. The
batting of Brouthers was tremendous, two doubles and a triple being his
contribution, while Kelly lined out two doubles and Nash a single and a
triple.

—Boston *Herald*

Chamberlain pitched one of the most remarkable games of the season yesterday against the Brooklyns, shutting them out by a score of 11 to
0. It was their third consecutive defeat, and gives the Browns an excellent
lead in the championship race. Until the sixth inning no Brooklyn player
reached first base. The only hits secured by Brooklyn were the two made
by Visner, and not a man reached base except in the sixth and eighth
innings, and they only had twenty-nine men at the bat in the entire game.

—St. Louis *Post-Dispatch*

The good people of Brooklyn are getting out telescopes to view the
pennant. It has moved so far west in the last few days that it is no longer
visible to the naked eye at the City of Churches.

—St. Louis *Post-Dispatch*

AMERICAN ASSOCIATION STANDINGS

	W	L	PCT.	GB		W	L	PCT.	GB
St. Louis	63	31	.670	—	Cincinnati	51	42	.548	11½
Brooklyn	58	33	.637	3½	Kansas City	38	53	.418	23½
Baltimore	53	38	.582	8½	Columbus	35	60	.368	28½
Athletic	50	37	.575	9½	Louisville	20	74	.213	43

NATIONAL LEAGUE STANDINGS

	W	L	PCT.	GB		W	L	PCT.	GB
Boston	53	30	.639	—	Chicago	43	45	.489	12½
New York	52	30	.634	½	Indianapolis	36	53	.404	20
Philadelphia	47	37	.560	6½	Pittsburg	35	53	.398	20½
Cleveland	47	40	.540	8	Washington	28	53	.346	24

Wednesday, August 14

On August 13, New York won at Cleveland 13–4 (Crane 10–7).
Boston lost at Pittsburg 0–9 (Daley 2–2).
Brooklyn won at Kansas City 3–2 (Terry 14–11).
St. Louis beat Columbus 12–3 (King 27–12).
NL: New York 53–30, Boston 53–31.
AA: St. Louis 64–31, Brooklyn 59–33.

Cleveland, Aug. 13—New-York won the game here this afternoon, and, as Boston lowered her colors to the Pittsburgs, the Giants stepped into first place, and to-night are the leaders in the League race.

—New York *Times*

Gracefully the Bostons yield the first position in the league race, which they have held continuously since the 17th of last May, to the men from New York. It has been a remarkable contest, and several times other clubs have been neck and neck with the Bostons, but have not been able to even tie them until now.

—Boston *Herald*

Thursday, August 15

On August 14, New York won at Cleveland 4–2 (Welch 21–7).
Boston won at Pittsburg 9–3 (Clarkson 30–13).
Brooklyn won at Kansas City 3–2 (Caruthers 26–7).
St. Louis lost to Columbus 0–13 (Chamberlain 25–10).
NL: New York 54–30, Boston 54–31.
AA: St. Louis 64–32, Brooklyn 60–33.

Cleveland, Aug. 14—There was an exciting scene at the ball grounds this afternoon. McAleer, for the Clevelands, in the fourth inning drove a ball to left field. He ran like a deer and reached second base in plenty time. Powers, the umpire, also ran to second, and after seeing McAleer safe on the base, returned to the home plate. There he was informed by "Buck" Ewing that McAleer had failed to touch first base, and he promptly called the runner out.

The pavilion was crowded, and nearly every man in it arose at once. "Ride him on a rail," cried several, and a dozen jumped into the field and started in the direction of Powers. Three policemen with drawn clubs and all the members of the Cleveland ball team hastened forward, and by sharp talk and some force drove the indignant spectators back. The field in the meantime was filling up, and 500 men were yelling their opinion of the umpire in chorus, and a hundred of them were shaking their fists and brandishing their canes at him. For ten minutes it seemed that a riot was certain, but Powers finally called the game and retired to a room under the grand stand. When he was out of sight the anger of the pavilion spectators cooled down, and on his return in a quarter of an hour he was merely assailed with words.

—New York *Times*

Friday, August 16

On August 15, New York lost at Pittsburg 2–9 (Keefe 16–9).
Boston lost at Cleveland 8–19 (Madden 9–8).
Brooklyn won at Kansas City 7–2 (Hughes 4–7).
St. Louis beat Columbus 17–11 (King 28–12).
NL: New York 54–31, Boston 54–32.
AA: St. Louis 65–32, Brooklyn 61–33.

Cleveland, O., Aug. 15, 1889—What a record Mr. Twitchell made— 6 hits, with a total of 16! It breaks the record of any one man in a single game in professional base ball, so good judges say. One single, one double, three triples and a home run is all that Mr. Twitchell did; and no telling what he would have done in the eighth inning had he had an opportunity to hit the ball instead of getting his base on balls.

In every inning the Clevelands got in at least one hit, and they also scored in every inning, breaking the record of the league in that respect.

—Boston *Herald*

Latham appears to be anxious to return to his old position. No doubt the actor-ball player is already commencing to feel the loss of his salary. He approached President Von der Ahe Wednesday and said he wanted to speak to him, but the boss President informed him he was busy as there was a game to be played that day. Yesterday Latham again approached him. He met with the same response and chilly reception. He wanted to know when Mr. Von der Ahe would have time to speak to him, and the Browns' President said there would be no game to-day, and if Latham called on him this afternoon he would listen to what he had to say. If he is taken back on the team at all, it will be under ironclad conditions.

—St. Louis *Post-Dispatch*

Saturday, August 17

On August 16, New York lost at Pittsburg 4–7 (Crane 10–8).
Boston won at Cleveland 13–0 (Clarkson 31–13).
NL: Boston 55–32, New York 54–32.

Cleveland, O., Aug. 16, 1889—Shortly after the noon hour today a horse passing the hotel at which the Bostons are stopping cast a shoe that was nearly a new one. Half of the Boston team rushed for it. Madden picked it up, and it was borne to the ball field in the carriage in which Clarkson, who was to do the pitching, rode. It was the omen of a great victory. There is considerable justifiable hilarity among the Boston players tonight, in marked contrast to the graveyard stillness that pervaded everywhere last evening, for, be it known, the Bostons completely turned the tables on the Clevelands, and, as the New Yorks succumbed for the second time to Pittsburg, the Hubites are again on top.

The game today was notable principally for two features, namely, the remarkable pitching by Clarkson, and the heavy hits of the visitors, that came in just at the right time. Twice the bases were full, and each time a three-bagger, one by Kelly and one by Brouthers, came in, and, with two men on bases, Brouthers got in a double that sent both men in.

—Boston *Herald*

Because the subject of Sunday ball games is of general interest the *Eagle* thinks it worth while to give place in its columns to the sentiments expressed in Queens County, where Ridgewood is situated. Editorially the rural Sunday Observance organ says:

> The hue and cry is against Sunday base ball at Ridgewood, which certainly is not a detriment to Brooklyn. And it cannot be offensive to the residents of Ridgewood, because they do not complain against it. Coney Island is in Kings County. Do we hear the Sunday Observance Association inveighing against Coney Island? Never a word. Yet there is more crime, debauchery, immorality and general devilry committed at Coney Island in one Sunday than in the whole of Queens County in a year of Sundays.

—Brooklyn *Daily Eagle*

Sunday, August 18

On August 17, New York lost at Pittsburg 10–15 (Welch 21–8).
Boston won at Cleveland 2–1 (Radbourn 13–7).
Brooklyn won at Louisville 10–0 (Caruthers 27–7).

St. Louis beat Athletic 4–1 (Chamberlain 26–10).
NL: Boston 56–32, New York 54–33.
AA: St. Louis 66–32, Brooklyn 62–33.

Pittsburg, Aug. 17—In the third inning Miller hurt himself by falling over Ewing's mask at the plate, and the crowd hissed the New-York catcher for having, as they believed, purposely place it there.

—New York *Times*

Boston was base ball wild yesterday. The admirers of the home team were exceedingly happy, not only because it was known that the Bostons would retain the lead even if the New Yorks won, but by reason of the fact that the New Yorks sank deeper into the consomme, and the Bostons increased their lead. The exultation that was displayed indicated everybody's confident belief that the home team would retrieve gloriously their slightly tarnished past. During the progress of the game Music Hall was thronged with an enthusiastic crowd, and when Stricker in the eighth inning led off with a three-base hit and was caught out by Quinn to Nash, the enthusiasm knew no bounds. The fair spectators in the gallery waved frantically their handkerchiefs, and the more boisterous spectators thumped and pounded with their canes and roared vociferous applause. To add to the situation, the bulletin chronicled the probable defeat of the New Yorks, and if any stranger imbued with traditional notions of the cultured city's calm temper had entered the hall at that time he would have gone away a doubting Thomas.

There isn't any doubt that there will be a large and enthusiastic crowd to welcome the Bostons on their return. The howling populace of Roman amphitheatre days weren't a marker to the crowds of base ball fever stricken Bostonians yesterday.

—Boston *Herald*

Louisville, Ky., August 17—The Brooklyns administered a coat of calcimine to the Kentuckians to-day. The Louisvilles never exerted themselves more for victory, but their efforts were unavailing, for Brooklyn had an easy time and won the game strictly on its merits.

—Brooklyn *Daily Eagle*

One of the largest week-day crowds that has been present at Sportsman's Park this season witnessed yesterday's game between the Browns and Athletics. The crowd guyed Capt. Stovey of the Athletics considerably for kicking, but he took it good naturedly, except when the bleaching boarders in left field threatened him. Then he asked for police protection and from that time on Stovey, a private watchman and a policeman, covered left field for the Athletics. The men with whom Stovey had trouble claimed that he and Welch called them vile names.

—St. Louis *Post-Dispatch*

Monday, August 19

On August 18, Brooklyn won at Louisville 6–3 (Terry 15–11). St. Louis beat Athletic 4–2 (King 29–12). AA: St. Louis 67–32, Brooklyn 63–33.

Clarkson has not his equal in the country. That man is simply a jewel, and he is not half appreciated. Look at the work he has done for the Boston club the past two seasons. It has been simply grand. He has had comparatively little help from his batsmen this season. It has been his good right arm that has been doing the work. That $10,000 the Bostons paid to get him was the biggest thing they ever did in the base ball line. Clarkson is a great worker, and he takes the greatest interest in the standing of his club. He is that sort of a rara avis who would go in and pitch six days in the week if it were necessary for the welfare

Harry Stovey, left fielder, Philadelphia Athletics (Library of Congress, Prints and Photographs Division [LOT 13163-05, no. 380]).

of the club. He is one of the best examples in the country of a headwork pitcher, and there isn't a player in the Boston nine who doesn't swear by him, and consider him the best pitcher in the country. Nine men of the Clarkson stamp would have the championship easy for Boston. It isn't his fault that his glorious record isn't higher than it is today. More power to him.

—Boston *Herald*

Now that the Bostons and New Yorks begin today a series of games on the South end grounds, which, while they will not by any means decide the championship, still will have an important bearing on the same, Capt. Ewing of the New York team comes in for a little special attention. Accompanying Boston on their western trip just closed, the writer heard in every city visited the most indignant protests against the conduct of Ewing in the games in those cities, conduct of which he has been equally guilty in Boston, and for which the umpire should have ordered him from the field. His conduct consists of a continual parrot-like talk with the umpire, players and spectators. The object thought by Ewing in acting thus is evidently to "work" the umpire, disconcert the players, and impress the spectators with his own smartness (?). In all this he fails, and the result is that he brings upon himself the utter contempt and indignation of the spectators. No one can complain of any decent, energetic and legitimate efforts on the part of Ewing to win a game for his side, but his practice of continual "chinning" with everybody is not legitimate, and he should be forced to stop. He does not care for fines, as he does not have to pay them, so he says, but he does dread the humiliation of being ordered out of a game.

Capt. Ewing is also guilty of practicing a trick as catcher that is one of the most contemptible and despicable introduced on the ball field. It is that, in the case of a base runner scoring from second or third base, of the catcher placing his mask on the home plate or on the base line near the plate, the object being to obstruct the runner in reaching the base. This act calls for severe condemnation and punishment, if for no other reason than that it endangers the limbs of the base runners. On Saturday last in Pittsburg Miller was scoring from second base, when Ewing placed his mask on the home plate. The result was that Miller, in touching the plate, became entangled with the mask, and his foot cut so badly that he was compelled to retire from the game. In one of the New York-Indianapolis games, Paul Hines jumped over the mask, but on securing his run he returned and jumped on the mask with both feet and ruined it. Should a Boston player be disabled by such a despicable act, as, for instance, Clarkson, or Nash, or Brouthers, or, in fact, any player, it would seriously weaken the playing strength of the team, and increase the chances of New York winning the pennant, as Ewing knows.

—Boston *Herald*

Tuesday, August 20

On August 19, New York tied at Boston 4–4.
Brooklyn won at Louisville 9–8 (Caruthers 28–7).
NL: Boston 56–32, New York 54–33.
AA: St. Louis 67–32, Brooklyn 64–33.

Never before, except on a holiday, have such scenes been enacted on the Boston grounds as were witnessed there yesterday afternoon. The game between the Bostons and New Yorks, the leaders in the contest, attracted the largest attendance ever seen on a non-festive day. Even the Boston directors were simply astounded at the size of the crowd that poured in through the three entrances. The spectators began to gather as early as 1 o'clock, and long after the usual hour of beginning the game the stream kept flowing. Fully three-quarters of an hour before play was to have been called every seat on the grand pavilion had been sold, and the result was that many ladies had to stand up during the game, while not a few were driven to the seats in centre field.

It was 3:57 when play was called, and by that time every seat on the grounds was occupied, and hundreds of people were standing against the right field fence. Spectators were standing several rows deep in the pavilion, and every point of vantage was taken. It was a sight that established the hold the game has upon the people of this city and vicinity. As some were heard to remark: "If this is the effect of those celebrated telegrams of Billings, he had better send some more the next time the club goes on a trip."

There was a great deal of cheering when the Bostons made the first run, but the air was fairly rent with the uproar that followed the making of the tying run in the eighth inning. Beside the applause and the wildest kind of cheering, arms, hats and handkerchiefs were waved in frantic excitement, and it took some time before order could be restored and the game go on.

—Boston *Herald*

AMERICAN ASSOCIATION STANDINGS

	W	L	PCT.	GB		W	L	PCT.	GB
St. Louis	67	32	.677	—	Cincinnati	53	45	.541	13½
Brooklyn	64	33	.660	2	Kansas City	40	56	.417	25½
Baltimore	56	40	.583	9½	Columbus	37	63	.370	30½
Athletic	52	40	.565	11½	Louisville	20	80	.200	47½

NATIONAL LEAGUE STANDINGS

	W	L	PCT.	GB		W	L	PCT.	GB
Boston	56	32	.636	—	Chicago	48	46	.511	11
New York	54	33	.621	1½	Pittsburg	40	54	.426	19
Philadelphia	50	39	.562	6½	Indianapolis	38	56	.404	21
Cleveland	48	45	.516	10½	Washington	29	58	.333	26½

Wednesday, August 21

On August 20, New York lost at Boston 2–12
(Keefe 16–10 and Radbourn 14–7).

Brooklyn won at Louisville 18–11 (Hughes 5–7).
St. Louis beat Athletic 14–2 (Chamberlain 27–10).
NL: Boston 57–32, New York 54–34.
AA: St. Louis 68–32, Brooklyn 65–33.

Boston, Aug. 20—The Bostons defeated the New-Yorks to-day with the greatest ease. In fact, the contest was so one-sided as to be robbed of all interest except that taken in the slugging of the Bostons. Keefe started to pitch for New-York, but at the end of the third inning, after the Bostons had made six hits and 4 runs off him, he retired and Welch was called in.

There is something wrong with Keefe and Welch. Both appear to have lost their effectiveness, and Crane is the only player who is pitching good ball. The other Giants are disappointed at the pitching of the two stars, and one mournfully remarked to-night: "Unless we get new pitchers or Keefe and Welch brace up we might as well give up the ship." In saying this he probably echoed the sentiment of the majority of the players.

—New York *Times*

Capt. Ewing's fondest hopes were most ruthlessly blasted yesterday. He came on the field as chipper as a lark, ready to show how easy it was to pull out a victory, for "we are the people," you know. The fact that Charles Radbourn was to pitch for the Bostons, and that great twirler, Keefe, was to pilot his forces, only tended to strengthen the belief that the Bostons would prove a "berry." This belief the New York captain shared with a great many Bostonians. The Bostons did prove to be a "berry"; but it was a very poisonous berry, and it made Mr. Ewing and his companions very sick.

—Boston *Herald*

There was an epidemic of slugging at Louisville yesterday. Darby O'Brien's two three baggers and one two bagger drove in no less than six of the eighteen runs.

—Brooklyn *Daily Eagle*

Chamberlain pitched another great game, and for the first six innings the visitors were unable to hit him safely more than two or three times; as the Browns then had the game almost won beyond peradventure, he let up his speed and took matters easy in the remaining innings.

—St. Louis *Post-Dispatch*

Thursday, August 22

On August 21, New York lost at Boston 4–10
(Crane 10–9 and Clarkson 32–13).
NL: Boston 58–32, New York 54–35.

Boston, Aug. 21—Crane struck out eleven men, but when his opponents hit the ball it was at a terrific pace. The attendance was 9,585, making nearly 32,000 for the three games. After the contest the New-Yorks started for home in an unhappy frame of mind. They were accompanied by a delegation of Gothamites who left some of their spare cash behind them.

—New York *Times*

There were plenty of ticklish situations in the contest. The most interesting was in the sixth inning, when the New Yorks had three men on bases with not a hand out, and the Bostons ahead, four runs to one. Clarkson centred all of his skill upon O'Rourke, who is as hard a man to dispose of on strikes as there is in the New York club. He accomplished the feat amid a storm of cheers, and the Bostons were lucky to get out of this hole with but one run for their opponents.

Bennett opened the seventh by sending a foul out of bounds. "New ball! New ball!" yelled Kelly. "The newer the ball, the harder we can hit it," said Ewing smilingly. Then Bennett smote that new ball for one of the longest home run hits ever made over that left field fence. With three balls and one strike on Kelly, that player leaned over the plate as if to draw a bad ball. The ball in play was the same on which Bennett had made a home run, and he "only" sent it flying in almost the same place as Bennett's. Two home runs in one inning set the crowd fairly wild with delight.

—Boston *Herald*

The balls come from Crane's hand as if from a catapult. He is a very powerfully built young fellow, and will turn the scales at about 220 pounds. Crane seems to be a terror for Dan Brouthers.

Charlie Bennett, catcher, Boston Beaneaters (Boston *Herald*, October 20, 1888).

He is the only pitcher who has succeeded in striking out the big man twice this season.

—Boston *Herald*

Cincinnati, O., August 22—The law which prohibits Sunday ball here is a State enactment, and the announcement that Brooklyn and Cincinnati would play at Hamilton next Sunday has stirred up some of the inhabitants of that place. The Tri State League Club has played there all the year on Sundays without interruption from the police authorities, but the announcement of the invasion of the association clubs has created, in the language of a special telegram from that place, general indignation that Butler County should be selected as a county where the law can be violated with impunity, and it may be that the authorities will interfere with the game and prevent it from taking place. The sheriff is being urged to use his authority and call out a posse, if necessary, to assert the dignity of the law. Taken altogether the situation looks rather squally for the crowd of Cincinnatians who are going to Hamilton to violate a law that they are compelled to obey in their own city. The base ball park is out of the city limits, and this prevents the city authorities from taking cognizance of the matter. Just how mad the sheriff is cannot be told at this writing.

—Brooklyn *Daily Eagle*

Latham has been reinstated. Several times since his suspension he has attempted to get back on the team, but Mr. Von der Ahe paid little heed to him. The third baseman was finally granted an interview last night, the Browns' President having informed him that he had left everything in Comiskey's hands and whatever he recommended would be done. The three met and on Latham's pledge to play winning ball hereafter and not to be guilty of any more indifferent work on the field, he was told he could resume his old position, and he will probably be seen on third base to-day. Comiskey lectured him severely, and no doubt Latham will hereafter be guilty of no more such exhibitions of ball playing as he gave for some weeks before his suspension. It is questionable, however, whether he can ever again become as popular as he was here before this unfortunate affair occurred.

—St. Louis *Post-Dispatch*

Friday, August 23

On August 22, New York beat Philadelphia 8–4 (Keefe 17–10).
Boston beat Washington 7–5 (Radbourn 15–7).

Brooklyn lost at Cincinnati 5–18 (Caruthers 28–8).
St. Louis lost to Baltimore 2–4 (King 29–13).
NL: Boston 59–32, New York 55–35.
AA: St. Louis 68–33, Brooklyn 65–34.

The Bostons climbed a bit higher yesterday on the league ladder toward that bit of bunting that is so temptingly displayed on top, though the tail-enders made a sort of attempt to keep them from ascending.

—Boston *Herald*

Cincinnati, Aug. 22—Caruthers was knocked out of the box in the third inning, and while playing first base was run into and knocked insensible by Duryea in the fifth inning. It is thought he is seriously injured.

—New York *Times*

Pinkney handled Duryea's ball cleanly, but he threw it low. As Caruthers stooped to get it the cyclone arrived and his knees struck the first baseman squarely in the stomach and he fell over unconscious. In a few moments he was carried to the directors' room, where he lay all during the game in a half dazed condition. On reviving he was sent to his hotel in a hack. He complained of severe pains in his shoulder, but Dr. Cromley, of the United States Marine Hospital Corps, who attended to him, declared that his internal organs were all right.

—Brooklyn *Daily Eagle*

Cincinnati, O., August 23—Caruthers was unconscious for quite a time. Prompt medical attendance was given him, and on returning to the hotel we resorted to heroic methods to give him relief from pain. He was carefully looked after last night and this morning. I am pleased to say he is as sound and plucky as ever, only a little sore. He will be able to do his share of work in a day or two. All the boys are well, full of confidence and determined. In spite of occasional painful setbacks we are going to land Brooklyn in first place if earnest effort, hard work and a "git there" spirit will accomplish it.

—Charles H. Byrne, Brooklyn *Daily Eagle*

T.J. Keefe, the crack pitcher of the New-Yorks, and J. Montgomery Ward, the Giants' short stop, are brothers-in-law. They became related on Monday past, when the genial pitcher was united in marriage to Mrs. Helm, a sister of Helen Dauvray, the wife of Ward. The marriage took place in Worcester while the club was in Boston.

—New York *Times*

Saturday, August 24

On August 23, New York beat and lost to
Philadelphia 7–3 and 2–11 (Welch 22–8; Crane 10–10).
Boston lost to Washington 7–8 (Daley 2–3).
Brooklyn won at Cincinnati 10–4 (Terry 16–11).
NL: Boston 59–33, New York 56–36.
AA: St. Louis 68–33, Brooklyn 66–34.

No base ball manager is a harder loser than President Von der Ahe. His team has taken the championship four times in succession, but he is as anxious as ever to win again. Now that the race has become so close he is kept wrought to the highest pitch of mental excitement, and whenever his team loses he becomes most dejected and furious. He feels like taking revenge out of the men whose poor play cost the club defeat, and it is safe to say that if the team does lose the championship this year several of the members who have been playing poorly will be given something that will make them remember the fact for many years to come.

—St. Louis *Post-Dispatch*

OLD JUDGE CIGARETTES Goodwin & Co., New York.

Elton Chamberlain, pitcher, St. Louis Browns (Library of Congress, Prints and Photographs Division [LOT 13163-13, no. 18]).

King does not appear to be the pitcher this season, he was last year. His arm seems to have lost its force and cunning. Early in the season he did some very good work, but for quite a while he has not been particularly effective. Chamberlain, on the other hand, has been doing remarkable work lately. Perhaps no pitcher in either Association or League is his equal in his present form. His pitching in several games has been on the phenomenal order, and if the Browns secure the championship it will be largely through his work.

—St. Louis *Post-Dispatch*

Sunday, August 25

On August 24, New York beat Philadelphia
twice 10–8 and 8–3 (O'Day 3–1; Keefe 18–10).
Boston beat Washington 9–3 (Clarkson 33–13).
Brooklyn won at Cincinnati 6–4 (Hughes 6–7).
St. Louis beat Baltimore 7–4 (Chamberlain 28–10).
NL: Boston 60–33, New York 58–36.
AA: St. Louis 69–33, Brooklyn 67–34.

Winning two games of baseball in one day is something of a novelty in diamond field circles, but the Giants performed that feat yesterday, and in consequence gained slightly on their Boston rivals. Harry Wright's Philadelphia players were the victims. They played all they knew how to win, but they couldn't on account of the superior batting of the muscular, broad-shouldered Giants.

—New York *Times*

The work of John G. Clarkson of the Boston Base Ball Club yesterday, following so closely upon the exhibition given the day before by Daley, was like the difference between the real article and the imitation. His was the polished gem, and the other was the crude material.

Kelly's base running was of his best. He stole four bases, one from third to home while Wilmot was trying to see whether the ball had been hurt by the knock that Nash had administered to it. The Boston captain was in his best mood, and he was awake all through the game. The men played, too, as if in sympathy with his vein.

—Boston *Herald*

Cincinnati, O., August 24—Mickey Hughes, who has been an easy mark for everybody, proved too much

Mickey Hughes, pitcher, Brooklyn Bridegrooms (New York *Clipper*, June 29, 1889).

for the Reds. Mickey wasn't faster than a narrow gauge limited express, but the Reds failed to transact business with him. The ball came floating up to the plate looking as big as a foot ball, but somehow or other the Reds could not line it out safely.

—Brooklyn *Daily Eagle*

Monday, August 26

On August 25, St. Louis beat Baltimore 16–9 (King 30–13).
AA: St. Louis 70–33, Brooklyn 67–34.

The 1st of August has long passed by with the Bostons in the lead, and the 1st of September is almost here and it looks as if the Bostons would still be in the lead by that time. Whether the club wins the championship or not, it has made a great fight this season and has done some elegant work. It has been shown that beyond a doubt there is championship material in the club.

After all the talk about the weakening of Pitcher Clarkson and his having his day, he keeps in the box, winning his games and leaving his rivals far in the rear. He has the greatest record of any pitcher in the country, and he isn't through yet.

—Boston *Herald*

Driven from home by the stern guardians of the law, the Cincinnati and Brooklyn clubs traveled up to Hamilton yesterday morning, twenty-five miles out on the C. H. and D. Railroad. On the grounds of the Tri State League club, just outside the city limits, the teams played yesterday in the presence of 5,000 spectators. Three big excursions were run up from the Queen City, and this crowd was swelled by a couple of thousand Hamiltonians. Before the games Managers Schmelz and McGunnigle and the players of both teams were taken out and arraigned before a white whiskered, red nosed country squire, who informed them that they were under arrest for violating the State law that forbids the playing of ball on Sunday. That was all of the legal interference at that time.

It was in the latter half of the fourth inning that a spectacle not on the bills occurred. Visner began business with a hit too hot to handle and Caruthers was at the bat when a commotion at the outer gate directed all eyes to that spot.

A battalion of police, eighteen in number, commanded by Chief Lindley, walked in. In a moment the field was crowded and play was suspended. The eighteen players were marched out to wagons and carriages and taken to the city building, where they were arraigned before Mayor Dirk. Not a word of testimony was heard, and his Honor simply fined them each $5 and costs, making the bill $159.30, which the Cincinnati Club had to foot. The interrupted game will be played at Brooklyn when the Reds reach here in September.

—Brooklyn *Daily Eagle*

Tuesday, August 27

On August 26, New York beat Washington 11–1 (Welch 23–8).
Boston won at Philadelphia 5–4 (Clarkson 34–13).
St. Louis lost to Kansas City 2–5 (Chamberlain 28–11).
NL: Boston 61–33, New York 59–36.
AA: St. Louis 70–34, Brooklyn 67–34.

Philadelphia, Pa., Aug. 26, 1889—It was a case of Kelly and the ball today in the minds of the Philadelphians. The ball in the pocket was one that Capt. Farrar wanted to take to first base on a claim that Johnston had not touched first in the 12th inning after he had made a stinging hit that brought in the winning run. Kelly, who was naturally entitled to it as captain of the winning nine, refused to give the ball up. The game was over, the umpire had left the field, the grounds were one great black mass of people; why should he have surrendered it? That claim of Farrar was sufficient to raise a small-sized riot. He has a propensity for that sort of thing. He leads the mobs here against visiting clubs and against the umpires, and he has made the city one of the most turbulent and noisy base ball cities in the country. Kelly will remember today for a long time to come. If he had not been quick and sharp, he would have been brutally assaulted. He got out of the way of the crowd just in time.

—Boston *Herald*

Another game was lost by the Browns yesterday, and now the Brooklyns are dangerously close to the top. Considering that the champions have to play nearly all of their remaining games away from home and that the Bridegrooms play a great majority of theirs in their home grounds, the latter team is in decidedly the more advantageous position of the two at the present time. There is now a difference of but .010 in the percentage of the two clubs. One day's play may tie the teams, as a defeat of the Browns and a victory by the Brooklyns would make their percentages .667 each.

—St. Louis *Post-Dispatch*

AMERICAN ASSOCIATION STANDINGS

	W	L	PCT.	GB		W	L	PCT.	GB
St. Louis	70	34	.673	—	Cincinnati	56	48	.538	14
Brooklyn	67	34	.663	1½	Kansas City	43	60	.417	26½
Baltimore	58	42	.580	10	Columbus	39	66	.371	31½
Athletic	55	43	.561	12	Louisville	22	83	.210	48½

NATIONAL LEAGUE STANDINGS

	W	L	PCT.	GB		W	L	PCT.	GB
Boston	61	33	.649	—	Cleveland	49	50	.495	10½
New York	59	36	.621	1½	Pittsburg	44	56	.440	19
Philadelphia	52	45	.536	6½	Indianapolis	42	58	.420	21
Chicago	51	49	.510	11	Washington	31	62	.333	26½

Wednesday, August 28

On August 27, New York lost to Washington 3–13 (Keefe 18–11).
Boston won at Philadelphia 13–6 (Radbourn 16–7).
Brooklyn lost at Baltimore 7–8 (Terry 16–12).
St. Louis beat Kansas City 19–0 (King 31–13).
NL: Boston 62–33, New York 59–37.
AA: St. Louis 71–34, Brooklyn 67–35.

New-York's aspirants for baseball honors encountered a set-back yesterday. They were badly beaten by the Senators from Washington, and as Boston came out ahead in the contest with Philadelphia the Giants were the recipients of an unwelcome "whip-saw." The results of the games yesterday were anything but pleasing to the "cranks" of this vicinity. To have the Giants beaten was bad enough, but Boston and St. Louis won and Brooklyn dropped a game, and the poor "crank" had nothing to console him.

The Giants played like so many schoolboys. Just what caused this state of affairs is a matter of conjecture, but it is more than probable that the absence of an efficient Captain had something to do with it. Ewing laid off to take a well-earned rest to get in condition for the Boston games, thinking that the boys could easily defeat Washington, but he was mistaken. The Giants without Ewing are like a ship without a rudder, and, while it is unfair to ask him to play every day, it must be done if New-York wants to win the pennant. Ewing is the best Captain in the profession, and his value can only be appreciated when somebody else attempts to fill his position.

—New York *Times*

Philadelphia, Pa., Aug. 27, 1889—The fact that Radbourn was to pitch for the Bostons made many think that Philadelphia would have an easy walkover. "You know he is a back number," said a prominent Philadelphia scribe to the writer. "You know that he is no good, and that his day has gone by. He is a back number." "I know nothing of the sort," was the answer. "I know that he can pitch great ball. He fooled the New Yorks the other day, and he is very apt to fool your people." "Oh, the New Yorks were not in condition," was the retort. "Well, we'll see," said the Bostonian.

It was "I told you so" for a few innings, but only for a few. Radbourn had hard luck to begin with, but as soon as the club began to bat he braced up and pitched splendid ball.

—Boston *Herald*

Thursday, August 29

On August 28, New York beat Washington
twice 16–3 and 7–5 (Crane 11–10; O'Day 4–1).
Boston lost at Philadelphia 3–4 (Radbourn 16–8).
Brooklyn lost at Baltimore 3–8 (Caruthers 28–9).
St. Louis tied Kansas City 9–9.
NL: Boston 62–34, New York 61–37.
AA: St. Louis 71–34, Brooklyn 67–36.

Washington's representatives suffered two defeats at the hands of the Giants yesterday, and as the Bostons lowered their colors to their Quaker friends the New-Yorks gained considerably on the leaders. In consequence to-day they are within hailing distance of "Mike" Kelly and his satellites, and it is safe to assert that when the two teams meet this afternoon the Polo Grounds will be the scene of one of the greatest baseball battles of the year.

—New York *Times*

The team to-day will probably be composed as follows:

New-York		*Boston*
Keefe	Pitcher	Clarkson
Ewing	Catcher	Bennett
Connor	First Base	Brouthers
Richardson	Second Base	Quinn
Whitney	Third Base	Nash
Ward	Short stop	Smith

New-York		Boston
O'Rourke	Left field	Richardson
Gore	Centre field	Johnston
Tiernan	Right field	Kelly

—New York *Times*

Philadelphia, Pa., Aug. 28, 1889—"We can win every day with 11 men," said a Philadelphian to a friend today at the close of the contest. "The Bostons were deliberately cheated out of two runs." It is all right for the stay-at-homes to talk about the continual harping upon the umpires, but when a Philadelphian can find it in his heart to make a remark such as the above, patience ceases to be a virtue and silence a jewel.

Richardson was clearly safe at the home plate in the fifth inning, and Radbourn in the ninth. In the latter case Sanders deliberately blocked Radbourn off at the plate so that he could not reach it. The trick succeeded.

—Boston *Herald*

Friday, August 30

On August 29, New York lost to Boston 4–6
(Welch 23–9 and Clarkson 35–13).
Brooklyn won at Baltimore 4–0 (Terry 17–12).
NL: Boston 63–34, New York 61–38.
AA: St. Louis 71–34, Brooklyn 68–36.

Just as the sun was going down over the Harlem meadows last evening a German band in one of the various concert halls on Washington Heights struck up "The Dead March," 10,000 baseball enthusiasts flied out of the New Polo Grounds with their hats pulled down over their eyes, and a feeling of sadness reigned in the vicinity. The Giants had met the Bostons and the latter had won the game by a score of 6 to 4. This series is regarded as the most important of the season, and the fact that the Giants had lost the opening game had anything but a cheerful effect on the vast army of "cranks" who reside in this city.

There was plenty of excitement, and for a time a panic was imminent. The new grand stand was taxed to its utmost capacity, and as soon as the game began and the crowds started to stamp and cheer, the upper portion of the structure settled. The spectators felt a shock and heard a noise occasioned by the cracking of timber. They made a rush for the stairway, and only for the interference of several cool-headed gentlemen there would certainly have been a bad crush. Inspector Conlin, who was on the grounds, took several policemen and rushed to the right wing of the grand stand.

"Sit down; there is no danger!" he yelled as loudly as he could. "Remain in your seats; everything is all right."

The spectators did as requested, and in a few moments the excitement was over and the game was continued. One of the big cross beams had slipped on account of a loose bolt, giving the spectators an unpleasant shock, although there was no danger of any accident to the structure.

In a few moments the excitement incident to the game made the spectators forget about the trouble and the battle progressed as smoothly as ever. Both teams played great ball and up to the eighth inning it was anybody's game. At that juncture, however, Welch, who had pitched a model game, made a bad throw, and 3 runs for Boston was the result. Hardie Richardson was on second and Nash on first, with one out. Ganzel hit a bounder to Welch, who threw to Whitney to make a double play, but the ball went wide of the mark, and the error lost the game.

—New York *Times*

New York, Aug. 29, 1889—Henry Chadwick, the father of base ball, was in ecstasies over Clarkson's pitching. "Beautiful, beautiful," he would mutter to himself, "such a change of pace, such command; he's a wonder." Before the contest began Mr. Chadwick called Clarkson to him and congratulated him upon his brilliant success this season. Mr. Chadwick remarked to the *Herald* correspondent that he had never seen better pitching in his life.

It was not a game of batting but of pitching, and the New York man had no reason to feel ashamed of his record, albeit his smile had to acknowledge the superiority of the Clarksonian frown. Boston did have some luck, and Mickey Welch had harder luck than he has had for some time. It was very unfortunate, after the way that Welch had pitched, that the loss of the game should be ascribed to him; yet such was the case.

—Boston *Herald*

Saturday, August 31

On August 30, New York beat Boston 7–2
(Keefe 19–11 and Radbourn 16–9).
Brooklyn beat Kansas City 14–4 (Caruthers 29–9).

St. Louis lost at Columbus 4–13 (King 31–14).
NL: Boston 63–35, New York 62–38.
AA: St. Louis 71–35, Brooklyn 69–36.

Good, clever pitching by Keefe and opportune batting by the Giants
won a game from the Bostons yesterday and sent 8,000 New-Yorkers
away from the New Polo Grounds in a cheerful mood. Keefe was at his
best, and pitched his greatest game of the year. The genial pitcher was
the stumbling block to the success of the gentlemen from the city of culture. "Mike" Kelly played with his usual dash and tried to get his boys
to winning form, but without base hits he couldn't get runs and of course
his efforts were useless. Some of Kelly's remarks while coaching his men
were very witty, and he caused no small amount of amusement.

—New York *Times*

New York has a "deadhead" hill. It is on Morningside drive, on the
crest of a rocky eminence overlooking the base ball grounds. It is distant
about a quarter of a mile, but commands an excellent view of the oper-
ations on the diamond. There is a rocky palisade reaching down to the
level of the grounds, but as it belongs to J.J. Coogan, who is also the owner
of the base ball field, that cannot be used as a vantage point.

—Boston *Herald*

The gentlemanly professional team from Kansas City put in an
appearance yesterday at Washington Park and they gratified the assemblage of over three thousand spectators, including hundreds of lady
guests of the home club, by not marring the contest with a single kick
against the decisions of the umpire. The game began promptly at 4 P.M.,
with Bushong acting as umpire, with the full approval of the Kansas City
manager, in the absence of Holland.

—Brooklyn *Daily Eagle*

Brooklyn is at its old tricks. When they play on their home grounds,
Byrne always makes it convenient for the regular umpires to be absent,
and he has some substitutes there that would beat any club on earth. At
the game yesterday the regular umpire was again absent and the Kansas
City Club accepted Bushong, one of the Brooklyn players, having more
confidence in his honesty than in the judgment of the substitute umpires.
Brooklyn has had more games umpired on its grounds by substitute
umpires than all the other clubs in the Association combined. There is
no use in attempting to win a game against any of them. It would not
seem necessary for the Brooklyns to put in substitute umpires for Byrne
has so strong a pull with the regular umpires that the club invariably gets

all the best of the decisions even when traveling. It is the umpires who have placed them where they are. Away from home they get the best part of the umpiring, and at home they get all of it. Is it any wonder they win games? The only strange thing is that they should be able to lose any.

—St. Louis *Post-Dispatch*

Sunday, September 1

On August 31, New York tied Boston 9–9.
Brooklyn beat Kansas City twice 11–4 and 8–2
(Terry 18–12; Hughes 7–7).
St. Louis lost at Columbus 1–4 (Stivetts 5–6).
NL: Boston 63–35, New York 62–38.
AA: Brooklyn 71–36, St. Louis 71–36.

New York, Aug. 31, 1889—A draw, 9 runs to 9. It would have been a great game to win, and it was a great game not to lose. What caused the game to be lost to the Bostons was an atrocious decision of Umpire Powers at the home plate on O'Rourke in the fifth inning. It was as clear an out as was ever seen on a diamond. The ball was fielded, Kelly to Smith to Bennett, and O'Rourke had no possible chance to get to the plate without being touched. The Boston public well knows Charlie Bennett. He is a player who makes no bluffs, and there never was a time when he was so exasperated as when Powers gave the man safe.

It was one of the greatest games ever seen on a base ball field. Kelly said that he never saw anything like it in all his life. There never was a game so full of quivering excitement. The crowd was fairly frantic, and such yelling was never heard on a ground before. There was no reason why the umpiring should not have been perfectly impartial and fair, but, as Clarkson says, New York is bound to get the better of it, and he never knew the time when he got a good showing in this city.

The day was one of the hottest of the season, and the long ride to the grounds could not have been much more wearisome, but such a trifle would not keep a New Yorker away, and the trains were fairly freighted with humanity. On the way up an excellent view of the old polo grounds was secured—grounds which could have been left to the New York club as well as not. The old grounds were occupied by throngs of youngsters.

When the writer reached the grounds at 3:20 o'clock there were fully 9000 people present. Almost every seat on the left field section was occupied. At an early hour every seat in the grand stand was filled, and the standing room was packed with rows of people several deep. After that no gentleman was admitted to the upper part of the stand unless accompanied by a lady. The ladies were out in force and greatly enlivened and beautified the scene. For the first time in the series there was need to use the ropes in right field, and the crowd was so great that it extended beyond these and into the field. So large was the police force and so excellent all arrangements for accommodating a big crowd that there was very little delay in beginning and playing the game.

When the gong rang the sight was one well worth witnessing. The crowd had rushed upon the embankment. Some stood up and others divested themselves of their coats and tried to make themselves comfortable. The free seats in right field were, indeed, bleaching boards, for the sun beat down upon them with all of its heat. In the grand stand the crowd was sitting on the rafters by the hundreds. Great care was taken not to overcrowd the upper part of the stand. "Deadhead" hill contained over 1500 people. In all, over 16,000 people must have witnessed the game.

—Boston *Herald*

Columbus, O., August 31—The champion Browns were again forced to lower their colors to-day to the Columbus Babies. Stivetts was put in by Capt. Comiskey to pitch, and in addition to being rather wild was batted hard by the home boys. President Von der Ahe was enraged over the team dropping two consecutive games here and scored the players roundly.

—St. Louis *Post-Dispatch*

Brooklyn, N.Y., August 31—The Brooklyns won two games from the Kansas City club here to-day. Two games were played to-day because the Sheriff of Queens County had declared he would permit no Sunday games at Ridgeway Park. Bushong of the Brooklyns umpired both games.

—St. Louis *Post-Dispatch*

The continued absence of Holland, the umpire scheduled for the games, led to the assignment of Bushong again, his work in the position the day before having been fair and impartial and satisfactory to Manager Watkins, the utmost good feeling prevailing between the two clubs and their respective players.

—Brooklyn *Daily Eagle*

Columbus, O., August 31—President Von der Ahe is very sore over his treatment by Umpire Ferguson and the very indifferent manner in which some of his men are playing ball. "There is one thing I would like to ask," said Mr. Von der Ahe, "and that is, why does not one of the two umpires, Holland and Goldsmith, who are both in the East, umpire the games at Brooklyn? Yesterday neither of them were in use, yet Bushong, one of the Brooklyn players, umpired the game and they won. I would like you to ask Mr. Wikoff why it happens in Brooklyn when it does not in other places."

—St. Louis *Post-Dispatch*

It is evident to the lovers of the national game in St. Louis that Charles H. Byrne, the head of the Brooklyn Club, is determined to win the pennant this year by hook or by crook. He will stop at nothing in the line of scheming to accomplish the desired result. Byrne has the umpires apparently at his command, and two of them are now very conveniently "sick," and the Brooklyn players are put in to help out. Of course they are under instructions to help their club win at all hazards. Byrne sees he cannot win the pennant unless aided by the umpires and he starts a couple of them off on short vacations, alleging sickness

Doc Bushong, catcher, Brooklyn Bridegrooms (Library of Congress, Prints and Photographs Division [LOT 13163-13, no. 10]).

as the cause of their absence. He is tricky, and will leave no stone unturned to beat the Browns out of the pennant.

—St. Louis *Post-Dispatch*

Monday, September 2

On September 1, St. Louis lost at Columbus 5–6
(Chamberlain 28–12).
AA: Brooklyn 71–36, St. Louis 71–37.

The tumble has come at last. It had to. Brooklyn had theirs last April, and it has turned out to be a lucky thing for them that it came then. The close of the August campaign saw them tied with St. Louis, and the

September campaign opens, auspiciously for Brooklyn, with our team in the van for the first time this season.

As for the morale of the team, they have no equals in the American arena, as they have a club to work for which, from its president down, has been more liberal and considerate with its players than any club either in the league or the association. In this important respect they are way ahead of St. Louis, as there is scarcely a man in the champion team who does not bear some grudge or other against the "boss manager," with just cause or without; and as for harmony in the champion team, it is something unknown, and at no time this season has it been less than now.

It is hoped that when Von der Ahe's men come to Brooklyn they will be considerately received, and that there will be no such exhibition of ruffianism as occurred on the St. Louis grounds when the home nine were playing there. Because a St. Louis crowd chooses to resort to the tactics of the "bulldozer," it does not follow that a Brooklyn gathering should do the same. Let the contrast in behavior speak for itself.

—Brooklyn *Daily Eagle*

> The championship is nigh over,
> You'll soon hear the victors' whoop.
> The Brooklyns are in the clover,
> And the Browns are in the soup.

—St. Louis *Post-Dispatch*

There is great hue and cry about the Bostons relying upon Clarkson. So they do, and largely, but not nearly so much as the New Yorks do on Ewing. Boston without Clarkson would be a far stronger nine than New York without Ewing, and the latter, a catcher, is far more likely to be placed hors du combat than a pitcher. Ewing is the great head of the New York club, and he is making every effort to win that championship.

—Boston *Herald*

The *Sporting Times* says: "The Boston Base Ball Club may be congratulated upon the showing it has made this season. It has shown itself to be a strong rival of the New York champions, and worthy of the patronage of the banner base ball city in the country. No city has a more brilliant or prouder record in the glorious game that millions love so dearly as the Athens of America. It possesses as fine grounds as there are in the country, with a grand stand unsurpassed in architectural beauty, equipment and costliness. The devotion of the patrons of the game is in keeping with the surroundings. Over 200,000 people have witnessed the games there up to date, and win or lose, the players receive a support that must have its effect upon the players.

—Boston *Herald*

South End Grounds, Boston (National Baseball Hall of Fame Library, Cooperstown, New York).

Tuesday, September 3

On September 2, New York beat Pittsburg twice 9–6 and 11–0
(O'Day 5–1; Keefe 20–11).
Boston beat Indianapolis twice 8–3 and 1–0
(Radbourn 17–9; Clarkson 36–13).
Brooklyn beat and lost to Cincinnati 7–4 and 4–11
(Caruthers 30–9; Terry 18–13).
NL: Boston 65–35, New York 64–38.
AA: Brooklyn 72–37, St. Louis 71–37.

Two games were played on the Polo Grounds yesterday between the New-York and Pittsburg Clubs, and the Giants managed to win both. Boston, however, succeeded in winning the same number from Indianapolis, and in consequence the standing of the leaders is the same today as it was last week. Over 12,000 persons witnessed the contests.

The field work of Richardson and Ward was of the gilt-edged order. Between them they made seventeen plays and failed to accept only one chance, the single error being made by Ward. Tiernan had a successful day at batting, making in the two games five hits, for a total of fourteen bases. His hits were a home run, two triples and two doubles.

—New York *Times*

The Bostons played great ball in the two games of yesterday, and delighted 18,693 people by the excellence of the exhibition.

Radbourn and Clarkson were on their mettle, and the former puzzled his opponents not a little. John Clarkson pitched his 36th winning game of the season in the afternoon. He pitched great ball, and the Indianapolis club was able to make but four hits off him in the contest, while not a fly ball was hit to the outfield. This latter fact makes the game one of the most effectively pitched in the league this year. But one run was made in the entire contest, and it was made by Richardson, the first batsman in the very first inning, on a ball that went over the fence very close to the foul line.

—Boston *Herald*

The Brooklyn team closed their holiday games yesterday with even figures, as far as victories were concerned, their morning victory being a triumph of the first water, while their afternoon defeat was so exceptional in its character as to be no discredit to them whatever as a team. It was Terry's weak pitching and nothing else which lost them yesterday's game.

—Brooklyn *Daily Eagle*

AMERICAN ASSOCIATION STANDINGS

	W	L	PCT.	GB		W	L	PCT.	GB
Brooklyn	72	37	.661	—	Cincinnati	59	52	.532	14
St. Louis	71	37	.657	½	Kansas City	44	64	.407	27½
Baltimore	62	44	.585	8½	Columbus	43	68	.387	30
Athletic	60	45	.571	10	Louisville	23	87	.209	49½

NATIONAL LEAGUE STANDINGS

	W	L	PCT.	GB		W	L	PCT.	GB
Boston	65	35	.650	—	Cleveland	51	54	.486	16½
New York	64	38	.627	2	Pittsburg	48	61	.440	21½
Philadelphia	54	49	.524	12½	Indianapolis	45	63	.417	24
Chicago	56	52	.519	13	Washington	34	65	.343	30½

Wednesday, September 4

On September 3, New York beat Pittsburg 9–4 (Welch 24–9).
Boston lost to Indianapolis 7–8 (Madden 9–9).
Brooklyn beat Cincinnati 13–8 (Caruthers 31–9).
St. Louis lost at Baltimore 1–7 (King 31–15).

NL: Boston 65–36, New York 65–38.
AA: Brooklyn 73–37, St. Louis 71–38.

The New-York champions defeated Pittsburg yesterday; Boston was whipped by Indianapolis, and in consequence to-day the Giants are only a few points behind the leader.

—New York *Times*

The toboggan slide which St. Louis struck in Kansas City on August 29 is still being ridden upon by the champions, and they do not relish it a little bit. From August 28 to September 3 inclusive the St. Louis team have played six games without winning one, a record new to their career this season.

—Brooklyn *Daily Eagle*

Baltimore, Md., September 4—The St. Louis players are badly demoralized by the result of yesterday's game and are despondent.

—St. Louis *Post-Dispatch*

Capt. Comiskey of the Browns says: "We are not afraid of Brooklyn or any other club. All we ask is a square deal from the umpires; this we may not get, but if we don't they will hear from us. We can beat Brooklyn on their own grounds just as easy as in St. Louis. This is not brag, but it's the truth."

—New York *Times*

Thursday, September 5

On September 4, New York beat Pittsburg 7–2 (O'Day 6–1).
Boston lost to Indianapolis 3–6 (Clarkson 36–14).
Brooklyn beat Cincinnati 12–1 (Lovett 14–8).
St. Louis won at Baltimore 4–2 (Chamberlain 29–12).
NL: Boston 65–37, New York 66–38.
AA: Brooklyn 74–37, St. Louis 72–38.

Hank O'Day was in the box for the home team and he pitched a superb game, mowing down the sluggers of the opposing team with the most consummate ease. It was, in point of fact, as fine an exhibition of twirling as has been witnessed on the Polo Grounds in many a day.

—New York *Times*

The best feature of the playing on the Bostons' side was the base running of Kelly. In the third inning he made a wonderful slide and stole second, and he followed this up by a daring steal of third, his great base running alone permitting the scoring of a run in the inning. He was loudly cheered for this brilliant work.

—Boston *Herald*

The home run hit of the game—and three were made—was that of Lovett in the fourth inning, which was decidedly the most effective hit of the kind made on the field this season. Two men were out, with all three bases occupied, when Lovett went to the bat. Burns was coaching on the bases, and thinking it was O'Brien's turn at the bat Tommy called out: "Here comes Darby; now, boys, look out sharp." But seeing Lovett

Tom Lovett, pitcher, Brooklyn Bridegrooms (New York *Clipper*, August 24, 1889).

step up to the bat instead of O'Brien, Burns said: "Well, here comes just as good a man, anyhow." and the words were no sooner out of his mouth than Lovett sent the ball from the bat clean out of the active Halliday's reach, and before he could get it out from the field back of the carriages Lovett had reached home easily, sending in four runs on the hit, something which has not come from a home run hit in any game at Washington Park this season.

—Brooklyn *Daily Eagle*

At last the Browns have won a game. They broke the ice yesterday at Baltimore by defeating the Orioles. While they were doing so, however, the Brooklyns were annihilating Cincinnati, so St. Louis gained nothing on the leaders. It is an uphill fight for the Browns, and nothing but marvelous playing from this time out will win them the pennant.

—St. Louis *Post-Dispatch*

President Von der Ahe telegraphed this morning from Baltimore that he had formally entered a protest with the Board of Directors of the American Association against the three Kansas City games with Brooklyn, played in Brooklyn last week, in which Bushong was allowed to umpire. The laws of the Association absolutely demand that, in the absence of a regular Association umpire, one of three substitute umpires, whose names must be furnished the President of the Association before the beginning of each season, must officiate. Not only did President Byrne see that no regular umpire was on hand, but his substitute umpires were employed in a neighboring graveyard and were dead to the world. He hid them away, and then with his ready tool Watkins, the Kansas City manager, proceeded to effect his scheme to get the lead in the Association race. Byrne "induced" Watkins to let Bushong umpire. Bushong did umpire, and Brooklyn won three games, hands down. Watkins did not even make a bluff to have one of his own men officiate with Bushong to give the series an air of fairness and respectability at least. In the face of this proceeding, evidently concocted against the St. Louis club, President Von der Ahe has filed his protest. If the Board of Directors of the American Association are fair minded and want to see fair play, they will throw out the three games in question and have them either played over in accordance with the rules, or serve a just rebuke to Byrne and his underhand methods by counting them against the Brooklyn club record.

—St. Louis *Post-Dispatch*

Friday, September 6

On September 5, New York lost to Indianapolis 3–5 (Keefe 20–12).
Boston lost to Pittsburg 4–10 (Radbourn 17–10).
Brooklyn beat Cincinnati 6–3 (Hughes 8–7).
St. Louis tied at Baltimore 5–5.
NL: Boston 65–38, New York 66–39.
AA: Brooklyn 75–37, St. Louis 72–38.

Since the Giants took possession of the Coogan estate and built their diamond on it Mr. James J. Coogan has become an ardent admirer of the game. Baseball, he judged from the large crowds that witnessed the contests on the new grounds, is a paying pastime, and several times he intimated that he would like to have some of the New-York Club's stock. After the game yesterday afternoon he called on President John B. Day and asked if any of the stock could be purchased.

"Oh yes," remarked Mr. Day in an off-hand manner, "it all depends on how much is offered."

Mr. Coogan thereupon said that he would give $200,000 for the franchise of the club. That offer caused Mr. Day to smile, and he informed Mr. Coogan that the sum was not big enough to secure a controlling interest. Since the Metropolitan Exhibition Company was formed in the Fall of 1880, the profits have been enormous, and it is said that the old Mets and the present New-York Club have cleared about $750,000. The diamond-field sport is increasing each year in public favor, and Messrs. Day, Dillingham, Appleton, and Gordon, the holders of the stock, are not inclined to sell. The former, however, who is a very shrewd business man, said that if he could get more than he thought his interest is worth he would part with it, but the sum would have to be much larger than the one offered by Mr. Coogan.

—New York *Times*

It was Ladies' day yesterday at Washington Park, and a most attractive scene was presented in the grand stand. Each week do the fair patrons of the game look forward to Thursday as the bright particular day of the week, and the Brooklyn team have come to regard that day as the one when victory smiles upon them most approvingly, for hitherto the team have invariably been invincible on Ladies' day. Apparently the presence of so many pretty girls on the grand stand, too, had an inspiring effect in the Cincinnati players, for they put up the strongest game of the series on the occasion.

The simple fact was that with the encouraging rays of light from the bright eyes of the fair assemblage on the grand stand the Bridegrooms saw points of play and made them which on ordinary occasions they lose sight of, while the effect on the visitors was to dazzle them somewhat.

—Brooklyn *Daily Eagle*

Evidently President Chris Von der Ahe, of the St. Louis Club, has lost his presence of mind, and he is rapidly approaching that mental condition when the services of an inquiring committee on lunacy will find their services needed. Not content with charging one of his most serviceable and honest players with crookedness, which he was utterly unable to prove, and demoralizing his team with experiments in engaging new players who turn out failures, but he really pitches into the captain of the team, who has actually been unscrupulous in his efforts to promote the success of the team by fair play or foul, and now that this demoralizing work of his yields it natural consequence in repeated defeats of his team he gnashes his teeth in rage and goes in like a bull against a locomotive in charging all kinds of dishonesty, first against one of the straightest umpires in the national game, and lastly against the president of the Brooklyn Club, whose integrity of character stands out in the association firmament like a bright particular star. Verily, "whom the gods would destroy they first make mad."

—Brooklyn *Daily Eagle*

Saturday, September 7

On September 6, New York lost to Indianapolis 4–5 (Welch 24–10).
Boston beat Pittsburg 5–0 (Clarkson 37–14).
St. Louis lost at Baltimore 2–3 (King 31–16).
NL: Boston 66–38, New York 66–40.
AA: Brooklyn 75–37, St. Louis 72–39.

It was not the fault of Clarkson that he did not have a clean score of victories this week. He is pitching great ball, and he is the cheapest salaried man in the club when the returns from his work are considered. He has been worth just about $70,000 to the Boston club this season. Bravo, John.

Clarkson says that he will break all records this season for games pitched, games won, and strike outs. There may be some question as to Clarkson's ability to take all these records, but there seems to be no question about one thing, and that is that Mr. Clarkson is troubled with a touch of expansion of the cranium.—[New York *Press*]. If there was ever an excuse for enlargement of the head, there seems to be one in this case. If Boston wins the championship, no man in the club can be said to have done so much toward securing it as Clarkson.—[Cleveland *Leader*].

—Boston *Herald*

George Pinkney beats the record in one thing, and that is persistency in playing every game. He has played no less than 645 consecutive championship games with his club, 586 straight of which have been at third base, the most remarkable case of steady play on record.

—Brooklyn *Daily Eagle*

To-day there opens at Brooklyn the most important series of the year in the American Association. On the result of the three games to be played there between the Browns and Bridegrooms to-day, Monday and Tuesday depends very largely the championship of the Association. Should the Browns take all three games at Brooklyn it would place them in the lead. With this lead the Browns should win the championship, as after playing the Athletics four games they come West, and from that time on play the weak Western clubs, while Brooklyn is brushing up against the strong teams of the East.

—St. Louis *Post-Dispatch*

Sunday, September 8

On September 7, New York beat Indianapolis 12–4 (O'Day 7–1).
Boston beat Pittsburg 5–3 (Daley 3–3).

Brooklyn declared forfeit winner over St. Louis 9–0.
NL: Boston 67–38, New York 67–40.
AA: Brooklyn 76–37, St. Louis 72–40.

Brooklyn, N.Y., September 7—The crowd was good-natured, well-behaved and full of enthusiasm. The people came from all quarters and represented almost every walk in life. In the long lines that were formed from the ticket windows as early as 1 o'clock, ministers elbowed politicians, the millionaire's toes were ruthlessly trodden on by the demonstrative bootblack, and the menial office boy took his turn on the line with as much importance as did his employer, yet all were content with their lot and strove only to get into the grounds as quickly as possible in order to get a seat. But only about half of them were successful. By 3 o'clock the stands were filled and all those who came later had to be content with a sofa of green turf or a stand against the ropes that encircled the field.

The exciting stage of the race and the fact that this was the first time the two clubs were to meet this season with Brooklyn in the lead was enough to draw a big crowd, but in addition the series has had more gratuitous advertising during the past week than the most ambitious star could wish for. Comiskey's and Von der Ahe's talk served well to keep the games uppermost in the people's minds.

The Browns are stopping at a New York hotel, and did not follow the example of the other Association clubs of driving to the grounds in uniform. They straggled in one by one, with their gripsacks, and received the hospitality of the Brooklyn Club's dressing room. At 3:15 the first bell was sounded and the Browns marched on the field to take their practice. A remarkably weak round of applause greeted them and this lack of enthusiasm was the more noticeable in that the Browns have always been heartily welcomed heretofore. But the crowds were evidently sore at Comiskey and the club for their unkind words and took this means of showing their resentment. The second bell, twenty minutes later, was the signal for the Brooklyns' appearance, and as the boys emerged from the old stone house a cheer and hurrah arose from the throngs that showed an appreciation of the team's brilliant work of late in an unmistakable and encouraging manner. The team was the same as has played regularly in every game for over two months without a break. Not a man of them had as much as a bruise to hinder good play, and all were in the pink of condition and a splendid looking lot of men they are too.

The second inning was one long to be remembered in Brooklyn. Both pitchers were on their mettle and six men gave evidence of the twirlers' ability. Clark, Smith and O'Brien struck out, leaving Caruthers

Washington Park, Brooklyn (Transcendental Graphics).

on second base. Caruthers duplicated Chamberlain's work by striking out Comiskey, Robinson and Duffee in order as they came to the bat.

—St. Louis *Post-Dispatch*

After unsuccessfully trying to bunt the sphere Latham mumbled to himself, walked around the home plate like a chicken with its head cut off and then tried again. Pinkney's fumble allowed him to reach the initial bag, but Clark's deadly throw to second rendered him hors de combat. How the crowd did guy him! Latham, the clown, who always caused unlimited merriment by his antics and hippodromes, did not begin his funny tricks until the sixth inning, when the St. Louis team had scored. He woke up then and made the spectators laugh at his witty sayings and repartee. At one time, while at the bat, he yelled to McGunnigle, the Brooklyn manager, who was showing signs of nervousness, to stop pulling his mustache and not to hoodoo him. Again, just as O'Neill was about to meet a ball, he said: "Oh! Look at that hit," and the remark was well timed, too, for the left fielder cracked out a ball which enabled one of his fellow players to cross the plate. When the Missourians tied the score he turned flipflaps, stood on his hands and rolled over the ground in a perfect paroxysm of delight. Of course, the spectators looked distressed, but they had to laugh at the clown's action nevertheless.

—Brooklyn *Daily Eagle*

The sixth inning ended with St. Louis in the van by 3 to 2. Now came the tug of war as Brooklyn went in to their seventh inning at 5:40

P.M. with a cloudy atmosphere, but the sun still well up in the west. The St. Louis captain now began his bulldozing tactics to delay the game into darkness and kept up arguments with the umpire, despite fines, for delay. It was now 5:50 P.M. and the umpire noted the time and got ready to call the game in case Comiskey did not resume play promptly. The eighth inning was then played with the result of blanks to both sides, and once more Comiskey and his gang tried to bulldoze the umpire. But he adhered to his determination to have the game played out as long as he himself could see the ball. Despite over half an hour's intentional delay by the visitors, it was only 6:18 P.M. when the Brooklyns went to the bat in their ninth inning, and when Smith reached base on an error by Milligan, Comiskey called his men in, who took up the bats and marched off the field, to the disgust of every impartial spectator on the field, he contemptuously disregarded the umpire's call to the St. Louis field to play ball. Goldsmith took his watch, waited the legal time, and, the St. Louis players not returning, he then and there gave the game to Brooklyn as forfeited by 9 to 0. And with this decision goes all bets, as also the penalty of the $1,500 fine which the St. Louis Club must pay to Brooklyn.

When the Western players marched off the field they were the recipients of such hooting, cat calls, hisses and adjectives not nice to print that it made them look around in alarm, and it is safe to say that they will never forget the scene, nor will their ears stop tingling for some time with the volume of sound which met them.

—Brooklyn *Daily Eagle*

Not in the history of professional ball playing in this city has the game received such a blow to its continued favor with the best patrons of the national game as was given it yesterday at Washington Park at the hands of the St. Louis Club players and the club's president, the latter of whom sat on the bench and aided and abetted Captain Comiskey and his gang in their ball playing tricks on the field and in their bold and impudent exhibition of the bulldozing work through which they have gained so many of their victories this season. Hundreds were present yesterday who, on witnessing the disgraceful conduct of the visiting team in the closing part of the contest, declared that if that was professional ball playing they would have nothing to do with it.

—Brooklyn *Daily Eagle*

Late last night President Von der Ahe telegraphed Secretary Munson that the St. Louis Browns would play no more games this season in Brooklyn owing to the insufficiency of protection for the team while on the field. He stated that McCarthy and other members of the Browns were mobbed by the crowd of excited Brooklynites who broke into the field during the trouble in yesterday's game. This action on the part of President Von der Ahe will be costly to the Brooklyn club, as it will lose them thousands of dollars. It is a settled fact that the Brooklyn team propose to win the pennant by hook or crook and President Von der Ahe is not the kind of man to stand idly by and see them do it.

—St. Louis *Post-Dispatch*

In exactly four weeks the league championship season of 1889 will be a thing of the past, and the question which has been uppermost in the minds of thousands of people for months will have been settled. It will be the fault of the Boston directorate, and of no one else, if the championship does not come to this city. Boston cannot rely solely upon the work of Pitcher Clarkson, and, as matters stand, this it will have to do if it wishes to be sure of victory. The other pitchers are not in his class, nor in the class with the fine group of twirlers who make the New York club so strong in the attack. From the beginning of the season Clarkson has been the only Boston pitcher who has been at all effective. The directors have been well aware of this fact and have done nothing to remedy matters.

President Day was in the best of humor this evening after the game when the *Herald* correspondent saw him, and he said: "This is the hardest fight I have witnessed in some years, and the question is not settled yet. We are not out of the race yet, and we will make things lively for the Bostons before the struggle is over." Just then Manager Mutrie came up, and the first thing he said was: "Oh, we are still the people, and we will get there yet. We have the pitchers, and that is going to tell in this race. Now, I am going to give you a pointer," continued the genial manager, "and you can put it down in black and white, we will be in the lead when we start on our last western trip, and the next time we get into the lead we will hold it until the end of the season."

—Boston *Herald*

Monday, September 9

On September 8, Brooklyn won by forfeit over St. Louis 9–0.
AA: Brooklyn 77–37, St. Louis 72–41.

A great crowd went out to Ridgewood Park yesterday to see the Brooklyn and St. Louis teams play the second game of their series. As President Byrne had received notice from Von der Ahe that his team would not go over and play, the gates were thrown open at 3 o'clock and everybody permitted to enter free.

At 3:30 Umpire Goldsmith took out his watch and gave notice that he would give the St. Louis men five minutes to appear. As they did not show up, he gave the game to Brooklyn, according to the rules, by a score of 9 to 0. The rule in the case is as follows:

Rule 26. A forfeited game shall be declared by the umpire in favor of the club not in fault at the request of such club in the following cases:

Section 1. If the nine of the club fail to appear upon the field, or being upon the field fail to begin the game within five minutes after the umpire has called "Play" at the hour appointed for the beginning of the game, or unless such delay in appearing or in commencing the game be unavoidable.

Constitution of the American Association.

Section 9. Any member shall be subject to expulsion under the following rules: First—for failure to play out the full schedule of championship games or for willfully failing to present its nine at the time and place agreed upon to play any championship game unless the failure is caused by an unavoidable accident.

The action of Von der Ahe in disappointing the spectators was generally denounced as a disgrace to baseball. There is nothing for the Association to do now but expel him. President Byrne received a telegram from W.C. Wikoff, President of the Association, saying that he had notified the "boss President" of the penalty. When Byrne was approached on the subject he said that he would push the case to the bitter end, for, while he was sorry to see such a dilemma arise, there was nothing to do but expel the club whose manager dared to break one of the most important rules in baseball.

Mr. Von der Ahe was seen at the Grand Central Hotel. He said that he was prepared to take the consequences, let come what may. "Why, my men would not go over to play ball for $1,000 apiece. They were afraid of their lives. We may play Tuesday if we are guaranteed good police protection."

—New York *Times*

New York, Sept. 8, 1889—True to his word, President Von der Ahe of the St. Louis team refused to take his team to Ridgewood today and play the game scheduled to be played at that place. It is the first instance on record that a club has failed to appear on the field through fear, for that is the reason the management of the club give for their refusal to go to the ball field. When Chris made his threats on Saturday night every one thought that he spoke in the heat of passion, and that he would change his mind after a night of rest. He did nothing of the kind.

Mr. Von der Ahe, being interviewed tonight, said: "If with their police arrangements at Washington Park on Saturday they could not protect us, how would they do it at Ridgewood without police? I was stoned at Ridgewood last year, and I don't want any more of it. My players told me last night that they would not go to Ridgewood for $1000 each. They were afraid of their lives. The crowd assaulted McCarthy, Robinson and Comiskey on Saturday, and things looked dangerous for me at one time. If I had had a pistol, I might have been tempted to use it. Goldsmith acknowledged to our men that he knew it was too dark to play that game on Saturday."

—Boston *Herald*

A period has been reached in the history of the American Association when it becomes a question of vital importance to the future welfare of the organization as to whether one individual member of the association is to be disciplined for the benefit of the remainder, or whether the offender is to be allowed to continue his objectionable methods with immunity from the legal punishment his misconduct has subjected him to. Mr. Chris Von der Ahe, the president of the St. Louis Club, has time and again created lots of trouble for the American Association by his reckless utterances while under the influence of an uncontrollable temper. But the worst breaks he has ever made have been those which have characterized his public utterances within the past month and especially the wild reckless action he has taken within the past week. Not content with injuring the well earned reputation the national game possesses, of being the most honestly conducted sport in vogue, by making charges of crookedness against his own players which have been shown to be false and grossly unjust, he adds insult to the injury by impugning the integrity of character of a well known member of the association's staff of umpires, whose lifetime honesty of conduct is as a household word. And to these offenses is to be added a gross violation of the rules of play governing the game, followed by the climax of an open and willful disregard of the constitutional law of the association he has done his worst to bring into public disrepute. This is the indictment which to-day brings the president of the St. Louis Club before the Board of Directors of the American Association to answer for such willful violation of its laws as is likely to damage its good name to the extent of a financial loss of thousands of dollars to the clubs most affected by the injurious effect of his discreditable conduct.

When Mr. Byrne was notified by telegraph that the St. Louis Club president would play no more games in Brooklyn he had a personal interview with him, and, to his surprise, was informed that the only conditions on which the St. Louis Club would again play in Brooklyn were that Mr. Byrne should treat the umpire's decision in regard to Saturday's game with contempt, allow that game to be recorded as won by St. Louis and ignore the $1,500 penalty the St. Louis Club had incurred. Could reckless assurance and impudent effrontery go further? It is needless to state that the offer was indignantly declined.

—Brooklyn *Daily Eagle*

Manage McGunnigle said: "I never saw a man make a greater mistake than Von der Ahe is making. He is a bad loser and has lost his head because he is in danger of losing the pennant. Comiskey has had his own way all his life and thought he could bulldoze and rob us on our ground as well as he did on his own. The St. Louis men were not mobbed, not injured and not in danger."

James Mutrie, manager of the New Yorks, said it was a disgrace to base ball for Von der Ahe to act as he did. "The association must expel the team," continued Mr. Mutrie, "for the sake of honest ball. If we were not protected by the strictest kind of rules the game would soon go to the dogs. I do not care how powerful a man is he cannot break the rules with impunity, and the sooner severe methods are adopted, why, the better it will be for the game. It does not seem that there is any way out of it but for Von der Ahe to go."

—Brooklyn *Daily Eagle*

New York, September 9—The row between the Brooklyn and St. Louis nines is the sensation of the day in sporting circles. Nothing else is talked about at the present hour. Von der Ahe and Byrne are in hiding somewhere in earnest conference trying to fix things up to play the game to-morrow. Von der Ahe remains firm and declares he is afraid of his nine being mobbed. There are lively times ahead in the American Association. The forfeited game of Saturday at Brooklyn has been more far reaching in its results than the big crowd had any idea of when it dispersed after its unpleasant conclusion. The St. Louis club has since committed itself in a way that lays it liable to expulsion from the American Association, and has created the biggest base ball sensation of the year. This is the most serious infraction that the rules and constitution of the American Association have ever suffered, and that organization will be compelled to take extreme measures in order to maintain its dignity, or else take water.

—St. Louis *Post-Dispatch*

The whole affair would appear to be a very poor piece of business management on the part of Mr. Von der Ahe. Undoubtedly there is something back of it all, however. From the opening of the season the Brooklyn Club in some mysterious manner has had all the umpires aiding them, and no doubt on the present trip the Browns have been given a pretty rough dose of it by those emissaries of Byrne. Mr. Von der Ahe evidently saw it was useless to endeavor to win against the evident intent of the umpires, and determined not to go through the form of playing games which it had been ordained beforehand they should lose. If the Association does not right the matter he will evidently enter the League with his club. He is not the man to pay the fines imposed upon him or to submit to games being forfeited against him. He knows the League will receive him with open arms, and, therefore, expulsion from the American Association has no terror for him. The withdrawal of the Browns from the Association would be a severe blow to that organization and a strong addition to the League. If the present trouble results in the Browns entering the League the people of St. Louis will be grateful it occurred, for it has been the desire here for years to have the team enter that organization, where the clubs are stronger and better able to cope with them.

—St. Louis *Post-Dispatch*

Tuesday, September 10

On September 9, New York beat Cleveland 11–5 (Keefe 21–12).
Boston tied Chicago 0–0.
NL: Boston 67–38, New York 68–40.

Apparently without any trouble the Giants won a game from their Cleveland opponents on the Polo Grounds yesterday afternoon. As Boston and Chicago played a "tie" game, the victory achieved by the Giants places them in close proximity to the leaders. They are now only 8 points behind Boston, and the result of one game in New-York's favor will place the latter in the lead.

The result of the game in Boston yesterday was eagerly watched in this city. In saloons crowds could be seen standing around tickers, and in places where bulletins were displayed the streets were thronged with diamond-field enthusiasts. As each inning was registered and scores put up for both clubs a series of "Ohs!" went up from the assemblage. When the result was announced the crowds wended their way homeward, pleased that the Bostons had not secured a victory.

—New York *Times*

The home base was a vainly coveted point for the members of the Boston and Chicago clubs yesterday. It was a battle of pitchers. Clarkson and Hutchinson were in fine form, and it seemed almost child's play for them to dispose of opposing batsmen.

—Boston *Herald*

New York, September 10—The twentieth and last game of the year between the St. Louis and Brooklyn clubs will be played at Washington Park this afternoon. The St. Louis President has made up his mind to play the game if police protection is accorded him. He informed President Byrne of that fact yesterday morning in the following telegram:

> *C.H. Byrne, Brooklyn:*
> If you will guarantee us sufficient police protection we will play.
> *Chris Von der Ahe.*

In reply to this Mr. Byrne sent the following:

> *C.Von der Ahe, Grand Central Hotel, New York:*
> The rules require us to furnish proper police to preserve order on our grounds. This we have always done and will continue to do so. The record of six years here shows how effectually we have done this.
> *C.H. Byrne.*

—St. Louis *Post-Dispatch*

Columbus, September 10—A reporter of the *Post-Dispatch* saw President Wikoff and asked what was going to be done about the Brooklyn-St. Louis controversy. The President was inclined to be uncommunicative regarding the matter, but said that as yet he had taken no action regarding the calling of a meeting, and would not do so until he saw the outcome of the game scheduled for to-day. If Von der Ahe refused to play then he will call a meeting for Thursday or Friday.

When asked as to his opinion of Von der Ahe's stand, he said he thought the St. Louis President had made a mistake, that he should have put in an appearance at Ridgewood Park on Sunday and played the game, protesting

Wheeler Wikoff, president, American Association (New York *Clipper*, April 6, 1889).

the one of Saturday if he thought the grounds sufficient for doing so, but that in staying away and openly refusing to play again in Brooklyn he weakened his case.

"What do you think of the possibility of his being made to surrender his charter?" was asked.

"I consider that part of the constitution virtually a dead letter. It would be impossible to enforce it without carrying the matter to the courts, and there the case would not hold. It would be compelling a man to give something for nothing. In regard to the whole matter I am very sorry that the difficulty has arisen and I am not anxious to hold a meeting until both parties in the controversy have had time to cool down somewhat."

—St. Louis *Post-Dispatch*

AMERICAN ASSOCIATION STANDINGS

	W	L	PCT.	GB		W	L	PCT.	GB
Brooklyn	77	37	.675	—	Cincinnati	60	55	.522	17½
St. Louis	72	41	.637	4½	Kansas City	47	67	.412	30
Baltimore	64	46	.582	11	Columbus	48	69	.410	30½
Athletic	62	48	.564	13	Louisville	24	91	.209	53½

NATIONAL LEAGUE STANDINGS

	W	L	PCT.	GB		W	L	PCT.	GB
Boston	67	38	.638	—	Cleveland	53	58	.477	17
New York	68	40	.630	½	Indianapolis	49	65	.430	22½
Philadelphia	58	51	.532	11	Pittsburg	49	66	.426	23
Chicago	58	55	.513	13	Washington	38	67	.362	29

Wednesday, September 11

On September 10, Boston beat Chicago 2–1 (Radbourn 18–10).
NL: Boston 68–38, New York 68–40.

Over 3700 people saw the Boston and Chicago nines engage in another great battle for supremacy yesterday afternoon, and when the run that put the Bostons ahead was made in the 13th inning, there was an almost unlimited amount of cheering and applause. The game abounded in brilliant plays on both sides, and few ever played upon the grounds have been more exciting.

Radbourn was on the cards to pitch, and few expected that he would make as brilliant an exhibition as was the case. Again and again he was applauded during the game, and when, in the 11th inning, he struck out

Duffy and Pfeffer and caused Anson to bat a fly ball to Johnston, he came in for a regular ovation.

The most exciting inning in the whole game was the 13th, and nine-tenths of the people present acted like lunatics and yelled in a manner that threatened with calamity throat and lungs.

—Boston *Herald*

Even when Brouthers is well he does not seem to play with his old-time animation. What is the matter with the big man? He plays little like the leading batsman in the country. Come, Dan, make a brace. This is just about the time for you to get your work in.

—Boston *Herald*

A letter was received from President Von der Ahe this morning in which several circumstances not known before are detailed. He says: "As I was leaving the players' bench to go to Byrne's office, some contemptible whelp threw a beer glass at me, and it came very near hitting me on the head. This is a pretty state of affairs to exist in the city of churches. As the Browns were on the way to the dressing room, a stone was hurled at McCarthy and it struck him in the face. He was unable to eat his supper, and I had to send for a surgeon to have him examined, fearful that his jaw was broken. While the players were dressing, cobble stones were fired through the windows at them, and it was only good fortune that saved them from being disabled, possibly for life. All the money in Brooklyn could not have induced me to take the Browns to Ridgewood on Sunday. The players positively refused to go, knowing that they were in danger of having bodily injury done to them. This terrible state of affairs is due to Byrne, and he alone must be held accountable for its existence."

—St. Louis *Post-Dispatch*

Thursday, September 12

No games were played on September 11.

Friday, September 13

On September 12, Boston beat Cleveland twice 3–2 and 5–0
(Clarkson 38–14;Clarkson 39–14).
NL: Boston 70–38, New York 68–40.

By defeating the Clevelands in both of the games played on the South end grounds yesterday afternoon, the Bostons increased their lead over the New Yorks to 18 points, and strengthened their position most materially. Clarkson pitched in both games, and in but one inning was he called upon to exert himself. In fact, he felt the strain of both games so little that he declared that he could have pitched in a third contest had it been necessary. Manager Hart remarked after the game that Clarkson was the pitching wonder of the age, and that the beauty of it was that his head was not at all swelled by his skill or success.

Dan Brouthers was warmly greeted upon his return, but he acted as if he had become rusty by his absence from the nine, and he did not bat with his usual vim, finding it a difficult matter to send the ball out of the diamond, and going out for the most part on easy fly balls. He went to the bat eight times and did not make one hit. And it was the sixth time he struck out this season.

—Boston *Herald*

At 10 o'clock to-morrow morning a special meeting of the American Association was to be held at the Continental Hotel, Philadelphia, to take action in the recent trouble between the Browns and Brooklyns, but the meeting has been postponed until the 23rd, when it will be held at Cincinnati.

—St. Louis *Post-Dispatch*

Saturday, September 14

On September 13, Boston lost to and tied Cleveland
0–3 and 4–4 (Radbourn 18–11).
St. Louis lost at Athletic 0–11 (Chamberlain 29–13).
NL: Boston 70–39, New York 68–40.
AA: Brooklyn 77–37, St. Louis 72–42.

Rad never smiled. The score stood 4 to 3 against the Bostons, and there were two men out in the ninth inning of the second game when he came to the bat. Smith and Bennett had both struck out, and the croakers in the grand stand and the army of the disappointed and poor losers groaned aloud. Many had left their seats and were on their way to the gate. A beat—and the second one of the day—was conceded. No one dreamed that Radbourn of all men would hit the ball safely. Why, he had not made a safe hit in the game, and had not batted the ball outside the diamond. He make a hit! Impossible.

It is the unexpected that always happens in base ball, and somehow

"Hoss" Radbourn, pitcher, Boston Beaneaters (shown here "tagging out" teammate Billy Nash). (Library of Congress, Prints and Photographs Division [LOT 13163-05, no. 16]).

Radbourn managed to connect with a ball that Pitcher Gruber gave to him, and that ball somehow wended its winged way over that left field fence, while 4000 people got up in their boots and made more noise than any like number had ever made on the South end grounds.

It took some of them a long time to get over their astonishment, and some are not over it yet. They yelled and howled, and for a time pandemonium was let loose. It was well worth while being present to witness this scene. The ladies were as much beside themselves as the gentlemen, and they so far forgot themselves as to join in the cheering, while the heightened color of their faces as they left the grounds showed how the excitement had told upon them. It was one of the most dramatic scenes ever enacted at the South end.

—Boston *Herald*

The Browns met with their usual defeat at Philadelphia yesterday, and it was a crushing one, too. The grounds were in miserable condition, and the water on them had to be swept with brooms and sawdust sprinkled freely all over them to enable the clubs to play.

—St. Louis *Post-Dispatch*

Once more the rumor that the Brotherhood is going to form a syndicate and manage the clubs of the League is going the rounds. The Chicago Club's grounds, it is said, have been leased by men representing the Brotherhood. The managers and stockholders of clubs, however, pay but little attention to the rumor. They regard it as one of the annual "strikes" for higher salaries.

—New York *Times*

Sunday, September 15

On September 14, New York beat Chicago twice 3–1 and 13–3
(Welch 25–10; Keefe 22–12).
Boston beat and lost to Cleveland 8–2 and 0–4
(Clarkson 40–14; Madden 9–10).
Brooklyn beat Louisville twice 6–2 and 6–3
(Caruthers 32–9; Hughes 9–7).
St. Louis won and tied at Athletic 5–1 and 4–4 (King 32–16).
NL: Boston 71–40, New York 70–40.
AA: Brooklyn 79–37, St. Louis 73–42.

Slowly but surely the Giants are creeping toward the winning goal.
To-day they are only four points behind Boston, and the result of one
game may place the champions in the lead for diamond field honors. This
state of affairs was brought about by the result of the games played yesterday. To the surprise but intense delight of all lovers of the game in
this city, Anson's aggregation of brawn and muscle from Chicago twice
bowed to the superiority of the Giants. In Boston it was different. After
losing one game, the little men from Cleveland known as the Infants
showed Bostonians what they knew about our popular sport by administering a defeat of the "whitewash" character to the haughty representatives of the "Hub." It was a hard defeat at this stage of the contest, and
it is safe to say that there is no joy in Boston.

—New York *Times*

Chicago, Ill., September 14—Hints of various kinds touching an
important move to be made by the brotherhood of base ball players have
been published recently, but none of them have covered the ground. The
Journal this afternoon publishes the following:
The report that the brotherhood of ball players intend to take the
game out of the hands of the present owners of the league clubs seems
to have some foundation. They are preparing to gobble the whole business, grounds, players, audiences and all. And what's more, they don't
propose to lose any time in doing it.
The plan of the brotherhood is to run the game, so far as the league
cities are concerned, on a sort of co-operative basis. It is proposed to
place the management of the whole affair in the hands of a general committee of eight, consisting of one representative of each league club.
These clubs will probably be formed in New York, Boston, Chicago,
Philadelphia, Brooklyn, Cincinnati, Washington and Cleveland or St.
Louis. Each club will have a stock capital of $20,000, some of which will
be taken by the players and the rest by the men who are to act as officers
and financial backers.

The players are to receive a small, but fair salary, and a percentage of the net profits. The receipts, after all expenses—including the players' salaries—are paid, are to be put into a pool and divided into eight equal parts, one share going to each club. It is hoped by this to bring the cities all on the same financial footing and do away with the claim that the strong cities are making money at the expense of the weak.

Another new feature will be the hanging up of big money prizes for the first and second and perhaps third club in the championship race. The amount has not been yet determined, but it has been suggested that each club put say $5,000 in the pot at the opening of the season. This would make $40,000 to play for, of which the winning team would take $25,000, the second $10,000 and the third $5,000. This would, it is believed, invest the game with an interest which does not now attach to the flying of a mere championship pennant.

—Brooklyn *Daily Eagle*

Monday, September 16

On September 15, Brooklyn beat Louisville twice 6–5 and 7–2
(Lovett 15–8; Terry 19–13).
St. Louis lost at Athletic 1–8 (Chamberlain 29–14).
AA: Brooklyn 81–37, St. Louis 73–43.

The contest at Ridgewood yesterday morning between the Brooklyn and Louisville teams began at 10:25 A.M. and it did not end until 1:20 P.M., during which time fourteen innings had to be played.

After the contest the hungry players of both teams, the umpire and the scribes were taken to the Ridgewood Hotel to dinner, during which time rain fell and it looked rather unpromising for the second game; but it was commenced at 2:45 P.M., with a drizzling sea fog rain falling, but it cleared up sufficiently to allow the game to be finished.

—Brooklyn *Daily Eagle*

The *Eagle*'s exclusive news yesterday that the Grand Jury in Queens County would begin an investigation of Sunday base ball at Ridgewood was verified this afternoon by the appearance in Queens County Court House at Long Island City of Charles H. Byrne, president of the Brooklyn Club. He was there under subpoena and very much against his will. In company with him were Messrs. Mayer and Wallace, of the Ridgewood Amusement Company, under whose auspices base ball is played on Sunday; Christian Homeyer, owner of the property included in the park grounds, and Deputy Sheriffs Robert Haslem and Joseph Siebert, who do duty at Ridgewood on Sunday.

It was regarded as an extraordinary proceeding to summon before the county inquisitors, with a view to making them witnesses, the men whom it is proposed to indict for misdemeanor, and it is questioned whether an indictment founded on the statements of the men themselves can stand.

—Brooklyn *Daily Eagle*

Everything indicates that Cincinnati will make an effort to get into the league this fall. The deal is being worked very quietly, but it is being worked all the same. It is going to take a great deal of money to arrange matters, but come it will. Then Brooklyn will step into the place of Washington. The trouble that St. Louis is making simply precipitates the arrangement. There will be some great surprises and changes in store for lovers of the game next season.

—Boston *Herald*

Tuesday, September 17

On September 16, New York won at Washington 12–4 (O'Day 8–1). Boston lost to Philadelphia 2–3 (Clarkson 40–15). NL: New York 71–40, Boston 71–41.

Washington, Sept. 16—The New-York-Giants achieved a double victory to-day. Through hard and consecutive batting, aided by several damaging errors, they experienced no trouble whatever in defeating the Senators. Then, too, Boston's defeat at the hands of Philadelphia displace the former club in favor of New-York, who secured the lead for the championship.

—New York *Times*

AMERICAN ASSOCIATION STANDINGS

	W	L	PCT.	GB		W	L	PCT.	GB
Brooklyn	81	37	.686	—	Cincinnati	62	57	.521	19½
St. Louis	73	43	.629	7	Kansas City	49	68	.419	31½
Baltimore	65	48	.575	13½	Columbus	50	71	.413	32½
Athletic	64	49	.566	14½	Louisville	24	95	.202	57½

NATIONAL LEAGUE STANDINGS

	W	L	PCT.	GB		W	L	PCT.	GB
New York	71	40	.640	—	Cleveland	55	61	.474	18½
Boston	71	41	.634	½	Indianapolis	52	66	.441	22½
Philadelphia	60	52	.536	11½	Pittsburg	49	67	.422	24½
Chicago	58	59	.496	16	Washington	39	69	.361	30½

Wednesday, September 18

On September 17, Boston beat Philadelphia 5–1 (Radbourn 19–11).
NL: New York 71–40, Boston 72–41.

In the second inning Smith made one of the finest plays ever seen
on the grounds, and the star play of the game. That fast runner, Fogarty,
hit a ball that bounded high from Radbourn's hand. Smith made a great
run across the diamond, clutched the ball between the first and second
bases, and threw it to first without trying to recover and got his man out.
It was a wonderful piece of work, and the spectators applauded for a long
time, as it deserved.

—Boston *Herald*

Thursday, September 19

On September 18, New York won twice at
Washington 7–4 and 10–4 (Keefe 23–12; Crane 12–10).
Boston beat Philadelphia 9–1 (Clarkson 41–15).
Brooklyn tied at Athletic 11–11.
St. Louis won at Kansas City 7–2 (King 33–16).
NL: New York 73–40, Boston 73–41.
AA: Brooklyn 81–37, St. Louis 74–43.

Washington, Sept. 18—In the first game the two Keefes were pitted
against each other, and up to the tenth inning both were equally effective.
The second game was poorly played on both sides, and was called at the
end of the sixth inning on account of darkness.

—New York *Times*

Fortune smiled kindly upon the Bostons yesterday afternoon, and
allowed a game to be played. There were 1848 people who were anxious
enough to take the chances of visiting the grounds and of being disappointed, and they were well repaid for their trouble. There were very few,
indeed, who had any idea that a game of ball would be played, for it had
been raining hard during the night and morning. It was not until late that
the placards announcing a game were put on the cars. Manager Hag-
gerty was busy all day doing all that he could to keep the grounds in playing condition, and he deserves great credit for the success that he
achieved. A plentiful supply of sawdust helped matters amazingly.

—Boston *Herald*

Saturday afternoon the Browns will meet the Cincinnatis at Sports-man's Park in the first of three championship games. The feeling between the two teams is of bitter nature, because of the openly expressed desire from Porktown of "Anything to beat St. Louis for the pennant."

—St. Louis *Post-Dispatch*

The Western papers have decided that the Cincinnati Club is to take Indianapolis' place in the league in 1890, the latter club being amalgamated with the Cincinnatis. This is owing to the stoppage of Sunday games. What Brooklyn will do in such case is not decided. Chicago, Cleveland, and Pittsburg want Brooklyn in the league, as does Philadelphia, but Day and Soden are opposed to it. Brooklyn would go if asked. If they do, they will buy out Washington and go in in that city's place, Washington and Indianapolis entering the American Association. Both those cities deny the two reports. The league would not have St. Louis again as a gift. Its pool rooms and Sunday games would prevent that, not to mention Von der Ahe.

—Brooklyn *Daily Eagle*

Friday, September 20

On September 19, New York won at Philadelphia 12–5 (O'Day 9–1). Boston won at Washington 6–2 (Clarkson 42–15). Brooklyn lost at Athletic 10–12 (Hughes 9–8). St. Louis won at Kansas City 13–3 (Chamberlain 30–14). NL: New York 74–40, Boston 74–41. AA: Brooklyn 81–38, St. Louis 75–43.

Philadelphia, Sept. 19—By a vigorous use of the bat the Giants succeeded in winning a ball from the League team of this city to-day. The feature of the game was the batting of Tiernan, who made two home runs and one single.

—New York *Times*

Mike Tiernan, right fielder, New York Giants (Library of Congress, Prints and Photographs Division [LOT 13163-05, no. 214]).

Washington, D.C., Sept. 19, 1889—The Bostons went into today's game with their spirits thoroughly aroused. The men had learned some very unpleasant rumors since they arrived in the city. These rumors related to the exhibition given by the Washingtons in their games this week with the New Yorks, and it is openly charged that in Monday's game and the second one of Wednesday the Washingtons played as though they did not care to win and were bent on assisting New York in the race for the pennant. These rumors and charges are heard on every hand. Hardly anything else is talked about but the indifference of the home players in the games referred to. The Boston men heard the stories almost as soon as they arrived at their hotel, and when in addition they read in a local paper an appeal to the home players to take their revenge out of the Bostons, they went to the grounds this afternoon with their blood stirred to a fever heat and a determination to win or make their opponents play great ball.

—Boston *Herald*

The game was made very uninteresting by the very long hits to the outfield—regular fungo hits—giving chances for catches. Of these outfield chances the Athletics accepted no less than seven and the Brooklyns ten. It was a heavy hitting game on both sides, with very little scientific play to make it worth looking at.

—Brooklyn *Daily Eagle*

Philadelphia, Sept. 19—The baseball event of the season here to-day was the published announcement that the Brooklyn and Cincinnati Clubs had determined to jump the Association and seek admission to the League. The Continental Hotel, at which the Brooklyn and New-York Clubs are stopping, presented a busy scene to-day. The fact that President Byrne of Brooklyn and President Day of New-York were on hand looking after their clubs' interests naturally added to the general excitement.

Mr. Byrne stated that the published accounts were a surprise to him. So far as Brooklyn was concerned, Mr. Byrne had to say only that Brooklyn was a club member of the American Association, and up to a very recent date had found its membership therein very agreeable. So long, therefore, as the interests of his club warranted it, and his club could feel protected in its rights, morally and financially, he saw no good reason for changing the club's membership.

"Furthermore," said Mr. Byrne, "we have not as yet been made to feel that we cannot be accorded full protection in the Association, and when that is denied us we can then determine what to do. We have made no overtures to the National League for membership in that body, and the League has made none to us. The Brooklyn Club represents a great city, and the attendance at our games this year places Brooklyn far in advance of any city in the country as a baseball town. We feel therefore we can take care of ourselves. All things being equal, the Association suits us admirably, as we naturally want to stand by the organization which first stood by us."

—New York *Times*

Saturday, September 21

On September 20, New York won and tied at
Philadelphia 5–1 and 4–4 (Keefe 24–12).
Boston won at Washington 4–3 (Clarkson 43–15).
Brooklyn won at Athletic 4–1 (Lovett 16–8).
St. Louis won at Kansas City 6–0 (Stivetts 6–6).
NL: New York 75–40, Boston 75–41.
AA: Brooklyn 82–38, St. Louis 76–43.

Philadelphia, Sept. 20—Two games were played here to-day between the champions and the Quakers. The feature of the game was the heavy batting of the Giants. They are hitting the ball in a lively manner and look like pennant winners. Keefe pitched both games, and, with proper support in the second, would have won both.

—New York *Times*

Washington, D.C., Sept. 20, 1889—There came very near being no game at all in this city today between the Washingtons and Bostons, and it was not until Manager Hart had agreed to play for one-half of the gate receipts, instead of the guarantee, that the Washington management consented to start the game. After a pleasant morning the clouds began to gather just before noon and threatened rain at any moment. It was not very cold, but very dark, and, owing to this and the fact that the interest in base ball has completely died out in this city, the attendance was ridiculously small. Just 16 persons, including both men and boys, occupied seats on the bleaching boards, while the entire attendance, counting in the grand stand, was just 271. A few minutes before the hour of starting the game, a light rain began to fall. Capt. Irwin had about concluded to avail himself of the privilege granted by the rules, which permits the captain of the home team to be the judge of the condition of the grounds before play commences, and he was about to decide them unfit to play on when Manager Hart began his diplomacy. He offered to play for one-half of the gate receipts. Owing to darkness, but eight innings were played, and when Manager Hart counted up his share of the receipts he found it amounted to but $67.50.

Manager Hart says that Clarkson will pitch tomorrow, and every day as long as he is willing to. This policy of pitching Clarkson in every game, while Radbourn is in good condition and ready to go in at any time, is open to criticism. It may turn out all right as long as Clarkson keeps up, but should he be weakened by the overwork, the result to Boston's chances would be liable to be disastrous.

—Boston *Herald*

Von der Ahe makes Byrne out to be the prime cause of all the evil. "As I told him," said he, "we never had any trouble in the Association until he came in. I organized the Association and got it going. I spent $1,500 in 1881 getting it in shape. Then in 1884 this man comes in and endeavors by his schemes to get charge of the whole thing. He talks of going into the League. Let him go. We would be glad to get rid of him. But he can't get into the League. They know him too well. I am told that Day says if they let him in the New York Club will draw out. If his record had been known he would never have been let into the Association."

—St. Louis *Post-Dispatch*

Sunday, September 22

On September 21, New York won at
Philadelphia 7–3 (Welch 26–10).
Boston tied at Washington 4–4.
Brooklyn beat Columbus 9–4 (Caruthers 33–9).
St. Louis lost to Cincinnati 4–5 (King 33–17).
NL: New York 76–40, Boston 75–41.
AA: Brooklyn 83–38, St. Louis 76–44.

Washington, D.C., Sept. 21, 1889—An angrier set of ball players never walked off the field at the end of a game than the Bostons at the close of today's 12-inning contest. It was because they had been deliberately robbed of two runs and a chance to make two more, and thereby lost an opportunity to add another much needed victory. While in some respects the Boston men did not exercise the best judgment in their stick work, still, with all their shortcomings in that respect, they would have won but for the execrable decisions of Umpire Powers.

—Boston *Herald*

With the score standing 4 to 1 against them, the Cincinnatis went in for their half of the ninth inning, in the game at Sportsman's Park, yesterday afternoon, and secured four runs and a victory. It was not through any particularly brilliant work on their own part, but through fieldwork on the part of the Browns that was marvelous in its wretchedness, that they won. There have been worse exhibitions of ball playing than that given by the Browns yesterday, but fortunately for the sport, they have been few and far between. Not a very large number of people were present to welcome the "champs," or, more correctly speaking, the "chumps" home, and those who were there wished they were somewhere else.

—St. Louis *Post-Dispatch*

Monday, September 23

On September 22, Brooklyn lost to Columbus 4–7 (Terry 19–14).
St. Louis lost to Cincinnati 6–17 (Chamberlain 30–15).
AA: Brooklyn 83–39, St. Louis 76–45.

Chicago, Sept. 22—Buying and selling of baseball players "for revenue only" will, it appears, end with this season, and the men dealing in that kind of "merchandise" may have to seek new employment when the individual members of each of the eight ball clubs of the League become stockholders and commence to "play ball" in earnest, instead of for an alleged pennant. A morning paper says:

"The transfer work is to be done by the Brotherhood of Professional Baseball Players, of which John M. Ward, short stop of the New-York Club, is President; Dennis Brouthers, first baseman of the Boston team, Vice President, and Timothy J. Keefe, the New-York Club's great pitcher, Secretary. Most of the details have been arranged and remain but to be carried out after the end of the present playing season and before the beginning of that of 1890. Every man in the League clubs of 1889, with the exception of half a dozen, among whom Anson, Williamson, and Burns are notable examples, is a member of the brotherhood, and sworn to stand by the new scheme. Its outlines are as follows:

"The new organization is to be known as the United Baseball Association. It is to be made up of eight clubs as follows: Boston, New-York, Brooklyn, Philadelphia, Pittsburg, Cleveland, Buffalo, and Chicago.

"In each city local capitalists are to operate teams formed and placed there by the brotherhood, giving a bond of $25,000 for the performance of their part of the work. Albert L. Johnson is the Cleveland capitalist, and his active participation in the deal as a missionary caused him to be mistaken for its national head. It has no national head at this time outside of the officers of the brotherhood. The players are guaranteed their salaries at the 1889 rate for 1890 and a share of the profits. All expenses and receipts are to be pooled for the general benefit and gate receipts divided equally between the clubs.

"Each club is to be governed by a board made up of eight men, four capitalists and four players, and the main body by a senate of sixteen, each club having two representatives, one a player and the other a capitalist. Each club is stocked for $20,000, half of which can be taken by the players. Of course the classification and reserve rules go with the present management. Score-card and general privileges are to be considered as profits and pooled as such. The association is to make and sell its own ball.

"Nearly all the work of rearing the fabric as it stands to-day has been done at Cleveland this Summer. The papers were sent to each League club and signed by the players. In each city capitalists are at work over grounds and plans for next season.

"The men figure that it will be to their interest to manage themselves, and a general surveillance will be kept up by the members of each team on their fellows. A man's interest in the association will be continued as long as he is a member of it. For bad work he will be released and his share turned over to his successor. A structure to last forever is to be reared by the brotherhood. The profits and losses being pooled, a general pooling of interests and players must follow.

"So the great baseball deal stands to-day. The players are united and present a strong case. They number about one hundred and thirty. The League club owners do not know, however, how broad the movement among the players is. They expect that only part of each team will go out. In this they are mistaken. In all the eight League clubs not ten men will be left.

"The League men say: 'If the brotherhood has any grievances we are ready to discuss and remove them.' The brotherhood leaders say: 'It is too late. We have been deceived before and will not be again.'"

—New York *Times*

Too much praise cannot be bestowed upon Clarkson. Few players would have done as much for their nine even with the promise of extra compensation. He has stamped himself as the greatest pitcher in the country. There may be men who have better averages, but for effectiveness with men on bases he has no peer. With all this, he is no star. He is quiet, unassuming in manner, and does not allow any feeling of importance to dominate him on account of success. He has been well worth $2500 more than he has been paid this season, for he has fully done the work of one of the other pitchers, who have been paid for sitting on the bench. This year he has already pitched in the extraordinary large number of 60 games, and he is not yet through.

—Boston *Herald*

John Clarkson, pitcher, Boston Bean-eaters (New York *Clipper*, May 3, 1890).

The Browns gave another disgraceful exhibition of ball-playing at Sportsman's Park yesterday and lost to the Cincinnatis by a score of 17 to 6. Chamberlain pitched miserably, and he, Robinson—who played very poorly—and Latham were hissed by the crowd.

Next Wednesday evening the play of several members of the Browns will be investigated at a special meeting of the Board of Directors of the club.

—St. Louis *Post-Dispatch*

Chicago, September 23—President A.G. Spalding of the Chicago Base Ball Club was interviewed last night regarding the big base ball trust. He said: "The League has existed for fifteen years, and the game is clean and on a healthy basis. Now all the purifying work is forgotten by the players, and 'long chance' capi-talists are ready to step in and assume the possible profits that may come through the game. Supposing the games are as pure and clean as those played under the National League's reign, will the public have any belief in its purity under the pooling system and auspices of an oath-bound secret organization of strikers which has plotted against the life of the League through the care of which it became a possibility? Certainly base ball can gain no immediate benefit if the plot thickens and out of it springs the Brotherhood's League. If such a league

A.G. Spalding, president, Chicago White Stockings (1890 *Spalding Guide*).

comes, the towns of small population at present in the National League will suffer, and may be forced to the wall."

—St. Louis *Post-Dispatch*

Tuesday, September 24

On September 23, New York won at Indianapolis 11–9 (Keefe 25–12).
Boston won at Chicago 8–3 (Clarkson 44–15).
Brooklyn lost to Columbus 2–3 (Lovett 16–9).
St. Louis beat Cincinnati 5–1 (Stivetts 7–6).
And Brooklyn's forfeit win over St. Louis from September 7th was overturned and the original score (2–4 in favor of St. Louis) was reinstated (Caruthers 33–10; Chamberlain 31–15).
NL: New York 77–40, Boston 76–41.
AA: Brooklyn 82–41, St. Louis 78–44.

Indianapolis, Ind., Sept. 23, 1889—John B. Day, the irascible president of the New York league club, was not in a very amiable frame of mind today over the publication of the plans for the formation of a new base ball organization intended to take the place of the league. He couldn't speak of the matter without getting mad. It was referred to in his presence as the "brotherhood scheme," and he exclaimed: "You mean the scheme of the cranks? That's what it is. The brotherhood hasn't anything to do with it." At first he was unwilling to talk about it except to denounce it as "all dead bosh," but later he became a little more tractable, and, in response to a question as to what he thought of the matter, said: "There is nothing in it; it's a fake, and I don't believe in advertising it. For this reason I don't care to talk. All the talk about it has been started by a few cranks and newspaper writers, and it hasn't any existence outside of their heads."

"Have you been assured by members of the brotherhood that there is no truth in the story?" was asked.

"No, but I know. I wouldn't insult the players by asking them if they had anything to do with it. I don't know that they need any defense, but I can state it as a fact: The statements connecting the brotherhood with the scheme are wholly unwarranted. The players are not fools."

—Boston *Herald*

Washington, D.C., Sept. 23, 1889—"It is the season for the annual baseball scare." said President Young of the national league, "and hence I was not at all surprised when I read the details of the Brotherhood of Base Ball Players' scheme in the papers this morning. So far as the league officials are concerned they will not pay any attention to the matter until the annual meeting in November. We have heard mutterings for several weeks about a big sensation that might be expected shortly in the league ranks, but the news has been discounted so far as we are concerned, and we shall simply proceed in our accustomed groove and do business at the old stand as usual."

—Boston *Herald*

In regard to the base ball trust scheme, which is the sensation of the day, John Ward, in an interview had with him at Indianapolis yesterday, said:

"Everybody takes it for granted that the brotherhood has definitely decided to leave the league. Such an idea is preposterous. The brotherhood has grievances against the league, for it has broken every promise it made to us. We have made up our minds to one thing, and that is the irksome rule giving the league the right to sell and exchange players at will must be suspended. That is the whole matter in a nutshell. The brotherhood and league will hold a joint meeting some time in November. The matter will then be brought up. We hope that the difference will be adjusted amicably. If the league will not yield to our demands it will then be time to consider our future course."

Keefe said:

"The brotherhood has no intention of leaving the league whatever. We have grievances, but they will be settled by our Executive Committee. If we had any idea of leaving the league it would take a solid year of agitation before we could get all the members to agree to it and to make other necessary arrangements."

That settles the story.

—Brooklyn *Daily Eagle*

The meeting at Cincinnati yesterday resulted in a decision dead against the Brooklyn Club. The report of the Board is as follows:

The Board of Directors of the American Association of Base Ball Clubs at its meeting held in Cincinnati decides, after a careful review of the evidence in the case, that the game played at Washington Park, Brooklyn, between the Brooklyn and St. Louis base ball clubs on September 7, 1889, and which was declared forfeited to Brooklyn by a score of 9 to 0 by Umpire Goldsmith at the beginning of the ninth inning, as provided for in Rule 26, Section 2, of the playing rules, be set back to the end of the eighth inning and the game awarded to the St. Louis Club, which at the time were in the lead by a score of 4 to 2. The Board, arriving at this decision, finds that at that time and previous thereto it had been too dark to continue to play, and the umpire should have so decided. The evidence absolutely shows that the members of each club conducted themselves in a manner unworthy of the profession and detrimental to the best interests of the national game, and they are hereby censured for needlessly delaying and prolonging the game instead of playing it to a finish in proper time. Mr. Goldsmith is hereby censured for his action in the case and his dismissal from the staff of umpires requested.

And, further, the Board finds that the decision of the umpire at Ridgewood Park on Sunday, September 8, in awarding the game scheduled for that day between the Brooklyn and St. Louis clubs to Brooklyn, because of the failure of the St. Louis Club to appear upon the field, be sustained as the correct ruling under Section 78 of the constitution of the American Association, and, as also provided for in said section, a fine of $1,500 is ordered collected from the St. Louis Club and paid to the Brooklyn Club.

Mr. Byrne is very indignant, but says it is about what he expected.
—Brooklyn *Daily Eagle*

The decision of the Board of Directors takes off a victory from the Brooklyn record of games with St. Louis and adds a defeat, and this makes a very important change in the percentage record—.667 for Brooklyn to .639 for St. Louis, giving Brooklyn a lead of but twenty-eight points, quite a falling off from the lead they had on Saturday night.
—Brooklyn *Daily Eagle*

AMERICAN ASSOCIATION STANDINGS

	W	L	PCT.	GB		W	L	PCT.	GB
Brooklyn	82	41	.667	—	Cincinnati	66	59	.528	17
St. Louis	78	44	.639	3½	Columbus	54	72	.429	29½
Athletic	68	50	.576	11½	Kansas City	51	72	.415	31
Baltimore	65	53	.551	14½	Louisville	26	99	.208	57

NATIONAL LEAGUE STANDINGS

	W	L	PCT.	GB		W	L	PCT.	GB
New York	77	40	.658	—	Cleveland	56	66	.459	23½
Boston	76	41	.650	1	Pittsburg	54	68	.443	25½
Philadelphia	61	57	.517	16½	Indianapolis	54	70	.435	26½
Chicago	61	62	.496	19	Washington	39	74	.345	36

Wednesday, September 25

On September 24, New York won at Indianapolis 16–12 (Crane 13–10). Boston won at Chicago 7–5 (Radbourn 20–11).

Brooklyn beat Columbus 10–0 (Caruthers 34–10).
NL: New York 78–40, Boston 77–41.
AA: Brooklyn 83–41, St. Louis 78–44.

Indianapolis, Ind., Sept. 24—Big Crane took Welch's place. His lightning curves checked the heavy hitting of the Hoosiers, enabling the champions to score a victory. Capt. Ewing showed good judgment in taking out Welch. He was apparently out of form, and if he had remained in the box the local players would probably have won. Ewing says that if possible he will catch every game until his club has a commanding lead.

—New York *Times*

Chicago, Ill., Sept. 24, 1889—Thanks to the base running and batting of Dick Johnston, the Bostons added another game today to their score of victories. He opened with a home run in the first inning when there was a man on base, made one of the three runs in the third, got in a single in the fifth, lined out a double in the eighth, went to third on a short passed ball, and by lively sprinting scored on a hit to the infield. He made three catches in the outfield, two of them of more than ordinary character.

—Boston *Herald*

Caruthers pitched with such telling affect throughout the contest and he was so ably assisted in every position that the visitors found it impossible to get in a single run in their nine innings' play, and the result was the signal defeat of the Columbus team by the score of 10 to 0.

—Brooklyn *Daily Eagle*

Director Appleton, of the New York Club, says he would like to see Brooklyn in the league. He says Mr. Day's objection to Brooklyn lies in his idea that the Brooklyn team would draw the crowd from New York when playing with the strong league teams. Mr. Appleton says that the Brooklyn-New York games would offset this loss.

—Brooklyn *Daily Eagle*

A special meeting of the Board of Directors of the St. Louis Base Ball Club is being held this afternoon to investigate the play of some of the members of the team. The work of Latham, King and Chamberlain has been most unsatisfactory and these players will all be brought up and given a hearing. The suspension of all of them is not unlikely and they may also have to pay fines.

—St. Louis *Post-Dispatch*

Thursday, September 26

On September 25, New York lost at Indianapolis 2–7 (Keefe 25–13).
Boston lost at Chicago 4–7 (Clarkson 44–16).
NL: New York 78–41, Boston 77–42.

Mr. Byrne returned home yesterday, and he is indignant over the
unjust treatment accorded him by the Board of Directors. He says: "Our
case was the strongest ever laid before an executive body, and we went
prepared to fight for our rights to the very end. But what was the result?
A contemptible compromise that is not only ridiculous, but makes the
association the laughing stock of the base ball world. To show you that
the compromise was premeditated I need only say that the Board refused
to consider the merits of the Saturday game until they had heard the evidence bearing on the Sunday game as well, and then rendered their decision on the two games."

—Brooklyn *Daily Eagle*

The predictions made in yesterday's *Post-Dispatch* that Latham, King
and Chamberlain would probably be punished by suspension or fines at
the meeting of the directors of the St. Louis Club held yesterday afternoon, was verified. Third baseman Arlie Latham was fined $200 and laid
off for the balance of the season, and Pitcher King was fined $100, and
also suspended for the remainder of the season. Chamberlain was rep-
rimanded and fined $100 and Robinson was reprimanded and fined a
similar sum, but was granted a stay of execution during good behavior.
Robinson was fined for improper conduct and also for poor field work,
while the others were all punished for very indifferent play, Latham also
getting an extra dose for bad conduct. The action of the directors created a decided sensation among the patrons of the game. It was the almost
universal sentiment that the men had not been doing the work of which
they were capable and that they deserved the punishment they received.
In fact there was a general feeling that extreme measures should be
adopted in dealing with the players as the Browns would have won the
championship easily if it was not for the strangely poor work of some
members of the club.

—St. Louis *Post-Dispatch*

Friday, September 27

On September 26, New York lost at Chicago 3–4 (Welch 26–11).
Boston won at Indianapolis 12–6 (Clarkson 45–16).

Brooklyn tied Columbus 7–7.
St. Louis beat Louisville 5–4 (Stivetts 8–6).
NL: New York 78–42, Boston 78–42.
AA: Brooklyn 83–41, St. Louis 79–44.

Chicago, Sept. 26—The result of the ball match played in this city to-day will add interest to the contest for supremacy in the League. New-York's aggregation of brawn and muscle dropped a game to Anson and company, and as the Bostons secured a victory in Indianapolis, the two clubs are even for first place. The record is seventy-eight victories and forty-two defeats each. New-York's players, however, are confident of winning. The defeat to-day has not damped their ardor in the least, and will, if anything, act as a stimulant.

—New York *Times*

Indianapolis, Ind., Sept. 26, 1889—The Bostons awoke from the batting lethargy under which they have labored for several weeks, and today put in one of their old time hitting games. The happiest man on the team tonight is Dan Brouthers. He has been hitting the ball hard lately, but not safely, and he was about discouraged. Dan says that, now the spell is broken, his friends may look for some batting on his part from this time out.

—Boston *Herald*

Mr. Day said that neither Brooklyn, Cincinnati nor St. Louis would be taken into the league, and he added that if Brooklyn went into the league New York would go out, which would forever bar the Bridegrooms from the league. Mr. Day talked plainly about St. Louis, and said the town would never be represented in the older organization as long as Mr. Von der Ahe was connected with the club.

—Boston *Herald*

Comiskey is now confident of winning the pennant. He says: "We have thirteen games yet to play, and we expect to win them all, while Brooklyn will certainly drop enough games to Baltimore, Columbus and the Athletics to land us first."

—Brooklyn *Daily Eagle*

Saturday, September 28

On September 27, New York won at Chicago 18–6 (Keefe 26–13).
Boston won at Indianapolis 15–8 (Clarkson 46–16).

Brooklyn beat Baltimore 2–0 (Caruthers 35–10).
NL: New York 79–42, Boston 79–42.
AA: Brooklyn 84–41, St. Louis 79–44.

Chicago, Sept. 27—The Giants won to-day's game as they liked. Keefe was very effective for the visitors, but both nines fielded very loosely. Altogether the Giants made twenty hits for a total of thirty-two bases.

—New York *Times*

Indianapolis, Ind., Sept. 27, 1889—Richardson, Kelly and Brouthers had a picnic with the bat. Their hitting was terrific. Joe Quinn and "Pop" Smith put up their usual fine game, and made some of the prettiest double plays imaginable.

—Boston *Herald*

Latham's fall down on the Browns has been pretty costly medicine to the rest of the team. He not only up to date knocked them out of winning $500 each as an extra bonus for winning the pennant, but he has knocked a good many of them out of all chances of an increase in salary, which had they won the pennant would naturally have been forthcoming. Latham has been a millstone around the neck of the St. Louis Browns since July 1, and his present predicament is not bringing him much practical sympathy.

—St. Louis *Post-Dispatch*

Sunday, September 29

On September 28, New York tied at Chicago 2–2.
Boston lost at Indianapolis 3–10 (Clarkson 46–17).
Brooklyn beat Baltimore 8–7 (Lovett 17–9).
St. Louis tied Louisville 2–2.
NL: New York 79–42, Boston 79–43.
AA: Brooklyn 85–41, St. Louis 79–44.

Chicago, Sept. 28—New-York's club didn't win to-day, but nevertheless it is in the lead for League honors. This state of affairs was brought about by a defeat administered to the Bostons by the Hoosiers. The Giants played a tie game with the Chicago Club this afternoon, and in consequence their percentage did not suffer, while Boston's defeat set them back five points. The percentage to-night is: New-York, 653; Boston, 648.

—New York *Times*

Indianapolis, Ind., Sept. 28, 1889—Radbourn was on the card to pitch for Boston, and that was the intention when the team left the hotel. It appears that at the last moment Radbourn informed Manager Hart that he had a lame shoulder and some trouble with his knee, and it would not be advisable for him to go in. Manager Hart then determined to try Clarkson again, even if he was hit, rather than trust to Madden or Daley.

—Boston *Herald*

The New York syndicate of the Brotherhood of Base Ball Players to-day leased of Mr. James J. Coogan two blocks of ground lying between One Hundred and Fifty-seventh and One Hundred and Fifty-ninth streets, Eighth and Ninth avenues, for a term of ten years at an annual rental of $24,000. The names of the persons comprising the syndicate and sureties are withheld.

—Brooklyn *Daily Eagle*

The disorganized and demoralized Browns played a ten-inning tie game with the tail-enders from Louisville, yesterday afternoon. In the tenth excitement ran high, and the small crowd present was on the tip-toe of expectation as each batter stepped to the plate. The Browns were retired in short order. Raymond was the first batter for Louisville. He hit a grounder to Fuller, which Shorty fumbled, and the batter took his base. Galligar bunted at the first ball pitched, and it bounded away toward the grand stand. Milligan thought it was a foul and started very leisurely after the sphere. Gaffney, however, called a "strike," and Raymond ran to third. Stivetts then showed his great nerve by striking out in succession Galligar, Tomney and Ewing, thus retiring the side without the run and saving the game. It was by this time quite hazy overhead, and Umpire Gaffney called the game on account of darkness.

—St. Louis *Post-Dispatch*

New York, Sept. 28—The remarkable struggle between the New York and Boston clubs for the National League base ball championship has been completely overshadowed during the last week by the reports stating that the Brotherhood of Base Ball Players would surely organize a league of its own next year. The players' move is past the bluff stage, and when met must be met with a lasting and business arrangement.

The talk about Cincinnati and Brooklyn coming into the League is wild. Neither club will come. Non-interference means self-preservation for the Association clubs, and non-interference will be their programme.

—St. Louis *Post-Dispatch*

Monday, September 30

Hub Collins, second baseman, Brooklyn Bridegrooms (New York *Clipper*, October 26, 1889).

On September 29, Brooklyn beat Baltimore 7–2 (Caruthers 36–10). AA: Brooklyn 86–41, St. Louis 79–44.

The feature of the contest was the remarkable work of Collins. He put out eight players—five by fine catches—and assisted five times in the fielding; he made two safe hits, stole two bases and scored four of the seven runs.

—Brooklyn *Daily Eagle*

There has never been so much excitement in a campaign as there has been this season. Go into Music Hall any afternoon and gaze about you. The character of the gentlemen that constitute the patrons will amaze you. The game has got its hold upon all, and the exciting character of the present struggle has intensified this fact. The ladies, too, have shown the greatest interest in the result. A peculiar feature of the game this year is that you will find readers of the *Herald*, both ladies and gentlemen, carefully read the base ball column, who never saw a professional contest in their lives. They show the greatest kind of local patriotism in so doing.

—Boston *Herald*

Tuesday, October 1

On September 30, New York tied at Pittsburg 3–3. Boston won at Cleveland 6–3 (Clarkson 47–17). St. Louis beat Louisville 6–3 (Ramsey 1–1). NL: New York 79–42, Boston 80–43. AA: Brooklyn 86–41, St. Louis 80–44.

Pittsburg, Sept. 30—New-York failed to win to-day. The game, however, resulted in a draw and the Giants are still in the lead by a small margin. This, of course, is a source of satisfaction, but the Bostons are getting too close now, and the champions will have to make a spurt to protect their laurels.

—New York *Times*

It is plainly evident that some of the smallest amount of lying is being done by the league players in regard to the conspiracy scheme or by the capitalists who are said to be leasing grounds for the syndicate clubs. On the one hand the players all deny complicity in the conspiracy, while the other fellows swear they are in it. By the time of the league meeting we shall know which side has been lying.

—Brooklyn *Daily Eagle*

AMERICAN ASSOCIATION STANDINGS

	W	L	PCT.	GB		W	L	PCT.	GB
Brooklyn	86	41	.677	—	Cincinnati	68	61	.527	19
St. Louis	80	44	.645	4½	Columbus	55	74	.426	32
Athletic	69	52	.570	14	Kansas City	53	74	.417	33
Baltimore	66	56	.541	17½	Louisville	26	101	.205	60

NATIONAL LEAGUE STANDINGS

	W	L	PCT.	GB		W	L	PCT.	GB
New York	79	42	.653	—	Cleveland	60	68	.469	22½
Boston	80	43	.650	—	Pittsburg	59	68	.465	23
Chicago	64	64	.500	18½	Indianapolis	56	73	.434	27
Philadelphia	61	62	.496	19	Washington	40	79	.336	38

Wednesday, October 2

On October 1, New York lost at Pittsburg 2–7 (Welch 26–12).
Boston won at Cleveland 8–5 (Clarkson 48–17).
St. Louis beat Louisville 7–4 (Stivetts 9–6).
NL: Boston 81–43, New York 79–43.
AA: Brooklyn 86–41, St. Louis 81–44.

Pittsburg, Oct. 1—After the game the Giants were a crestfallen lot of athletes. When the news of the victory of the Bostons reached here it added discomfort to the visitors, and sadness reigns to-night in the ranks of the New-Yorkers. Capt. Ewing is, perhaps, the most hopeful. He tried to cheer up the boys with words of encouragement. "Well, boys," he said, after the game, "we've got everything to win and nothing to lose now. Take all chances hereafter, and if we fall let it be after a hard fight."

Judging from the feelings of the men they will play desperate ball until the season closes.

—New York *Times*

Cleveland, O., Oct. 1, 1889—While the sixth inning was in progress in this city today the bulletin board announced that the Pittsburg-New York game stood 6 to 2 in favor of Pittsburg. The Boston men were quick to learn the news, and, with the score 4 to 3 against them, they passed the word along the line to brace up and go in to win, for a victory for them probably meant first position in the league race and the championship. Capt. Kelly set the example, and infused more life into his team than he has before displayed on a single occasion, and his men responded nobly in the seventh inning and settled the game then and there. Before the teams left the grounds the full score of the Pittsburg game was bulletined, and it was a joyful aggregation of players that filed into the hacks of the Boston party.

—Boston *Herald*

On all sides in Boston hilarity prevailed last evening, and the great topic of discussion was the victory of the Bostons and the most unexpected defeat of the New Yorks. In every place where score cards were displayed crowds stood and stared in silent delight. There were over 3,000 cranks in Music Hall yesterday afternoon, and when the returns began to come in they were about as glum a collection of individuals as one would care to see. It was gall and wormwood to them to see the New Yorks take the lead and the Bostons striding on to defeat. When the tying and winning runs came in the crowd let itself loose, and there was the biggest kind of pandemonium for the next few minutes. The cup of happiness was full to overflowing when the ninth inning at Pittsburg showed a gain for the home club and nothing for the New Yorks. All New England shared the happy result with Boston last evening.

—Boston *Herald*

Brockton, Oct. 1, 1889—Manager William H. McGunnigle of the Brooklyn ball team arrived in this city yesterday, on a visit to his family, and his friends called in large numbers at his residence, to congratulate him on the success of his club. "Mac" feels quite elated over the position now held by the "bridegrooms," and says that they will surely capture the much desired piece of bunting this season. When asked which club in the league he would rather win the pennant, the manager brightened up with a smile, and said: "Why, Boston of course. I was born in the Hub and naturally I take some pride in the club, which I think is far superior to any team in the league. It makes very little difference to the

Brooklyn management whether Boston or New York is our competitor in the world championship series."

"Does Brooklyn intend to leave the association and join the league, in view of the treatment in the late Brooklyn-St. Louis dispute?"

"President Byrne of Brooklyn is a man who tells me considerable about his business affairs, and I don't think that he will desert the association next year. It is true Brooklyn didn't receive a fair deal in the St. Louis-Brooklyn affair, but that is no reason why the latter club should leave the association."

—Boston *Herald*

Thursday, October 3

On October 2, New York won at Pittsburg 6–3 (Crane 14–10).
Boston lost at Cleveland 1–7 (Clarkson 48–18).
St. Louis beat Kansas City 15–5 (Ramsey 2–1).
NL: New York 80–43, Boston 81–44.
AA: Brooklyn 86–41, St. Louis 82–44.

Pittsburg, Oct. 2—All is joy in the camp of the Giants to-night. The boys are in high glee and it is safe to predict that if they didn't have to play good ball for a few days longer they would indulge in a little town painting to-night. The cause of this change was a victory here to-day over Pittsburg and the news of the defeat of Boston in Cleveland. In sporting parlance they "whip-sawed" the turn, and to-night are ahead again for first honors.

—New York *Times*

Cleveland, Oct. 2—"Mike" Kelly, the high-priced star of the Boston Ball Club, created a scene at League Park to-day. Kelly did not play, but sat muffled up in an overcoat on the bench of the Cleveland players and made comments on the game as it progressed. When Cleveland was 3 runs ahead he ventured to inform the members of his club in a loud tone of voice that they could not win.

Mike "King" Kelly, captain and right fielder, Boston Beaneaters (New York *Clipper*, February 26, 1887).

"You never win," said he with characteristic modesty, "when I don't play. Kelly is king. I am a king."

No attention was paid to his little pleasantries, which were muttered at times and shouted at others. In Boston's half of the sixth Richardson was touched out at the plate. Kelly did not like Umpire McQuaid's decision, and when the inning was over strode toward McQuaid with blazing eye and inflamed face. He told the umpire that he had come West to rob Boston of the pennant and at the same time drew back his fist to strike McQuaid. Two policemen sprang into the field and grappled with Kelly, who broke away and made for McQuaid again. The officers took the pugilist in hand, however, and after choking him a trifle to subdue his untamed spirit, dragged him through the gate and left him there. Lighting a cigarette, he strode into the street with the dejected air of Napoleon in exile. He attempted to enter the grounds again, but found the gate locked, and the fence was too high to vault. Small boys chided him, and the gentlemen on the bleachers suggested that he buy a ticket and break in by way of the turnstiles.

—New York *Times*

Friday, October 4

On October 3, New York won at Cleveland 9–0 (Keefe 27–13).
Boston won at Pittsburg 7–2 (Clarkson 49–18).
Brooklyn beat Athletic 17–0 (Caruthers 37–10).
St. Louis beat Kansas City 7–5 (Stivetts 10–6).
NL: New York 81–43, Boston 82–44.
AA: Brooklyn 87–41, St. Louis 83–44.

Cleveland, Oct. 3—New-York began the last of the series here to-day in a manner that would send a thrill of joy to the hearts of the admirers of the champions. Keefe pitched the finest game seen here this season, the Giants batted and fielded in good form, and from the outset Cleveland never had a chance to win.

Just as the game finished here news of the victory of Boston at Pittsburg was posted on the bulletin board, but it didn't seem to annoy the New-Yorkers. They are confident of winning first place again.

—New York *Times*

Pittsburg, Pa., Oct. 3, 1889—A local paper of this city, in its announcement of today's Pittsburg-Boston game, made a statement that Clarkson had been seriously overworked, that he was beginning to feel the strain, and that he had a "dead" arm. What must have been the astonishment of the readers of that paper who saw the game to see the way that "dead" arm manipulated the sphere. It was simply marvelous. Clarkson gave another exhibition of his wonderful endurance physically, as well as of his complete mastery of the art of pitching.

—Boston *Herald*

The Brooklyn team played ball yesterday as they have not done before this season. It was not the fact that they defeated their strong opponents by a large score, but it was the exceptional way in which they did it, that made the contest so noteworthy. Yesterday's victory was the result of exceptional skill at the bat as well as effective battery work and splendid field support, in addition to which there was a "vim" about their work, a spirit of determination and an energy which they have not exhibited for a month past.

There is no questioning the fact that Ladies' Day at Washington Park is Brooklyn's lucky day. Not a game have they lost on any of these days when the bright eyes of their lady guests shone on them from the grand stand, and the brilliant gathering of the fair sex in the grand stand yesterday stirred them up to do wonders on this last Ladies' day of the season.

—Brooklyn *Daily Eagle*

An enthusiastic admirer of Brooklyn's ball players sends the following to the *Eagle*:

Champions of the World.

It now becomes all Brooklynites, especially "base ball cranks,"
To call a meeting and to give the Grooms a vote of thanks.
For they have done so nobly, I'm sure we can't refrain
From giving them a "blow off" and fill them with champagne.

There's Darby out in left field, a whole team in himself,
And with Bobby in the pitcher's box, he never once gets left.
Bob Clark there up behind the bat, the base stealers he downs
Especially when they're playing Comiskey's tricky Browns.

George Smith plays short stop splendidly, and Collins second base,
And with Pinkney playing at the third why it's a settled case;
Our own Dave Foutz on first base takes all that comes his way,
And with Honest John in center field makes many a double play.

No matter who is in the box, be it Lovett, Hughes or Terry,
The way the visitors fan the air—it makes us all feel merry.
There's Tommy Burns in coacher's box, to us he's also dear;
He rattles opposing batteries until they fan the atmosphere.

Brooklyn Bridegrooms, 1889. *Standing, left to right:* George "Germany" Smith, "Pop" Corkhill, Will "Adonis" Terry, Dave Foutz, Darby O'Brien, Doc Bushong, Joe Visner. *Sitting on chairs, left to right:* George Pinkney, Bob Caruthers, Hub Collins, Manager Bill McGunnigle, Tom "Oyster" Burns, Bob Clark, Tom Lovett. *Sitting on the ground:* Mickey Hughes (National Baseball Hall of Fame Library, Cooperstown, New York).

Reynolds, Visner and Bushong, their catching is quite great;
The way they stick to all foul flies has settled many a fate.
We never bluff the umpire nor call him out of place.
And now we claim with pleasure to be leaders in the race.

If Boston wins that other flag it's settled that she'll die,
And if New York should win it—why, we don't want better pie.
Before the end of this month our flags will be unfurled
And we will prove to you that we are Champions of the World.

—Brooklyn *Daily Eagle*

The aspirant organization of ball tossers from the city by the Kaw played the second game of the present engagement with the Browns at Sportsman's Park this afternoon. The players from the Western suburb came on to St. Louis to stop the home team in its triumphant march. Yesterday was their Waterloo.

—St. Louis *Post-Dispatch*

Saturday, October 5

On October 4, New York won at Cleveland 6–1 (Welch 27–12).
Boston won at Pittsburg 4–3 (Madden 10–10).
NL: New York 82–43, Boston 83–44.

Cleveland, Oct. 4—This afternoon the New-Yorks again easily defeated the local club and entered on the last lap of the great struggle for baseball supremacy. The deciding games will be played in this city and Pittsburg to-morrow. At present the Giants have two to one the best of it. If the New-Yorks and Bostons win the Giants will be champions. If they both lose the Giants will be champions. In order to lose the championship Boston will have to win and New-York will have to lose. The members of the New-York team are jubilant to-night and are confident of success.

Keefe and Ewing will form the Giants' battery to-morrow. Keefe says that he never felt better and that he will pitch the game of his life.

—New York *Times*

Pittsburg, Pa., Oct. 4, 1889—It looked at one time today as though the jig was up. The telegraph indicated that the New Yorks were winning at Cleveland. The Pittsburgs were playing like fiends against the Bostons, and a defeat for the latter meant a settlement of the championship problem right off. It was not till after two men were out in the ninth inning, with the bases full, that jolly Dan Brouthers made one of his terrific ground hits past third base and the game was won.

And on the eve of the last day of the season the championship is unsettled, for if on the morrow Boston wins and New York loses, Boston wins the pennant. Clarkson will pitch for Boston.

—Boston *Herald*

Tim Keefe, pitcher, New York Giants (Library of Congress, Prints and Photographs Division [LOT 13163-05, no. 195]).

Sunday, October 6

On October 5, the last day of the season in the National League,
New York won at Cleveland 5–3 (Keefe 28–13).
Boston lost at Pittsburg 1–6 (Clarkson 49–19).
Brooklyn lost to Athletic 2–10 (Lovett 17–10).
St. Louis beat Kansas City 7–2 (Chamberlain 32–15).
NL: New York 83–43, Boston 83–45.
AA: Brooklyn 87–42, St. Louis 84–44.

Cleveland, Oct. 5—After a six months' conflict on the diamond field
the aggregation of brain and muscle known as the New-York Giants won
the deciding game here to-day, and they will sport the pennant emblem-
atic of the League championship for another year. The deciding game
was a grand one. With a determination surpassing anything ever seen
here the New-Yorkers started on the last lap of the pennant struggle.
They took a lead in the opening inning and were never headed, although
the Clevelands made matters rather interesting in the fifth inning.

The Giants played like pennant winners. They were in championship form. For eight innings they handled the ball without an error of
any description, but in the ninth little Richardson fumbled a grounder
and spoiled a perfect game. And the pitching! When Keefe said yesterday that he would pitch the game of his life he told the truth. From the
outset he shot the ball across the plate with rare speed and accuracy and
had the Cleveland batters completely at his mercy. Beads of perspiration
dropped from his brow, but he continued his telling work until the last
man was retired in the ninth inning. Tiernan made the prettiest hit of
the game—a home run—and started the scoring. Everybody here wanted
to see the Giants win, and when the game ended a cheer that surprised
the New-Yorkers went up from the assemblage.

—New York *Times*

Pittsburg, Pa., Oct. 5, 1889—The Bostons made an unusually early
start for the ball grounds this afternoon and put in a half-hour of good
solid practice. During the preliminary work Manager Hart sent the following dispatch to Manager Loftus of the Cleveland team: "We will give
$1000 to your team if we win the championship, $500 to the battery and
the balance to the rest of the team." This was signed by Mr. Hart and
Clarkson. There were 400 people present at the game. On the fence in
the left field a large bulletin announced the progress of the Cleveland-
New York game by innings. The Bostons were evidently overconfident
and overanxious. They played very badly in the first part of the game
and lost the contest in the very first inning. In the ninth, Brouthers flied

Boston Beaneaters, 1889. *Standing, left to right:* Joe Quinn, Tom Brown, "Pop" Smith, Dan Brouthers, Charlie Ganzel, Charlie Bennett. *Sitting on chairs, left to right:* Hardy Richardson, Hoss Radbourn, John Clarkson, Manager James Hart, Mike "King" Kelly, Dick Johnston, Billy Nash. *Sitting on the ground, left:* Bill Daley; *right:* "Kid" Madden (National Baseball Hall of Fame Library, Cooperstown, New York).

to Fields for the third time, Johnston flied to Miller, Quinn fouled to Carroll, and the season of 1889 was over.

—Boston *Herald*

The Giants once more claim the proud title of champion and the small army of "cranks" who occasionally transform the staid precincts of upper New-York into a modern Bedlam are at peace with the world. It was a hard struggle and the Giants can justly feel proud of their achievement. During the season they had a great many drawbacks. In fact they were handicapped to such an extent at times that success looked like an impossibility.

To begin with Keefe did not play in the early series, and when he was finally induced to sign a contract he suffered from lack of practice. Then Welch seemed to give out, and Capt. Ewing and Hatfield were forced to do some curving. The champions lost their grounds and were

OLD JUDGE CIGARETTES Goodwin & Co., New York.

William "Buck" Ewing, captain and catcher, New York Giants and team mascot (Library of Congress, Prints and Photographs Division [LOT 13163-13, no. 2])

forced to meet their rivals in the marshes of New-Jersey. Arrangements were finally made so that they could occupy the old Metropolitan diamond at St. George. Finally the present ground was secured, and the champions, after playing on two strange grounds, got a permanent diamond.

Every man connected with the club, from President Day down to the mascot, can justly claim credit for the success of the team, but the giant's share belongs to Capt. Ewing. The genial back-stop played great ball this year. His whole heart was in his work, and his aim was to capture the pennant. He has succeeded, but it was a difficult task, and it was only gained by remarkable skill and endurance on his part. Day after day he caught the curves of Keefe and Welch and the speedy pitching of Crane when his hands were sore and painful. But he stuck to his work like a Trojan, and his reward is the proud distinction of being the Captain of the championship team. Ewing is a great ball player. It is safe to assert that without his services the Giants could never win first place.

—New York *Times*

Interest in the struggle for the League baseball pennant this season has been sustained to the very end by the extraordinary closeness of the contest. At the time when the leading contestants took the field against their opponents in Cleveland and Pittsburg yesterday afternoon it was still undecided whether the trophy was to stay in New-York another year or be borne hence by the Boston players. A little luck on the part of the Bostons, a few errors on the part of the New-Yorks, in the concluding games, and the pennant would have gone to Boston, perhaps to be displayed above the golden dome of the State House. But the result was determined by skill and merit, not by luck and blunders. New-York wins the pennant.

—Editorial Page, New York *Times*

The agony is over, and everybody is glad of it. If the boys did not win the first place they were as close to it as they possibly could be, and they surprised many people by the plucky way they stuck to the lead during the season, and resisted all attempts to shake them off. They have led the class almost during the whole of the campaign, and now they have had to give way at the very end to a claimant that has been near the front all along. The winners have earned their laurels. They have played with great vim and determination, and have made a fight that few clubs could have made.

—Boston *Herald*

The work of Clarkson has been of the finest possible description. Not only has he pitched in a larger number of contests than any pitcher in the league or the American association, but no pitcher has a larger number of victories to his credit. What has been most remarkable has been his untiring effort, his willingness to pitch whenever there was a call for his services, and his phenomenal endurance. All through the season the cry was raised about his giving out, his inability to stand the strain, but he remained at his post to the very end, and triumphed over all his would be detractors.

Brouthers of the Bostons, despite his great falling off in batting at the end of the season, leads the league.

—Boston *Herald*

The general feeling about Boston when the result of the Pittsburg-Boston game became known last evening was one of unconcealed disgust and universal soreness. Admirers of base ball were deep in the consomme, while those who take only a slight interest in the game were depressed merely out of local pride, and yet, withal, there was a graceful tendency among all Bostonians to yield complacently to the inevitable. At the clubs, about hotel corridors, at all the sporting resorts and along the avenues and sidewalks, in fact everywhere that base ball talk prevailed, the sentiment was often expressed: "They overworked one pitcher."

President Soden of the triumvirates took the defeat very philosophically, and in the set lines of his "property smile" could be read the thought, "We played good ball and the pennant should be ours," even though he didn't say so. What he did say was this: "We're licked, and we submit gracefully. I wish the result was reversed in our favor, that's all."

—Boston *Herald*

It looked like old times to see Elton Chamberlain back in his effective form, pitching a winning game, as he did against Kansas City yesterday at Sportsman's Park. He not only showed conclusively that when he is in condition he can pitch against and down any club whom he may face, but he helped win the game on his good, hard, clean hitting.

—St. Louis *Post-Dispatch*

A week from tomorrow the Association race closes. The Brooklyns have an excellent lead, but there is still a fighting chance for the Browns. Brooklyn has played one game more than the Browns and has three more victories and two less defeats, giving them a lead of .018. St. Louis still has seven games to play. Including to-day's contest, the Brooklyns still have eight games to play. If they lose three out of their eight and if the Browns should win all of their games, the Browns would win by .002 per cent., or if the Brooklyns lose half of their games and the Browns lose only one, St. Louis would win by .003. While not probable, it is by no means impossible that St. Louis should again secure the pennant this year.

—St. Louis *Post-Dispatch*

FINAL NATIONAL LEAGUE STANDINGS

	W	L	PCT.	GB		W	L	PCT.	GB
New York	83	43	.659	—	Pittsburg	61	71	.462	25
Boston	83	45	.648	1	Cleveland	61	72	.459	25½
Chicago	67	65	.508	19	Indianapolis	59	75	.440	28
Philadelphia	63	64	.496	20½	Washington	41	83	.331	41

Monday, October 7

On October 6, Brooklyn beat Athletic 9–0 (Caruthers 38–10).
St. Louis beat Kansas City 9–4 (Ramsey 3–1).
AA: Brooklyn 88–42, St. Louis 85–44.

As the Western express rolled in to the station of the Erie Railroad last evening a shout went up that could be heard for a radius of half a mile. Among the passengers were the members of the New-York Club returning from their victorious tour, and about seven hundred enthusiasts were there to give them a rousing welcome. Ball players in civilian dress are as a rule hard to recognize, but everybody seemed to know Capt. Ewing. He was cheered to the echo, and hundreds rushed forward to grab his hand.

Manager Mutrie came in for a good share of the applause. He was

Jim Mutrie, manager, New York Giants (Library of Congress, Prints and Photographs Division [LOT 13163-05, no. 202]).

all smiles, and felt as proud as a small boy with a new pair of boots. "It was a hard struggle," he said with a sigh, "and I'm mighty glad it's over. For weeks I have passed sleepless nights, and now that we are champions I can rest contentedly. Our last trip has been one of the most remarkable ever made by a ball nine. We played ball that surpassed anything that I ever witnessed. That last game in Cleveland was the greatest ever played. The spirit of the boys manifested itself there. They went to do or die, and they would have risked a limb to score a run. On that occasion I really felt proud of the boys, for I realized that I had the management of the greatest aggregation of ball players on earth. This contest has been a grand one, and the Bostons deserve credit for the close race they gave us. The Bostons are good players, but we are the people."

—New York *Times*

A nine of Clarksons would have won that pennant. What endurance, what indefatigability, what skill and what steadiness! His work this season has excited greater admiration than that of any other player. If every member of the nine had worked as faithfully as he during the season, the Bostons would have got there.

John M. Ward: "I'd hate to be in their (Boston's) place tonight. They've made a great fight, but they have lost, and losers never get the credit they deserve. Clarkson would have been a god had they won, and he's a hero as it is."

New York *World*: "The principal feature of the Boston Club's campaign was the well-nigh phenomenal showing of Pitcher John Clarkson. For weeks he has been the mainstay of his club, and he has done his work day in and day out with unflinching energy and will. There is but one parallel to his work since base ball was adopted, and that was the record made by Radbourn with the Providence club in 1884. The latter's work, though, pales to insignificance when compared with Clarkson's, for in those days the strain was not nearly so great on a pitcher as it now is, and the limitations not nearly so exacting. Boston may well be proud of her citizen and the Boston club of its pitcher. That $10,000 will never cause a sigh of regret."

—Boston *Herald*

The home team had the best of it, owing to the remarkable command of the ball shown by Caruthers. It did not look as if it were possible to play ball yesterday afternoon with the day opening with rain and continuing with small intervals until night, and consequently none but the enthusiastic class of patrons known as the cranks went out to Ridgewood. But nearly three thousand of these enthusiasts went there and saw the home team "chicago" their opponents for the third time this season.

—Brooklyn *Daily Eagle*

Tuesday, October 8

On October 7, Brooklyn lost at Baltimore 2–3 (Terry 19–15).
AA: Brooklyn 88–43, St. Louis 85–44.

The Brooklyn team yesterday played in Baltimore, a day before they were expected there, and the result was an attendance of 249 spectators. The game played yesterday was originally scheduled for Friday, but for reasons best known to Messrs. Byrne and Barnie it was changed to yesterday. The dispatch from Baltimore last night said that "wild throws by Clark and O'Brien gave the Baltimores two of their three runs and the game to-day." This apparently tells the story of the defeat. Why the weakest throwing catcher of the team is so persistently put in behind the bat is one of those mysteries of the management which "no feller can find out."

—Brooklyn *Daily Eagle*

It is beginning to look as if the contest for the pennant would be marked by as close a finish almost as that of the league. Brooklyn will have to brace up. The Columbus Club's manager has it in for them to beat them every game there. The Brooklyns are now but thirteen points ahead of St. Louis and only one less defeat is now charged, with but three more victories to their credit. The margin is getting smaller by degrees. To-day's contest will tell a tale. If St. Louis wins and Brooklyn loses, Brooklyn will lead by .667 to .662 only.

—Brooklyn *Daily Eagle*

AMERICAN ASSOCIATION STANDINGS

	W	L	PCT.	GB		W	L	PCT.	GB
Brooklyn	88	43	.672	—	Cincinnati	71	61	.538	17½
St. Louis	85	44	.659	2	Columbus	55	76	.420	33
Athletic	72	55	.567	14	Kansas City	53	78	.405	35
Baltimore	70	58	.547	16½	Louisville	26	105	.198	62

Wednesday, October 9

On October 8, Brooklyn won at Baltimore 12–9 (Caruthers 39–10).
St. Louis won at Louisville 9–3 (Stivetts 11–6).
AA: Brooklyn 89–43, St. Louis 86–44.

The result of to-day's games does not make any material difference in the Association championship race, as both the Browns and Brooklyns won. The Bridegrooms lead the Browns by .012. If Brooklyn had been defeated by Baltimore to-day, as would surely have happened but for the wretched work of shortstop Ray of Baltimore, Brooklyn's percentage would have been .677, leaving them a lead of but .005 over St. Louis.

—St. Louis *Post-Dispatch*

Thursday, October 10

On October 9, Brooklyn won at Baltimore 17–9 (Caruthers 40–10).
St. Louis won at Louisville 8–4 (Chamberlain 33–15).
AA: Brooklyn 90–43, St. Louis 87–44.

With a well broken up team to play against, the Brooklyn club had an easy time in defeating the once strong Baltimores, at Baltimore, yesterday. Brooklyn played in pennant winning style. Caruthers, who pitched his second successive game, was hit hard at times, but held them down at critical stages.

—Brooklyn *Daily Eagle*

Early this morning Caruthers, the Brooklyn's star pitcher, received a telegram from home conveying the pleasing intelligence that he was the father of a bouncing boy, and that mother and child were doing well. With a smile that took in both ears Bob hastened into the august presence of President Byrne to acquaint him of the arrival of another pitcher. After the usual congratulations had passed, the Brooklyn manager settled down to business. "Of course," said he, "under the present circumstances I cannot expect you to remain with the club just now. An event of this kind is not an every day occurrence and you will want to go home. We cannot well spare you, but nevertheless I will grant you leave of absence." Rather to President Byrne's surprise Caruthers declined to avail himself of the generous offer. Said he: "The telegram says that my wife is doing well, and I know that in case I should go home and the club should then lose games she as well as I would be worried, and that might do more harm than if I remained away. I will therefore stay with the club until the season closes."

This devotion to duty made Byrne feel good, and he went to the grounds feeling as happy as Caruthers. The latter, though he had pitched in yesterday's game, again went into the box to celebrate the occasion by winning another game.

—Brooklyn *Daily Eagle*

Jocko Milligan, catcher, St. Louis Browns (Library of Congress, Prints and Photographs Division [LOT 13163-13, no. 24]).

Louisville, Ky., Oct. 9— Milligan, the Browns' big catcher, won the game to-day, knocking out two home runs and driving in five tallies.

—St. Louis *Post-Dispatch*

The Browns' chances of winning the pennant are growing beautifully less. The Brooklyns must now lose two out of their remaining four games and the Browns must win all of the four games they still have to play to give the pennant to St. Louis. All of the Baltimore pitchers were put in against Brooklyn yesterday, so that there is little hope of the Orioles winning to-day. Why Barnie should have exhausted all of his pitching material yesterday on a game he had no chance to win is a mystery, unless he wanted the Brooklyns to capture to-day's contest.

—St. Louis *Post-Dispatch*

Friday, October 11

On October 10, Brooklyn won at Baltimore 7–2 (Terry 20–15). St. Louis won at Louisville 9–1 (Stivetts 12–6). AA: Brooklyn 91–43, St. Louis 88–44.

The game yesterday at Baltimore was won by Brooklyn in the seventh inning, after the sixth had ended with the score at 2 to 2. The feature of the game was the all around work of Clark, who made a record of four hits, four runs, two steals, seven put outs, one assist and one error. The team is full of ginger and left for Columbus last night with the determination to bring back the pennant to Brooklyn.

Bob Clark, catcher, Brooklyn Bridegrooms (New York *Clipper*, November 24, 1888).

—Brooklyn *Daily Eagle*

Manager Mutrie is so confident that Brooklyn will beat St. Louis in the Association race that he is ready to make terms with Mr. Byrne in regard to the world's championship series. He wants to play eleven games, the first of which must be on the New Polo Grounds. When one club wins six games the series will close.

In regard to the financial division, he says that Mr. Byrne can decide that matter in any way he wishes. The winning club can take all the receipts daily or half, whichever suits the Brooklyn manager. He would like the winning club to take all the money.

—New York *Times*

Pitcher Keefe of the New York Base Ball Club was in the city yesterday. Mr. Keefe is the secretary of the Brotherhood of League Players, and it is natural that his opinion on the war that seems to be impending between the players and the magnates should be sought. He said: "We want the abolition of the classification of the players, and we want the sale of the players entirely done away with."

"Do you think that the brotherhood could make a success of the movement?"

"I do not see why not. The public will go to see the best ball playing, no matter who is at the head of the movement. If Clarkson is to pitch for the brotherhood club in this city, the public will go see him play, no matter if there is another club charging but 25 cents admission."

Speaking of the season just over, Mr. Keefe said: "It was the closest season I ever saw. We had to play great ball to win, and make no mistake about it, Clarkson did powerful work. It is too bad that he and the nine could not have been successful after the splendid stand they made. And Radbourn pitched finely, too. He did his share to bring the club to the position it occupied at the close of the season."

—Boston *Herald*

Saturday, October 12

No games were played on October 11.

In the association constitution of 1887 article 65 provided that "postponed games might be played off at any time prior to the 17th day of October." It appears that this clause, though not embodied in the revised constitution by specific date, has, by tacit consent, been continued in force ever since, and consequently, though the scheduled season, under the constitution, extends only to the 14th of October, the three days' grace for the playing off of postponed games still exists. This will enable the St. Louis Club to play off their three postponed games with the Athletics, and as Brooklyn has only one postponed game possible to be played off—that with Columbus—the St. Louis Club have an advantage which the Brooklyns are deprived of. But even these postponed games will not save the St. Louis team if they lose two out of the three in Cincinnati and the Brooklyns win two out of their three at Columbus.

—Brooklyn *Daily Eagle*

Manager Mutrie has been coolly arranging all of the details of the world's series of games with the Brooklyns as if there was no such person in existence as Charles H. Byrne. Mutrie says that he will select the association umpire, leaving Mr. Byrne to choose the one for the league. This is one thing that will not be done. The Brooklyn Club will select its own umpire, leaving New York to do likewise.

The first game will draw the largest crowd, and it would be a financial loss to play it at the New Polo Grounds, which cannot hold as many as Washington Park by 10,000.

A correspondent writing to the *Sun*, in comparing the Brooklyn and New York teams as competitors in the world's series, says: "They outrank New York in fielding, and, although they may be beaten by them in team batting, in all around work they are fully the equals of the New York team. In Caruthers we have a pitcher who will rank in the first three in the country. I presume that New York will use Keefe and Welch in most of the games, but they will find foemen worthy of their steel in Caruthers and Terry, with Hughes and Lovett as side issues to offset Crane and O'Day. I do not see how New York can get more than two or three games at the most from such pitchers, backed as they will be by such superb fielding support as only the Brooklyn Club is capable of. I claim that the title of the king of pitchers will be carried over to Brooklyn this Fall and presented to Caruthers, for his record was never equaled by Keefe in his palmiest days."

—Brooklyn *Daily Eagle*

From present appearances the benefit to be tendered to the Giants at the Broadway Theatre on Oct. 20 promises to be a grand success. In the mail yesterday was the following letter of acceptance from the Captain of the Giants.

> *Messrs. Digby Bell and De Wolf Hopper, Five A's Club, 43 West Twenty-eighth-street, New-York:*
> *My Dear Boys:* In behalf of the players of the New-York Baseball Club I write this to accept your very kind offer to get us up a benefit on the occasion of the presentation of the pennant, as you did last year.
> This, of course, is merely a formal acknowledgement of thanks from us, as we have long understood that should we succeed in bringing back the flag you boys would do what you so kindly did for us last year. We appreciate more the kindly feeling and good fellowship which prompts our two celebrated "baseball cranks," Bell and Hopper, to get up this testimonial than we do any pecuniary benefit which may be realized to us personally. I need not say that the boys are all with you, and if there is anything that we can do outside of appearing, which we will do en masse on that occasion for the first time in public since winning the pennant, you may call upon us, not forgetting that "we are the people." Yours truly, *William Ewing*, Captain New-York Baseball Club.
> New-York, Friday, Oct. 11, 1889.

—New York *Times*

There are now in progress of arrangement two different receptions to be given the returning coming champions next week, the first of which is the welcome to be given the team on Tuesday evening next, on their arrival by the annex boat at Fulton Ferry at 5 P.M., while the second is the public reception and banquet which will take place at the Academy of Music Assembly Rooms on Wednesday night week. Of course these receptions depend upon the fact of the Brooklyn team leaving Columbus on Monday night and as champions—a contingency which, though very probable, is not yet a certainty.

The details of the Tuesday night reception embody the appointment of a reception committee to meet President Byrne, Manager McGunnigle and the players at Fulton Ferry and take them in carriages to the Washington Park Ball Grounds, escorted by members of local base ball clubs in uniform, carrying torches and led by a military band, pyrotechnic displays en route being a feature. A special committee will meet the teams at Jersey City and escort them to Brooklyn, where the public will take them in hand. As it will be the first event of the kind in the history of the game in this city it should be made specially interesting.

—Brooklyn *Daily Eagle*

Sunday, October 13

On October 12, Brooklyn lost at Columbus 5–7 (Caruthers 40–11).
AA: Brooklyn 91–44, St. Louis 88–44.

It was dollars to doughnuts in the ninth that Columbus would not win. As Johnson came to bat the excitement was intense. Columbus needed one to tie and two to beat their opponents. It had been a game for blood throughout, and as Johnson sent a ball whizzing into Corkhill's territory the immense crowd arose and watched its flight. Corkhill misjudged the ball and it bounded over his head, Dailey and Crooks scoring. The winning run had been made and a scene of wild excitement ensued. The bleachers arose as one man and showered cushions and hats into the diamonds in clouds. Play had to be stopped for fully ten minutes. Never before in Columbus had such a scene been witnessed. Byrne attributes the loss of the game to Corkhill.

—Brooklyn *Daily Eagle*

That was a hard game for the Brooklyns to lose at Columbus yesterday. Their defeat was a godsend for St. Louis, as it improves the Browns's chances most decidedly. They are now within .007 of the Bridegrooms, being tied with them in the matter of games lost and three games behind them in the games won. As there is scarcely any chance of the authorities at Cincinnati permitting the teams to play to-day, St. Louis will have two postponed games there to make up. At the special meeting of the American Association held in Cincinnati a short time ago, the championship was lengthened three days, up to and including October 17, to enable the clubs to play off postponed games. It has been Mr. Von der Ahe's intention in case the Browns are behind the Brooklyns in percentage after to-morrow's game to play off their three postponed games with the Athletics at Philadelphia. They could reach Philadelphia in time to play Wednesday and would play either two games on that day and one on Thursday, or vice versa. Of course the club would not play any more than would be necessary to place them in the lead.

—St. Louis *Post-Dispatch*

Monday, October 14

On October 13, Brooklyn won at Columbus 2–1 (Terry 21–15).
AA: Brooklyn 92–44, St. Louis 88–44.

Thanks to Terry's effective pitching at the most critical period of the Brooklyn Club's closing campaign, the pennant was virtually won yesterday, the victory scored in Columbus on Sunday leaving Brooklyn with a credit of four more victories than St. Louis, the defeats being equal. No game was played at Cincinnati yesterday, and consequently, under the rules, the St. Louis team will have to remain over in Cincinnati on Tuesday and Wednesday to play off the postponed game of Saturday and yesterday's scheduled game, and this will leave them but Thursday afternoon to play off their postponed game with the Athletics. In the interim the Brooklyn team, if necessary, will stop en route home on Tuesday to play off their postponed game with the Athletics, which game, however, will not be necessary if Brooklyn wins to-day. The pitchers in to-day's game will most likely be Baldwin and Caruthers and another close contest is looked for. It is not likely that St. Louis will win more than one game in Cincinnati and if they lose one that ends their chances.

—Brooklyn *Daily Eagle*

In baseball circles the topic of conversation is on the coming world's series. From present appearances New-York and Brooklyn will do battle for the honors. The Association race is not over yet, however, and St. Louis may make things unpleasant for the boys across the bridge.

On the whole the chances are in favor of Brooklyn. Bets have already been made on the world's series, so sure are the admirers of the Bridegrooms that their club will win. In most quarters the Giants rank as favorites, but numbers of bets were made last week on even terms. As soon as the Association race is finished, and if the Brooklyns come out ahead, it is safe to say that large sums will be wagered on the contest between the champions. The rivalry between New-York and Brooklyn is so great that the "cranks" of both cities are willing to wager their last dollar on their favorites. It is safe to predict that the games will be largely attended, and if the weather is fine all records in that respect may be broken.

The players and managers of both the New-York and Brooklyn teams feel confident of success. Manager Mutrie was spoken to yesterday on the subject and he appeared to be very enthusiastic. "Why, my dear boy," he said, "we'll win the series from Brooklyn or any other club on earth. The Giants are world-beaters. Brooklyn or the cream of all the players in the American Association can't compare with the Giants. We can outbat them, outfield them, outrun them, and outgeneral them. Now, how in the name of common sense can they win? Before the series is over Brooklyn will gain some knowledge of baseball, or rather the delicate points of the game. Some of our team-work plays will open their eyes. I may be mistaken, but, my dear boy, I seldom make an error."

President Byrne of Brooklyn is in Columbus with his team. "In case we win, I think we would find it easier to beat the New-Yorks than the Bostons," he said, in reference to the world's series. "In last Spring's series Mutrie's club won two games out of three from us, but it was chiefly due to accident. We made more base hits, fewer errors, and played a steadier game than they. As soon as the Association struggle is over I will arrange the world's series at once. Of course, the New-York 'cranks' think that they will have a soft snap, but we may fool them. I think that Brooklyn can beat New-York, or, in fact, any club in the League or Association. The Giants may beat us and surprise me. If they do it will be after the hardest struggle of their lives. The Brooklyns are ball players, every man of them, and they are in championship form now. If we meet the great Giants they had better look to their laurels as we propose to show them who are the people!"

"Mike" Kelly is an ardent admirer of the Giants. He is of the opinion that nothing short of an accident can make the New-Yorks lose the series. "Baseball is uncertain, " he remarked, "but if things break even or near it the New-Yorks will win to a certainty. Why, Brooklyn is not in the same class with New-York. That catcher of the New-York Club is a team by himself. He is not an ordinary ball player; he is a wonder of the nineteenth century. There is only one great ball player in the country, and he is William Ewing. He stands head and shoulders above all others. In other words, Ewing is in a class by himself. The New-York Captain knows more about baseball in one second than the majority of ball players will learn in a dozen seasons. Only for Ewing I would be Captain of the champion team. He is half of the New-York Club, and without him New-York would be third or fourth in the League race. Ewing is a good ball player, an unassuming gentleman, and, above all things, his hat always fits him.

"No man, past or present," continued the Boston idol, " has any right to be put in his class, and I don't think we shall ever see his like again. He is to the average ball tosser what Napoleon was compared to his lieutenants, what Booth is to a Bowery 'ham fatter,' what the Statue of Liberty is to a toothpick, and I am proud to be his understudy."

—New York *Times*

Day wants Brooklyn to win the championship, as no price will be too great for that city to pay for first honors, and the crowds will be immense, even if it is cold enough to freeze. It would not be at all surprising if the average attendance at the games in Brooklyn were 8000. It does not look quite so nice for the Brooklyns now as it did a few weeks ago. What stayers those St. Louis men are, to be sure! Think, too, that they have crept this close to the leaders with Latham out of the club and King in disgrace.

—Boston *Herald*

Tuesday, October 15

On October 14, Brooklyn won at Columbus 6–1 (Terry 22–15).
St. Louis won at Cincinnati 5–1 (King 34–17).
AA: Brooklyn 93–44, St. Louis 89–44.

Yesterday's contest may be regarded as one marked by the most noteworthy victory the Brooklyn team have achieved this season. Every circumstance was against them in the contest. They were on their enemies' ground, opposed by a team determined to use every possible effort to beat the Brooklyns, and with the crowd of spectators dead against the visitors, Buckenberger having carried out his threat to employ hoodlums to insult the Brooklyn players. Under such a condition of things to win as they did was a double triumph.

Will Terry has, by his gentlemanly conduct on all occasions, by his strictly temperate habits, determined pluck and perseverance in the face of difficulties, and earnest effort to do his best for the welfare of the club, long ago earned a reputation second to that of no one in the professional fraternity. But in the effective work he did in the box in the last two critical contests in Columbus he added laurels to his wreath which make him the star of his company in the closing battles of the campaign.

—Brooklyn *Daily Eagle*

Cincinnati, O., Oct. 14—The St. Louis and Cincinnati teams opened the first game of their last series at the Cincinnati Ball Park this afternoon in the presence of 2,000. The weather was cold, raw and cheerless, but the great interest manifested in the outcome of the game has overcome all weather drawbacks.

The Browns won, beating the Cincinnatis by a one-sided score, but Brooklyn kept up its beastly way of winning, taking a game from Columbus. The Browns are no nearer to the pennant than they were this morning.

—St. Louis *Post-Dispatch*

When this morning's papers conveyed the intelligence of the arrangements the Cincinnati and Athletic clubs had made to deprive Brooklyn of their well earned laurels a howl of righteous indignation went up from the entire Metropolis, as it was then plainly to be seen that the conspiracy which had deprived the Brooklyn Club of its rights in the forfeited game lost to Brooklyn by St. Louis had been further extended to include the three days of grace given the clubs after the close of the regular season, which ended yesterday. That the arrangements to play the extra games entered into by the Cincinnati and Athletic clubs have been made solely with a view to down the Brooklyn team at any cost is too apparent to be questioned for a moment, and it is but a fitting climax to the discreditable action taken by the Board of Directors at their Cincinnati meeting.

Here is what Mr. Byrne, in a letter to the public at large, has to say about it:

Columbus, O., October 14.

Under the schedule adopted by the American Association, limiting games from April 17 to October 14, we have won the American Association championship. Under the form of law the directors of the association deprived Brooklyn of a game it was justly entitled to from St. Louis. The combination to deprive Brooklyn of its victory is still operating. Two games are to be played by St. Louis in Cincinnati to-morrow to enable St. Louis to get to Philadelphia to play off its postponed games there. This, if done, simply makes our championship race a farce. If we are deprived of the victory we have honestly earned by these methods we must trust our cause to an honest press and public sentiment.

—Brooklyn *Daily Eagle*

AMERICAN ASSOCIATION STANDINGS

	W	L	PCT.	GB		W	L	PCT.	GB
Brooklyn	93	44	.679	—	Baltimore	70	64	.522	21½
St. Louis	89	44	.669	2	Columbus	59	78	.431	34
Athletic	75	58	.564	16	Kansas City	55	82	.401	38
Cincinnati	74	62	.544	18½	Louisville	27	110	.197	66

Wednesday, October 16

On October 15, the last day of the season
in the American Association, St. Louis lost and
won at Cincinnati 3–8 and 2–1
(Stivetts 12–7; Chamberlain 34–15).
AA: Brooklyn 93–44, St. Louis 90–45.

Cincinnati, O., Oct. 15—Two thousand people saw the two games between St. Louis and Cincinnati this afternoon. Both sides were in for blood. The first contest began at 1:30 o'clock with Duryea and Keenan as the battery for Cincinnati and Stivetts and Milligan for the visitors. Hits by McPhee, Reilly and Carpenter's double gave Porkopolis three runs in the first. Bad errors by Stivetts and Milligan gave Cincinnati two more in the second. The ex-champions seemed to go to pieces in the fourth and bad errors by Milligan and Boyle gave the Reds a run. The Reds put another nail in St. Louis' coffin by an earned run in the sixth on McPhee's double and steal, and Holliday's sacrifice.

In the ninth, St. Louis went to the bat for the last time. The jig was up and they played as if they thought so. Boyle struck out and Duffee followed suit. Fuller ended the agony with a fly to Tebeau and all chances of St. Louis were gone.

President Von der Ahe, who had arranged to take his team to Philadelphia in case he won both games here, decided not to go. He was very much broken up over his defeat.

—St. Louis *Post-Dispatch*

The fortune of baseball has smiled on New-York and vicinity this season. A week ago the Giants came home winners of the League pennant, and yesterday Col. Byrne and his band of Brooklyn players returned to their native heath winners of the championship honors of the American Association. It has been a great season for the national game in his vicinity, and stockholders, managers, players, and enthusiasts are all happy.

When the news reached Brooklyn that St. Louis had been beaten at

Cincinnati, the flags were run up over the City Hall and the other public buildings. Shortly after 5 o'clock the Brooklyn players, accompanied
by a score of friends, arrived in town, and were driven up Fulton-street
in open carriages. They were surrounded by hundreds of people and
cheered heartily as they went up town. They are to be given a dinner at
the Academy of Music, at which Mayor Chapin will preside.

—New York *Times*

Yesterday's games decided the American Association championship.
Brooklyn gets the pennant and St. Louis finishes a fair second. It was a
hard race to lose, as St. Louis had a team which, had they played ball,
could have won with a margin of twelve or fifteen games. For the first
time since the team has been in the Association there has been serious
dissension in the ranks. There have been slight quibbles before in the
club but not till this season has the trouble been of so serious a character as to interfere with the play of the organization. The first trouble
arose when Robinson was fined. At that time the club had a good lead
which it was daily increasing. A strike was threatened by the players when
the second baseman was fined and the club went to Kansas City and purposely dropped three games, which, had they won as they could have
done, would have made them champions. From that time on there was
more or less trouble in the team. They played good ball for awhile and
assumed a commanding lead and then they again fell off in their play
and it became painfully evident to all that some of the men were not trying to play ball. About the 1st of July Latham commenced his peculiar
work, and King became very ineffective. On their last Eastern trip in
September the work of some of the men was such that all the League
players are said to have talked of the crooked work going on in the team.
After their return home the poor work was kept up and the fining and
suspension of King and Latham and fining and reprimanding of Chamberlain and Robinson followed. With Latham off the club they invariably played much better ball, despite the fact that he is one of the best
players in the country when he tries to play. At the close of the season
the club made a grand rally and hard fight for the bunting, winning twelve
consecutive games before they finally met with their fatal defeat at Cincinnati yesterday.

Not only did the club have to contend with dissension in its own
ranks, but suffered straight along from the umpiring which was strongly
favorable to Brooklyn from the outset. Such favoritism to a club as the
Association displayed to Brooklyn this season was never before known
in any League. Not only were the umpires favorable to Brooklyn, but
some clubs played very strange ball when pitted against them. The whole
thing looks very suspicious, and if the Brooklyn management were not

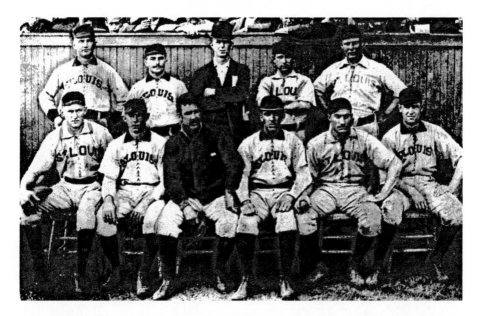

St. Louis Browns, 1889. *Standing, left to right:* "Silver" King, Tommy McCarthy, Manager Charlie Comiskey, "Yank" Robinson, Jocko Milligan. *Sitting, left to right:* Jack Boyle, Charlie Duffee, Arlie Latham, "Shorty" Fuller, Jack Stivetts, "Tip" O'Neill (National Baseball Hall of Fame Library, Cooperstown, NY).

guilty of underhand work they are certainly surrounded by an unfortunate chain of circumstances which looks decidedly bad. The number of games won by Brooklyn where they have been outplayed by their opponents has a peculiar look to say the least.

—St. Louis *Post-Dispatch*

Washington, D.C., Oct. 15, 1889—Cincinnati will in all probability be admitted to membership in the league at the November meeting, in the event of Washington's withdrawal. Brooklyn would be delighted to join the league ranks, but something must be done to strengthen the western circuit, as Chicago is now the only drawing city in that section. The eastern clubs all prefer Brooklyn to any other city that has been mentioned, but the western contingent insist that Cincinnati is a more desirable city from their standpoint. Should the Cincinnatis retire from the American association during the month of November, they can take with them into the league all of the members of their present team, if they so desire, a privilege granted them in sec. 6 of the national agreement.

—Boston *Herald*

Final American Association Standings

	W	L	PCT.	GB		W	L	PCT.	GB
Brooklyn	93	44	.679	—	Baltimore	70	65	.519	22
St. Louis	90	45	.667	2	Columbus	59	78	.431	34
Athletic	76	58	.567	15½	Kansas City	55	82	.401	38
Cincinnati	75	63	.543	18½	Louisville	27	110	.197	66

Thursday, October 17

To-morrow afternoon the Giants and the Bridegrooms will begin the great diamond-field struggle to determine which is the champion club of the year. It required but a few moments to arrange matters. New-York wanted to meet Brooklyn, and the latter was equally anxious to face the great Giants. The meeting to arrange the games was held in the office of the *Sporting Times* yesterday afternoon. President Day and Manager Mutrie represented the New-Yorks, while President Byrne and Major Abel looked after the interests of the Brooklyns.

It was decided at once to play eleven games. As soon as one club wins six the contest will end. It was decided to charge the regular League rate to all games—50 cents admission and 25 cents for the grand stand. The opening game will be played on the Polo Grounds on Friday afternoon. After that the contests will alternate between New-York and Brooklyn until the requisite number is won. The gate money will be evenly divided, while each club will keep the grand stand money of the home games.

Betting among baseball enthusiasts is very brisk. New-York is a slight favorite, but Brooklyn backers can be found in all quarters. At Washington Park next Saturday it is safe to say that New-Yorkers will be able to lay their money at even figures.

—New York *Times*

The world's series of contests which begin to-morrow will be the struggle of the season and the most exciting series of games ever played in New York and Brooklyn ball fields, far surpassing in public interest and excitement the old time battles on the Union Grounds between the Atlantic and Mutual clubs of twenty years ago.

—Brooklyn *Daily Eagle*

When the players refuse to sign the contracts next Monday, the League clubs will break the national agreement and proceed to gobble up the best players in the Western Association, International League,

New England League and other minor associations. No attempt will be made to secure players from the American Association. The latter association is too strong, and the League cannot afford to undertake to fight it and the Brotherhood at the same time, as such a contest could only result in their own destruction. On the other hand they will endeavor to make an ally of the American Association and try to influence them to join them in the fight on the minor leagues. It is very doubtful whether the association can be drawn into such a trap. Its wisest policy is clearly to hold hands off and let the League fight its own battle with the Brotherhood and minor leagues.

—St. Louis *Post-Dispatch*

Friday, October 18

Now is the day and now is the hour for the great base ball event of the season, viz., the first game of the grand series of contests for the base ball championship of the United States—and necessarily for that of the world—between the champion teams of the National League and the American Association, and the two competing teams which will face each other to-day at the Polo Grounds, and their order of batting, will be as follows:

New York	Brooklyn
Gore, c.f.	O'Brien, l. f.
Tiernan, r. f.	Collins, 2b.
Ward, s. s.	Foutz, 1b.
Richardson, 2b.	Burns, r. f.
Connor, 1b.	Pinkney, 3b.
O'Rourke, l. f.	Corkhill, c. f.
Ewing, c.	Visner, c.
Keefe, p.	Caruthers, p.
Whitney, 3b.	Smith, s. s.

Unluckily the chances are for a great deal of kicking, there being so much betting on the result of the contests that the crowd will be an unusually prejudiced one, as there is not a man who has a bet on the result who will be apt to view any decision of the umpires which works against his side with impartiality. This is an invariable rule. But it is to be hoped that the fair and impartial spectators of the crowd will control the betting people on the occasion.

—Brooklyn *Daily Eagle*

The opening contest of the great world series of base ball games is in progress on the Polo Grounds, in New York. Of course every lover of the national pastime in Brooklyn hopes that the Bridegrooms will come out victors in the initial contest, while it is equally safe to assume that their brethren of the Metropolis are confident of the success of the Giants.

At noon the elevated and surface cars, the bridge cars and the ferryboats, by reason of their largely increased cargoes of humanity, gave proof of the great interest felt in this city for the success of the home players. Staid business men vacated their offices, privileged clerks left their desks, sly messengers and office boys became suddenly ill, and even the reverend guardians of our welfare in the hereafter joined the jostling throngs at the bridge and at the river. The late comer to the Polo Grounds fared badly if he had corns because, as an observant newsboy expressed it, he had to sit on his feet. So much care has been taken by Presidents Day and Byrne to eliminate from the arrangements any element which could possibly beget friction that it is proper to aver that during the entire series the lovers of the game will be treated to exhibitions devoid of trickery, bullyism, or ungentlemanly conduct on the part of the bat handlers.

It is needless to say that the Bridegrooms feel that they are the cynosure of eager eyes all over the continent and that they will go into the struggle with a determination to exercise all the skill begotten of a season's campaign and to do credit to the city whose name they bear. In the words of one of their most enthusiastic Hibernian admirers: "More power to their elbows."

—Brooklyn *Daily Eagle*

The *World* this morning says that "Dave Foutz cashed in $245 yesterday in bets made during the past season. He immediately placed $100 of it on to-day's game and made an agreement with Caruthers whereby, if the latter pitches, he will give him $50 if he wins, or Caruthers will give him $50 if he loses." This, if true, ought to be stopped by Mr. Byrne. It makes players too anxious about their bets to play coolly in a match.

—Brooklyn *Daily Eagle*

Saturday, October 19

On October 18, Brooklyn beat New York 12–10
at the Polo Grounds (Terry 1–0; Keefe 0–1).
Brooklyn 1, New York 0.

Baseball enthusiasts, like every other class of people, have their ups and downs in this world. For the past two weeks joy has reigned supreme among the ballmen of the diamond-field sport of this city, caused by the grand victory achieved by the Giants in the race for the League pennant. The big Giants, however, received a setback in the shape of a defeat from Brooklyn yesterday in the opening game for the world's series, and to-day there is mourning in the camp of their admirers.

Defeat from any other quarter would be bad enough, but the stigma was intensified because Brooklyn made the mighty Giants lower their colors. The rivalry between New-York and Brooklyn as regards baseball is unparalleled in the history of the national game. It is not confined to the players or the attaches of the clubs, but the patrons take part in it. Old men, middle-aged men, beardless youths, small boys, and even members of the gentler sex have the fever, and when the champions of the two teams meet heated arguments as to the merits of the nines are sure to follow. Just 8,445 persons paid to see the contest between the two champions yesterday on the New Polo Grounds. About nine-tenths of that number were of the class generally known as "cranks." While the New-Yorkers seemed to be in the majority, there was a good share of Brooklynites present, and for two hours they made matters rather lively in the upper portion of Manhattan Island. They shouted, cheered, hissed, yelled, stamped their feet, clapped their hands, and acted as only baseball "cranks" can. Every minute point of the game was watched with eager eyes, and no play worthy of applause went by unnoticed. In fact, every play, commonplace or otherwise, was cheered to the echo, and the contestants could not complain of lack of enthusiasm. If anything, there was too much, and at times the coachers made themselves heard only with difficulty.

It was a most peculiar contest. Brooklyn started out with a total of 5 runs in the opening inning, and for a time it looked as though they would make a runaway game of it. The Giants, however, checked them in short order. Then they began to overhaul the leaders. They crept up run by run until the seventh inning, when they made a spurt of 5 runs and jumped into the lead. They only held it for a short time, however. In the eighth inning Brooklyn got to another streak of batting and scored 4 runs, which won for them the game. It was very dark, however, when the runs were scored and several of the hits would have been captured by fielders, if there had been sufficient light. Little Richardson, who had played a remarkably brilliant game, made an unfortunate error for New-York. He failed to stop a grounder batted by O'Brien, which would have retired the side. This would have ended the game with New-York in the lead by 2 runs. It was a costly error, and the popular little second baseman realized it. Last night he was in an unhappy frame of mind, and, although his colleagues tried to cheer him up, he felt that the loss of the game rested on his shoulders.

The winners also showed good judgment in some respects. Players as a rule like to make a reputation by stealing bases off a catcher of the caliber of Ewing. But the Brooklyns proved that they are not gaited that way. They stuck to their bases, and not in one instance did they attempt to steal a base. They have seen and heard too much of the abilities of the New-York Captain and his fondness for throwing out swift runners, and they did not care to afford him any amusement. It was a wise move. In batting Collins led both teams. He made a home run, two doubles, and a single, an achievement that he has reason to be proud of, considering that he faced one of the best, if not the best, pitcher in the profession.

The umpiring, too, was anything but favorable to New-York. Messrs. Gaffney and Ferguson, two American Association men, officiated. It was nine League players against eleven Association men. Gaffney's work gave general satisfaction, but Ferguson's rulings greatly displeased the New-York players and their friends. He is a lifelong resident of Brooklyn. Everybody appeared to know it, and close attention was paid to his work. He will not officiate to-day. President Day said that he would not allow his men to play under him again.

The friends of the Giants could hardly realize that they had been defeated. They looked on in silence while the Brooklyn contingent yelled as loudly as their lungs would permit. Capt. O'Brien was hoisted on the shoulders of a dozen enthusiasts and carried triumphantly off the field, while the Giants made their way to the clubhouse with measured steps.
—New York *Times*

It is the unexpected that happens in base ball almost invariably, and it is this very uncertainty as to the results of contests in the national game which is one of its greatest attractions to the public at large. In the opinion of the great majority of the residents of Manhattan Island it was decidedly the unexpected which happened yesterday at the Polo Grounds on the occasion of the first meeting between the contesting teams for the world's championship honors, for to the New York base ball cranks the outcome of yesterday's game was regarded as certain victory for their pet team. Were they not the twice pennant winners of the National League? Did they not hold the world's championship emblem, won easily from the four time pennant winners of the American Association? Had they not whipped Boston's great batting team? What warrant was there, therefore, for supposing that "that village nine from Long Island" could cross the river and meet with anything but defeat at the hands of the great base ball giants of New York, headed by the great "Buck" Ewing? It was gross presumption on the part of Byrne's team to think for a moment that they would have the least chance of success on the occasion, especially in view of the fact that New York would be on its own camping ground, and would be backed by its own crowd of patrons in the contest. Nevertheless, the unexpected did happen, and Brooklyn's David knocked out New York's great Goliath and took the initiatory steps for becoming giant killers, to the intense disgust of the New York cranks of every description, and especially to the chagrin of the city's betting crowd, who had backed New York to win at large odds.

—Brooklyn *Daily Eagle*

Sunday, October 20

On October 19, New York beat Brooklyn 6–2 at Washington Park (Crane 1–0; Caruthers 0–1). Brooklyn 1, New York 1.

By four runs the New-York Giants showed their superiority over the Brooklyn team yesterday. In consequence the army of baseball cranks in this city is happy, and the Brooklyn enthusiasts who indulged in some town painting on Friday evening are correspondingly sad. It was a great game. Brooklyn tried hard to win, but the odds were against the Bridegrooms. They stubbornly contested every inch of ground, and were only defeated because of the Giants' superior skill on the diamond.

Although beaten the Brooklyn boys are entitled to some credit. They proved beyond doubt that they possess gameness and know how to play ball, but the contract on their hands is one that the Brooklyn or any other team is unable to fulfill. They were forced to meet the strongest aggregation of baseball talent in the country, and it was odds against them that they could not win. The friends of Brooklyn watched, waited, and hoped, and never lost faith in the ability of their champions to win until the third hand was out in the ninth inning.

Washington Park, on Fifth-avenue, Brooklyn, where the contest took place, was a study for an artist. For nearly two hours before the game began the turnstiles at the gates kept clicking continuously, and the lovers of outdoor sports passed through by the hundreds. In a short time all the seats were taken and standing room was at a premium. The spectators were forced to take to the field, where they formed a horseshoe of human heads around the playing line. Old men, young men, small boys, with a young lady here and there, formed the assemblage. The banks were crowded and hundreds of small boys, in order to get a bird's-eye view of the game, clambered to the top of the fence and watched the struggle to their hearts' content. It was a grand sight. Thousands of human faces could be seen in all directions, and save a few tilts, in which dyed-in-the-wool "cranks" took part, the best of good nature prevailed. When the game was half over and the turnstiles had finished their work they

CRANE, P., New Yorks
COPYRIGHT BY GOODWIN & CO., 1888.
OLD JUDGE
CIGARETTE FACTORY.
GOODWIN & CO., New York.

Ed "Cannonball" Crane, pitcher, New York Giants (Library of Congress, Prints and Photographs Division [LOT 13163-05, no. 165]).

registered 16,100. This is the second largest crowd that has ever assembled on the grounds.

As to the game, it was one that will long be remembered. Crane pitched as perhaps he never did before. He sent the ball over the plate with the speed of a cannon ball, and it was only with the greatest of difficulty that the Brooklyn men could gauge its course. And Ewing. He caught one of his best games. His work as a backstop and Captain provoked favorable comments in all quarters and he was given the lion's share of the applause. The task of catching Crane's speedy pitching is not an easy one by any means, but Ewing kept pluckily at his work.

In the second inning Collins took first on balls and was stealing to second. Ewing made a feint as if to throw to Richardson, but sent the ball to Whitney like a rifle shot. The latter caught "Pop" Corkhill off third base and three hands were out. Cries of "Ewing! Ewing!" could be heard everywhere, while the Brooklynites looked on in amazement. The play was something of a novelty to them. "There's a great ball player," said "Bob" Ferguson, pointing to Ewing after he had made the play. "He is without an equal as a ball player. He plays with his hands and head, particularly the head."

—New York *Times*

It was well that the Saturday game was scheduled for the Brooklyn grounds, for the Polo Grounds would not have held half the attendance and play would have been impossible. As early as 1 o'clock, when the gates were opened, the streets surrounding the park were crowded with cranks clamoring for admission, while the street cars kept pouring out more rooting humanity on their way to see the great game. At 2:30 every seat on the grounds was occupied, while every bare spot and the ground outside the ropes in far center field were crowded with expectant enthusiasts, impatient for the contest to commence. When space on the field was unavailable a crowd of youngsters and men took up points of vantage on top of the fences, perching themselves like so many sparrows.

The New Yorks took the field for practice at 2:30 o'clock under the lead of the great Ewing, the king pin of the diamond, and all were heartily cheered. As the association champions marched to the field the concourse of spectators rose and cheered as one man. This lasted several minutes and a monster horseshoe of roses presented by a local furniture company was placed conspicuously in the field.

Horns were plentiful on the grounds and were used frequently; in fact every good play brought out a blast which was heard a block away. A misplay of any of the opposing teams also caused a loud blast of derision. The New Yorkers had small tin horns, but the Brooklynites went further and procured fog horns which were heard every time a Bridegroom made a good hit or a fine play.

A large crowd surrounded the New Yorks as they left the field victorious and cheered them to the echo. Ewing left the field in the midst of an admiring throng, who gazed at him curiously. They were mostly Brooklynites who had never seen the only Buck before.

—Brooklyn *Daily Eagle*

New York, Oct. 19—The New York and Brooklyn base ball patrons are at present enjoying a treat, the like of which was never known—the New York and Brooklyn teams arrayed in battle for the world's championship. For years this event has been looked forward to with eagerness by everyone who cares for base ball in the two cities, and now at last their hopes are being realized.

Many Brooklyn people will be prevented from going to see the games in New York by reason of the long journey home, which will consume more than an hour and a half. On the other hand, Washington Park is within twenty minutes reach of the New York side of the big bridge, and New Yorkers may see the games in Brooklyn and get home in time for supper.

—St. Louis *Post-Dispatch*

Monday, October 21

New York, Oct. 20, 1889—Mr. Byrne was a proud man Saturday, and well he might have been. He wanted to show what a grand base ball city is Brooklyn, and he did it. It is an open secret that he desires to gain admission to the league. He wants to come in badly. The league needs him, too. Washington cannot be compared to Brooklyn in any respect as a base ball city. Mr. Byrne is one of the ablest of the association officials, and he has done a great deal for that body since he became connected with it. He is sick of the company, however. There is very little ability there. Von der Ahe, Barnie, Sharsig, Stearn, are not men of the Spalding, Day, Brush, Nimick, Soden stripe. The league is head and shoulders ahead, as far as brains are concerned, and Byrne knows it. He is an able, energetic, pushing man, ambitious to a high degree. He would be a valuable man. The opposition to him comes from the New York club, and is said to be directed against the man rather than the club. Mr. John B. Day does not like Charles H. Byrne. The rivalry between New York and Brooklyn would be of immense financial advantage to both clubs.

—Boston *Herald*

Tuesday, October 22

Over three thousand people wended their way to One Hundred and Fifty-fifth street yesterday to see the third game of the series between the New York and Brooklyn teams at the Polo Grounds, only to find to their chagrin that the grounds were too muddy from the rain of the early morning to be played upon. No notice was sent to the down town stations that there was no game, as it was expected that if the sun came out warm the ground would dry up sufficiently.

—Brooklyn *Daily Eagle*

Wednesday, October 23

On October 22, Brooklyn beat New York 8–7
at the Polo Grounds (Hughes 1–0; Welch 0–1).
Brooklyn 2, New York 1.

"It's a hundred dollars to a toothpick that we win to-day," said Capt. Ewing just before the New-York and Brooklyn champions began the third of the series yesterday. But ball players, like other human beings, are not infallible, and the Captain who had so skillfully piloted the Giants to victory this season made a big error. The toothpick end of the bet won, or in other words, the players from the other side of the bridge made the haughty Giants lower their colors once more.

Welch from the outset had little or no speed, and the Brooklyns hit the ball hard and often. Then Capt. Ewing called in O'Day. He pitched great ball, retiring the Association men without a hit or a run. The Brooklyns can hit slow pitching, and if the Giants want to win they will have to let Crane and O'Day do the pitching in the future.

In the latter part of the game the crowd grew disgusted at the antics of the Brooklyn men. They delayed the game at every opportunity, so that darkness would end the contest while they were in the lead. It is an old trick, and the spectators discovered the object in an instant. They hissed the Brooklyn men frequently. "The days of such tactics are gone by," said Manager Mutrie, "and it comes with poor grace for the Brooklyn men to resort to them. Such methods are disgusting and do not tend to elevate the national pastime. The Brooklyns played like schoolboys. I would sooner lose a game than win as they did this afternoon."

—New York *Times*

A fine day and the promise of an exciting contest should have led to another 8,000 crowd yesterday at the Polo Grounds, but apparently the first day's experience of wretched management by the elevated railroad company last Friday and the disappointment occasioned by being allowed to take the long trip up to One Hundred and Fifty-fifth street on Monday for nothing had a disastrous effect on the attendance and the result was that there were plenty of seats to be had at 3 P.M. yesterday at the Polo Grounds, alike in the grand stand and on the bleaching boards. In fact, the great majority of the patrons of the two clubs prefer a visit to Washington Park to the long trip to Manhattanville judging from the attendance at the two grounds thus far, and under the circumstances, the New York Club will find it to their pecuniary advantage to play Saturday's game in Brooklyn instead of at the Polo Grounds as now scheduled.

In the ninth inning, which was commenced at 5 P.M., Connor led off with a base hit, but he was forced out by Richardson. Then O'Rourke and Whitney were given their bases on balls. By this time it was 5:07 o'clock and the sun was due to set at 5:13 P.M. and Umpire Gaffney called the game on account of darkness. This left the score at the end of the eighth inning to decide the contest, and as that was 8 to 7 in favor of Brooklyn, they left the field victors.

—Brooklyn *Daily Eagle*

New York, Oct. 22—It is definitely ascertained that the annual meeting of the Brotherhood of Base Ball Players is to be held in this city on Monday, November 4. This is ten days previous to the League meeting, and whatever schemes the Brotherhood have in process of incubation will be popped at their coming congress. In course of a conversation yesterday, John M. Ward was asked, "What do you think of the statement made by the League officers and others that the Brotherhood scheme will fall through?" was asked.

"I do not know what Brotherhood scheme you refer to," replied Ward. "As far as their statements are concerned I think they are as foolish as can be. They jump before the public and postulate a theory or a scheme which they call a 'Brotherhood plan.' Then they tear it to pieces and claim that it will never work. If the base-ball players of the League should make up their minds to play ball for men with just as much money and an amount of brains equal to that possessed by the League people, can they be prevented? I think not. You see I do not bring the Brotherhood into the case at all. I am merely supposing a case. The team can reserve players within League limits, but they can no more prevent a player from playing with another organization than they can prevent him from earning a livelihood by keeping a hotel or driving a dray."

—St. Louis *Post-Dispatch*

Thursday, October 24

On October 23, Brooklyn beat New York 10–7 at
Washington Park (Terry 2–0; Crane 1–1).
Brooklyn 3, New York 1.

The change in the weather made it very uncomfortable at the Brooklyn ball grounds yesterday. It was a chilly day for the spectators, chilly for the Bridegrooms, but a very cold day for the New-Yorks. They went to Brooklyn fully confident of whipping the Association winners, and came back last night with another defeat charged against them. The score is now 3 to 1 against the Giants, and unless they brace up in short order the Association champions will snatch the championship from the big League club.

The New-Yorks were handicapped by the rulings of the umpires. Mr. Gaffney, in particular, made one decision that affected the result and perhaps won the game for Brooklyn. He declared Gore out in the sixth inning, when his run, according to the rules, should have counted. The wrangle that ensued delayed the game, and, in consequence, only six innings could be played. It was so dark when the Brooklyns were at the bat in the sixth inning that O'Rourke was unable to see a fly ball batted by Burns. This play gave Brooklyn three runs and the game.

"I am sick and tired of the methods resorted to by the Brooklyns," said Capt. Ewing last evening. "We have played like men, but the Brooklyns have disported themselves like schoolboys. Their work throughout has been of the sneaky order. They have made use of tactics that my men would not stoop to. And the umpires! I don't know what to make of them. In every game they have handicapped us, but it must be stopped.

In the future Gaffney and Lynch will have to umpire the games strictly on their merits or I will know the reason why. It's an outrage the way we have been treated. Of course, the boys have not been playing good ball, but if the umpiring had been just we should have won three games."

—New York *Times*

Those who failed to be present at Washington Park yesterday missed seeing the most exciting game of the world's series thus far, beside which they failed to witness ocular demonstration and the utter absurdity of the charge of "hippodroming" made against the two contesting teams, for never did two rival nines in a championship contest "play ball for blood" as the teams of New York and Brooklyn did yesterday. The visitors came over confident of victory with their "lightning pitcher" Crane in the box, while the home team felt just as much confidence in being able to do up the Giants again with Terry in the box.

When in the sixth inning the visitors made a successful assault on the home battery, almost carrying it by storm, the New York and Boston scribes in the press box made up a kicking reserve corps who out Heroded Herod in the free use of vile and abusive epithets addressed to the umpires, such terms as "robbers," "thieves," etc., being bandied about with the freedom of old Billingsgate days. From the talk of these impartial scribes—who all had New York spectacles on, of the regular partisan color—one would have supposed that the league club teams were models of deportment, while those of the association were neither more nor less than corner lot loafers. In fact, wild abuse ran rampant in the press box for about a quarter of an hour, so mad were the majority at the defeat their pets had sustained.

—Brooklyn *Daily Eagle*

Friday, October 25

On October 24, New York beat Brooklyn 11–3 at
Washington Park (Crane 2–1; Caruthers 0–2).
Brooklyn 3, New York 2.

One of the runaway games for which the Giants are peculiar was played yesterday, and the Brooklyns looked on in astonishment. They saw the curves of their favorite pitcher, Mr. Caruthers, batted unmercifully, and watched Giant after Giant touch the base plate and score. It was a one-sided game. The League champions played in their old form, and at no stage did the Brooklyns stand a chance to win. They were like amateurs in the hands of the brawny and skillful Giants.

Left: Willard "Big Bill" or "California" Brown, catcher, New York Giants (Library of Congress, Prints and Photographs Division [LOT 13163-05, no. 157]). *Right:* John B. Day, president, New York Giants (Transcendental Graphics).

At his request Crane pitched again and showed rare speed. He was handicapped by poor umpiring, but he overcame that obstacle and pitched a great game. Ewing reported sick early in the day, and substitute Brown was forced to put on the mask. And he was an acceptable substitute. He received the swift delivery of big Crane in a skillful manner, and kept a sharp lookout for the young men who are in the habit of pilfering bases. In fact, Brown's work was one of the features of the game, and the big Californian was warmly applauded. All the boys played great ball, and, judging from the manner in which they disposed of their opponents, they have struck their gait.

Before the game began yesterday Presidents Day and Byrne, Capt. O'Brien, Acting Captain Richardson, and Umpires Lynch and Gaffney had a conference in President Byrne's office. Mr. Day said that the work of the umpires was of the worst possible character in the four games that had been played. He attributed the poor success of the New-Yorks to one-sided umpiring and dirty tactics on the part of the Brooklyn players. "I want," he continued, "only what belongs to me, and I will have it or know the reason why. If the Brooklyns resort any longer to the dirty tactics that have characterized them in the games already played, and if the umpires continue to favor Brooklyn, the series will end with to-day's game. I will not allow my team to compete against a club that insists on playing dirty ball." The Captains were ordered to abide by the decision of the umpire and not delay the game by questioning and arguing points. Before the game yesterday, Mr. Day said that he was surprised at the work of Mr. Gaffney. He thinks the latter is either incompetent or "crooked."

—New York *Times*

The contest at Washington Park yesterday was preceded by a very important meeting in Mr. Byrne's office, at which those in attendance were Presidents Day and Byrne and Umpires Lynch and Gaffney. The two umpires expressed themselves as justly indignant at the charges of partiality made against them by the betting members of the press who had backed New York to win at odds, and especially did they personally object to the alleged charges of "robbery" said to have emanated from one of the league officials. In fact, it would only have taken another such an outrageous scene as that of Wednesday to have led them to retire from further umpiring in the series. Mr. Day was plainly made to understand that the charges made by his team players would no longer be submitted to and it was finally decided that in the concluding games of the series every man who disputed a decision of the umpire should be promptly fined, and if the offense were repeated the culprit or culprits should be removed from the field. The two captains were then called in and distinctly told by Presidents Day and Byrne that no more kicking would be permitted by either of them.

—Brooklyn *Daily Eagle*

It is doubtful whether better material for real social enjoyment was ever gathered together in the Assembly Rooms than last night clustered about the banquet tables where distinguished citizens of this city entertained President C.H. Byrne, the officers, managers and members of the victorious Brooklyn Base Ball Club. Every man present was an enthusiastic admirer of the game and anxious to do honor to the collection of players whose prowess and skill upon the diamond have brought honor and glory to Brooklyn town. A long table in the center of the room was reserved for the "Bridegrooms."

The pennant winners entered the dining room in a body about ten minutes after the rest of the guests had been assigned to their places. The coming of the gallant boys of Washington Park was the signal for a greeting which for genuine enthusiasm one could rarely see equaled. The band played a triumphal march, 150 napkins were waved in the air and 150 voices shouted welcome. Again and again the applause was renewed. It was a proud moment for the Bridegrooms, a proud moment for President Byrne, a proud moment for all the lovers of the national game that were present.

—Brooklyn *Daily Eagle*

The New Yorkers who charged President Von der Ahe of resorting to "the baby act" when he complained that the Brooklyns were winning the championship through the favoritism of umpires are now howling themselves hoarse about Byrne's trickery and the manner in which the umpires have been robbing the Giants. President Day very truly states that his club has lost its three games by trickery on the part of the Brooklyns, and says that unless the games are played on their merits he will not permit his team to play any more. He also volunteered the statement that the ball playing the Brooklyns had been doing and the umpiring done in their interest were enough to kill the game.

—St. Louis *Post-Dispatch*

Chicago, Oct. 24—Chris Von der Ahe, President of the St. Louis Club, is in this city and held a conference yesterday with President Spalding of the Chicago Club. The supposition is that the talk referred to the proposed independent move of the Brotherhood of Baseball Players. After the conference Mr. Von der Ahe said to a reporter:

"The Association will have to stand by the League. I don't speak officially as President of the St. Louis Club, but I believe that is the inevitable outcome of the fight. It is a question of capital against labor, and capital must stick by capital. The Brotherhood may think it can command capital on its side, but it will get left on that point. To mention nothing else, there are not six men in the whole Brotherhood who have an ounce of business brains. They are good ball players, but they can't manage. They can't even take care of the salaries they are now getting. And capitalists are not going to trust their money in such hands, and right here let me emphasize the fact that it takes capital, and big capital, to run the ball business. I exhaust this point when I say that A.G. Spalding is the only instance in the history of the game of a ball player developing into a successful manager."

"Johnny Ward," he continued, "no doubt, thinks he could manage. Johnny also calls himself a lawyer. Why doesn't he practice law, then? Simply because he is a ball player—nothing more—and couldn't make enough money at law in a year to pay one week's board."

—New York *Times*

The issue of the *Sporting News*, which will appear to-morrow, will contain a rather startling article on how the League intends to fight the Brotherhood. The scheme is nothing more nor less than the consolidation of the National League and American Association into one organization of ten or twelve clubs, the unprofitable cities of both bodies being dropped.

This one-association idea has long been a pet scheme of President Von der Ahe of the Browns and he is known to have been at work on it for a year past. Should the consolidation of the two associations take place, as now seems assured, it will unquestionably be owing to his efforts. He was in Chicago Wednesday in consultation with President Spalding of the League club there, and after being closeted for some time with him gave an interview to the newspaper reporters in which he stated that he was in favor of the American Association joining hands with the League in the fight against the Brotherhood. His visit there and subsequent statements to the reporters gave rise to the story that he intended selling the Browns to Chicago. It has also been stated elsewhere that the Anheuser-Busch Brewing Association was to purchase the club, but there is nothing in either story. Mr. Von der Ahe has been offered a place in the National League, and will go in on condition that there is a consolidation of the National League and American Association, the stronger clubs of each organization being taken in as members.

—St. Louis *Post-Dispatch*

Saturday, October 26

On October 25, New York beat Brooklyn 2–1 in
11 innings at the Polo Grounds (O'Day 1–0; Terry 2–1).
Brooklyn 3, New York 3.

After a struggle that lasted eleven innings yesterday, the New-Yorks won the sixth of the games for the world's championship, and to-day are even with Brooklyn for the honors. It was a contest that will long be remembered by baseball enthusiasts. There have been exciting scenes on the diamonds of the old Union and Capitoline Grounds; gray-haired followers of the game are wont to relate the struggles for victory that have taken place on the Elysian Fields, when the Atlantics, Eckfords, and Mutuals were in their prime, but the game in which the representatives of New-York and Brooklyn took part yesterday surpasses, perhaps, anything ever seen on a baseball field.

From start to finish the contestants played with rare vim and determination. Cheered on by the plaudits of the spectators every inch of ground was stubbornly contested, and when the game was finally won a scene that will long be remembered took place. For eight innings the Brooklyns held a lead of 1 run, and when the New-Yorks began the ninth their chances of winning were very slim. For eight innings they had failed to send a player around the bases and a defeat of the worst character— a "whitewash"—stared them in the face. Tiernan was the first batter up in the ninth. He sent up a fly ball which Corkhill grasped fondly. Ewing, the reliable, failed to alleviate the sufferings of the crowd. He sent a bounder, which Davis took care of. Then "Our John" Ward came to the bat. He was stern and resolute and perhaps the coolest man in the enclosure. John is noted for doing the proper thing in close games, and every eye was riveted on him. He hit the ball with all his might and it went past Foutz and Collins and was stopped by Burns just as Ward reached first base. Visions of home runs, three baggers, doubles, and even beggarly singles arose before the gaze of all present as Connor, the best of the Giants as regards batting, walked to the plate. Before he had a chance to strike Ward darted for second. He got there. Flushed with success, he never waited to get breath, but made a dash for third and reached that point in safety. Then Connor was implored to hit the ball and he did. It went straight at Davis, the short stop, who in his excitement failed to get the sphere and it rolled out to centre field. Meanwhile Ward rushed for home, touched the plate, and the game was saved.

This was the signal for an outburst of enthusiasm. From the outset the New-York "cranks" were compelled to hold their peace and listen to the exultant remarks and shouts of the Brooklynites. Their corked-up enthusiasm knew no bounds, and they shouted as only metropolitan "cranks" can. Hats, canes, and umbrellas were thrown in the air; old men, young men, middle-aged men, and small boys slapped each other on the back, and a feeling of joy pervaded the atmosphere. During the excitement somebody shouted "Ward—Ward—Johnny—Ward!" It was taken up by the vast assemblage, and nothing but the name of the favorite short stop could be heard for some minutes.

Slattery scored the run that won the game in the eleventh inning. He made a base hit, and after Tiernan had hit a fly to Burns, Ewing sent a grounder to Collins, allowing Slattery to go to second. As Ward faced Terry he was greeted with cheers on all sides. He sent a slow-bounding ball to Davis. It was a race between the ball and the fleet-footed player. Davis picked up the buckskin, threw it, but too late. Ward had reached the bag and couldn't be put out. During the struggle between Ward and the ball, Slattery, unobserved, had run down to third, and before Foutz could recover his equilibrium, had gained the home plate. He scored his run and one of the greatest games of ball on record was won. Again the New-York "cranks" shouted. Ward, Slattery, and nearly every member

OLD JUDGE CIGARETTES Goodwin & Co., New York.

John M. Ward, shortstop, New York Giants (Library of Congress, Prints and Photographs Division [LOT 13163-13, no. 8]).

of the team came in for a share, but above all could be heard the shout, "Ward, Ward, Johnny Ward!"

—New York *Times*

Never was a victory more plainly achieved by brilliant base running and strategic batting than in the ninth and eleventh innings of the contest by Ward. But for him Brooklyn had the game sure. Ward is an awfully dangerous man for an opposing team to face in a critical emergency like this.

—Brooklyn *Daily Eagle*

Sunday, October 27

On October 26, New York beat Brooklyn 11–7
at the Polo Grounds (Crane 3–1; Lovett 0–1).
New York 4, Brooklyn 3.

Few people believed Manager Mutrie in the early part of the week when he said that the Giants would be in the lead by Saturday. But they were, and the genial gentleman who piloted the Giants to victory must be considered something of a baseball prophet. The New-Yorks took the lead yesterday when they won their third successive game from Brooklyn.

Unlike the contest of Friday, yesterday's game was a one-sided one. The last half of the second inning was a Waterloo for Brooklyn. New York made 8 runs and settled all doubts as to the game.

—New York *Times*

The threatening aspect of the weather and the doubt as to whether a game would be played kept thousands from the grounds, and the result was the smallest attendance at any Saturday game of the season at the Polo Grounds, not three thousand people being present. The grounds were wet and muddy in some places, but not as bad as usual after a rain, so it was determined to play the game even under the drawback of a poor field and threatening weather.

—Brooklyn *Daily Eagle*

New York, Oct. 26—Lawyer James O'Rourke saved the New York club from defeat to-day by terrific batting and magnificent fielding. He came to bat twice in the second inning, the first time making a two-bagger and the second time a home run high over the center field fence, pronounced the longest hit ever made on the grounds. He drove in runs enough to win the game. Then in the fifth inning Brooklyn had the bases full and only one man out, when Smith smashed the ball into the left-field seats for what nine times out of ten would be a home run, but O'Rourke scaled the inside fence, climbed the seats, secured the ball and shot it, true as a bullet, to Ewing at the home-plate in time to put Smith out, who had driven in three men ahead of him.

—St. Louis *Post-Dispatch*

Boston, Mass., Oct. 26— President Soden was interviewed this morning in regard to the St. Louis rumor that the two big associations were to consolidate in order to make a fight against

George "Germany" Smith, shortstop, Brooklyn Bridegrooms (New York *Clipper*, February 20, 1886).

Arthur Soden, president, Boston Beaneaters (Transcendental Graphics).

the Brotherhood. He said: "There is nothing in it. I think it is all bosh, and on a par with the Minneapolis fake published a few days ago. The League can fight its own battles without any help from the American Association. Besides we have enough weak financial cities in the League now without carrying along such places as Columbus, Kansas City and Baltimore. St. Louis and Von der Ahe we don't want in the League anyway; games there do not pay except on Sunday, and we don't play Sunday games; neither do we wish for partners men who conduct themselves as Von der Ahe does. Now, what I think would be a good scheme would be to drop Washington and Indianapolis and take in Brooklyn and Cincinnati. That would strengthen us greatly. In regard to the Brotherhood, I am not worried at all. I think they are playing a great game of bluff. But nothing will be known until after the meetings of the two organizations, which will be held in about two weeks. For my part I am willing to make all reasonable concessions, and we shall ask the Brotherhood to make a few also."

—St. Louis *Post-Dispatch*

Monday, October 28

With only two games to win to capture the world championship, Mutrie's Giants are facing the Bridegrooms at Washington Park to-day. The latter have three of the necessary six games already to their credit, and it is not unreasonable to assume that they may make a tie race of the contest this afternoon. The home team has at least demonstrated one fact—they can play ball with a vigor and ability that made the New York rooters hold their breath twice last week. The gabble about the Giants using the association champions as brooms to figuratively sweep the Polo

Grounds has suddenly ceased and the only voicing that metropolitan enthusiasm now gets is confined to a low toned assurance that the league players will get there, but that their triumph will not be so easily acquired as was at first believed.

—Brooklyn *Daily Eagle*

The statement made in the New York *World's* article on the Brotherhood League that Comiskey will play with the Chicago member of the organization will receive little credence in this city. If there is one player on the Browns who would not desert Von der Ahe that man is Comiskey or else his employer is greatly mistaken in the man. Comiskey has always been satisfied here and was not willing to go elsewhere, even when an enormous salary was hung out as an inducement. He feels that he has made his reputation here and can remain with Mr. Von der Ahe as long as he cares to play ball, whereas if he went elsewhere and his work was not satisfactory there would be a howl, and things would be made decidedly disagreeable for him.

—St. Louis *Post-Dispatch*

"I see that Soden of the Boston Club comes out in a statement that the League does not want any assistance from the American Association in the League fight against the Brotherhood, and he takes occasion at the same time to go out of his way to cast a slur upon the St. Louis Club and myself," said President Von der Ahe this morning upon his return from Kansas City. "I don't believe in the first place that Soden would stoop to refer to me in the manner in which he has been reported, and I have written him demanding an explanation. I want to know whether or not he was guilty of giving utterance to the statements credited to him, especially in his allusions to myself."

"What do you think of the statement that Comiskey will captain and manage the Brotherhood club in Chicago next year?"

"It is about as probable as that Comiskey will manage the *Post-Dispatch* or the London *Times* next year. He has assured me that he will not. Comiskey will go up to Chicago to look after some property that he has there. All stories of his being connected with the Brotherhood are rank nonsense, as he will tell you himself."

—St. Louis *Post-Dispatch*

Tuesday, October 29

On October 28, New York beat Brooklyn 16–7
at Washington Park (Crane 4–1; Terry 2–2).
New York 5, Brooklyn 3.

Brooklyn, N.Y., Oct. 28, 1889—There is mourning in Brooklyn tonight. The base ball club of that city was disgracefully beaten by the New York Giants today, and was out of the race from the start. "Adonis" Terry was in the box and he was pounded terrifically. It has become apparent that the Brooklyns haven't a show against their strong antagonists. They acted today as if afraid.

—Boston *Herald*

Ward was very successful. In five times to bat he made three singles, got his base on balls, and was hit with a pitched ball. He scored 4 runs and was credited with four stolen bases. Crane was again an enigma to the Brooklyn batters. His speedy curves were too much for them, and they retired one after another in disgust.

—New York *Times*

The series will probably end to-day, unless New York should go in overconfident of victory after yesterday's easy task, and in such case the Brooklyns may work in an unexpected victory. The fact is, the New York team have shown better teamwork at the bat and more headwork in their play in the series than their opponents, and that is the main cause of their success.

The attendance was the smallest of the series in Brooklyn, hundreds of people being in doubt whether any game would be played yesterday. Whatever the outcome of the series may be the Brooklyn team have shown their league rivals that they were not to be beaten as easily as the St. Louis team were in 1888.

—Brooklyn *Daily Eagle*

Wednesday, October 30

On October 29, in the final game of the world's series,
New York beat Brooklyn 3–2 at the Polo Grounds
(O'Day 2–0; Terry 2–3).
New York 6, Brooklyn 3.

New-Yorkers ought to feel proud of their baseball nine. The Giants have once more proved their supremacy in diamond field matters and again claim the distinction of the being the world's champions. It is the highest honor that can be bestowed upon a baseball club, and was won yesterday when the New-Yorks finished the series with Brooklyn.

As regards the game, while the score, 3 to 2, was a close one, New-York won easily. O'Day pitched a good game of ball. Only four hits were made off him, and two of these were secured in the first inning. As the game wore on, he appeared to grow stronger. His speed, if anything, increased, and his work in the last inning was better than that of the first.

In the ninth Smith took his base on an error by O'Day. He was put out with Bushong on a neat double play. The latter hit a liner to Whitney, who threw to first in time to catch Smith. O'Brien got his base on balls, but was thrown out while trying to steal second. This ended the series and the Giants were proclaimed champions of the world.

—New York *Times*

Thursday, October 31

Manager McGunnigle of the Brooklyns will sport a handsome gold watch and chain and a diamond-studded locket. It is the gift of the players of his team. When the manager made his appearance at the clubhouse yesterday morning he was met by first baseman Foutz, who presented the gift in the presence of all the boys. He said:

Bill McGunnigle, manager, Brooklyn Bridegrooms (National Baseball Hall of Fame Library, Cooperstown, New York).

"Mr. McGunnigle: I have the honor of representing the Brooklyn Baseball Club in the performance of a duty which affords me the greatest satisfaction. Recognizing, as we all do, your capability as a manager, and your many sterling traits of character as a man and an associate, we desire to present you with a substantial token of our regard. In accepting this watch, chain, and charm, it is our desire that you shall feel that, though the gift is of costly material and fine workmanship, it is yet but a small memento of our regard. Hoping your heart will beat long after the machinery of this watch has rusted into dust, we remain your friends and admirers, the Brooklyn Baseball Club."

Mr. McGunnige blushed like a schoolgirl while the tall first base-man was making the address. After glancing at the token he replied:

"Boys, you caught me unprepared. Of course, I can't tell you how much I appreciate your kindness. It is sufficient for me to say that I value the feeling which prompted you in this act much more than I do the intrinsic expression of it. I hope each one of you will put yourself in my place and attribute your feelings under such circumstances to me. I can assure you that whatever happens the watch will never visit 'my uncle'; it will be kept in a chamois case. And that it will always be carried in the pocket over my heart."

—New York *Times*

"Will Comiskey play first base in Fred Pfeffer's brotherhood team in Chicago next season?" asks the Chicago *News*.

That is a question which few, perhaps, excepting Pfeffer and Comiskey themselves, are able to answer. President Von der Ahe in all proba-bility would turn stark mad should he find that his valiant Captain and manager was about to desert him and come to Chicago to fill "Old" Anson's place in the Brotherhood nine. Yet even "der poss bresident" is not wholly ignorant of the scheme.

The thing has been a subject of gossip in St. Louis for some time, and it is argued that Von der Ahe has already begun to tear his hair at the bare prospect of such a calamity befalling "der poss glub." A cir-cumstance which lends color to such a move is the fact that Comiskey has long desired to come to Chicago. In fact, there was a time when Von der Ahe and Spalding were discussing a trade which was to result in the transfer of the St. Louis Captain to the White Stockings. The present need for just such a man for Anson's place to complete the Brotherhood team was the first necessity recognized by the section "A" men backing Pfeffer in his rival project. Comiskey's was the first name proposed for the place and correspondence with the great Association player was opened at once.

He is reported to have replied that the proposition would not be dis-tasteful to him, providing he could have some substantial assurance of the success of the new club. He was well aware that his "jumping" the Association for the new league would forever bar him from returning to that organization, as he would be blacklisted. The proscription would also more than likely extend to the National League and in the event of the failure of the Brotherhood scheme would prevent him from holding a position with any team in the League, for a time at least.

Of course a man with the experience and recognized ability of Comiskey could not long be out of a job, because of his valuable acquire-ments and acknowledged drawing powers. Capt. Comiskey has long been styled the Anson of the Association, and by his admirers has been considered second to none in the country.

Everything now hinges on the action to be taken by the League men at their annual conference. Should they consent to call in the Brotherhood and give what is demanded in the way of mutual legislation that body will lay its League baby on the shelf for the time and each man will come up to the secretary's office and sign the 1890 contract. Otherwise the Brotherhood bull will be sent forth to be tacked on to the gate of every base-ball park in the country. The names of all the players will be made public, and Capt. Comiskey will be put down as first baseman of the Chicago team.

—St. Louis *Post-Dispatch*

Saturday, November 2

Secretary Keefe of the ball Players' Brotherhood yesterday officially announced the outline of the meeting to be held in the Fifth-Avenue Hotel on Monday. The League magnates will not be consulted. In other words, the players intend to go it alone. Already arrangements have been made for grounds in this city, Brooklyn, Boston, Philadelphia, Chicago, Buffalo, Cleveland, and Pittsburg, and next week it is the intention of the ball players to begin business by electing officers for the new organization.

The new grounds in New-York will be at One Hundred and Fifty-seventh-street and Eighth-avenue, just above the present diamond of the Giants. James J. Coogan will be one of the stockholders of the club.

It is the intention of President Ward to place all the teams on an even playing strength, or as near it as can possibly be done. The Brotherhood does not particularly care to tread on the toes of the American Association, but there may be a row in Brooklyn when a Brotherhood team is placed there. Row or no row, however, it has been decided to put a team there. Secretary Keefe remarked yesterday that Brooklyn was big enough for two clubs. A site has been secured on the line of the elevated road. It is about half an hour's ride from City Hall in this city.

—New York *Times*

Ward has been an assiduous worker and investigator in each city, and he has come to the conclusion that there will be a great deal of money in base ball for others than those who are now conducting the business. The question that agitates a great many of the interested ones is will the players stick? Unquestionably most of them will, and the period of their continuing service will depend upon the success of the new league. There will be some who will remain by the old flag, and among these has been mentioned Pitcher Clarkson of the Bostons. It is said that he will pitch for the league club in this city and will not go to the brotherhood organization.

—Boston *Herald*

Sunday, November 3

While the members of the Baseball Brotherhood were busy making arrangements for the meeting which is to be held to-morrow the League magnates were not idle. They have been consulting lawyers in regard to the legality of the reserve rule. The latter is an agreement entered into by a player when he signs a contract to the effect that he will play with the same club for the year following the one for which the contract is made. According to the recognized rule in baseball fourteen men can be held from year to year.

Players have always contended that the step was necessary to keep a club together, but they were of the opinion that such a contract would not stand in court, as it virtually binds a man for life or until any time that the club managers may feel inclined to give him his discharge. The members of the Brotherhood consulted their legal adviser on that point and he concurred in their judgment. President Day of the New-York Club, however, retained Mr. J.F.C. Blackhurst, who was formerly the attorney for the Brotherhood, and his opinion was in direct opposition to that of the present lawyer of the Brotherhood.

—New York *Times*

When the last game for the championship of the world was played at New York there were a great many people who exclaimed: "Thank heaven! We shall hear nothing more about base ball for a long time to come." They little knew that one of the greatest storms was brewing that ever beset the base ball world. Just now all who are interested in the national game, and their number is legion, are anxious to know what the Brotherhood of National League Base Ball Players is going to do at the meetings that it will hold at the Fifth Avenue Hotel in New York during the week at hand. This sort of a movement is something entirely new. It is the first time that the players of an organization have taken matters into their own hands and determined to break from their late employers. It is a matter that the brainiest of ball players, John Montgomery Ward, of the New York Base Ball Club, has been studying out for a very long time.

Mr. Ward is a very ambitious young man, far above the common order of ball players. He was anxious while with the Providence nine to be something above the common order of his tribe, and when he joined the New York club, that opportunity was given him. He was a student of Columbia College and a graduate of the law school. The knowledge he gained of the law he applied to his profession, and he was fully conversant with the game in its history and all its bearings. His book on the game of base ball showed great originality and ability, and the products of his pen have commanded a high price in the literary market. It is well known that he married Helen Dauvray at a time when she was a favorite actress, and at his intercession she retired from the stage. His wife is as ambitious as himself, and she quickly recognized in the proposed move a grand opportunity for her husband, and was not slow to sanction it with her most cordial approval. Ward worked at the scheme

John M. Ward, shortstop, New York Giants (Library of Congress, Prints and Photographs Division [LOT 13163-05, no. 218]).

during the past season, and busies himself with enlisting all of his brethren, and with the greatest success, so that the players, even if they do not break away from the existing state of things, can obtain the concessions from the league that they will demand.

—Boston *Herald*

President Von der Ahe received a letter yesterday from President Soden of the Boston club in reply to one sent to him demanding an explanation of him regarding an alleged interview with Soden, in which the latter is made to say some unkind things of the Browns' President. The correspondence covering the case is as follows:

St. Louis, Oct. 28, 1889.
A.H. Soden, Esq., President Boston Base Ball Club, Boston, Mass.:

I enclose herewith clipping sent out from Boston, which appeared
in St. Louis papers of last Sunday, purporting to be an interview with
you. I demand an explanation of your reference to me. The attack
upon myself, as reported, is contemptible and I cannot for an instant
believe that you made it. Awaiting an early reply, I am yours respect-
fully, *Chris Von der Ahe.*

President Soden replied as follows:

Boston, Oct. 31, 1889.
Chris Von der Ahe, President St. Louis Club:
    Dear Sir—The statements in enclosed clipping, referring to you,
were not authorized or uttered by me. Truly yours, *A.H. Soden.*

—St. Louis *Post-Dispatch*

Tuesday, November 5

As was predicted in these columns, the members of the Brotherhood
deserted the League clubs at the meeting held yesterday in the Fifth-
Avenue Hotel. This in defiance of the threat of the officials, means
another baseball war. The players are determined and feel assured of success. The magnates are bitter and declare that they will spare neither
pains nor expense to kill the movement and punish the ringleaders. Yesterday's meeting was a most harmonious gathering. The business was
conducted in a quiet orderly manner, and John Ward, who presided, did
so with the grace that characterizes his work in the short field. Genial
"Tim" Keefe acted as Secretary. He threw ink with as much skill and
proficiency as he curves an out-shoot.

All day long the corridors of the hotel were crowded with baseball
men of all calibers from the high and mighty Managing Director to the
small boy whose ambition is to carry the bat of some big hitter. The sole
topic of conversation, of course, was baseball, and the "cranks" had a
feast boring each other. Ward, O'Rourke, Pfeffer, Hanlon, and Brouthers
were selected a committee to draw up a statement for presentation to the
public. The following was adopted:

To the Public: At last the Brotherhood of Baseball Players feels at liberty to make known its intentions and defend itself against the asper-
sions and misrepresentations which for weeks it has been forced to suffer
in silence. It is no longer a secret that the players of the League have
determined to play next season under different management, but for reasons, which will, we think, be understood, it was deemed advisable to
make no announcement of this intention until the close of the present

season; but now that the struggles for the various pennants are over, and the terms of our contracts expired, there is no longer reason for withholding it.

In taking this step we feel that we owe it to the public and to ourselves to explain briefly some of the reasons by which we have been moved. There was a time when the League stood for integrity and fair dealing; to-day it stands for dollars and cents. Once it looked to the elevation of the game and an honest exhibition of the sport; to-day its eyes are upon the turnstile. Men have come into the business for no other motive than to exploit it for every dollar in sight. Measures originally intended for the good of the game have been perverted into instruments for wrong. The reserve rule and the provisions of the national agreement gave the managers unlimited power, and they have not hesitated to use this in the most arbitrary and mercenary way.

Players have been bought, sold, and exchanged as though they were sheep, instead of American citizens. "Reservation" became with them another name for property right in the player. By a combination among themselves, stronger than the strongest trust, they were able to enforce the most arbitrary measures, and the player had either to submit or get out of the profession in which he had spent years attaining proficiency. Even the disbandment and retirement of a club did not free the players from the octopus clutch, for they were then peddled around to the highest bidder.

That the player sometimes profited by the sale has nothing to do with the case, but only proves the injustice of his previous restraint. Two years ago we met the League and attempted to remedy some of these evils, but through what has been politely called "League diplomacy" we completely failed. Unwilling longer to submit to such treatment, we made a strong effort last Spring to reach an understanding with the League. To our application for a hearing they replied "that the matter was not of sufficient importance to warrant a meeting," and suggested that it be put off till Fall. Our committee replied that the players felt that the League had broken faith with them; that while the results might be of little importance to the managers, they were of great importance to the players; that if the League would not concede what was fair, we would adopt other means to protect ourselves; that if postponed until Fall we would be separated and at the mercy of the League, and that, as the only course left us required time and labor to develop, we must therefore insist upon an immediate conference.

Then upon their final refusal to meet us we began organizing for ourselves, and are in shape to go ahead next year under new management and new auspices. We believe that it is possible to conduct our national game upon lines which will not infringe upon individual and

natural rights. We asked to be judged solely by our work, and believing
that the game can be played more fairly and its business conducted more
intelligently under a plan which excludes everything arbitrary and
un–American, we look forward with confidence to the support of the
public and the future of the national game.

The National Brotherhood of Ball Players

—New York *Times*

When the "King of the diamond," Kelly, walked into the Fifth-
Avenue Hotel, he was at once made the centre of an admiring group. He
wore a tight-fitting pair of imported trousers, a tall silk hat, a beaver overcoat, patent leather shoes with russet uppers, and he sported a bright-
red boutonniere. He was radiant with smiles and seemed pleased to shake
hands with old friends. While he was engaged in conversation he suddenly caught sight of George Billings, a son of one of the leading stockholders of the Boston Club—the Kelly aggregation. "Well, sonny," he said
to young Billings, "tell pop that I'm sorry for him. If he wants a job next
season, I'll put him to work on one of my turnstiles. I'm one of the bosses
now and the triumvirate—well, to be frank, they are my understudies.
The whirligig of time brings ball players to their level. Next year they
will be in command and the former Presidents will have to drive horse
cars for a living and borrow rain checks to see a game. Goodbye, chap-
pie, I'm going inside to manipulate the wires that will startle the baseball world." and he left the awe-stricken young man to commune with
himself.

—New York *Times*

Wednesday, November 6

Washington, D.C., Nov. 5, 1889—The declaration of war upon the
part of the brotherhood was more generally discussed here today than
the political battles going on in the various states. At league headquar-
ters President Young was found busily engaged over the New York papers,
gleaning the details of yesterday's meeting at the Fifth Avenue Hotel.

In reply to a question from the *Herald* correspondent he said: "I
have just concluded a hasty reading of the brotherhood's proclamation,
and I must say that I am greatly surprised at the weak and empty style
of its construction. I have for several weeks been convinced that they
intended to declare war against the league, and I have prepared myself
to receive a startling and forcible presentation of their side of the case.
There is not a single sentence in their address that appeals to the

sympathy of the base ball public but what can be overturned by the league without any misstatement on the latter's part."

—Boston *Herald*

Thursday, November 7

New York, Nov. 6, 1889—In relation to Nick Young's letter President John M. Ward said: "It's all stuff. His pay was raised to $4000 last season, and our movement may endanger his position. He may think our manifesto a weak affair. He would have found it so, no matter what was its form. That's what he is paid for. His interview is, however, very weak. He says the league has always lived up to its pledges. He knows this is false. We are ready to try the issue. I am sure that the public is on our side. The league will try to undermine our position by specious arguments and talk. I am confident the public will wait until next spring and judge us by the exhibitions we will give on the ball field."

—Boston *Herald*

Friday, November 8

When the Players' National League was organized it was intended to engage only members of the Brotherhood for the clubs and to pay no attention whatever to the American Association. The latter, however, has showed a tendency to assist the League magnates, and in consequence the Brotherhood will break into the ranks of the Association. Charley Comiskey, the first baseman and Captain of the St. Louis Browns, will join the Chicago Club. He has been in sympathy with the new movement from the start and wants to get stock in one of the clubs. Comiskey prefers Chicago because it is his home.

Comiskey is perhaps the most popular player in the American Association and he would add considerably to the strength of the new scheme. It has been due to his skill, generalship, and faculty of handling men that the Browns have been successful. Even last season, with a far inferior team, he gave the Brooklyns a close race for first honors. Comiskey is not the only man wanted. If possible, Latham, King, and Robinson of the Browns, Collins of Brooklyn, and Stovey and Welch of the Athletics will be secured.

—New York *Times*

Sunday, November 10

The late meeting of the ball players' brotherhood in New York has attracted much attention here in Brooklyn, mainly for the reason that the Brotherhood had announced publicly its intention of not interfering with the American Association, its clubs or its players, providing the association kept its hands off in the fight between the players of the league and the clubs of the league. Immediately following this announcement came the notice that the brotherhood intended to place a club in Brooklyn— that is to say, the brotherhood, while asking the Brooklyn association club to keep aloof from its fight with the league, determined to invade but one association club's territory, and that was Brooklyn. In addition thereto, with a view to bolster up their strike, it was announced, inroads would be made upon the ranks of the association's players, so as to cripple the association in case a united effort was made by the league and association to defeat the brotherhood. The only club the brotherhood dreaded in a fight was the champion Brooklyn organization, whose president, Mr. C.H. Byrne, has taken a bold and open stand against the strikers. Hoping to intimidate him, the cry of a raid upon the association players was raised. Mr. Byrne understood the situation fully and very quietly went to work. He deemed it proper to put under contract for next season the men he wanted, and the moment he asked his men to sign it was a question as to who should have the honor to sign first, as an evidence of faith in the Brooklyn Club and an appreciation of the courtesy and consideration extended to the men.

—Brooklyn *Daily Eagle*

Monday, November 11

One does not know what day startling events may occur which will change the entire aspect of things alike in the association as well as the league. The present position of affairs is anomalous in the history of all the professional clubs, and it is going to test the innate strength of both the league and the association to make things harmonious for the season of 1890.

—Brooklyn *Daily Eagle*

Wednesday, November 13

There promises to be baseball war in earnest this Winter. When the League players jumped out and declared their intention of going it alone words of sympathy were received by the magnates from their American Association brethren. While delivering these messages the Association men probably laughed in their sleeves and congratulated themselves on having smooth sailing in their ranks. But things have changed. There is a big row in the Association that threatens that organization.

Brooklyn and Cincinnati want to withdraw and have asked for admission in the League. The Athletic, St. Louis, Columbus, Kansas City, and Louisville managers, it appears, have been jealous of their colleagues in Brooklyn, Cincinnati, and Baltimore. They have been working in private to get the plums of the Association next year. The plums are generally regarded as good dates and large percentages of gate receipts.

When President Byrne heard of the deal he coolly informed the "kickers" that he would not tolerate such treatment. Mr. Stern of Cincinnati, too, said that before he would be imposed upon he would resign from the Association. Messrs. Byrne and Stern held a conference, and they resolved to ask for admission into the League.

In view of the situation in the League rank caused by the action of the Brotherhood, it was thought that the request would be complied with instantly. Brooklyn could take the place of Washington and Cincinnati could step into the shoes of Indianapolis, and the League would be armed for a conflict with the Brotherhood.

As soon as the St. Louis faction, as the bolters are called, heard of the movements of Byrne and Stern they immediately held a caucus and determined to take action. The result was that they sent word to the League men that in the event of Brooklyn and Cincinnati being admitted to the League they would immediately join forces with the Brotherhood and work tooth and nail to drive the League out of existence. This threat had some effect. The League men do not think that they can be driven out of the business, but they are opposed to doing anything that will in any way benefit the Brotherhood. The Association men could no doubt render the Players' League some valuable assistance and in that way injure the League to some extent. On the whole, it was thought advisable to wait for a day or two before taking action. The probabilities are, however, that if Brooklyn and Cincinnati want to join the big organization they will be admitted.

—New York *Times*

Thursday, November 14

The annual meetings of both the League and American Association were held in the Fifth-Avenue Hotel yesterday and, as was predicted in *The Times*, there was a lively row at the Association gathering. Never before in the history of the Association has such bitterness been shown. The St. Louis men say that they are determined to throw off the Byrne yoke, while the Brooklyn men are equally sanguine of sitting down on the Dutchman, a name applied to President Von der Ahe of the St. Louis Browns. They claim that, instead of being ignorant of the rules pertaining to the management of clubs, Von der Ahe is a sly fox and has been deceiving his colleagues. His actions, they say, have been a detriment to the Association, and it is about time that something was done to correct his habits. The St. Louis people, while they do not charge Byrne with being ignorant, claim that he is a trickster of the first water, who resorts to all sorts of petty devices to further his own ends.

—New York *Times*

Friday, November 15

Brooklyn and Cincinnati having grown tired of the workings of the American Association, yesterday made formal application to join the League. They were admitted, and next year the organization will be composed of ten clubs—five in the East and a like number on the West.

Brooklyn and Cincinnati are very good baseball cities. Brooklyn particularly is considered the best baseball city of its size in the country. Big crowds are averaged on week days, and on a holiday the largest attendance of the season is credited to that city. Just how the increase in tariff—from 25 to 50 cents—will affect the patrons is a matter of conjecture, but it is safe to say that Brooklyn will support a first-class club at any price. The city across the bridge is the cradle of the national game. When it was in its infancy the largest of crowds attended the contests that took place there.

Charley Byrne, the President of the Bridegrooms, said that he has been anxious to join hands with the League for some time past, but was fearful of doing so because he didn't think that he had a team strong enough to cope favorably with the League nines. Now, however, he thinks that his club is second to none, and he will make a big effort to carry off the pennant next season. Yesterday he began to gather his men in the fold. "Tom" Burns was the first to sign a regular League contract. The heavy batter said that he was tired of the slow work in the Association and was glad to join a first-class organization.

Just what step the American Association men will take is hard to determine. They have not decided on any course as yet. The threat to join hands with the Brotherhood is a silly one. In that event the League men would declare war and take all the first-class players in their ranks.

They could be secured, too, as the League clubs can afford to pay bigger salaries than the Association nines. The Association men know that, and they will probably think again before joining hands with the Brotherhood.

—New York *Times*

New York, Nov. 14, 1889—John Ward, president of the brotherhood, said the loss of Brooklyn and Cincinnati would kill the association. He thought the matter had long been cut and dried. Of course it would make the league stronger, and the result would be that there would be two strong ball organizations—the brotherhood and the league. He was not prepared to state how the brotherhood men would meet any attempt on the part of the remaining clubs of the association to combine with the brotherhood. All of the league magnates think they have taken a wise step in admitting Brooklyn and Cincinnati. In all the deliberations of the day the brotherhood was hardly mentioned.

—Boston *Herald*

As the Mikado might say in Gilbert's opera,

> See how the Fates their gifts allot,
> Byrne is happy—Chris is not.

What glorious news this entry of Brooklyn into the league will be to "the boys" of the Brooklyn Club team; and how they will rejoice to think that they had the good sense to sign with the old club as they did before leaving for home. What pleasant news it will be, too, to the patrons of the game in Brooklyn to find that we are to have no more of the rowdy tactics of the St. Louis bullies of the Comiskey and Robinson class. And how the veteran habitués of the ball grounds will be pleased to learn that we shall now have a return in the near future to a series of contests marked by the old time rivalry between New York and Brooklyn in place of the secondary class of contests we have hitherto been obliged to be content with. Truly are good times in store now for the best class of patrons of the game in this city, brought about by the blindness of the would be leaders of the American Association, aided by selfish effort at self-aggrandizement of the class of seceding players of the league. It is now plain sailing for the National League of Professional Base Ball Clubs of America, which by the grand coup d'etat of yesterday has with one jump become the ruling professional organization of the base ball world.

—Brooklyn *Daily Eagle*

New York, Nov. 14—Kansas City has withdrawn from the American Association and ten minutes later was admitted to membership in the Western Association.

—St. Louis *Post-Dispatch*

Saturday, November 16

In St. Louis the feeling just now is strongly in favor of the Brotherhood. The people want to see Mr. Von der Ahe enter the Browns into the Brotherhood, which would be glad to receive them. The Athletics would then combine with the Philadelphia Brotherhood team, and the Columbus and Louisville and Baltimore Clubs could also be taken in. This would give the weak Brotherhood players confidence, and they would all sign Brotherhood contracts and a new Association would be formed, which would completely annihilate the old League.

The only way for St. Louis to have good ball playing is for Mr. Von der Ahe to go in with the Brotherhood. Then it would be such sweet revenge on his old associates who played him so false.

—St. Louis *Post-Dispatch*

Monday, November 18

The patrons of gentlemanly ball playing in this city scarcely have an idea of what a treat there is in store for them during the season of 1890, so many are the advantageous changes which will be brought about at Washington Park next year through the recent transfer of the Brooklyn Club and its team from the American Association to the ranks of the National League. In the first place, under league laws, no beer or liquor will be allowed to be sold within the enclosure, and the annoyance of having waiters passing to and fro on the grand stand will be got rid of. Then the opponents of the Sunday ball playing under the auspices of the club will have their wishes gratified, as the league does not admit of its club teams playing ball on Sunday. To see the League teams play, however, we shall have to pay 25 cents more for admission. But this additional fee is in return for decent ball playing in lieu of the dirty work of the St. Louis gang and their imitators.

The facilities for reaching the grounds from New York will be greater than ever next season, as the Union Elevated road will run special trains on match days under a schedule of but twelve minutes from the bridge depot, and by its system of transfers patrons of the game can easily reach the grounds from the most distant suburbs of the city for one fare.

—Brooklyn *Daily Eagle*

Tuesday, November 19

The following base ball "pome" received the first prize in the *Sporting Times* verse tourney which ended last week:

The Malcontent's Soliloquy

To sign, or not to sign—that is the question.
Whether 'tis braver in man's eyes to suffer
The wrongs of a classification rule
Or to take up arms against a host of magnates,
And by opposing, end it. To kick—to fight
No more—to fight—to say we end
The class rule and a dozen other ills
Now heaped upon us. 'Tis a consummation
Devoutly to be wished. To sign—to play.
To play—perchance to muff. Aye, there's the rub.
As by this classing rule each muff doth count
When averages are figured up at season's close,
Must give us pause. There's the respect
That makes calamity of playing ball.
For who would bear the scolding manager,
The magnates' wrongs, the reporters' contumely,
The pangs of unearned sneers for some misplay;
When he himself might his own magnate be,
By winning in the fight. Who would contracts keep,
To grunt and sweat under a tyrant's rule,
But that the fear of some great after clap,
Some breaking up in this new scheme which looks
So bright to our eyes just now—puzzles the will
And makes us rather bear those ills we have,
Than fly to others we know not of.
Thus scheming doth make blowhards of us all.
And thus the present style of ebullition,
Is simmered down by the pale cast of thought,
And this enterprise of great pith and moment
With this regards its chances fade away
And lose the name of action.

—Brooklyn *Daily Eagle*

Monday, November 25

Michael J. Kelly, the Captain of the Boston Baseball Club, better known, perhaps, as the "Ten-Thousand-Dollar Beauty," or the "King of the Diamond," attached his signature to a Brotherhood contract this morning shortly after midnight. This is considered a victory for the Brotherhood. Kelly is, perhaps, one of the most prominent players on the diamond. He has a following second to none, and it is supposed that many who are at present on the fence will shortly follow his example.

Kelly has been in sympathy with the new movement from the outset, but he did not take an active part in the formation of the clubs for private reasons. He assured the boys that he was with them, heart and soul, and that when called upon to render assistance he would respond at once.

Without any ceremony he attached his signature to the document. Kelly will get a yearly salary of $5,000 for three years. He will captain the Boston team, and it is generally understood that he will also act in the capacity of manager.

—New York *Times*

New York, Nov. 24, 1889—"You have no idea," said Kelly, "what a weight has been lifted from my mind since I signed that contract. I want to go now and take hold of that Boston team, and if I am permitted to do it, I will work harder than ever I did in my life. Furthermore, I will pledge my word and honor that not a drop of liquor shall pass my lips throughout the season."

Kelly is confident that all of the old league team will stand true to the brotherhood. The Boston triumvirate have been very busy among their players, but very little impression seems to have been made. Brouthers thus far is the only one who has signed a brotherhood contract, but now that Kelly has come into the fold, there is great confidence that Clarkson and the balance of the team will follow suit.

—Boston *Herald*

Saturday, November 30

Columbus, Nov. 29—Unless the present baseball deal miscarries the American Association and the Brotherhood will make common cause against the National League in ten cities next season. The preliminary arrangements have been concluded, and the only thing now necessary is a formal acceptance of the proposed plan of amalgamation by a committee of the Brotherhood, who will meet at the Tremont House, Chicago, for that purpose within a few days, or, at least, sometime before the meeting of the American Association in Columbus on Dec. 10.

The proposition is to combine the present Brotherhood teams in Chicago, Pittsburg, Buffalo, New-York, Philadelphia, Boston, Cleveland, and Indianapolis with Association teams at Columbus and St. Louis, merging the Athletic and Brotherhood Clubs in Philadelphia, and dropping the Louisville and Baltimore Clubs entirely. The National League did its best to wreck the Association by inducing Cincinnati, Kansas City, and Brooklyn to leave its ranks, and now it has come to a survival of the fittest. The Association clubs concerned in this deal will sign all their men and then make open war upon the National League by joining the Brotherhood at its December meeting.

—New York *Times*

Wednesday, December 4

San Francisco, Cal., Dec. 3, 1889—The first man "King" Kelly struck to sign a brotherhood contract after completing his long journey from Boston yesterday was John Clarkson. But Kelly was doomed to disappointment. Clarkson wants more money than the brotherhood offers him, and, besides, has not much faith in the financial success of the scheme. Kelly offered the much sought twirler $500 out of his own pocket to sign, but Clarkson refused, and thus the matter stands. If Clarkson doesn't wilt when the "Only Mike" and his fellow players have exhausted their oratorical powers, he will indeed be considered headstrong and cold-hearted in the extreme.

—Boston *Herald*

Sunday, December 8

There is a strong impression that the American Association will join the Brotherhood movement, while some think that the remnants of the organization will join hands with the League and fight the new organization. In Philadelphia, however, the Athletics are in sympathy with the players, and there is a strong probability of their joining the Players' League. Rumors of all sorts are current. The latest is that the St. Louis Browns will take the place of the old Chicago Club and that the National League will declare war on both the Brotherhood and the American Association. One thing, however, is certain—there are lively times ahead in baseball.

—New York *Times*

Friday, December 13

Messrs. Soden, Conant and Billings, the famous triumvirate who own the Boston Base Ball Club, were made very happy last evening by receiving a dispatch that contained news of a most cheery and important nature. The dispatch was from San Francisco. It was signed by John Clarkson, and stated that he had signed a contract with the Boston league club.

Clarkson was not secured without a hard struggle and a large outlay of money. His record for last season easily stamped him as the king pitcher of the country. The brotherhood was determined to secure him for the players' league and bent every energy in that direction. Mike Kelly was dispatched to California as a special agent to secure the signatures of the Boston men, and he had special instructions to secure Clarkson above all men. But before leaving for California, terms between Clarkson and the Boston club had been practically agreed upon, and although fabulous offers were made to him by Kelly in behalf of the brotherhood, he could not be swerved from his purpose to play with the men who had acted squarely by him in the past, and against whom he had no cause of complaint.

The signing by Clarkson of a Boston league club contract is a great disappointment and a severe blow to the hopes of the brotherhood backers, not only in this city, but throughout the country.

—Boston *Herald*

In a telegram from New Orleans Capt. Comiskey of the Browns is quoted as saying that there is no hope of the American Association surviving, and that he will play first base for the Chicago Players' Club next season. He states that even if the Association does succeed in filling its vacancies it would be a very weak organization, and the new clubs would not be drawing cards. The crack Captain remarks that he has always played in first-class company, and he does not care now to drop down into a second-class organization.

—St. Louis *Post-Dispatch*

Tuesday, December 17

New York, Dec. 16, 1889—Early this forenoon the capitalists and players who are interested in the Players' National League of Base Ball Clubs began to assemble at the Fifth Avenue Hotel. Although the hour set for the adjourned meeting of the league was 10 o'clock, it was over two hours later when the accredited delegates were called to order. The moving of the entire machinery was powerless in the absence of one man, John M. Ward. He was away on other business, and the progress of the entire movement was completely at a standstill until he showed up. For a long time Mike Kelly has been named the king of the diamond, but he must now yield that title to John Montgomery Ward, for if there ever was a ball player who held unlimited sway over his professional associates, that one is Ward.

At 12 o'clock Ward put in an appearance, and 20 minutes later the players' league was called to order. The objects of the league as set forth are:

To encourage, foster and elevate the game of base ball; to enforce proper rules for the exhibition and conduct of the game; to protect the mutual interests of professional base ball players and base ball clubs, and to establish the championship of the world.

—Boston *Herald*

Postscript

The 1890 season saw three leagues competing for "cranks." The Players' League won the battle but lost the war. Their attendance figures were the highest of the three leagues, but most of the capitalists who backed the league lost money and got out at the end of the season. The Players' League, a "structure to last forever," lasted only one year.

The National League added Brooklyn and Cincinnati, while the Indianapolis and Washington teams disbanded, leaving the League with eight teams. The pennant was won by newcomer Brooklyn, as the Bridegrooms had virtually the same roster they had had in their Association championship season of 1889 but the competition had been depleted by the defection of so many quality players to the Players' League (which had 15 future Hall of Fame players in its ranks in 1890, while the National League had only 11).

Baltimore joined Brooklyn, Cincinnati, and Kansas City in withdrawing from the American Association, forcing the Association to add four new teams to its roster: Syracuse, Rochester, Toledo, and a new Brooklyn club. But chaos reigned in the Association during 1890, as the Brooklyn team disbanded in August, forcing the Association to replace the team with a club from Baltimore, and the quality of players was by far the lowest of the three leagues, best evinced by the fact that Louisville, the doormats of 1889, won the pennant in 1890. A year after the Player's League died, so, too, did the American Association, an outcome precipitated by the mid-season defection of Mike "King" Kelly from the Association's Boston Reds to their cross-town rival Beaneaters of the League. Only the National League was left standing in 1892.

Index

Numbers in *italics* indicate photographs.